Company's Coming for Christmas

Holiday Magic for Your Table

All New Recipes by Jean Paré

Company's Coming for Christmas

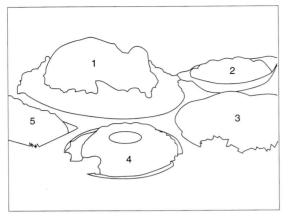

Pictured on divider:

1. Roast Turkey, page 138
   with Sausage Stuffing, page 141
2. Sauced Broccoli, page 168
3. Table Bread Wreath, page 58
4. Cranberry Mold, page 154
5. Christmas Cake, page 87

It is my most sincere wish that this book becomes part of your family's Christmas tradition as it has with mine.

Jean Paré

Company's Coming For Christmas was created thanks to the dedicated efforts of the people and organizations listed on this page.

COMPANY'S COMING PUBLISHING LIMITED

Author	Jean Paré
President	Grant Lovig
Research Assistant	Helen Urwin

Production Department:

Production Manager	Kathy Knowles
Design	Derrick Sorochan
Typesetting	Marlene Crosbie
Proofing	Hollie Heroux
Copy Writing	Cathie Bartlett

THE RECIPE FACTORY INC.

Managing Editor	Nora Prokop
Research Assistant	Lynda Elsenheimer

Test Kitchen Staff:
- Mary Boratynec
- Betty Boychuk
- Ellen Bunjevac
- Pam Klappstein
- Audrey Thomas
- Pat Yukes

Photo Studio:

Photographer	Stephe Tate Photo
Prop Stylist	Gabriele McEleney
Food Stylist	Nora Prokop

Our special thanks to the following businesses for providing extensive props for photography.

The Bay
Chintz & Company
Eaton's
Enchanted Kitchen
Enchanted Forest

Additional thanks to:

Call The Kettle Black
Dare Foods
Edmonton Wedding & Party Centre
IKEA
La Cache
Le Gnome
Libicz's kitchen essentials
Mystique
One Island Antik Ltd.
Sears
Sissy Walker's Country Interiors
Stokes
When Pigs Fly
Zellers
Zenari's

Table of Contents

Breads & Quick Breads
Easy Cinnamon Knots, page 66

Beverages   Traditional Eggnog, page 57

Cookies & Confections
Beer Nuts, page 99
Nutty Cherry Shortbread, page 91
Chocolate Drop Cookies, page 99

Main Courses
Cauliflower Ham Bake, page 142

Salads
Tomato Shrimp Aspic, page 155

Foreword

Of all the special occasions during the year,
Christmas is truly the most wonderful—a time
when young and old gather to celebrate the season
in a spirit of joy and goodwill.

★

The cherished traditions that bind family and friends
together are what make Christmas so special.
It's reassuring and comforting to carry on the
memorable traditions of your parents and grandparents
and to teach your own children these beloved customs.
Christmas is also a time to build on these traditions,
so be open to change and new ideas.

★

Each family celebrates Christmas in its own way. When
looking through old pictures and home movies or more
recent photos and videos, you can't help but notice that
much of Christmas celebration happens around
the tree and the table.

★

The food that goes on that table is an important
part of the holiday as well. Of all the meals you'll serve or
consume throughout the year, Christmas dinner
has to be the one that stands out the most.

Mealtime is an important part of any event over
the Yuletide season. That holds true whether a
meal is the focal point of the occasion—such as supper
on Christmas Eve, dinner on Christmas Day or brunch on
Boxing Day—or following an activity such as skating or
carolling. Indeed, foods such as turkey and cranberry
sauce, Christmas cake and pudding have become
synonymous with the word "Christmas."

★

At Company's Coming we are believers in
tradition and that is why we put this book together.
Company's Coming for Christmas is an exciting
new venture for us—a keepsake book that involves
all aspects of the Christmas menu and
all manner of Yuletide occasions.

★

No doubt you already have your own treasured
Christmas recipes collected from family and friends or
clipped from newspapers and magazines over the years.
Company's Coming for Christmas is here
not to intrude, but to supplement your repertoire
and to offer old favorites with a different twist.

You'll find several kinds of Christmas cakes and puddings, salads that are pleasing to the eye and even better to eat, and favorite vegetables in rejuvenated form. There's new focus on breads and soups. Main dishes and desserts have their day with a range that will delight everyone.

★

To top it off, we help you to set a fine table with suggestions for centerpieces, decorations and settings for a truly memorable occasion.

★

We don't stop there! Experience the spirit of giving with Baskets Of Gifts. Enjoy social occasions through Exchanging With Friends.

As well, we want to help you tackle situations that may be new to you. Cooking for a crowd or holding a brunch may be a departure from the sorts of get-togethers you usually hold. Our tips, suggestions, sample menus and recipes will take the guesswork out of the preparations and make these holiday gatherings the enjoyable events they should be.

★

More than 250 new recipes were created especially for this book. Every recipe is pictured and all have been painstakingly tested in our own kitchen. The result is quick and easy recipes from everyday ingredients—and the results will make you proud.

★

More than anything else, we at Company's Coming want this book to become a part of your family's Christmas tradition for years to come. From everyone at Company's Coming, we wish you all the best this festive season. May all your Christmas dreams come true.

Jean Paré

Baskets Of Gifts

A gift basket is a wonderful thing— especially when it's filled with something special and topped off with a holiday bow or two.

★

A gift basket shows you care because of the time and thought you put into selecting the appropriate contents. Gift baskets are perfect because they are so easy to personalize. Food makes an excellent gift because it is appreciated and enjoyed by everyone.

★

Best of all, the scope is endless—from one item in a tiny basket to a much larger basket overflowing with a potpourri of goodies. Your "basket" can be a bowl, a colander, a sleigh or any other suitable container.

★

Theme baskets are particularly effective, letting you build around a favorite food group. Pasta noodles and special utensils make a good start toward a pasta basket. For the citrus fan, a few jars of jam or marmalade nestled inside colorful napkins would be nice. Consider yourself blessed if there is a "sweet tooth" on your list!

A Christmas tin full of cookies or confections is quick, easy and oh-so appreciated.

★

These recipes are included because the results look good and keep well—two prerequisites for gift baskets. Feel free to call on other sections of this book for more recipes to round out your special selections.

★

Have fun creating your holiday masterpieces!

Seasoned Tomato Sauce

Adjust the spices to personal preference. Seal in decorative jars for gift-giving.

Canned tomatoes, chopped	4 × 28 oz.	4 × 796 mL
Worcestershire sauce	1 tbsp.	15 mL
Salt	2 tsp.	10 mL
Whole oregano	1½ tsp.	7 mL
Onion powder	1 tsp.	5 mL
Seasoned salt	½ tsp.	2 mL
Garlic powder	¼ tsp.	1 mL
Celery salt	¼ tsp.	1 mL
Sweet basil	¼ tsp.	1 mL
Cayenne pepper	¼ tsp.	1 mL
Brown sugar	2 tbsp.	30 mL

Put tomatoes and remaining ingredients in large pot. Heat, stirring often, until mixture boils. Boil, stirring often, for about 25 minutes until thick. For a smooth sauce, cool a bit and run through blender. Return purée to pot. Return to boil. Pour boiling sauce into hot sterilized pint jars to within ½ inch (1 cm) of top. Place sterilized metal lids on jars and screw metal bands on securely. For added assurance against spoilage, you may choose to process in a boiling water bath for 10 minutes. This may also be cooled and frozen. Makes 6 pints sauce.

Pictured on page 8.

Meaty Tomato Sauce

Before serving, add about ½ to ¾ pound (250 to 375 g) scramble-fried lean ground beef to 1 pint Tomato Spaghetti Sauce.

Pictured on page 8.

1. Meaty Tomato Sauce, page 9
2. Seasoned Tomato Sauce, page 9

Freezer Zucchini Marmalade

Pretty light yellow. Use decorative jars.

Peeled and grated zucchini	8 cups	2 L
Oranges, quartered and seeded	6	6
Lemons, quartered and seeded	2	2
Crushed pineapple, well-drained	19 oz.	540 mL
Granulated sugar	5 cups	1.25 L
Orange-flavored gelatin (jelly powder)	2 × 3 oz.	2 × 85 g
Lemon-flavored gelatin (jelly powder)	1 × 3 oz.	1 × 85 g

Put zucchini into large pot. Grind oranges and lemons including rind. Add to pot. Add pineapple and sugar. Heat, stirring often, until mixture boils. Boil 15 minutes.

Add gelatin powders. Stir to dissolve. Cool. Pour into containers, leaving 1 inch (2.5 cm) headroom. Freeze. Makes 12 cups (3 L) or 6 pints marmalade.

Pictured on page 11.

Freezer Strawberry Jam

Make in the fall, well in advance of holiday company.

Crushed strawberries, fresh or frozen whole	3 cups	750 mL
Granulated sugar	5 cups	1.25 L
Water	1 cup	250 mL
Pectin crystals	1 × 2 oz.	1 × 55 g

Stir strawberries and sugar together in bowl. Let stand for 10 minutes.

Combine water and pectin crystals in saucepan. Heat and stir until mixture reaches a boil. Boil for 1 minute, stirring continually. Remove from heat. Pour over strawberries. Stir for 2 minutes. Fill freezer containers, leaving 1 inch (2.5 cm) headroom. Let stand on counter for 24 hours to set. Freeze. Makes 7 cups (1.75 L) jam.

Pictured on page 11.

Orange Marmalade

Always popular on toast or biscuits.

Oranges, quartered and seeded	2	2
Lemon, quartered and seeded	1	1
Grapefruit, cut in eights and seeded	1	1
Water, 3 times as much as fruit		
Granulated sugar, equal to amount of fruit mixture		

Grind first 3 fruits including rind. Measure then put into large saucepan.

Add water. Boil, stirring occasionally, for 20 minutes. Let stand at room temperature for 24 hours.

Measure fruit mixture and return to saucepan. Add sugar. Heat, stirring often, until mixture boils. Boil until it jells. This will take about 1¼ hours. Fill hot sterilized half pint jars to within ¼ inch (0.5 cm) of top. Place sterilized metal lids on jars and screw metal bands on securely. For added assurance against spoilage, you may choose to process in a boiling water bath for 10 minutes. Makes 8 half pints marmalade.

Pictured on page 10 and on page 76.

Peach Zucchini Jam

Wonderful yellow color with red specks of cherry.

Grated and peeled zucchini, 4 lbs. (1.8 kg)	11 cups	2.75 L
Granulated sugar	6 cups	1.5 L
Unsweetened crushed pineapple, well-drained	19 oz.	540 mL
Red maraschino cherries, quartered (add more if desired)	12	12
Peach-flavored gelatin (jelly powder)	3 × 3 oz.	3 × 85 g

Combine zucchini and sugar in large saucepan. Heat and stir until sugar dissolves and mixture comes to a boil. Boil for 15 minutes.

Stir in pineapple. Boil for 5 minutes. Remove from heat.

Add cherries. Stir. Cut off corners of gelatin packages so you can pour granules in slowly as you keep stirring to dissolve. Fill hot sterilized pint jars to within ½ inch (1 cm) of top. Place sterilized metal lids on jars and screw metal bands on securely. For added assurance against spoilage, you may choose to process in a boiling water bath for 10 minutes. Makes 5 pints jam.

Pictured on page 10/11.

Irish Cream

So rich and creamy!

Rye whiskey	1½ cups	375 mL
Sweetened condensed milk	11 oz.	300 mL
Light cream (half and half)	1 cup	250 mL
Large eggs	2	2
Instant coffee granules	1 tsp.	5 mL
Dry chocolate drink mix (such as QUIK)	1 tsp.	5 mL
Vanilla	1 tsp.	5 mL

Measure all ingredients into blender. Process until smooth. Pour into bottle or jar to store in refrigerator. If using as a gift, be sure it's fresh with a label stating to keep refrigerated and to use within 2 weeks. Makes 4½ cups (1 L) liqueur.

Pictured below.

Mock Crème De Menthe

Just like the real thing!

Granulated sugar	1½ cups	375 mL
Boiling water	2 cups	500 mL
Peppermint flavoring	½ tsp.	2 mL
Vodka	2 cups	500 mL
Green food coloring	⅛ tsp.	0.5 mL

Stir sugar into boiling water in bowl until sugar dissolves. Cool.

Add flavoring, vodka and food coloring. Pour into containers. Let stand in cool spot for 2 weeks. Ready for use or for gifts. Makes approximately 4¾ cups (1 L) liqueur.

Pictured below.

Irish Cream

Mock Crème De Menthe

Antipasto

Make this well in advance of the holiday season.
Great to give as a hosting gift.

Pickled onions, drained and halved	1 cup	250 mL
Canned mushroom pieces, drained and chopped	2 × 10 oz.	2 × 284 mL
Red pepper, seeded and chopped	1	1
Green pepper, seeded and chopped	1	1
Green pimiento stuffed olives, chopped	1 cup	250 mL
Pitted ripe olives, chopped	1 cup	250 mL
Chopped dill pickles	1 cup	250 mL
Canned tuna, drained and flaked	2 × 6½ oz.	2 × 184 g
Ketchup	2½ cups	625 mL
White vinegar	¼ cup	60 mL
Olive oil or cooking oil	¼ cup	60 mL
Canned cut green beans, drained	14 oz.	398 mL

Place all ingredients in large saucepan. Heat, stirring often, until mixture comes to a boil. Simmer for 20 minutes, stirring often. Cool. Fill freezer containers, leaving 1 inch (2.5 cm) at the top to allow for expansion. Freeze. Makes 13 cups (3.2 L) antipasto.

Pictured on page 15.

1. Salsa, page 16
2. Antipasto, page 14
3. Hot Pepper Jelly, page 16

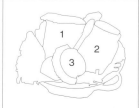

Salsa

Tangy and hot. Make it hotter by adding more cayenne.

Canned tomatoes	2 × 28 oz.	2 × 796 mL
Tomato sauce	2 × 7½ oz.	2 × 213 mL
Red pepper, seeded and chopped	1	1
Green peppers, seeded and chopped	2	2
Chopped onion	2 cups	500 mL
White vinegar	⅔ cup	150 mL
Granulated sugar	3 tbsp.	50 mL
Coarse (pickling) salt	2 tsp.	10 mL
Paprika	2 tsp.	10 mL
Garlic powder	½ tsp.	2 mL
Whole oregano	½ tsp.	2 mL
Cayenne pepper, to taste	¼-1 tsp.	1-5 mL

Measure all ingredients into large saucepan. Heat, stirring often, until mixture starts to boil. Boil slowly, uncovered, for about 1½ hours until thickened. Pour into hot sterilized half pint jars to within ¼ inch (0.5 cm) of top. Place sterilized metal lids on jars and screw metal bands on securely. For added assurance against spoilage, you may choose to process in a boiling water bath for 5 minutes. Makes 7 half pints salsa.

Pictured on page 15.

Hot Pepper Jelly

Great colors for Christmas. Serve over a block of softened cream cheese.

Medium red or green peppers, seeded and chopped	2	2
Cider vinegar	1½ cups	350 mL
Granulated sugar	6½ cups	1.45 L
Hot pepper sauce (add more, if desired)	1 tsp.	5 mL
Liquid pectin	6 oz.	175 mL
Drops of red or green food coloring, if desired	3-4	3-4

Put peppers and vinegar in blender. Process until smooth. Pour into large saucepan.

Add sugar and hot pepper sauce. Heat and stir until sugar dissolves and mixture starts to boil. Boil for 3 minutes.

Stir in pectin. Return to a full rolling boil on medium-high. Boil hard for 1 minute. Remove from heat. Skim off foam.

Add a bit of food coloring if desired. You can also add more hot pepper sauce. Pour into hot sterilized half pint jars to within ¼ inch (0.5 cm) of top. Place sterilized metal lids on jars and screw metal bands on securely. For added assurance against spoilage, you may choose to process in a boiling water bath for 5 minutes. Makes 6 half pints jelly.

Pictured on page 15.

No-Cook Cranberry Relish

Couldn't be easier. Quite tangy.

Cranberries	2 cups	500 mL
Apple, peeled and cored	1	1
Orange, quartered and seeded	1	1
Part of lemon, seeds removed	½	½
Granulated sugar	1¼ cups	300 mL

Put first 4 ingredients, including orange and lemon rind, through coarse blade of food chopper.

Add sugar. Stir well. Chill overnight. Makes 3 cups (750 mL) relish.

Pictured below.

Cranberry Relish

Superb color for the Christmas dinner table.

Cranberries, fresh or frozen	2 cups	500 mL
Sultana raisins	1 cup	250 mL
Apple, peeled, cored and diced	1	1
Orange, peeled and diced	1	1
Prepared orange juice	¼ cup	60 mL
Granulated sugar	1 cup	250 mL
Cinnamon stick, 4 inch (10 cm)	1	1
Whole cloves	6	6
Whole allspice	6	6
Rum flavoring	1 tsp.	5 mL

Measure first 6 ingredients into large saucepan.

Tie cinnamon stick, cloves and allspice in double layer cheesecloth. Add to saucepan. Bring to a boil, stirring often. Boil slowly for about 15 minutes until thickened. Discard spice bag.

Stir in rum flavoring. Pour into hot sterilized pint jars to within ½ inch (1 cm) of top. Place sterilized metal lids on jars and screw metal bands on securely. For added assurance against spoilage, you may choose to process in a boiling water bath for 10 minutes. May also be frozen. Makes 1 pint relish.

Pictured below.

No-Cook
Cranberry Relish

Cranberry Relish

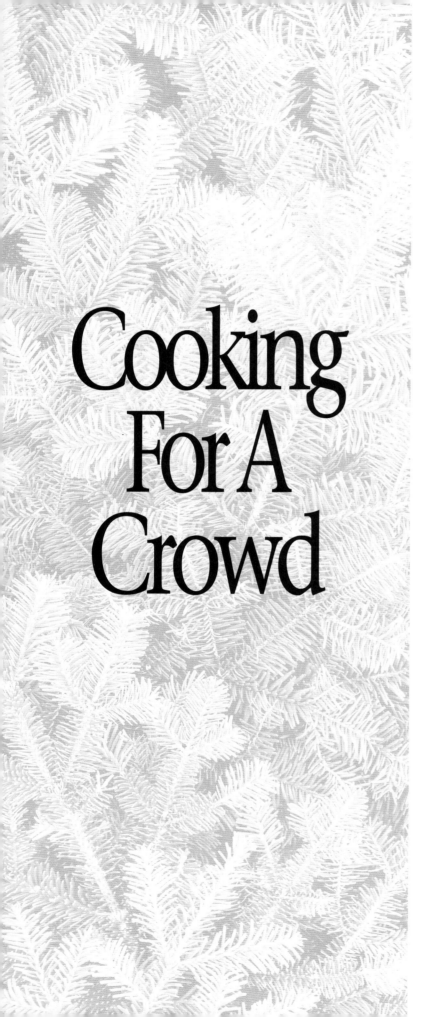

Cooking For A Crowd

Holiday gatherings are so much fun for everyone.

But feeding a crowd can be daunting. Most recipes are intended to serve four to six, or maybe six to eight. Suddenly you're having twelve for dinner, or a holiday buffet for even more—what to do?

Start planning, that's what! With a bit of advance work you can put on a repast that memories are made of and still enjoy the festivities.

★

Handling a crowd calls for different considerations in planning the menu, preparing and serving the food. When choosing recipes keep in mind that you want to offer a choice of colors and textures as well as tastes.

When deciding the menu, keep in mind several factors:

1. How many guests will there be?

2. What ages are the guests—any teens or young children?

3. How many people can I seat at the table?

4. Can I split my guests up between the dining room and kitchen tables? Do I want to?

5. Can my guests sit down and use a fork and knife,or will most be standing requiring fork-only food?

6. How many serving dishes, plates and utensils do I have or need? Can I increase my settings by borrowing, renting or using disposable products?

★

When choosing the recipes, remember that some of your favorite recipes may not double or triple well. A smorgasbord of several dishes is one option. Set out two or three meat dishes, complemented with a side selection of lighter dishes.

A second option is to double, or even triple one recipe and serve with two or three salads, rolls and a choice of two desserts. Either make the recipe in a larger dish that will accommodate the large quantity (foil roasting pan works well) or divide it into two or three smaller dishes.

Recipes that are particularly well-suited to cooking and serving in large quantities, especially buffet style are:

Cauliflower Ham Bake, page 142
Lazy Ravioli, page 138
Gourmet Burgers, page 70
Sausage Rice Casserole, page 145
Seafood Deluxe, page 144
Seafood Lasagne, page 145
Tamale Casserole, page 135
Triple Seafood Noodles, page 144
Turkey Au Gratin, page 132
Turkey Wizard, page 140

Now get out your pad and pencil, draw up your checklist and come the big day, the compliments from happy guests around the table will be music to your ears.

Exchanging With Friends

Sharing the bounty of the kitchen with friends and neighbors is as old as time. So it's only logical that exchanging food has become part of Christmas.

★

An exchange lets you add variety to your stock of Christmas goodies. Most cookie recipes yield four to six dozen, making it cumbersome to bake more than two or three kinds. An exchange provides the opportunity to make just one recipe (doubled or tripled) and end up with the same amount but in a variety of six to twelve different kinds.

★

You can ask participants to attach the recipe to each individually wrapped dozen or to give recipe cards to each participant. Remind your guests to pack their items for safe travel home to prevent breaking or squashing.

You can give a little or a lot of direction as to what is to be exchanged. Do you simply want cookies, or narrow it down to shortbread or Christmas cake? Do you want a specific kind from each person or go potluck-style and make it a surprise?

Plan to have no less than six and no more than twelve participants (including yourself). How many dozen each person provides can be determined in several ways:

1) If there are ten people, each person brings ten times one dozen; for six people each person brings six times one dozen and so on;

or

2) If there are ten people, each person brings a predetermined number (say eight dozen) and a large empty container. Everyone walks around and around the table taking an agreed number of each kind until everything has been divided up.

★

Traditionally cookies have been exchanged but in recent years appetizers and squares have joined the scene. Squares make an excellent exchange. Lining the pan with foil makes removal and cutting much easier.

★

Christmas cake is another possibility. Granted, the ingredients are expensive and making the cake can be time-consuming. But a tray of light and dark cakes in a variety of shapes is so attractive and appealing.

★

Generally recipes for Christmas cake make two or three large loaves. By baking them in 19 ounce (540 mL) cans or mini loaf pans, a single or double recipe could suffice for an exchange.

★

If exchanging appetizers, they should be made fresh and be suitable for storing in the freezer.

★

Get in on the holiday fun early and play host to an exchange. Circle a date on the calendar, cover the dining room table with a festive tablecloth, and make way for friends bearing boxes of luscious treats.

★

Recommended Cookies/Confections

Almond Roca, page 103
(approximately ½ lb., 225 g per participant)

Jolly Fruit Drops, page 89
(1 dozen per participant)

Breton Brittle, page 102
(approximately ½ lb., 225 g per participant)

Peanut Brittle, page 103
(approximately ½ lb., 225g per participant)

Cherry Surprise, page 101
(1 dozen per participant)

Rum Balls, page 101
(1 dozen per participant)

Christmas Fudge, page 96
(⅓ pan per participant)

Scotch Shortbread, page 98
(1 dozen squares per participant)

Christmas Trees, page 94
(1 dozen per participant)

Shortbread Squares, page 98
(1 dozen squares per participant)

Condensed Fudge, page 96
(⅓ pan per participant)

Special Chocolate Fudge,
page 96 (⅓ pan per participant)

Dipped Vanillas, page 105
(1 dozen per participant)

Spritz, page 91
(1 dozen per participant)

Divinity Drops, page 95
(1 dozen per participant)

Sugar Cookies, page 95
(1 dozen per participant)

Merry Fruit Cookies, page 90
(1 small unbaked roll or 1 dozen baked
cookies per participant)

Whipped Shortbread, page 89
(1 dozen per participant)

Recommended Appetizers

Baked Cheese Balls, page 45
(1 dozen per participant)

Salty Caraway Sticks, page 44
(1 dozen per participant)

Curried Nuts, page 51
(2 cups, 500 mL per participant)

Snackies, page 51
(2 cups, 500 mL per participant)

Fun Party Mix, page 50
(2 cups, 500 mL per participant)

Spinach Squares, page 42
(¼ pan per participant)

Lazy Sausage Rolls, page 37
(1 dozen slices per participant)

Welsh Cakes, page 45
(1 dozen per participant)

Onion Tarts, page 44
(1 dozen mini tarts per participant)

Zucchini Squares, page 32
(¼ pan per participant)

Recommended Christmas Cakes & Puddings

Carrot Pudding, page 86
(1 can per participant) *

Steamed Fruit Pudding,
page 80
(1 can per participant) *

Orange Gumdrop Loaf,
page 83
(1 mini loaf per participant) *

White Fruitcake, page 81
(1 mini loaf per participant) *

Plum Pudding, page 81
(1 per participant) *

* See: For Gift Giving, page 86

1. Sugar Cookies, page 95
2. Chocolate Spritz, page 91
3. Baked Cheese Balls,
   page 45
4. White Fruitcake, page 81
5. Steamed Fruit Pudding,
   page 80

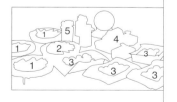

Make-ahead Recipe Ideas

★

You're looking at photographs or videos of Christmas

past when you realize that someone significant

is missing. Where is the cook?

★

Out in the kitchen, that's where. There's so much to

do to pull this special dinner together that he or she

can't join the others until the food is on the table.

★

Some aspects of Christmas dinner are part of the day

itself, such as the smell of the turkey as it roasts to

perfection. But much of the work can be done ahead,

reducing stress and clutter and allowing the cook

to enjoy conversation with family and guests.

★

Baking ahead clears the oven for the big bird and

means you're not cooking and cleaning up all day.

So go through the menu with a view to what can be done

ahead. Make sure dishes prepared well ahead of time

will freeze well. Clear the refrigerator for those

dishes you make the day before.

★

With some effort beforehand you'll be relaxed

and smiling on the big day and you'll even

make it into the Christmas video!

★

Appetizers

Appetizers can be made in November or early
December and put in the freezer. Broiling is best done
at the last minute, but do everything up to the
broiling step then freeze. Sauces and dips
are best left to the day before.

Remember that appetizers are much smaller in
individual size and will dry out somewhat in the freezer.
Wrap them well and remove as much air as
possible. To give you flexibility, spread individual
items like Oriental Meatballs, page 33, Sesame Wings,
page 36 or Sausage Balls, page 36, on a baking
sheet and freeze for three hours. Place in freezer
bag or container and refreeze. They will remain
separated so that you can take out as many as
you need for any one occasion.

Beverages

Most punches can be made the day before, but add carbonated or sparkling liquids just prior to serving. Any beverage containing eggs should be made close to serving time. Liqueur recipes can be made two weeks to two months in advance.

Breads And Quick Breads

All the recipes in this section, with the exception of Lemon Spread, page 66, can be made in advance and frozen. If you won't need large quantities at any one time, cut loaves in half and wrap each half individually. All loaves should be cooled completely before freezing, wrapped airtight in plastic wrap and wrapped a second time in foil.

Brunches

The Baked Omelet, page 71, Lobster Fantans, page 75, Eggs Lyonnaise, page 77 and Oven Apple Pancake, page 77 must be made on the day of serving. However, Make-Ahead Eggs Benedict, page 68, Quick Fruit Bowl, page 69, Orange Fruit Dip, page 73, Overnight Oven French Toast, page 76 and Sausage Strata, page 77 can all be made or partially made the day before. The rest of the recipes in this section can be frozen well in advance.

Christmas Cakes And Puddings

With the exception of the sauces, all these recipes can be frozen. As with breads and quick breads, they should be wrapped airtight in plastic wrap and wrapped again in foil. All the sauces can be made several days ahead of time then reheated quickly in the microwave just before serving.

Christmas Cookies And Confections

Absolutely every recipe in this section can be made in November, or even October! Most can be frozen (without icing), others can be stored in airtight containers at room temperature or in the refrigerator. Make squares in foil-lined pans. To freeze, remove from pan, fold foil over top edges and wrap with a second layer of foil.

Desserts

The recipes in this category are all make-aheads with the exception of Sherry Trifle, page 114 and Fluffy Frosting, page 122. Most of the recipes can be frozen; the rest are best if made the day before serving. Cool squares completely and then either cut and freeze, or freeze first then cut when ready to use. Some squares cut better when partially frozen. Remember, this is the season to serve a tray of mixed goodies, so cut pieces a bit smaller than you might when serving only one or two choices.

Main Courses

This may be the one section you concentrate on the day of entertaining. But just in case you'd rather visit, most can be frozen several weeks in advance or assembled the day before and heated just before serving. You may choose to do Beef Roast In Gravy, page 135, Roast Goose, page 140, Golden Glazed Ham, page 132 and Roast Turkey, page 138 one week ahead. Remove the meat, slice it and freeze. Be sure to wrap it airtight.

Pies And Tarts

These are fancy desserts that can be frozen ahead for the most part. Add any whipped topping the day of serving, but only after pie has completely thawed. Some pies will slice better when still partially frozen.

Salads

Molded (or jellied) salads can easily be made the day before. Keep chilled in mold and cover exposed area with plastic wrap to prevent drying. Unmold up to one hour before serving but keep chilled. To help with the tossed or creamy salads, make dressings a day or two in advance. Wash and tear lettuce or spinach several days ahead and store airtight, wrapped in paper towel in plastic bag. Drain or cut fruit the day before but add bananas and apples at the last minute.

Soups

Freeze all the soups if you wish. When reheating, do so over low to medium heat, stirring fairly often.

Vegetables

Most of these dishes are best done a few days before serving. Vegetables can be washed and cut and kept in cold water. Some of these recipes can be assembled the day before and cooked the day of, and some can be cooked two to three days in advance and reheated just before serving.

Menus

More often than not "menu" means you're dining out. But home cooking is just as worthy of a menu, especially during the holiday season when you want to put your best foot forward. So before you start cooking, take the time to draw up your own list from the kitchen.

Make your menu suit the occasion. An afternoon of tobogganing or skating calls for something hot and substantial, while nibblies are fine to munch on as you and your guests sit around the fireplace for an evening of carols.

Take into account how many you are serving and the age range. Don't forget that looks are important, so consider color in addition to texture and flavor, and hot versus cold. Remember to add a festive touch wherever possible—turning out a cranberry jellied salad, or decorating chocolate cupcakes with miniature candy canes and so on.

These sample menus span a range of occasions. Try the menus as is, adjust them a little or a lot, or take out pen and paper and start from square one. Planning is the key to success and in the kitchen the menu is the plan.

Cookie Decorating Party

Gingerbread Figures, page 100
Sugar Cookies, page 95
Cocoa Cookies, page 91
Quick Fruit Punch, page 56

Cookie Exchange Brunch

Perked Wassail, page 54
Shrimp Dip, page 49 (served with veggies and crackers)
Cottage Salad, page 156
Sausage Strata, page 77
Chocolate Truffle, page 109

Tree-Trimming

Perked Wassail, page 54
Creamy Cranberry Punch, page 53
Crab Ball, page 42 (served with crackers)
Last Minute Appetizer, page 46
Creamy Stuffed Mushrooms, page 40
Artichoke Strudel, page 37
Tray of assorted cookies and squares

Neighborhood Carolling

Christmas Punch, page 56

French Silk Chocolate, page 54

Stuffed Edam, page 48 (served with crackers)

Mushroom Nappies, page 38

Sausage Rice Casserole, page 145

Creamy Chilled Dessert, page 116

Celebrate The Snowman (Kids)

French Silk Chocolate, page 54

Cinnamon Crisps, page 50

Banana Pancakes, page 76

Cookies 'N Cake, page 114

Christmas Eve Gathering

Traditional Eggnog, page 57

Christmas Punch, page 56

Lobster Chowder Feed, page 164

Potato Rolls, page 59

Lazy Ravioli, page 138

Just For The Elves

Quick Fruit Punch, page 56

Fancy Macaroni, page 136

Drop Cheese Biscuits, page 61

Frozen Peanut Butter Pie, page 148

Christmas Morning Brunch

French Silk Chocolate, page 54

Rhubarb Cocktail, page 56

Orange Fruit Dip, page 73 (served with fresh fruit)

Make-Ahead Eggs Benedict, page 68

Overnight Oven French Toast, page 76

Holiday Brunch Cake, page 60

Cranberry Orange Muffins, page 67

Christmas Day Dinner

Shrimp Cocktail, page 43

Roast Turkey, page 138, with Gravy, page 133

(served with mashed potatoes)

Sausage Stuffing, page 141

Sweet Potato Bake, page 170

Sauced Broccoli, page 168

Cranberry Mold, page 154

Table Bread Wreath, page 58

Plum Pudding, page 81

Rum Sauce, page 87

Boxing Day Brunch

Open House

Fork-Food Buffet

Après Ski

Skating/Tobogganing Party

Mistletoe Magic

Scallop Attraction, page 43

Citrus Salad, page 156

Chicken Breasts Florentine, page 142

Carrot Medley, page 171

(served with oven-roasted potatoes)

Chocolate Crêpes, page 111

Irish Cream, page 13

Mock Kahlua, page 53

Wine & Nibblies

Mulled Wine, page 52

Perked Wassail, page 54

Baked Cheese Balls, page 45

Nutty Cheese Ball, page 46 (served with crackers)

Dilled Carrot Sticks, page 44

Antipasto, page 14

Sausage Balls, page 36

Shrimp Stuffed Mushrooms, page 40

Almond Roca, page 103

Dipped Vanillas, page 105

Cherry Pound Cake, page 64

New Year's Eve

Champagne Punch, page 53

Shrimp Canapés, page 41

King Artichoke Dip, page 44 (served with veggies)

Beer Nuts, page 99

Cajun Spareribs, page 130

(served with rice)

Broccoli Casserole, page 170

Mock Black Bottom Pie, page 152

New Year's Day Casual

Mulled Cranberry Juice, page 54

Tomato Cabbage Soup, page 165

Green Pepper Salad, page 155

Lobster Fantans, page 75

Festive Savory Cheesecake, page 74

Golden Glazed Ham, page 132

Hasselback Potatoes, page 168

Dressed Peas, page 168

Glimmering Slice, page 119

Butter Tarts, page 149

Appetizers

The festive season sees many kinds of social occasions, and that makes appetizers especially appropriate at this time of the year. As part of a dinner menu they are an extra touch that adds to the special atmosphere. For a casual get-together a tray of appetizers is the perfect way to provide that little something to nibble on.

Appetizers are wonderfully easy to prepare and they look good, offering your guests a sampler of tastes and textures. Moreover, they're convenient. Make them ahead, refrigerate or freeze until needed, heat them up, arrange on a tray and voila—another happy holiday event is under way!

Top: Oriental Meatballs, page 33
Center: Sausage Balls, page 36
Bottom: Zucchini Squares, page 32

Bruschetta

A great blend of flavors. Make filling the day before and chill. Spread on bread just before baking.

Salad dressing (or mayonnaise)	½ cup	125 mL
Grated mozzarella cheese	1 cup	250 mL
Medium tomatoes, halved, seeded and finely diced	2	2
Chopped ripe pitted olives	¼ cup	60 mL
Grated fresh Parmesan cheese (or 2 tbsp., 30 mL dry)	¼ cup	60 mL
Whole oregano	1 tsp.	5 mL
Pepper	½ tsp.	2 mL
Sweet basil	¼ tsp.	1 mL
Baguette (must be fresh), about 2½ inches (6 cm) round, 24-27 inches (40-48 cm) long	1	1
Butter or hard margarine, softened	⅓ cup	75 mL

Mix first 8 ingredients in small bowl.

Cut baguette into 1 inch (2.5 cm) slices. Butter each slice on 1 side. Arrange, buttered side up, on ungreased baking sheet. Divide tomato mixture among slices and spread. Bake in 350°F (175°C) oven for 15 minutes until hot and cheese is melted. Serve warm. Makes 24 to 27 appetizers.

Pictured on page 33.

Zucchini Squares

Such a pretty light green. Freeze and cut when partially thawed.

Large eggs	4	4
Parsley flakes	1 tsp.	5 mL
Whole oregano	½ tsp.	2 mL
Seasoned salt	½ tsp.	2 mL
Garlic powder	½ tsp.	2 mL
Salt	¼ tsp.	1 mL
Cooking oil	½ cup	125 mL
Biscuit mix	1 cup	250 mL
Grated zucchini, with peel	3 cups	750 mL
Finely chopped onion	½ cup	125 mL
Grated medium Cheddar cheese	½ cup	125 mL
Grated Parmesan cheese	¼ cup	60 mL

Beat eggs in mixing bowl until smooth.

Add next 7 ingredients. Mix well.

Add remaining ingredients. Stir until mixed. Pour into greased 9 x 13 inch (22 x 33 cm) pan. Bake in 350°F (175°C) oven for 40 to 45 minutes until set and golden brown. Serve warm or cool. Cuts into 54 squares.

Pictured above.

When serving both hot and cold appetizers at the same time, plan to have two to three times more hot appetizers than cold for each person. The total number of appetizers per person will depend on how long you plan to serve appetizers, whether there is other food on the menu and what type of function you are holding.

Oriental Meatballs

The tangy flavor of the sauce will agree with everyone.
Make the meatballs ahead and freeze.

Meatballs:

Lean ground beef	1 lb.	454 g
Large egg	1	1
Worcestershire sauce	1 tsp.	5 mL
Finely chopped onion	1/4 cup	60 mL
Sour cream	1/2 cup	125 mL
Fine bread crumbs	1/3 cup	75 mL
Salt	3/4 tsp.	4 mL
Pepper	1/4 tsp.	1 mL

Sweet And Sour Sauce:		
Brown sugar, packed	2/3 cup	150 mL
Cornstarch	3 tbsp.	50 mL
Dry mustard powder	2 tsp.	10 mL
Pineapple juice	1 cup	250 mL
White vinegar	1/2 cup	125 mL
Ketchup	1/2 cup	125 mL
Water	1/2 cup	125 mL
Soy sauce	1/2 tsp.	2 mL

Meatballs: Measure all ingredients into bowl. Mix well. Shape into 1 inch (2.5 cm) balls. Arrange on baking sheet. Bake in 350°F (175°C) oven for 15 minutes.

Sweet And Sour Sauce: Stir brown sugar, cornstarch and mustard powder together in saucepan.

Stir in pineapple juice. Add vinegar, ketchup, water and soy sauce. Heat and stir until it boils and thickens. Sauce can be served separately for dipping or can be poured over meatballs to serve from chafing dish. Makes 64 meatballs and 2 1/3 cups (575 mL) sauce.

Pictured on page 32.

Bruschetta, page 32

Bacon Cheddar Dip

Everybody raves over this. Easy to spread or dip.

Salad dressing (or mayonnaise)	1 cup	250 mL
Buttermilk	1 cup	250 mL
Grated medium Cheddar cheese	1 cup	250 mL
Onion flakes	1/4 cup	60 mL
Bacon bits	1/3 cup	75 mL
Garlic salt	3/4 tsp.	4 mL

Mix all 6 ingredients in bowl. Cover. Chill for 30 minutes. Serve with raw vegetables and assorted crackers. Makes 2 1/3 cups (575 mL) dip.

Pictured below.

Simple Shrimp Dip   Bacon Cheddar Dip

Simple Shrimp Dip

Lots of flavor for dipping. Also delicious with
raw vegetables.

Sour cream	2 cups	450 mL
Chili sauce (or ketchup)	1/4 cup	60 mL
Canned broken or small shrimp, drained and mashed	4 oz.	113 g
Lemon juice, fresh or bottled	1/2 tsp.	2 mL
Worcestershire sauce	1/2 tsp.	2 mL
Minced onion	1 tsp.	5 mL
Beef bouillon powder	1/2 tsp.	2 mL

Combine all 7 ingredients in bowl. Mash or beat together well. Serve chilled with chips and assorted crackers. Makes 2 1/2 cups (575 mL) dip.

Pictured above.

Turkey Appetizers

Assemble these the day before. Chill then bake just before serving.

Butter or hard margarine	1 tbsp.	15 mL
Canned pineapple chunks, drained and patted dry	16	16
Prepared orange juice	1 cup	250 mL
Granulated sugar	1/3 cup	75 mL
Cranberries, fresh or frozen	32	32
Cooked turkey cubes	16	16
Savory Sauce:		
Ketchup	1 cup	250 mL
Mild molasses	1/4 cup	60 mL
Cider vinegar	1/4 cup	60 mL

Melt butter in frying pan. Add pineapple. Quickly brown both sides. Remove to plate.

Heat and stir orange juice and sugar in saucepan until mixture boils.

Add cranberries. Return just to a boil. Drain. Pour onto a separate plate.

To arrange on skewers, start with a cranberry, then a turkey cube, followed by a cranberry in center, then a pineapple chunk, another cranberry, another pineapple chunk, another turkey cube and ending with a cranberry. Chill until ready to add sauce. Makes 8 appetizers.

Savory Sauce: Mix all 3 ingredients together. Lay chilled skewers on greased baking sheet. Brush or dab sauce on skewer contents. Heat in 425°F (220°C) oven for 5 to 10 minutes until hot. Use remaining sauce for dipping. Other dips could be orange marmalade or cranberry chutney. Makes 1 1/2 cups (375 mL) sauce. Makes 8 skewers.

Pictured on page 36.

1. Sauced Crab Ball, page 42
2. Shrimp Canapés, page 41
3. Favorite Clam Dip, page 49
4. Crab Ball, page 42
5. Dilled Carrot Sticks, page 44
6. Shrimp Dip, page 49

Bottom Left: Lazy Sausage Rolls, page 37 | Bottom Center: Turkey Appetizers, page 35 | Top Center: Sesame Wings, page 36

Sausage Balls

Serve with cocktail picks and a dipping sauce.
Try Sweet And Sour Sauce, page 33.

Sausage meat	½ lb.	225 g
Cayenne pepper	⅛ tsp.	0.5 mL
Grated sharp Cheddar cheese	2 cups	500 mL
Biscuit mix	1½ cups	375 mL

Scramble-fry sausage meat and cayenne pepper in frying pan. Drain off fat.

Add cheese. Stir until it melts.

Stir in biscuit mix. Remove from heat. Shape into 1 inch (2.5 cm) balls. Place about 1 inch (2.5 cm) apart on ungreased baking sheet. Bake in 400°F (205°C) oven for 10 to 12 minutes. To reheat frozen balls, heat in 325°F (160°C) oven for 10 minutes until hot. Makes 32 appetizers.

Pictured on page 32.

Sesame Wings

Always popular, these can be made ahead,
frozen and reheated in oven.

Cornstarch	½ cup	125 mL
All-purpose flour	¼ cup	60 mL
Granulated sugar	¼ cup	60 mL
Soy sauce	⅓ cup	75 mL
Cooking oil	¼ cup	60 mL
Sesame seeds	2 tbsp.	30 mL
Salt	1½ tsp.	7 mL
Garlic powder	¼ tsp.	1 mL
Large eggs	2	2
Chicken drumettes, or whole wings	3 lbs.	1.3 kg

Measure first 9 ingredients into bowl that has a tight fitting lid. Mix well.

Add drumettes. (If using whole wings, discard tips. Cut wing apart at joint.) Add to marinade. Put lid on tightly. Rotate bowl to coat all pieces. Turn bowl often as wings marinate. Refrigerate at least 2 hours. Remove from marinade. Discard marinade. Arrange chicken on foil-lined baking sheet. Bake in 350°F (175°C) oven for about 30 minutes until tender. Makes about 3 dozen hot appetizers.

Pictured above.

Variation: Deep dry in hot oil for 8 minutes instead of baking in oven.

Bottom Right: Sauerkraut Balls, page 38

Lazy Sausage Rolls

These have an attractive pinwheel design. Try a combination of the basic recipe plus some of each of the variations. All freeze well.

Biscuit mix	2 cups	500 mL
Onion powder	1 tsp.	5 mL
Water	1/2 cup	125 mL
Pork sausage meat, mild or hot	1 lb.	454 g
Cayenne pepper	1/2-1 tsp.	2-5 mL

Stir biscuit mix and onion powder together. Add water. Mix until it forms a ball. Turn out onto lightly floured surface. Knead 6 to 8 times. Roll out into a rectangle about 15 × 18 inches (30 × 45 cm).

Mash sausage meat with fork to make it more pliable. Mix in desired amount of cayenne pepper. Spread over dough. Roll up dough like a jelly roll, beginning at long end. Slice 3/8 inch (9 mm) thick. Arrange on greased baking sheet, cut side down, about 1 inch (2.5 cm) apart. Bake in 450°F (230°C) oven for about 15 minutes. Makes about 3 dozen appetizers.

Variation: Brush tops with beaten egg and sprinkle with poppy seeds, sesame seeds or parsley flakes. Bake as above.

Pictured on page 36.

Artichoke Strudel

Fussy but fantastic! Can be frozen.

Butter or hard margarine	1/4 cup	60 mL
Finely chopped onion	1 cup	250 mL
Garlic powder	1/2 tsp.	2 mL
Cream cheese, softened	8 oz.	250 g
Creamed cottage cheese	1 cup	250 mL
Large eggs	3	3
Garlic salt	1 tsp.	5 mL
Parsley flakes	1 tsp.	5 mL
Tarragon	3/4 tsp.	4 mL
Pepper	1/2 tsp.	2 mL
Jars of marinated artichokes, drained and chopped	3 × 6 oz.	3 × 175 mL
Grated fresh Parmesan cheese (or 2 tbsp., 30 mL dry)	1/4 cup	60 mL
Cracker crumbs	1/2 cup	125 mL
Filo pastry dough sheets	15	15
Butter or hard margarine, melted	1/2 cup	125 mL

Melt first amount of butter in frying pan. Add onion. Sauté until soft. Do not brown.

Add garlic powder. Stir.

Beat cream cheese and cottage cheese in bowl until cheese is mixed in. Beat in eggs 1 at a time. Add garlic salt, parsley, tarragon and pepper. Beat to mix. Add onion with any leftover drippings.

Add artichokes, Parmesan cheese and cracker crumbs. Stir.

Lay out filo sheets. Brush with melted butter. Stack 5 sheets on top of each other, making 3 stacks. Spoon 1/3 artichoke mixture down one end of each stack. Roll up, tucking end edges of sheets around filling. Arrange rolls on greased baking sheet. Bake in 350°F (175°C) oven for 30 to 40 minutes until nicely browned. Cut each roll into 10 pieces. Serve warm or room temperature. Makes 30 appetizers.

Pictured below.

Artichoke Strudel

Mushroom Nappies

An incredible edible. Mixture can be made ahead and frozen.

Butter or hard margarine	3 tbsp.	50 mL
Chopped onion	1 cup	250 mL
Chopped fresh mushrooms	2 cups	500 mL
Grated mozzarella cheese	1 cup	250 mL
Grated Parmesan cheese	¼ cup	60 mL
Parsley flakes	1 tsp.	5 mL
Large egg	1	1
Whole oregano	½ tsp.	2 mL
Salt	½ tsp.	2 mL
Pepper	¼ tsp.	1 mL
Bread Nappies:		
White bread slices	12	12
Butter or hard margarine, softened	⅓ cup	75 mL
Yellow cheese slices	3	3

Melt butter in frying pan. Add onion and mushrooms. Sauté until soft.

Stir in next 7 ingredients. Stir for 1 minute. Remove from heat.

Bread Nappies: Cut off crusts from bread slices. Roll each slice lightly with rolling pin to flatten. Butter slices. Cut each slice into 4 squares. Press, buttered side up, into tiny muffin tins. Fill with mushroom mixture using about 1½ tsp. (7 mL) for each one.

Cut each cheese slice into 16 small squares. Put 1 square on top of each tart. Bake in 350°F (175°C) oven for 20 to 25 minutes. Makes 4 dozen appetizers.

Pictured above.

Sauerkraut Balls

Crunchy on the outside and creamy on the inside.

Pork sausage meat	½ lb.	225 g
Finely chopped onion	⅓ cup	75 mL
All-purpose flour	1 tbsp.	15 mL
Canned sauerkraut, well drained and finely chopped	14 oz.	398 mL
Cream cheese, softened, cut up	4 oz.	125 g
Prepared mustard	1 tsp.	5 mL
Parsley flakes	1 tsp.	5 mL
Salt	⅛ tsp.	0.5 mL
Garlic powder	¼ tsp.	1 mL
Pepper	¼ tsp.	1 mL
Coating:		
All-purpose flour	⅓ cup	75 mL
Large eggs	2	2
Water	2 tbsp.	30 mL
Fine dry bread crumbs	1 cup	250 mL

Fat, for deep-frying

Scramble-fry sausage meat and onion in frying pan until no pink remains in meat and onion is soft.

Sprinkle flour over top. Mix. Add sauerkraut, cream cheese, mustard, parsley, salt, garlic powder and pepper. Stir until blended. Chill until it will hold its shape. Roll into 1 inch (2.5 cm) balls.

Coating: Measure flour into small bowl.

Beat eggs and water with a fork in another bowl.

Roll balls in flour to coat. Dip in egg mixture. Coat with bread crumbs.

Carefully drop 1 at a time until there are about 4 in hot 385°F to 400°F (195°C to 205°C) fat. Deep-fry until browned, about 3 minutes. Remove with slotted spoon to tray lined with paper towels to drain. These may be made ahead and heated in 400°F (205°C) oven for 8 minutes until hot. If frozen, heat in 350°F (175°C) oven for 12 minutes until hot. Makes about 30 appetizers.

Pictured on page 37.

Scallop Attraction, page 43

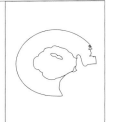

Left: Salmon Canapés, page 41
Center: Shrimp Stuffed Mushrooms, page 40
Right: Creamy Stuffed Mushrooms, page 40

Shrimp Stuffed Mushrooms

This is a stuffed mushroom that is served chilled rather than the usual broiled or baked type.

Large whole mushrooms	24	24
Lemon juice, fresh or bottled	¼ cup	60 mL
Granulated sugar	2 tbsp.	30 mL
Cream cheese, softened	4 oz.	125 g
Sour cream	2 tbsp.	30 mL
Broken shrimp, drained and chopped (or use fresh cooked)	4 oz.	113 g
Green onions, finely chopped	4	4
Hot pepper sauce	¼ tsp.	1 mL
Paprika, sprinkle		

Remove stems from mushrooms and save for another recipe. Mix lemon juice with sugar in bowl with tight-fitting cover. Add mushrooms. Cover and marinate 3 to 4 hours, shaking bowl often. Drain well.

Mix cream cheese and sour cream together well. Add shrimp, onions and pepper sauce. Stir together. Stuff mushroom caps. Garnish with additional tiny shrimp if desired.

Sprinkle with paprika. Serve chilled. Makes 24 cold appetizers.

Pictured on this page.

Creamy Stuffed Mushrooms

Always popular. The fresher the mushrooms the better.

Large mushrooms	24	24
Cream cheese, softened	4 oz.	125 g
Grated Parmesan cheese	¼ cup	60 mL
Finely chopped green onion	2 tbsp.	30 mL
Reserved mushroom stems, chopped		
Salt	⅛ tsp.	0.5 mL
Dill weed	⅛ tsp.	0.5 mL
Garlic powder	1/16 tsp.	0.5 mL

Gently twist stems from mushrooms. Reserve stems.

Mash cream cheese and Parmesan cheese together using fork. Add onion, mushroom stems, salt, dill weed and garlic powder. Stuff mushroom caps. Arrange on ungreased baking sheet. Broil on second rack down from broiler until golden brown. Serve hot. Makes 24 appetizers.

When placing stuffed mushrooms on baking sheet, dab the bottoms in the filling to help "glue" onto the sheet. This helps keep them level while baking and keeps them from sliding around.

Pictured on this page.

Shrimp Canapés

There is a nice nip to the flavor of these quick appetizers.

Jar of Old English cheese spread	⅓ cup	75 mL
Butter or hard margarine, softened	¼ cup	60 mL
Salad dressing (or mayonnaise)	2 tsp.	10 mL
Lemon juice, fresh or bottled	½ tsp.	2 mL
Cayenne pepper, just a pinch		
Onion powder, just a pinch		
Canned broken or tiny shrimp, rinsed and drained	4 oz.	113 g
English muffins, split	4	4

Put first 6 ingredients into small bowl. Beat until smooth.

Add shrimp. Beat on low just to mix.

Spread on 8 muffin halves. Broil until lightly browned. These may be frozen whole before broiling then broiled from the frozen state. Cut each muffin half into 8 pieces to serve. Makes 64 tiny appetizers.

Pictured on page 34.

Salmon Canapés

Serve these à la carte—let everyone make their own.

Canned salmon (red, such as Sockeye, is best for color)	2 × 7.5 oz.	2 × 213 g
Cream cheese, softened	8 oz.	250 g
Canned ham flakes	6½ oz.	184 g
Lemon juice, fresh or bottled	2 tsp.	10 mL
Horseradish	1 tsp.	5 mL
Liquid smoke	1 tsp.	5 mL
Onion powder	¼ tsp.	1 mL
Paprika (use with pink salmon)	2 tsp.	10 mL
Crackers or small bread rounds		

Drain salmon. Remove skin and round bones. Flake salmon in bowl.

Add next 7 ingredients. Mash and work together. Spread on crackers or bread rounds. Makes 3 cups (700 mL) spread.

Pictured on page 40.

Ripe Olive Canapés

Make the olive mixture the day before. Or spread on toasted bread slices and freeze. Broil when thawed.

Chopped ripe olives	14 oz.	398 mL
Grated medium Cheddar cheese	1 cup	250 mL
Salad dressing (or mayonnaise)	¼ cup	60 mL
Onion powder	¼ tsp.	1 mL
Curry powder	¼ tsp.	1 mL
Sandwich bread slices, crusts removed	8	8

Mix first 5 ingredients in small bowl.

Arrange bread slices on ungreased baking sheet. Toast 1 side under broiler. Spread olive mixture on untoasted side. Broil for about 2 or 3 minutes until bubbly. Cut each slice into 4 squares or 4 triangles. Makes 32 appetizers.

Pictured below.

Left: Ripe Olive Canapés, page 41
Center: Baked Cheese Balls, page 45
Right: Spinach Squares, page 42

Welsh Cakes, page 45   Date Nut Log, page 48

Crab Ball

Covered in nuts and parsley, this has a nice sharp flavor.
Serve with assorted crackers. Freezes well.

Cream cheese, softened	8 oz.	250 g
Hot pepper sauce	¼ tsp.	1 mL
Salt	½ tsp.	2 mL
Pepper	¼ tsp.	1 mL
Chopped green onion	2 tbsp.	30 mL
Crabmeat (or 1 can 4 oz., 113 g, drained, membrane removed)	1 cup	250 g
Finely chopped walnuts	¼ cup	60 mL
Chopped fresh parsley (or 2 tsp., 10 mL, parsley flakes)	2 tbsp.	30 mL

Mash cheese with fork in bowl. Add pepper sauce, salt, pepper and onion. Mash well.

Add crabmeat. Mash to mix. Chill for 30 minutes or more before shaping into a ball. It will remain fairly soft.

Mix walnuts and parsley on large plate. Roll ball in mixture. Cover and chill. Makes 1 ball about 3½ inches (9 cm) in diameter.

Pictured on page 35.

Spinach Squares

Make these well in advance and freeze.
Cut when partially thawed.

Butter or hard margarine	2 tbsp.	30 mL
Chopped fresh mushrooms	2 cups	500 mL
Chopped onion	1 cup	250 mL
Large eggs	4	4
Dry bread crumbs	¼ cup	60 mL
Grated Parmesan cheese	⅓ cup	75 mL
Salt	¼ tsp.	1 mL
Pepper	⅛ tsp.	0.5 mL
Ground nutmeg	⅛ tsp.	0.5 mL
Ground oregano	⅛ tsp.	0.5 mL
Sweet basil	⅛ tsp.	0.5 mL
Frozen chopped spinach, thawed and squeezed dry	2 × 10 oz.	2 × 300 g
Condensed cream of mushroom soup	10 oz.	284 mL

Melt butter in frying pan. Add mushrooms and onion. Sauté until soft.

Beat eggs in bowl until frothy. Measure in remaining ingredients. Mix. Add mushroom mixture. Spoon into greased 9 x 13 inch (22 x 33 cm) pan. Bake in 350°F (175°C) oven for about 35 minutes until set and browned. Cool. To reheat frozen squares, arrange on ungreased baking sheet. Heat in 325°F (160°C) oven for about 12 minutes. Makes 54 appetizers.

Pictured on page 41.

Sauced Crab Ball

Recipe can be made several days ahead and can easily be doubled. Serve with assorted crackers.

Cream cheese, softened	4 oz.	125 g
Canned crabmeat, drained, membrane removed, flaked	4 oz.	113 g
Lemon juice, fresh or bottled	1 tsp.	5 mL
Onion powder	¼ tsp.	1 mL
Hot pepper sauce, just a dash		
Seafood cocktail sauce	⅓ cup	75 mL

Beat cheese, crabmeat, lemon juice, onion powder and hot pepper sauce together well. Shape into ball. Cover and chill.

Just before serving, pour seafood sauce over crab ball. Add more seafood sauce as needed. Makes 1 small ball.

Pictured on page 34.

Scallop Attraction

Picture perfect and so easy!

Hard margarine (butter browns too fast)	2 tbsp.	30 mL
Thin slices of small zucchini, with peel	2	2
Medium tomatoes, halved, seeded and diced	3	3
Whole oregano	1/4 tsp.	1 mL
Sweet basil	1/8 tsp.	0.5 mL
White wine	1/4 cup	60 mL
Large scallops, cut in 3 slices each	1 lb.	454 g
Sauce:		
Butter or hard margarine	2 tbsp.	30 mL
All-purpose flour	2 tbsp.	30 mL
Evaporated skim milk (or light cream)	2/3 cup	150 mL
Reserved liquid from scallops	1/3 cup	75 mL
Red pepper or pimiento, for garnish		

Melt first amount of margarine in frying pan. Add zucchini. Sauté about 5 minutes until it looks lightly browned. Remove to warm plate.

Put tomatoes in frying pan. Sauté briefly until tomato skin wrinkles a bit. Sprinkle with oregano and basil. Stir. Remove to warm plate.

Add wine to frying pan. Poach scallop slices in wine until just done, stirring occasionally. Remove to warm plate. Reserve liquid.

Sauce: Melt butter in small saucepan over medium heat. Stir in flour. Whisk in reserved liquid. Add milk slowly. Whisk until smooth and thickened.

To assemble, overlap 1/4 zucchini slices in a circle on individual salad plate. Spoon 1/4 tomato pieces on top. Overlap 1/4 scallop slices on tomatoes. Lay 1 scallop slice on top. Pour 1/4 cup (60 mL) sauce on top. Garnish with red pepper or pimiento. Repeat for remaining 3 plates. Serves 4.

Pictured on page 39.

Shrimp Cocktail

Sauce is just right for this traditional dinner appetizer. So elegant in appearance. Set at each place before calling guests.

Seafood Sauce:		
Chili sauce	1/2 cup	125 mL
Ketchup	1/3 cup	75 mL
Sweet pickle relish	2 tbsp.	30 mL
Prepared horseradish	1 tsp.	5 mL
Worcestershire sauce	1/2 tsp.	2 mL
Lemon juice, fresh or bottled	1/2 tsp.	2 mL
Seasoned salt	1/4 tsp.	1 mL
Torn lettuce, lightly packed	2 cups	500 mL
Cooked jumbo shrimp, peeled, deveined, tail intact	40-48	40-48

Seafood Sauce: Stir first 7 ingredients in small bowl. Chill until ready to assemble. Makes 3/4 cup (175 mL) sauce.

Divide lettuce among 8 sherbet dishes. Spoon about 2 tbsp. (30 mL) seafood sauce in center. Hook 5 or 6 shrimp around top outside edge of each sherbet with tails hanging downward. Serves 8.

Pictured below.

Shrimp Cocktail

Dilled Carrot Sticks

Pickled flavor with a crunchy texture.

Small carrots, peeled and quartered lengthwise	8	8
Dill pickle juice	1 cup	250 mL

Simmer carrots and pickle juice in covered saucepan for 20 to 25 minutes until you pierce them with tip of paring knife. Cool in juice. Chill in juice in refrigerator overnight. Makes 32 sticks.

Pictured on page 35.

Jean's Favorite

King Artichoke Dip

Yummy! Wonderful blend of cheese, bacon, spinach and artichoke. Looks pretty, too.

Bacon slices, diced	8	8
Finely chopped onion	1 cup	250 mL
Garlic cloves, minced	2	2
Canned artichoke hearts, drained and chopped	14 oz.	398 mL
Cream cheese, softened	8 oz.	250 g
Sour cream	1/2 cup	125 mL
Bunch of fresh spinach, finely chopped	1	1
Worcestershire sauce	1/4 tsp.	1 mL
Milk, optional		
Baguette, sliced and quartered	1	1

Sauté bacon, onion and garlic in frying pan until bacon is done and onion is soft.

Add artichoke hearts. Sauté for 1 minute more.

Beat cream cheese and sour cream in bowl until smooth. Add bacon mixture. Stir.

Mix in spinach and Worcestershire. Thin with milk if desired.

Serve with bread chunks for dipping. Makes 3 cups (750 mL) dip.

Pictured on page 45.

Onion Tarts

These can be baked then frozen. Reheat in oven, not microwave, to keep pastry flaky.

Hard margarine (butter browns too fast)	1/4 cup	60 mL
Medium onions, finely diced	4	4
All-purpose flour	2 tbsp.	30 mL
Large eggs	4	4
Milk	1 cup	250 mL
Seasoned salt	1 tsp.	5 mL
Pepper	1/8 tsp.	0.5 mL
Bacon slices, cooked crisp and crumbled	5	5
Grated Edam cheese	2 cups	500 mL
Pastry, your own, or a mix, enough for 3 shells		

Melt margarine in frying pan. Add onion. Sauté until onion is soft.

Sprinkle with flour. Mix. Remove from heat.

Beat eggs in mixing bowl. Add milk, seasoned salt and pepper. Stir in onion, bacon and cheese.

Roll out pastry. Cut and fit into ungreased mini muffin cups. Fill with onion mixture. Bake in 350°F (175°C) oven for 15 to 20 minutes. Makes about 4 dozen mini tarts.

Pictured on page 45.

Variation: Bake the filling in 9 inch (22 cm) unbaked pie shell and serve for a brunch or sit-down dinner.

Salty Caraway Sticks

A wonderful little breadstick appetizer. The caraway is a nice savory blend with other more zippy appetizers.

Packaged refrigerator biscuits (10 to a tube)	1	1
Crisp rice cereal, crushed	1 1/4 cups	300 mL
Caraway seed	1 1/2 tbsp.	25 mL
Salt	1 tsp.	5 mL
Milk	1/2 cup	125 mL

Cut each biscuit in half. Roll each half into a pencil shape.

Mix cereal, caraway seed and salt in shallow bowl.

Dip each roll into milk, then roll in seed mixture. Arrange on greased baking sheet. Bake in 450°F (230°C) oven for 10 minutes. Makes 20 appetizers.

Pictured on page 45.

Welsh Cakes

A nice change from crackers. Serve with
Date Nut Log, page 48.

All-purpose flour	2 cups	450 mL
Granulated sugar	1/3 cup	75 mL
Baking powder	2 tsp.	10 mL
Salt	1/2 tsp.	2 mL
Ground nutmeg	1/4 tsp.	1 mL
Ground cinnamon	1/4 tsp.	1 mL
Butter or hard margarine	1/2 cup	125 mL
Cut glazed mixed fruit (see Note)	3/4 cup	175 mL
Large egg	1	1
Milk	1/3 cup	75 mL

Measure first 6 ingredients into large bowl. Cut in butter until mixture is crumbly.

Add fruit. Stir.

Beat egg with fork in separate bowl. Stir in milk. Add egg and milk to flour mixture. Stir just until moistened. Roll out 1/4 inch (6 mm) thick on lightly floured surface. Cut into 2 inch (5 cm) rounds. Grease frying pan for first round of cakes. It shouldn't need greasing again. Fry on medium-low, browning both sides. Makes about 24 small cakes.

Pictured on page 42.

Note: Red and green glazed cherries can be used in place of the fruit.

Baked Cheese Balls

Shortbread-like texture. Freezes well.

Grated sharp Cheddar cheese	1 cup	250 mL
All-purpose flour	1 cup	250 mL
Butter or hard margarine, softened	1/2 cup	125 mL
Salt	1/2 tsp.	2 mL

Poppy seeds
Toasted sesame seeds

Mix cheese, flour, butter and salt in small bowl. Shape into 1/2 inch (12 mm) balls.

Roll in your choice of seeds. Arrange on greased baking sheets. Bake in 350°F (175°C) oven for about 20 to 25 minutes. Makes 36 appetizers.

Pictured on page 41 and on page 23.

1. Salty Caraway Sticks, page 44
2. Chestnuts In Jackets, page 48
3. All-Season Dip, page 49
4. Onion Tarts, page 44
5. King Artichoke Dip, page 44

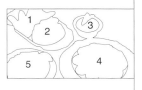

Nutty Cheese Ball

Serve with assorted fruit and crackers. Somewhat softer ball.
Make the day before.

Crushed pineapple, well-drained	14 oz.	398 mL
Cream cheese, softened	12 oz.	375 g
Salt	1 tsp.	5 mL
Onion powder	1/4 tsp.	1 mL
Chopped pecans	3/4 cup	175 mL
Chopped green pepper	2 tbsp.	30 mL

Combine pineapple, cream cheese, salt and onion powder in bowl. Beat slowly to mix well.

Mix in pecans and green pepper. Chill overnight. Shape into a ball. Serve with fruit and assorted crackers. Makes 1 medium cheese ball.

Pictured on page 47.

Round Cheese Spread

Nice strong curry flavor.

Cream cheese, softened	8 oz.	250 g
Salad dressing (or mayonnaise)	1 tbsp.	15 mL
Curry powder	1 1/2 tsp.	7 mL
Worcestershire sauce	1 tsp.	5 mL
Seasoned salt	1/4 tsp.	1 mL
Salt	1/4 tsp.	1 mL
Paprika	1/4 tsp.	1 mL
Chutney, your choice	1/2 cup	125 mL

Beat first 7 ingredients together on medium. Shape into a flattened ball. Chill.

When ready to use, place cheese round on serving plate. Spoon chutney over top allowing some to run down sides, using more chutney if desired. Makes 1 small ball.

Pictured on page 47.

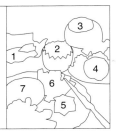

Cheese Pastries

Keep these in an open container to retain crispness.

All-purpose flour	1 cup	250 mL
Cornmeal	2 tbsp.	30 mL
Garlic powder	1/4 tsp.	1 mL
Salt	1/8 tsp.	0.5 mL
Cayenne pepper	1/8 tsp.	0.5 mL
Butter or hard margarine	1/4 cup	60 mL
Grated sharp Cheddar cheese	1 cup	250 mL
Grated Parmesan cheese	2 tbsp.	30 mL
Water	5 tbsp.	75 mL

Put first 5 ingredients into bowl. Cut in butter until crumbly.

Add both cheeses. Toss. Sprinkle with water. Mix into a ball. Roll out on lightly floured surface to 16 × 5 inch (40 × 12 cm) rectangle. Cut in 1/2 inch (12 mm) wide strips crosswise, making 32 strips. Place on greased baking sheet. Bake in 400°F (205°C) oven for about 10 minutes until golden. Cool on rack. Makes 32.

Pictured on page 47.

Last Minute Appetizer

Horseradish gives an unexpected tang.

Apple or crabapple jelly	1/2 cup	125 mL
Pineapple or apricot jam	1/2 cup	125 mL
Prepared horseradish	1 tbsp.	15 mL
Dry mustard powder, generous measure	1/4 tsp.	1 mL
Cream cheese, softened	8 oz.	250 g

Put first 4 ingredients into small bowl. Stir well.

Place cheese on serving dish. Top with jam mixture, allowing it to run down sides. Serve with assorted crackers. Makes 1 cup (250 mL) sauce plus 1 block cream cheese.

Pictured on page 47.

Chestnuts In Jackets

A bit fussy to make but the outcome is like a Cheddar shortbread. Freeze uncooked in plastic container.

Canned whole water chestnuts	2 x 8 oz.	2 x 227 mL
Butter or hard margarine, softened	½ cup	125 mL
Grated sharp Cheddar cheese	2 cups	500 mL
Sesame seeds	2 tbsp.	30 mL
Garlic salt	½ tsp.	2 mL
Paprika	½ tsp.	2 mL
Cayenne pepper, just a pinch		
All-purpose flour	1½ cups	375 mL

Drain chestnuts. Dry with paper towels. Let stand to dry even more while making "jackets".

Beat butter and cheese in medium bowl. Add sesame seeds, salt, paprika and cayenne. Beat. Gradually work in flour until mixture holds together. Mold about 1 tbsp. (15 mL) dough around each chestnut. Cover and chill or freeze. Bake, chilled, in 425°F (220°C) oven for 15 to 20 minutes. If baking frozen, lower temperature to 400°F (205°C) and bake about 15 minutes longer. Makes 36 hot appetizers.

Pictured on page 45.

Stuffed Edam

Serve at room temperature but can be made the day before. Very tasty.

Edam cheese, with red wax coating (or Gouda)	1 lb.	454 g
Cream cheese, softened	8 oz.	250 g
Apricot jam	¼ cup	60 mL
Onion powder	½ tsp.	2 mL
Paprika	⅛ tsp.	0.5 mL
Milk	1-2 tbsp.	15-30 mL
Finely chopped red pepper	⅓ cup	75 mL
Chopped chives	1 tsp.	5 mL

Cut a thin slice from top of cheese. Use a sharp knife to cut a zig zag edge if you like. Use a spoon or melon baller to scoop out cheese, leaving shell intact. Dice cheese into fine pieces.

Beat cream cheese, jam, onion powder and paprika together in small bowl. Add diced cheese. Stir. Process in food processor 1 minute. Add milk. Process another 20 seconds. Remove to bowl.

Add green pepper and chives. Stir. Spoon into red shell. Serves 10.

Pictured on page 47.

Spinach Dip

This can be served in the bread loaf or as a separate heated dip with bread, crackers and fresh veggies.

Salad dressing (or mayonnaise)	½ cup	125 mL
Cream cheese softened	2 x 8 oz.	2 x 250 g
Grated medium or sharp Cheddar cheese	1 cup	250 mL
Frozen chopped spinach, thawed, squeezed dry	10 oz.	300 g
Chopped fried bacon, 6 slices	½ cup	125 mL
Finely chopped onion	¼ cup	60 mL
Dill weed	2 tsp.	10 mL
Garlic powder (or 1 clove, minced)	¼ tsp.	1 mL

Beat salad dressing and cream cheese together in small bowl until smooth. Stir in next 6 ingredients. Makes 3 cups (750 mL) dip.

Variation: Cut top off round bread loaf. Hollow out loaf leaving shell 1 inch (2.5 cm) thick. Reserve removed bread for dipping. Pour spinach mixture into hollow. Wrap in foil. Heat in 325°F (160°C) oven for 2 hours. Remove from oven. Turn back foil. Serve with bread pieces taken from loaf to use as dippers. Slice baguette for extra dippers. As dip disappears, break off sides for dippers. Good warm and also good as it cools. Makes 1 loaf.

Pictured on page 47.

Date Nut Log

Good on Welsh Cakes, page 45, or serve with assorted crackers.

Cream cheese, softened	8 oz.	250 g
Corn syrup	2 tbsp.	30 mL
Maple flavoring	½ tsp.	2 mL
Chopped dates	¾ cup	175 mL
Chopped walnuts	½ cup	125 mL
Finely chopped walnuts	¾ cup	175 mL

Beat cheese, corn syrup and maple flavoring in small bowl until smooth.

Stir in dates and first amount of walnuts. Chill overnight. Shape into log.

Roll in remaining walnuts. Chill until ready to serve. May be frozen. Makes 1 log about 1½ inches (4 cm) in diameter.

Pictured on page 42.

> M ost dips taste best if made the day before and chilled. Flavors seem to blend better. For best results serve at room temperature.

Favorite Clam Dip

The name says it all. It's mild but always popular.

Cream cheese, softened	8 oz.	250 g
Minced clams, drained, juice reserved	2 × 5 oz.	2 × 142 g
Lemon juice, fresh or bottled	1 tbsp.	15 mL
Worcestershire sauce	1 tsp.	5 mL
Onion salt	1/4 tsp.	1 mL
Onion powder	1/4 tsp.	1 mL
Reserved juice, as needed	5 tbsp.	75 mL

Beat first 6 ingredients together in small bowl.

Add a bit of reserved juice a small amount at a time until mixture is of dipping consistency. Makes 2 1/2 cups (600 mL) dip.

Pictured on page 34.

All-Season Dip

This tangy dip will be a hit! Serve with assorted raw vegetables.

Salad dressing (or mayonnaise)	1 cup	250 mL
Chili sauce	1 cup	250 mL
Onion flakes	3 tbsp.	50 mL
Water	2 tbsp.	30 mL
Mustard seeds	2 tsp.	10 mL
Horseradish	2 tbsp.	30 mL

Put all 6 ingredients into small bowl. Stir together well. Chill at least 2 hours. Makes 2 cups (500 mL) dip.

Pictured on page 45.

Shrimp Dip

Very shrimpy tasting with the zip of cayenne. Serve with an assortment of crackers and veggies.

Canned broken shrimp, drained, mashed with fork	1 × 4 oz.	1 × 113 g
Salad dressing (or mayonnaise)	1/2 cup	125 mL
Onion powder	1/4 tsp.	1 mL
Sherry (or alcohol-free sherry)	2 tbsp.	30 mL
Cayenne pepper	1/8 tsp.	0.5 mL
Salt	1/4 tsp.	1 mL
Pepper	1/16 tsp.	0.5 mL
Milk	1 tbsp.	15 mL

Stir all 8 ingredients together in small bowl. Chill. Makes 1 cup (250 mL) dip.

Pictured on page 34.

Fruit Dip

Very quick. Dip can be prepared a day ahead. This has a nice hint of cinnamon.

Frozen whipped topping, thawed	2 cups	500 mL
Brown sugar, packed	1/4 cup	60 mL
Ground cinnamon	1/4 tsp.	1 mL
Apple slices, cored, with peel		
Pear slices		
Grapes		
Water	1 cup	250 mL
Lemon juice, fresh or bottled	2 tbsp.	30 mL

Stir whipped topping with brown sugar and cinnamon.

Combine fruit with water and lemon juice. Let stand about 30 minutes. Drain. Place dip in small dish. Arrange fruit around dip. Makes 2 cups (500 mL) dip.

Pictured on page 47.

Fun Party Mix

*Double or triple this recipe and store in fridge
or freezer for unexpected guests.*

Crispix cereal	6 cups	1.35 L
Mini pretzels	1 cup	250 mL
Salted dry roasted peanuts	1 cup	250 mL
Butter or hard margarine	6 tbsp.	100 mL
Brown sugar, packed	¾ cup	175 mL
Honey	¼ cup	60 mL
Vanilla	1 tsp.	5 mL

Put cereal, pretzels and peanuts into large bowl. Stir gently.

Measure next 3 ingredients into saucepan. Heat on medium and stir until mixture boils. Boil gently on medium-low without stirring for 5 minutes.

Stir in vanilla. Remove from heat. Pour hot syrup over cereal mixture. Stir well to coat. Transfer to large greased roaster. Bake for 1 hour in 250°F (120°C) oven, removing every 15 minutes to stir. Cool. Store in airtight container. Freezes well. Makes 8 cups (2 L) snack mixture.

Pictured on page 51.

Cinnamon Crisps

*A great snack or appetizer. Take in the car if you're traveling
or to the skating rink.*

Butter or hard margarine, melted	½ cup	125 mL
Flour tortillas, 10 inch (25 cm) diameter	10	10
Granulated sugar	½ cup	125 mL
Ground cinnamon	1 tbsp.	15 mL

Brush tops of tortillas with melted butter. Spread remaining butter over jelly roll pan. Cut tortillas into 13 wedges each for a total of 130 "chips". Fit as many chips as close together as you can.

Mix sugar and cinnamon in small bowl. Sprinkle over chips. Bake in 325°F (160°C) oven for about 10 to 12 minutes until golden. Cool. Store in covered container. Makes 130 small pieces.

Pictured above.

Variation: Substitute 1 package (16 oz., 454 g) of wonton wrappers for the tortillas. Cut each wrapper diagonally into 4 wedges. Proceed as above, baking for 8 minutes. Makes 288 small pieces.

1. Snackies, page 51
2. Cinnamon Crisps, page 50
3. Curried Nuts, page 51
4. Fun Party Mix, 50

Snackies

Be prepared to refill the bowl often once guests get started on these.

Sultana raisins	1 cup	250 mL
Bite size shredded wheat cereal	2 cups	450 mL
Bite size shredded corn cereal	2 cups	450 mL
Oat squares cereal	2 cups	450 mL
Corn bran cereal	2 cups	450 mL
Pecan halves	1 cup	250 mL
Coating:		
Butter or hard margarine	½ cup	125 mL
Corn syrup	¼ cup	60 mL
Brown sugar, packed	1½ cups	375 mL
Ground cinnamon	1 tsp.	5 mL
Salt	¾ tsp.	4 mL
Vanilla	1 tsp.	5 mL

Combine raisins, cereals and pecan halves in large greased bowl.

Coating: Stir all ingredients in saucepan until mixture comes to a boil. Boil slowly for 3 minutes. Pour over cereal mixture. Stir well to coat all pieces. Spread on 2 greased baking sheets. Cool until firm. Break into pieces. Store in airtight container. Makes 2½ pounds (1.1 kg) or about 13 cups (3.2 L) snack mix.

Pictured on page 50.

Curried Nuts

The curry flavor is not too strong. Adjust curry powder as desired.

Butter or hard margarine	¼ cup	60 mL
Curry powder	1 tsp.	5 mL
Salt	1 tsp.	5 mL
Mixed nuts such as pecans, almonds, peanuts, walnuts, filberts	4 cups	1 L

Melt butter in large saucepan. Stir in curry powder and salt. Add nuts. Stir to coat. Turn into ungreased 10 x 15 inch (25 x 30 cm) jelly roll pan. Bake in 350°F (175°C) oven for 10 to 15 minutes. Stir occasionally while baking. Cool. Makes 4 cups (1 L) nut mixture.

Pictured on page 50.

Beverages

Certain foods have come to represent Christmas. Certain beverages play the same role. With their rich colors and inviting hues, these flavorful drinks are significant additions to any holiday occasion.

Hot and cold, traditional and contemporary selections are included for an extra special touch on your Yuletide table.

Mock Mint Julep

As green as green can be. Adjust mint flavoring as desired.

Lemon-lime drink mix (2 quart , 2 L size each, such as Kool-Aid)	2	2
Mint flavoring	¼ tsp.	1 mL
Lemon-lime soft drink	4 cups	1 L
Maraschino cherries, for garnish		

Make drink mix according to directions on envelope.

Stir in mint flavoring and soft drink. Pour over ice in glasses.

Garnish with cherries. Makes 160 oz. (5 L).

Pictured on this page.

Raspberry Liqueur

So smooth and sweet. Perfect color for Christmas.

Frozen raspberries, in syrup	15 oz.	425 g
Ground cinnamon	⅛ tsp.	0.5 mL
Brandy or kirsch	2 cups	500 mL
Vodka	2 cups	500 mL
Granulated sugar	½ cup	125 mL

Put all ingredients into jar. Put on lid. Let stand at room temperature for 6 weeks. Shake jar once a week. After 6 weeks, strain and bottle. Makes 5 cups (1.25 L) liqueur.

Pictured on page 53.

Mulled Wine

Full-bodied mulled flavor. Double the recipe for a larger crowd.

Cranberry cocktail juice	3 cups	750 mL
Whole cloves	10	10
Cinnamon sticks (about 2 inch, 5 cm length)	3	3
Ground nutmeg	¼ tsp.	1 mL
Honey	¼ cup	60 mL
Orange, sliced	1	1
Lemon slices	3	3
Dry red wine	3 cups	750 mL

Pour juice into large saucepan.

Add next 6 ingredients. Stir to dissolve honey. Simmer on low for about 1 hour.

Add wine. Heat and serve hot. Makes 8 cups (2 L).

Pictured on page 55.

Mock Mint Julep

Left: Mock Kahlua, page 53
Bottom Center: Raspberry Liqueur, page 52

Top Center: Champagne Punch, page 53
Right: Creamy Cranberry Punch, page 53

Mock Kahlua

Wow! It tastes very close to the real thing.
Lasts in the fridge for several months.

Granulated sugar	4 cups	900 mL
Water	4 cups	900 mL
Instant coffee granules	⅔ cup	150 mL
Rye whiskey	25 oz.	750 mL
Vanilla bean	1	1

Heat and stir sugar, water and coffee granules in saucepan until mixture boils. Boil 3 minutes without stirring. Cool. Pour into 3 quart (3 L) jar.

Add rye and vanilla bean. Cover. Let stand for 3 weeks. Remove vanilla bean. Makes 9 cups (2.25 L) liqueur.

Pictured above.

Creamy Cranberry Punch

Very refreshing and not too sweet. Different from traditional clear punches.

Cranberry cocktail, chilled	1⅓ cups	325 mL
Frozen whole strawberries, thawed	20 oz.	600 g
Small bananas, cut up	3	3
Plain yogurt	1⅓ cups	325 mL
Granulated sugar	½ cup	125 mL
Cranberry cocktail, chilled	5½ cups	1.4 L
Prepared orange juice	⅓ cup	75 mL

Put first 5 ingredients in blender. Process until smooth. Pour into punch bowl.

Add remaining cranberry cocktail and orange juice. Stir. Makes 10 cups (2.5 L) punch.

Pictured above.

Champagne Punch

Keep champagne chilled and add just before serving for most bubbly effect.

Champagne or sparkling white wine	25 oz.	750 mL
Cointreau	6 oz.	170 mL
Ginger ale	8 cups	2 L
Orange or lime slices, for garnish		

Pour champagne, cointreau and ginger ale into punch bowl. Garnish with fruit slices or add Ice Ring, below. Makes 96 ounces (3 L) punch.

Pictured above.

Ice Ring

Fill a 3 or 4 cup (750 or 1 L) ring mold with sugar free ginger ale. Freeze. Do not use ginger ale with sugar as it melts quickly.

Perked Wassail

Very nice—warming! Great for a crowd after skiing or skating.
Or serve while you decorate the Christmas tree.

Oranges	2	2
Lemons	2	2
Water	2 cups	500 mL
Apple cider	4 qts.	4 L
Whole allspice	1 tbsp.	15 mL
Cinnamon sticks, 4 inch (10 cm)	3	3
Whole cloves	1 tsp.	5 mL
Reserved sliced oranges		
Reserved sliced lemons		
Granulated sugar	1 cup	250 mL
Boiling water	2 cups	500 mL

Squeeze oranges and lemons to get juice. Remove any seeds. Pour juices into percolator at least 24 cup (6 L) size. Slice remaining fruit and reserve. Add first amount of water and apple cider to percolator.

Put next 5 ingredients into coffee basket. Perk until hot.

Stir sugar in boiling water until dissolved. Pour into basket. Serve hot. Makes 25 cups (5.2 L).

Pictured on page 55.

Mulled Apple Drink

Nice amber color with a spicy taste.

Apple juice	4 cups	1 L
Brown sugar, packed	1/3 cup	75 mL
Salt	1/8 tsp.	0.5 mL
Whole cloves	6	6
Whole allspice	6	6
Cinnamon sticks, 4 inch (10 cm)	2	2

Measure all ingredients in large saucepan. Heat, stirring often until it comes to a boil. Simmer for 10 minutes. Strain into punch cups. Makes almost 4 cups (1 L).

Pictured on page 55.

Mulled Cranberry Juice

Double or triple this recipe. Beautiful red color.

Cranberry cocktail	4 cups	1 L
Lemon juice, fresh or bottled	2 tbsp.	30 mL
Granulated sugar	1/4 cup	60 mL
Whole allspice	10	10
Cinnamon stick, 4 inch (10 cm)	1	1

Combine all ingredients in saucepan. Bring to a boil. Boil 5 minutes. Pour through strainer into punch cups. Makes 4 cups (1 L).

Pictured on page 55.

French Silk Chocolate

Fluffy and light with a silky smooth texture.
Creamy chocolate flavor. Delicious.

Semisweet chocolate chips	3/4 cup	175 mL
White corn syrup	1/2 cup	125 mL
Water	1/3 cup	75 mL
Vanilla	1 tsp.	5 mL
Whipping cream	2 cups	500 mL
Milk	8 3/4 cups	2 L

Combine chocolate chips, syrup, water and vanilla in saucepan. Heat, stirring often, on low until smooth and all chocolate is melted. Refrigerate until cold.

Beat whipping cream until it is beginning to thicken just a little. Add chocolate mixture gradually while continuing to beat. Beat until mixture will mound. Chill.

Heat milk in heavy saucepan. Pour 6 ounces (175 mL) hot milk into mugs. Add chocolate mixture to taste. Stir well. An 8 oz. (250 mL) mug would take about 4 heaping tbsp. (60 mL). Makes 20 servings, 8 oz. (250 mL) each.

Pictured on page 55.

Left: Quick Fruit Punch with Punch Ice Ring   Right: Christmas Punch

Quick Fruit Punch

*This recipe doubles easily. Nice and sweet
for children and adults alike.*

Canned cranberry jelly	14 oz.	398 mL
Granulated sugar	½ cup	125 mL
Boiling water	1 cup	250 mL
Prepared orange juice	½ cup	125 mL
Lemon juice, fresh or bottled	½ cup	125 mL
Cold water	2 cups	500 mL

Stir cranberry jelly, sugar and boiling water in bowl to dissolve sugar and melt jelly. Beat on medium if necessary.

Add remaining ingredients. Stir. Pour into punch bowl. Carefully add Punch Ice Ring, page 56. Makes 6½ cups (1.5 L).

Pictured above.

Rhubarb Cocktail

Lovely rosé color. Great and refreshing!

Finely chopped rhubarb, fresh or frozen	6 cups	1.5 L
Boiling water	6 cups	1.5 L
Frozen concentrated lemonade	12 oz.	355 mL
Lemonade cans of water	2	2
Granulated sugar	½ cup	125 mL
Ginger ale, chilled	9 cups	2.2 L

Measure rhubarb into large bowl. Pour boiling water over top. Cover. Let stand overnight. Strain through cheesecloth into pitcher. Store for a few hours or 5 to 6 days in the refrigerator or freeze until needed.

When ready to make punch, thaw rhubarb juice and pour into punch bowl. Stir in concentrated lemonade, cans of water and sugar. Stir until sugar dissolves. Chill.

To serve add ginger ale. Pour over ice in glasses. Makes 18 cups (4.5 L).

Pictured on page 69.

Christmas Punch

Beautiful Christmassy red. Double or triple this recipe.

Cranberry cocktail	8¾ cups	2 L
Frozen concentrated lemonade, thawed	12 oz.	340 mL
Lemon-lime soft drink	8¾ cups	2 L
Lime slices, orange slices, maraschino cherries, for garnish		

Stir cranberry cocktail, concentrated lemonade and lemon-lime soft drink together in punch bowl.

Float fruit slices or cherries on top. Makes 18 cups (4.5 L).

Pictured on this page.

Punch Ice Ring

*Any assortment of fruit or glazed cherries can be used.
Be creative.*

Distilled water, 1 inch (2.5 cm) depth		
Strawberries, halved	4	4
Mandarin orange sections	8	8
Distilled water, ⅛ inch (3 mm) depth		
Distilled water, 1 inch (2.5 cm) depth		
Distilled water, 1 inch (2.5 cm) depth		

Pour first amount of water into ring pan using a salad mold or a bundt pan. Freeze.

Arrange strawberries, cut side down around top as well as orange sections and holly leaves. Pour just barely enough water to freeze them in place. If you add too much water at this stage, fruit will float. Freeze.

Pour third amount of water over fruit. Freeze.

Add final layer of water. Freeze. Unmold to use in punch. Makes 1 ring.

Pictured on this page.

Note: For less dilution of punch as ring thaws, use a sugar-free drink such as diet 7-UP or diet ginger ale. If you use a soft drink containing sugar, ice will thaw too fast.

Traditional Eggnog

Creamy, foamy layer on top. Just stir a bit if it lessens.

Egg whites, large	12	12
Granulated sugar	1 cup	250 mL
Egg yolks, large	12	12
Salt	½ tsp.	2 mL
Whipping cream	3 cups	750 mL
Granulated sugar	2 tbsp.	30 mL
Vanilla	1 tbsp.	15 mL
Milk	7 cups	1.75 L
Light rum	2 cups	500 mL
Whiskey (rye or scotch)	1 cup	250 mL
Nutmeg, sprinkle		

Beat egg whites in large bowl until they start to thicken. Add first amount of sugar. Beat until thick.

In second large bowl beat egg yolks and salt until thick. Add egg whites. Beat until mixed and thick.

In third large bowl beat cream until it starts to thicken. Add remaining sugar and vanilla. Beat until thick. Add egg mixture slowly as you stir in.

Add milk, rum and whiskey, beating continually. Chill.

Serve in a punch bowl or a pitcher. Garnish with a sprinkle of nutmeg. Makes 20 cups (5 L).

Pictured below.

Traditional Eggnog

Coffee Nog

A wonderful combination of two favorite beverages.

Instant coffee granules	2 tbsp.	30 mL
Boiling water	2 tbsp.	30 mL
Eggnog	8¾ cups	2 L
Brown sugar, packed	⅓ cup	75 mL
Ground cinnamon	¼ tsp.	1 mL
Kahlua or Tia Maria liqueur, (optional)	1 cup	250 mL
Topping:		
Whipping cream (or 1 envelope topping)	1 cup	250 mL
Granulated sugar	1 tbsp.	15 mL
Vanilla	½ tsp.	2 mL
Nutmeg, sprinkle		

Stir coffee granules into boiling water in large bowl. Add eggnog, brown sugar and cinnamon. Beat to dissolve sugar. Stir in Kahlua. Pour into punch bowl.

Topping: Beat cream, sugar and vanilla until thick. Spoon over top.

Sprinkle whipped cream with nutmeg. Makes about 18 servings 5 oz. (140 mL) each or 10 cups (2.5 L).

Pictured on page 72.

Easy Eggnog

Very easy to prepare. Not quite as rich as the Traditional Eggnog on this page.

Large eggs	12	12
Granulated sugar	1½ cups	375 mL
Salt	¾ tsp.	4 mL
Homogenized milk (for richness)	12 cups	3 L
Vanilla	3 tbsp.	50 mL
Brandy (see Note)	2 cups	500 mL
Rum (see Note)	½ cup	125 mL
Ground nutmeg, sprinkle		

Beat eggs in extra large bowl until light. Continue beating while adding sugar and salt gradually. Beat until sugar is dissolved.

Add milk and vanilla. Add brandy and rum. Adjust strength by increasing or decreasing liquor. Stir. May be refrigerated up to 24 hours before serving or stored, covered, in refrigerator for 6 days. To serve, run through blender to foam.

Garnish with a sprinkle of nutmeg. Makes 28 servings, 5 oz. (140 mL) each.

Pictured on page 72.

Note: Liquor may be left out and 5-6 tbsp. (75 to 100 mL) rum flavoring added instead.

Breads & Quick Breads

Bread is important all year. But at Christmas this staple becomes as special as the season itself.

A yeast bread woven into a wreath has a place of its own on a holiday brunch or supper table. Breads filled with cherries, raisins and other goodies are just as enticing to the eye as they are to the palate. Quick breads like tea loaves and muffins are easy to make and wonderfully convenient for drop-in guests.

So don't overlook the potential of the bread group and do make room for these special breads and quick breads.

Table Bread Wreath

Table Bread Wreath

Very attractive. Use for a buffet or brunch.

Warm water	1 cup	225 mL
Granulated sugar	2 tsp.	10 mL
Active dry yeast	2 x ¼ oz.	2 × 8 g
Butter or hard margarine, softened	¾ cup	175 mL
Granulated sugar	½ cup	125 mL
Large eggs	2	2
Salt	1 tsp.	5 mL
All-purpose flour	2 cups	450 mL
Cut glazed mixed fruit	1 cup	250 mL
Raisins	½ cup	125 mL
All-purpose flour, approximately	2¾ cups	625 mL
Large egg, fork-beaten	1	1
Glaze:		
Icing (confectioner's) sugar	1½ cups	375 mL
Water	2½ tbsp.	40 mL
Vanilla	½ tsp.	2 mL
Glazed red or green cherries, for garnish		
Chopped walnuts, for garnish		

Stir warm water and first amount of sugar in small bowl. Sprinkle yeast over top. Let stand 10 minutes. Stir.

Cream butter and second amount of sugar in large bowl. Beat in eggs 1 at a time. Add salt and yeast mixture. Add first amount of flour. Beat on medium about 2 minutes until smooth.

Mix in glazed fruit and raisins. Work in remaining flour with a spoon. Turn out onto lightly floured surface. Knead for 5 to 8 minutes until smooth and elastic. Put into large greased bowl, turning once to grease top. Cover with tea towel. Let stand in oven with light on and door closed for about 2 hours until doubled in bulk.

Punch dough down. Divide into 3 equal portions. Roll each portion on lightly floured surface until it reaches 2 feet (60 cm) in length. Pinch 3 ends together on greased baking sheet. Braid the 3 ropes. Shape into a wreath, joining ends and pinching together. Cover with tea towel. Let stand in oven with light on and door closed for about 1 hour until doubled in size. Brush with beaten egg. Bake in 375°F (190°C) oven for 40 to 45 minutes until browned. Cool on rack.

Glaze: Mix icing sugar, water and vanilla, adding more water if needed to make a barely pourable glaze. Brush over wreath.

Garnish with cherries or nuts. Makes 1 wreath.

Pictured on this page and on front cover.

Christmas Braid

Rich golden appearance. Not too sweet. Very showy.

Granulated sugar	1 tsp.	5 mL
Warm water	¼ cup	60 mL
Active dry yeast	1 × ¼ oz.	1 × 8 g
Milk, scalded and cooled to lukewarm	1½ cups	375 mL
Salt	1 tsp.	5 mL
Butter or hard margarine	¼ cup	60 mL
Granulated sugar	6 tbsp.	100 mL
Large egg, beaten	1	1
Cardamom	¼ tsp.	1 mL
All-purpose flour	3 cups	750 mL
All-purpose flour, approximately	2½ cups	625 mL
Large egg, beaten	1	1

Stir first amount of sugar into warm water in small bowl. Sprinkle yeast over top. Let stand for 10 minutes. Stir to dissolve yeast.

Measure next 6 ingredients into large bowl. Mix. Add yeast mixture. Stir well.

Mix in first amount of flour.

Work in enough remaining flour as needed to make a soft dough. Place in greased bowl, turning once to grease top. Cover with greased waxed paper and tea towel. Let stand in oven with light on and door closed for about 1½ hours until doubled in bulk. Punch dough down. Using about ½ the dough, roll into rectangle 10 x 15 inches (25 x 38 cm). Place on greased baking sheet.

Prepare Prune Filling, below. Spread ½ down center using ⅓ of space. Cut sides almost to filling in strips about 1 inch (2.5 cm) wide. Turn each side strip over filling alternately as though braiding. Seal ends. Repeat with remaining dough and filling. Cover with greased waxed paper and tea towel. Let stand in oven with light on and door closed for about 40 minutes until doubled in size. Brush with beaten egg. Bake in 350°F (175°C) oven for 30 to 40 minutes. Decorate with Glaze, page 58 and cherries.

Pictured on this page.

Prune Filling

Dry pitted prunes	3 cups	750 mL
Water	½ cup	125 mL
Chopped walnuts	¾ cup	175 mL
Ground cinnamon	½ tsp.	2 mL

Simmer prunes in water for 10 to 15 minutes. Drain. Mash slightly. Stir in walnuts and cinnamon. Cool completely. Makes 3 cups (750 mL), enough for 2 Christmas Braids.

Pictured on this page.

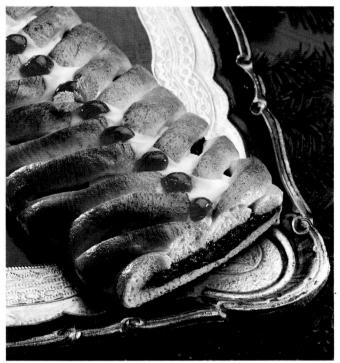

Christmas Braid with Prune Filling

Potato Rolls

Golden brown rolls. Good with any meat or casserole.

Butter or hard margarine	½ cup	125 mL
Granulated sugar	½ cup	125 mL
Salt	½ tsp.	2 mL
Hot potato water, drained from cooked potatoes	1 cup	250 mL
Granulated sugar	1 tsp.	5 mL
Warm water	¼ cup	60 mL
Envelope active dry yeast	1 × ¼ oz.	1 × 8 g
Large eggs, fork beaten	2	2
All-purpose flour	4 cups	1 L

Stir first 4 ingredients together in large bowl until butter is dissolved. Set aside to cool to lukewarm.

Stir second amount of sugar into warm water in small bowl. Sprinkle yeast over top. Let stand 10 minutes. Stir to dissolve yeast. Add to potato mixture.

Beat in eggs. Add flour. Mix. Knead on floured surface about 7 to 10 minutes until smooth and elastic. Place in greased bowl, turning once to grease top. Cover with tea towel. Let stand in oven with light on and door closed about 2 hours until doubled in bulk. Punch dough down. Shape into rolls the size of eggs. Arrange on greased baking sheet. Cover with tea towel. Let stand in oven with light on and door closed about 1 hour until doubled in size. Bake in 350°F (175°C) oven for 15 to 18 minutes. Makes 24 rolls.

Pictured on page 141.

Holiday Brunch Cake

A real winner! Make this ahead and freeze.
Glaze just before serving.

Frozen bread loaves, thawed	2	2
Butter or hard margarine, softened	2 tbsp.	30 mL
Granulated sugar	½ cup	125 mL
Ground cinnamon	1 tsp.	5 mL
Chopped red glazed cherries	⅔ cup	150 mL
Butter or hard margarine, softened	2 tbsp.	30 mL
Large egg, beaten	1	1
Sliced almonds	⅓ cup	75 mL
Icing Drizzle:		
Icing (confectioner's) sugar	1 cup	250 mL
Vanilla	¼ tsp.	1 mL
Water	1 tbsp.	15 mL

Combine the 2 loaves then divide into 3 equal portions. Roll out 1 portion to fit greased 12 inch (30 cm) deep dish pizza pan.

Spread with first amount of butter.

Mix sugar, cinnamon and cherries in small bowl. Sprinkle ½ over first dough layer in pan. Roll out second portion. Lay it over top.

Spread with second amount of butter. Scatter second ½ cherry mixture over top. Roll out third portion of dough. Place over top. Position a 2 to 2½ inch (5 to 6.5 cm) cookie cutter in center of top. Mark dough in quarters, then mark each quarter in 4 wedges. This makes a total of 16 wedges. Using a sharp knife cut through marks to the bottom, taking care not to cut past the cookie cutter. Twist each wedge 5 times and arc slightly, twisting all in the same direction. Cover with greased waxed paper and tea towel. Let stand in oven with light on and door closed about 1 hour until doubled in size.

Brush with egg. Sprinkle with almonds. Bake in 375°F (190°C) oven for about 30 minutes until golden brown.

Icing Drizzle: Mix all ingredients together, adding more water if needed to make a drizzle consistency. Drizzle over warm coffee cake. Serve warm or cold. Makes 1 coffee cake.

Pictured on page 69.

Easy Overnight Buns

Have lots of these in the freezer for holiday guests.

All-purpose flour	2 cups	500 mL
Butter or hard margarine, softened	½ cup	125 mL
Granulated sugar	½ cup	125 mL
Large egg	1	1
Cold water	2 cups	500 mL
Salt	½ tsp.	2 mL
Baking powder	½ tsp.	2 mL
Active dry yeast	1 × ¼ oz.	1 × 8 g
All-purpose flour, approximately	4 cups	1 L

Put first 5 ingredients into large bowl. Beat slowly to moisten.

Sprinkle with salt, baking powder and yeast. Let stand for 1 minute. Beat well.

Work in enough remaining flour to make a stiff dough. Place in greased bowl, turning once to grease top. Cover with greased waxed paper and tea towel. Let stand on counter overnight. In the morning punch down dough. Shape into buns, using greased palms if necessary. Arrange in greased pan. Let stand in oven with light on and door closed for 2 to 3 hours until doubled in size. Bake in 375°F (190°C) oven for about 35 to 40 minutes until golden brown. Yield: about 20 medium buns.

Pictured on page 137.

Christmas Tree Buns, page 61

Christmas Tree Buns

Pretty as a picture for Christmas buffet or brunch table.

Granulated sugar	1 tsp.	5 mL
Warm water	¼ cup	60 mL
Active dry yeast	1 × ¼ oz.	1 × 8 g
Milk, scalded and cooled to lukewarm	1½ cups	375 mL
Salt	1 tsp.	5 mL
Butter or hard margarine, melted	¼ cup	60 mL
Granulated sugar	6 tbsp.	100 mL
Large egg, beaten	1	1
Cardamom	¼ tsp.	1 mL
All-purpose flour	3 cups	750 mL
Currants or dark raisins	¼ cup	60 mL
Sultana raisins	½ cup	125 mL
Cut mixed glazed fruit	½ cup	125 mL
All-purpose flour, approximately	2½ cups	625 mL
Candied cherries, for garnish	¼ cup	60 mL

Stir first amount of sugar into water in small bowl. Sprinkle yeast over top. Let stand 10 minutes. Stir.

Mix next 6 ingredients in large bowl. Add yeast mixture. Stir.

Beat in first amount of flour.

Add currants, sultana raisins and fruit. Stir.

Work in enough flour as needed to make a soft dough. Knead until smooth and elastic. Place in greased bowl turning once to grease top. Cover with tea towel. Let stand in oven with light on and door closed for about 1½ hours until doubled in bulk. Punch dough down. Make into small buns. Arrange on greased baking sheet in shape of a Christmas tree. Set buns fairly close together allowing some room to rise. Let stand in oven with light on and door closed about 1 hour until doubled in size. Bake in 350°F (175°C) oven for 30 to 40 minutes until golden. Cool. Ice thinly or drizzle with Glaze, page 59.

Use candied cherries to garnish tree. Makes 2 large trees.

Pictured on page 60.

Drop Cheese Biscuits

Light and flaky texture. So easy and quick to make.

All-purpose flour	2 cups	500 mL
Baking powder	4 tsp.	20 mL
Salt	¾ tsp.	4 mL
Butter or hard margarine	½ cup	125 mL
Water	1 cup	250 mL
Grated sharp Cheddar cheese	1½ cups	375 mL

Measure flour, baking powder and salt into medium bowl. Cut in butter until crumbly.

Add water and cheese. Stir to moisten. Drop by rounded tablespoonfuls about 2 inches (5 cm) apart onto greased baking sheet. Bake in 425°F (220°C) oven for about 15 minutes. Makes 16 biscuits.

Pictured below.

Left: Raisin Biscuits, page 62
Right: Drop Cheese Biscuits, page 61
Top Center: Lemon Spread, page 66

Banana Bran Nut Loaf

Moist and delicious and so nutritious.

Butter or hard margarine, softened	¼ cup	60 mL
Granulated sugar	¼ cup	125 mL
Large egg	1	1
All-bran cereal (100%)	1 cup	250 mL
Mashed banana (3 large, or 4 medium)	1½ cups	375 mL
Chopped pecans or walnuts	½ cup	125 mL
Vanilla	1 tsp.	5 mL
All-purpose flour	1½ cups	375 mL
Baking powder	2 tsp.	10 mL
Baking soda	½ tsp.	2 mL
Salt	½ tsp.	2 mL

Cream butter and sugar in large bowl. Beat in egg.

Add cereal, banana, pecans and vanilla. Beat until smooth.

Stir flour, baking powder, baking soda and salt together in separate bowl. Add. Stir or beat on lowest speed just to moisten. Turn into greased 9 x 5 x 3 inch (22 x 12 x 7 cm) loaf pan. Bake in 350°F (175°C) oven for about 1 hour until an inserted wooden pick comes out clean. Let stand for 15 minutes. Turn out onto rack to cool. Makes 1 loaf.

Pictured on page 63.

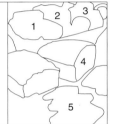

Eggnog Bread

Eggnog flavor comes through nicely.

Granulated sugar	1 cup	250 mL
Large egg	1	1
Butter or hard margarine, melted	¼ cup	60 mL
Egg nog	1½ cups	375 mL
All-purpose flour	3 cups	750 mL
Baking powder	1 tbsp.	15 mL
Salt	1 tsp.	5 mL
Cinnamon	½ tsp.	2 mL
Nutmeg	½ tsp.	2 mL
Chopped pecans or walnuts	⅔ cup	150 mL
Cut glazed mixed fruit	1 cup	250 mL

Beat sugar and egg in mixing bowl. Beat in melted butter. Add egg nog. Mix.

Sift flour, baking powder, salt, cinnamon and nutmeg over egg nog mixture. Stir until moistened.

Mix in pecans and fruit. Turn into greased 9 x 5 x 3 inch (22 x 12 x 7 cm) loaf pan. Bake in 350°F (175°C) oven for about 1 hour until an inserted wooden pick comes out clean. Let stand 20 minutes. Turn out onto rack to cool. Makes 1 loaf.

Pictured on page 63.

Raisin Biscuits

Nice flaky layer. Serve with cheese slices.

All-purpose flour	3 cups	750 mL
Granulated sugar	2 tbsp.	30 mL
Cream of tartar	2 tsp.	10 mL
Baking powder	1 tbsp.	15 mL
Baking soda	1 tsp.	5 mL
Salt	1 tsp.	5 mL
Ground cinnamon	½-1 tsp.	2-5 mL
Butter or hard margarine	½ cup	125 mL
Raisins or currants	1 cup	250 mL
Milk	1⅓ cups	325 mL

Measure first 7 ingredients into bowl. Stir well.

Cut butter into flour mixture until crumbly.

Add raisins and milk. Stir with a fork to form a soft ball. Knead on lightly floured surface 8 to 10 times. Roll or pat dough 1 inch (2.5 cm) thick. Cut into 2½ inch (6 cm) circles. Arrange about 2 inches (5 cm) apart on greased baking sheet. Bake in 425°F (220°C) oven for 20 to 30 minutes until risen and browned. Serve warm with butter, jam or Lemon Spread, page 66. Makes 18 biscuits.

Pictured on page 61.

Left: Lemon Cheese Loaf, page 64   Top Center: Raspberry Cream Muffins, page 67
Bottom Center: Holiday Banana Loaf, page 64   Right: Cherry Pound Cake, page 64

Lemon Cheese Loaf

Flavor is tangy. Texture is moist. Cream cheese
cubes show evenly throughout.

Butter or hard margarine, softened	½ cup	125 mL
Granulated sugar	1¼ cups	300 mL
Large eggs	2	2
Milk	¾ cup	175 mL
Grated rind of 1 lemon		
All-purpose flour	2 cups	450 mL
Baking powder	2 tsp.	10 mL
Salt	¾ tsp.	4 mL
Cream cheese, cut in ¼ inch (6 mm) cubes	8 oz.	250 g
Chopped walnuts	½ cup	125 mL
Topping:		
Juice of 1 lemon		
Granulated sugar	¼ cup	60 mL

Cream butter and sugar. Beat in eggs 1 at a time. Mix in milk and lemon rind.

Stir flour, baking powder and salt together in bowl. Add to batter. Stir just to moisten.

Fold in cream cheese and walnuts. Turn into greased 9 x 5 x 3 inch (22 x 12 x 7 cm) loaf pan. Bake in 350°F (175°C) oven for about 1 hour and 20 minutes, until an inserted wooden pick comes out clean.

Topping: Stir lemon juice and sugar in small saucepan. Heat and stir until sugar dissolves. Poke 8 or 10 holes in top of loaf with toothpick. Spoon syrup over hot loaf. Let stand for 10 minutes. Turn out onto rack to cool. Makes 1 loaf.

Pictured above.

Holiday Banana Loaf

Double this recipe to have enough for smaller gift loaves.

Butter or hard margarine, softened	½ cup	125 mL
Granulated sugar	1 cup	250 mL
Large eggs	2	2
Vanilla	1 tsp.	5 mL
All-purpose flour	1¾ cups	425 mL
Baking soda	1 tsp.	5 mL
Baking powder	1 tsp.	5 mL
Salt	½ tsp.	2 mL
Chopped walnuts	¼ cup	60 mL
Fine coconut	½ cup	125 mL
Chopped cherries	½ cup	125 mL
All-purpose flour	¼ cup	60 mL
Mashed banana (about 3)	1 cup	250 mL

Cream butter and sugar well. Beat in eggs, 1 at a time, beating well after each addition. Add vanilla. Stir.

Measure first amount of flour, baking soda, baking powder and salt into separate bowl. Stir.

Toss walnuts, coconut and cherries with second amount of flour in third bowl.

Add flour mixture to egg mixture in 3 additions alternately with banana in 2 additions, beginning and ending with flour mixture. Add fruit mixture. Mix only until blended. Do not over mix. Turn into greased 9 x 5 x 3 inch (22 x 12 x 7 cm) loaf pans. Bake in 350°F (175°C) oven for 50 to 60 minutes until an inserted wooden pick comes out clean. Let stand for 20 minutes. Turn out onto rack to cool. Makes 1 loaf.

Pictured on this page.

Cherry Pound Cake

Rich and buttery. Very colorful.

Butter or margarine, softened	1 cup	250 mL
Granulated sugar	1 cup	250 mL
Large eggs	3	3
All-purpose flour	2¼ cups	550 mL
Glazed red and green cherries, halved	1 cup	250

Cream butter and sugar in large bowl until light and fluffy. Beat in eggs 1 at a time.

Mix flour and cherries in separate bowl to coat cherries. Stir into butter mixture until moistened. Turn into greased 9 x 5 x 3 inch (22 x 12 x 7 cm) loaf pan. Bake in 325°F (160°C) oven for 1½ hours until an inserted wooden pick comes out clean. Turn out onto rack to cool. Makes 1 loaf.

Pictured on this page.

Strawberry Bread

Light cake-like texture. Flecks of red jam throughout.

Butter or hard margarine	½ cup	125 mL
Granulated sugar	¾ cup	175 mL
Large eggs	2	2
Vanilla	¾ tsp.	4 mL
Lemon juice, fresh or bottled	¼ tsp.	1 mL
Strawberry jam, stirred	⅓ cup	75 mL
Sour cream	¼ cup	60 mL
All-purpose flour	1½ cups	350 mL
Cream of tartar	½ tsp.	2 mL
Baking soda	¼ tsp.	1 mL

Cream butter and sugar well in mixing bowl. Beat in eggs 1 at a time, beating well after each addition. Mix in vanilla and lemon juice.

Stir jam and sour cream together in small bowl .

Sift remaining 3 ingredients together. Add flour mixture in 3 parts alternately with jam mixture in 2 parts, beginning and ending with flour mixture. Stir only enough to moisten. Turn into greased 8 x 4 x 3 inch (20 x 10 x 7 cm) loaf pan. Bake in 350°F (175°C) oven for about 55 to 60 minutes until an inserted wooden pick comes out clean. Let stand for 20 minutes. Turn out onto rack to cool. Makes 1 loaf.

Pictured below.

Chocolate Zucchini Loaf

Make several in the fall when zucchini are more plentiful. Freeze and bring out for Christmas.

Butter or hard margarine, softened	6 tbsp.	100 mL
Granulated sugar	1 cup	225 mL
Large egg	1	1
Vanilla	1 tsp.	5 mL
Grated zucchini, with peel	1 cup	250 mL
All-purpose flour	1½ cups	375 mL
Cocoa	¼ cup	60 mL
Baking powder	1¼ tsp.	6 mL
Baking soda	¾ tsp.	4 mL
Salt	½ tsp.	2 mL
Ground cinnamon	½ tsp.	2 mL
Milk	¼ cup	60 mL
Chopped walnuts	½ cup	125 mL

Cream butter and sugar in mixing bowl. Beat in egg. Add vanilla and zucchini. Stir with spoon.

Add next 6 ingredients. Stir to moisten.

Add milk and walnuts. Stir slowly to mix in. Turn into greased 9 x 5 x 3 inch (22 x 12 x 7 cm) loaf pan. Bake in 350°F (175°C) oven for about 60 minutes. An inserted wooden pick should come out clean. Let stand for 10 minutes. Turn out onto rack to cool. Makes 1 loaf.

Pictured below.

Left: Strawberry Bread
Right: Chocolate Zucchini Loaf

Easy Cinnamon Knots

Experiment with different types of knots or twists. These will be popular.

Water	2²/₃ cups	650 mL
Granulated sugar	²/₃ cup	150 mL
Cooking oil	²/₃ cup	150 mL
Salt	1¼ tsp.	6 mL
All-purpose flour	2 cups	500 mL
Instant yeast	2 tbsp.	30 mL
Large eggs	4	4
All-purpose flour, approximately	7½ cups	1.8 L
Coating:		
Ground cinnamon	3 tbsp.	50 mL
Granulated sugar	3 cups	750 mL
Butter or hard margarine, melted	1 cup	250 mL

Heat first 4 ingredients in large saucepan stirring until sugar is dissolved. It should be very warm but you should be able to hold your hand on side of pan.

Stir first amount of flour with yeast in medium bowl. Add to warm mixture. Stir.

Beat eggs in small bowl. Stir into batter in saucepan.

Add enough remaining flour until it pulls away from sides of bowl. Place in greased bowl, turning once to grease top. Cover with greased waxed paper and tea towel. Let stand in oven with light on and door closed for about 25 minutes until doubled in bulk. Punch dough down. Divide dough into 4 equal portions. Roll each into a rope. Mark off and cut each rope into 12 pieces. Roll each piece into a 10 inch (25 cm) rope.

Coating: Mix cinnamon and sugar. Brush working surface with butter. Roll each rope in butter to grease, then in cinnamon mixture. Tie each rope into a loose knot. Arrange on greased baking sheets. Cover with tea towel. Let stand in oven with light on and door closed about 30 minutes until doubled in size. Bake in 350°F (175°C) oven for 20 to 25 minutes. Makes 4 dozen buns.

Pictured below.

Easy Cinnamon Knots

Carrot Pineapple Muffins

Golden with flecks of carrot and pineapple showing. Good all year round.

All-purpose flour	2 cups	500 mL
Granulated sugar	³/₄ cup	175 mL
Baking powder	1 tsp.	5 mL
Baking soda	1 tsp.	5 mL
Ground cinnamon	1 tsp.	5 mL
Salt	½ tsp.	2 mL
Large eggs, well-beaten	2	2
Cooking oil	½ cup	125 mL
Finely grated carrot	1 cup	250 mL
Crushed pineapple, with juice	½ cup	125 mL
Vanilla	1 tsp.	5 mL

Mix first 6 ingredients in large bowl.

Add eggs, cooking oil, carrot, pineapple, juice and vanilla. Beat on low until just moistened. Spoon into greased muffin cups, filling ²/₃ full. Bake in 350°F (175°C) oven for 20 to 25 minutes. Makes 12 muffins.

Pictured on page 63.

Bake muffins in pretty "Christmas theme" paper muffin cups. Do not grease muffin pans. Place 1 or 2 papers in each cup. Fill and bake according to recipe. Remove immediately from muffin pan to minimize moisture build-up on paper.

Lemon Spread

So refreshing. A nice change from butter and jam.

Hard margarine, softened	½ cup	125 mL
Granulated sugar	½ cup	125 mL
Finely grated rind of 1 orange		
Finely grated rind of 1 lemon		
Juice of 1 orange		
Juice of 1 lemon		

Beat margarine in small bowl until light-colored. Add sugar very gradually while beating. Add rinds and juices. Spread on raisin bread, Raisin Biscuits, page 62, or Welsh Cakes, page 45. Makes 1 cup (250 mL) spread.

Pictured on page 61.

Christmas Fruit Muffins

Fill a basket with these for Christmas morning breakfast. Very colorful.

All-purpose flour	1¾ cups	425 mL
Baking powder	1 tsp.	5 mL
Baking soda	1 tsp.	5 mL
Salt	½ tsp.	2 mL
Glazed red pineapple ring, diced	1	1
Glazed green pineapple ring, diced	1	1
Glazed yellow pineapple ring, diced	1	1
Chopped pecans	½ cup	125 mL
Butter or hard margarine, softened	½ cup	125 mL
Granulated sugar	1 cup	250 mL
Large eggs	2	2
Vanilla	1 tsp.	5 mL
Milk	⅔ cup	150 mL

Measure first 8 ingredients into large bowl. Stir. Make a well in center.

Cream butter and sugar in separate bowl. Beat in eggs 1 at a time. Add vanilla and milk. Stir. Pour into well. Stir just to moisten. Fill greased muffin cups almost full. Bake in 400°F (205°C) oven for 15 to 20 minutes until an inserted wooden pick comes out clean. Let stand 5 minutes before removing from pan. Makes 12 muffins.

Pictured on page 63.

Cranberry Orange Muffins

The melding of these flavors is wonderful.

Large egg	1	1
Cooking oil	¼ cup	60 mL
Granulated sugar	½ cup	125 mL
Chopped cranberries	1 cup	250 mL
Grated rind of 1 large orange		
Juice of 1 large orange, plus frozen condensed orange juice, to make	¾ cup	175 mL
All-purpose flour	2 cups	500 mL
Baking powder	2 tsp.	10 mL
Baking soda	½ tsp.	2 mL
Salt	½ tsp.	2 mL

Beat egg in large bowl. Add cooking oil and sugar. Beat to mix. Add cranberries, orange rind and juice. Stir.

Stir flour, baking powder, baking soda and salt together in separate bowl. Add to liquid ingredients. Stir just to moisten. Fill greased muffin cups almost full. Bake in 400°F (205°C) oven for 15 to 20 minutes. Let stand 5 minutes before removing from pan. Makes 12 muffins.

Pictured on page 63.

Raspberry Cream Muffins

Raspberry Cream Muffins

Strong raspberry flavor and red Christmas color. Serve at brunch, afternoon tea or as a late evening snack.

All-purpose flour	2 cups	500 mL
Baking powder	1 tsp.	5 mL
Baking soda	½ tsp.	2 mL
Salt	½ tsp.	2 mL
Ground cinnamon	¼ tsp.	1 mL
Butter or hard margarine, softened	½ cup	125 mL
Granulated sugar	⅔ cup	150 mL
Large eggs	2	2
Sour cream	½ cup	125 mL
Vanilla	1 tsp.	5 mL
Coarsely chopped frozen raspberries	1 cup	250 mL

Measure first 5 ingredients in bowl. Stir well.

Beat butter and sugar in medium bowl. Beat in eggs 1 at a time. Add sour cream and vanilla. Beat to mix. Add flour mixture. Stir just until moistened.

Fold in raspberries. Fill greased muffin cups almost full. Bake in 350°F (175°C) oven for 30 to 35 minutes until golden. An inserted wooden pick should come out clean. Let stand 10 minutes. Remove from pan to cool on rack. Makes 12 large muffins.

Pictured above and on page 64.

Brunches

Well-suited to hectic holiday schedules, the brunch bypasses those busy evenings, drawing on the late morning and early afternoon hours instead. It's a great way to bring family and friends together on Boxing Day and other special days over the Yuletide season.

Because it combines breakfast and lunch dishes, the brunch offers great scope. Hot and cold entrées, salads, breads and sweets are all welcome on the brunch table.

Call on the various sample menus we've included (page 28-31) to help you put your holiday brunch together, or explore the other sections of our book for more recipe suggestions.

Make-Ahead Eggs Benedict

Yes, the poached eggs are still slightly runny when served! This is a Christmas morning tradition!

English muffins, split	4	4
Bacon slices	16	16
Water		
Large eggs	8	8
Sauce:		
Butter or hard margarine	¼ cup	60 mL
All-purpose flour	¼ cup	60 mL
Paprika	1 tsp.	5 mL
Pepper	¼ tsp.	1 mL
Ground nutmeg	⅛ tsp.	0.5 mL
Milk	2 cups	450 mL
Grated Swiss cheese	2 cups	450 mL
White wine (or alcohol-free)	½ cup	125 mL
Topping:		
Butter or hard margarine	1 tbsp.	15 mL
Crushed corn flakes	½ cup	125 mL

Arrange muffin halves, cut side up, in greased 9 x 13 inch (22 x 33 cm) pan.

Fry bacon in frying pan until crisp. Blot on paper towel. Put 2 slices on each muffin half.

Left: Make-Ahead Eggs Benedict, page 68

Heat water in large saucepan until it simmers. Carefully break in eggs to poach until just set. Transfer and center each egg on bacon using slotted spoon.

Sauce: Melt butter in saucepan. Mix in flour, paprika, pepper and nutmeg. Stir in milk until it boils and thickens.

Add cheese and wine. Stir until cheese melts. Spoon sauce over eggs.

Topping: Melt butter in small saucepan. Stir in corn flakes. Sprinkle over top of sauce. Cover and chill overnight. In the morning, remove cover. Bake in 375°F (190°C) oven for 20 to 25 minutes until heated through. Makes 8 servings.

Pictured above.

Bottom Center: Holiday Brunch Cake, page 60   Top Center: Rhubarb Cocktail, page 56   Right: Quick Fruit Bowl, page 69

Quick Fruit Bowl

This is a mix and match delight! Sauce adds just the right sweetness.

Canned sliced peaches or apricots, drained, juice reserved	14 oz.	398 mL
Canned pineapple chunks, drained, juice reserved	14 oz.	398 mL
Canned pears, drained, juice reserved	14 oz.	398 mL
Canned mandarin orange sections, drained, juice discarded	12 oz.	341 mL
Canned grapefruit sections, drained, juice discarded	14 oz.	398 mL
Maraschino cherries, halved or quartered	15	15
Reserved juices plus water, if needed, to make	2 cups	450 mL
Cornstarch	2 tbsp.	30 mL
Granulated sugar	¼ cup	60 mL

Place sliced peaches into bowl. May be cut in half crosswise for smaller pieces. Add pineapple chunks. Slice pears, cutting in half crosswise for smaller pieces if desired. Add orange sections. Add grapefruit, cutting in half crosswise for smaller pieces, if desired. Add cherries. Toss.

Stir reserved juices, cornstarch and sugar in saucepan. Heat and stir until it boils and thickens. Cool. Stir into fruit. Add more drained fruit, if desired. Makes 5 cups (1.1 L).

Pictured above.

Gourmet Burgers

These are real winners! A nice change of flavor from ordinary hamburgers.

Lean ground beef	1 lb.	454 g
Finely chopped onion	2/3 cup	150 mL
Finely chopped celery	3/4 cup	175 mL
Salted soda crackers, crushed	7	7
Hand-crushed corn flakes	1 cup	250 mL
Large egg	1	1
Plum sauce	1 tbsp.	15 mL
Hickory smoke sauce (liquid smoke)	2 tsp.	10 mL
Soy sauce	1 tsp.	5 mL
Whole oregano	1/2 tsp.	2 mL
Salt	1/2 tsp.	2 mL
Pepper	1/4 tsp.	1 mL
All-purpose flour	1 tbsp.	15 mL
Hamburger buns, split and buttered	6	6
Condiments such as ketchup, relish, cheese, tomatoes, pickles		

Combine first 5 ingredients in bowl. Mix well.

Beat egg with fork in small bowl. Add next 7 ingredients. Beat well with fork. Add to beef and mix in. Shape into 6 patties. Let stand in refrigerator for at least 1 hour before cooking to allow flavors to mingle. Fry or grill about 3 minutes per side until no pink remains in meat.

Insert 1 patty in each bun. Let everyone help themselves to the condiments. Makes 6 burgers.

Pictured on page 75.

Blueberry Streusel Cake

Blueberry Streusel Cake

Wrap well and freeze ahead of time. Take out of freezer the night before your brunch. Heat just before serving.

Butter or hard margarine, softened	1/2 cup	125 mL
Granulated sugar	3/4 cup	175 mL
Large eggs	3	3
Vanilla	1 tsp.	5 mL
Milk	1 cup	250 mL
All-purpose flour	3 cups	750 mL
Baking powder	1 tbsp.	15 mL
Ground cinnamon	1/2 tsp.	7 mL
Ground nutmeg	1 tsp.	5 mL
Salt	1 tsp.	5 mL
Blueberries (thaw if using frozen)	3 cups	750 mL
Streusel Topping:		
All-purpose flour	3/4 cup	175 mL
Quick cooking rolled oats	3/4 cup	175 mL
Brown sugar, packed	3/4 cup	175 mL
Butter or hard margarine	1/2 cup	125 mL

Cream butter and sugar in mixing bowl. Beat in eggs 1 at a time. Add vanilla and milk. Mix.

Add flour, baking powder, cinnamon, nutmeg and salt. Stir slowly to moisten. Continue to stir until smooth. Spread in greased 9 x 13 inch (22 x 33 cm) pan.

Sprinkle with blueberries.

Streusel Topping: Measure flour, rolled oats and brown sugar into bowl. Cut in butter until crumbly. Spread over blueberries. Bake in 350°F (175°C) oven for 40 to 50 minutes. Serves 15.

Pictured on this page.

Pastry Biscuits

These look like cookies but taste like biscuits. Serve with jam or jelly.

Butter or hard margarine, softened	1/2 cup	125 mL
Cream cheese, softened	4 oz.	125 g
All-purpose flour	1 cup	250 mL

Cream butter and cream cheese well. Mix in flour. Shape into 1 roll about 1 1/2 inches (4 cm) in diameter and 7 inches (18 cm) long. Roll up in waxed paper. Chill all day or overnight in refrigerator. Cut into 1/4 inch (6 mm) slices. Place on ungreased cookie sheet. Bake in 400°F (205°C) oven for about 10 minutes until browned. Makes 20 to 24 biscuits.

Pictured on page 72.

Cranberry Corn Bread

Cranberry Corn Bread

So quick to make. Savory corn bread flavor with the sweetness of cranberry. Freezes well.

Butter or hard margarine, melted	6 tbsp.	100 mL
Brown sugar, packed	½ cup	125 mL
Large egg	1	1
Buttermilk, fresh or reconstituted from powder	1 cup	250 mL
Coarsely chopped cranberries	1 cup	250 mL
Cornmeal (yellow)	1 cup	250 mL
All-purpose flour	1 cup	250 mL
Baking powder	1 tbsp.	15 mL
Salt	½ tsp.	2 mL
Chopped walnuts	⅔ cup	150 mL

Beat melted butter, brown sugar and egg together in mixing bowl. Mix in buttermilk. Add cranberries. Stir.

Add cornmeal, flour, baking powder and salt. Stir to moisten. Turn into greased 9 x 9 inch (22 x 22 cm) pan.

Sprinkle with walnuts. Bake in 400°F (205°C) oven for about 25 minutes until an inserted wooden pick comes out clean. Best served warm. Cuts into 16 pieces.

Pictured above.

Baked Omelet

Lovely golden brown on top. Serve with a tossed lettuce or spinach salad and rolls or toast.

Cream Sauce:		
Butter or hard margarine	6 tbsp.	100 mL
All-purpose flour	½ cup	125 mL
Salt	1½ tsp.	7 mL
Pepper	⅛ tsp.	0.5 mL
Milk	1½ cups	375 mL
Milk	1½ cups	375 mL
Large eggs	6	6
Diced cooked ham	1 cup	250 mL
Grated medium or sharp Cheddar cheese	1 cup	250 mL
Canned sliced mushrooms, drained	½ x 10 oz.	½ x 284 mL

Cream Sauce: Melt butter in large Dutch oven. Mix in flour, salt and pepper. Stir in first amount of milk until it boils and thickens.

Whisk in second amount of milk. Mixture can be refrigerated at this point until the next day.

Beat eggs in small bowl until smooth. Stir into cream sauce.

Add ham, cheese and mushrooms. Mix well. Pour into greased 8 x 8 inch (20 x 20 cm) pan. Bake in 350°F (175°C) oven for about 1½ hours. An inserted knife should come out clean. Let stand 10 minutes before cutting. Serves 9.

Pictured below.

Baked Omelet

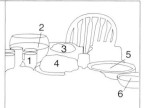

Breakfast Pull-Aparts

Nice and gooey! Lots of cinnamon.

Butter or hard margarine	6 tbsp.	100 mL
Granulated sugar	½ cup	125 mL
Ground cinnamon	1 tbsp.	15 mL
Frozen bread dough buns	20	20
Sliced almonds	½ cup	125 mL
Halved glazed cherries	½ cup	125 mL
Corn syrup	⅓ cup	75 mL
Remaining butter		

Melt butter in small saucepan.

Stir sugar and cinnamon in small bowl.

Dip frozen dough buns in butter. Roll in sugar mixture. Put 10 in greased 12 cup (2.7 L) bundt pan.

Sprinkle with ½ almonds and ½ cherries. Repeat.

Mix corn syrup with remaining butter. Drizzle over top. Cover with damp tea towel. Let stand on counter for 6 to 8 hours or overnight. Bake in 350°F (175°C) oven for about 30 minutes. Let stand 5 minutes. Turn out onto plate. Makes 20 servings.

Pictured on page 72.

Orange Fruit Dip

Serve with a platter of assorted fresh fruits.

Sour cream	1 cup	250 mL
Brown sugar	1 tbsp.	15 mL
Grand Marnier liqueur (or other orange flavored liqueur)	1 tbsp.	15 mL

Stir all together. To make without liqueur, add more sugar to taste. Makes 1 cup (250 mL) dip.

Pictured on this page.

Jean's Favorite

Golden Cheesecake

Provide a small paté knife and serve with assorted breads and crackers.

Fine dry bread crumbs	3 tbsp.	50 mL
Grated cheese product (powdered Cheddar)	2 tbsp.	30 mL
Cottage cheese	1 cup	250 mL
Canned ham flakes, drained	6½ oz.	184 g
Cream cheese, softened, cut up	3 × 8 oz.	3 × 250 g
Grated sharp Cheddar cheese	3 cups	750 mL
Chopped green onion	¼ cup	60 mL
Large eggs	4	4
Onion powder	½ tsp.	2 mL
Garlic powder	¼ tsp.	1 mL
Hot pepper sauce	¼ tsp.	1 mL

Stir bread crumbs and dry cheese together in small bowl. Grease sides and bottom of 9 inch (22 cm) springform pan. Coat with crumb mixture, shaking out excess.

Run remaining ingredients through blender until smooth. This may need to be done in 2 parts. Pour into prepared pan. Bake in 325°F (160°C) oven for 1 to 1½ hours. Center will quiver slightly when you shake pan. Place on rack. Immediately run sharp knife around top edge so cheesecake can settle evenly. Cool, then chill for 3 to 4 hours or overnight. Serves 15 to 20.

Pictured below.

Golden Cheesecake

Festive Savory Cheesecake

For blue cheese lovers. Pleasant blend of cheese and bacon flavors with crunchy surprise from pecans.

Crust:

Butter or hard margarine	½ cup	125 mL
Saltine cracker crumbs	1½ cups	375 mL
Grated Parmesan cheese	¼ cup	60 mL

Filling:

Cream cheese, softened	3 × 8 oz.	3 × 250 g
Blue cheese, crumbled	4 oz.	125 g
Large eggs	4	4
Sour cream	¾ cup	175 mL
Hot pepper sauce	¼ tsp.	1 mL
Onion powder	½ tsp.	2 mL
Salt	¼ tsp.	1 mL
Pepper	⅛ tsp.	0.5 mL
Bacon slices, diced	8	8
Medium onion, finely chopped	1	1
Finely chopped pecans	½ cup	125 mL
Finely chopped green onion	½ cup	125 mL

Topping:

Sour cream	1 cup	250 mL
Pimiento strips, for garnish		
Parsley sprigs, for garnish		

Crust: Melt butter in saucepan. Stir in crumbs and Parmesan cheese. Press firmly into bottom of ungreased 9 inch (22 cm) springform pan. Bake in 350°F (175°C) oven for 10 minutes. Cool.

Filling: Beat cream cheese, blue cheese and 1 egg in mixing bowl until light. Beat in remaining eggs, 1 at a time. Add sour cream, pepper sauce, onion powder, salt and pepper. Beat just to mix in.

Sauté bacon in frying pan for 4 to 5 minutes. Add onion, continuing to sauté until onion is soft. Drain off excess fat. Mix in pecans and green onion. Stir. Add to cream cheese mixture. Stir well. Pour over cooled crust in springform pan. Bake in 325°F (160°C) oven for 1 to 1½ hours. Center will quiver slightly when pan is shaken. Set on rack. Immediately run knife around top edge to allow it to settle evenly. Cool. Chill for 1 to 2 hours.

Topping: Spread top with sour cream. Decorate with pimiento strips and parsley sprigs. Serves 15 to 20.

Pictured on page 75.

Festive Savory Cheesecake, page 74   Lobster Fantans, page 75   Gourmet Burgers, page 70

Ham Quiche

Very tasty. Can be frozen and reheated just before serving.

Hard margarine (butter browns too fast)	1 tbsp.	15 mL
Finely chopped onion	¹/₂ cup	125 mL
Finely chopped cooked ham	1 cup	250 mL
Grated Swiss cheese	³/₄ cup	175 mL
Grated medium or sharp Cheddar cheese	³/₄ cup	175 mL
Unbaked 9 inch (22 cm) deep dish pie shell, your own or a mix	1	1
Large eggs	3	3
Evaporated skim milk (or light cream)	1¹/₂ cups	350 mL
Prepared mustard	1 tsp.	5 mL
Salt	¹/₂ tsp.	2 mL
Pepper	¹/₄ tsp.	1 mL
Ground nutmeg	¹/₈ tsp.	0.5 mL

Melt margarine in frying pan. Add onion. Sauté until soft. Do not brown.

Spread ham and both cheeses in pie shell. Sprinkle onion over top.

Beat eggs in bowl until smooth. Mix in remaining ingredients. Pour into pie shell. Bake on bottom rack in 375°F (190°C) oven for 30 to 35 minutes until a knife inserted near center comes out clean. Makes 1 quiche. Serves 6 to 8.

Pictured on page 73.

Lobster Fantans

Make filling first thing in the morning then assemble before serving. Quite showy.

Canned lobster, drained, broken up	5 oz.	142 g
Grated Swiss cheese (or your favorite)	¹/₂ cup	125 mL
Chopped green pepper	3 tbsp.	50 mL
Minced onion	2 tbsp.	30 mL
Salt	¹/₂ tsp.	2 mL
Salad dressing (or mayonnaise)	¹/₄ cup	60 mL
Lemon juice, fresh or bottled	1 tsp.	5 mL
Soft rolls, about 4 × 3 inch (10 × 7.5 cm) size	5	5
Butter or hard margarine, softened	2 tbsp.	30 mL

Place first 5 ingredients in bowl. Toss together.

Stir salad dressing and lemon juice together in cup. Pour over lobster mixture. Stir lightly.

Make 3 cuts from top to bottom in each roll, not cutting through bottom. Spread inside cuts with butter. Spread lobster mixture between cuts. Wrap each roll in foil. Heat in 350°F (175°C) oven for about 20 minutes until hot. Serves 4 to 5.

Pictured above.

Banana Pancakes

Definitely befitting a houseful of overnight guests.
Serve hot with butter and maple syrup.

All-purpose flour	2 cups	500 mL
Granulated sugar	2 tsp.	10 mL
Baking powder	1 tbsp.	15 mL
Salt	½ tsp.	2 mL
Large eggs	2	2
Butter or hard margarine, melted	2 tbsp.	30 mL
Milk	1¾ cups	425 mL
Bananas, quartered lengthwise and thinly sliced (see note)	2	2

Measure flour, sugar, baking powder and salt into bowl. Stir. Make a well in center.

Beat eggs in separate bowl. Mix in butter and milk. Pour into well in flour mixture. Stir to moisten. Don't try to smooth out small lumps. Add more milk or flour to make thicker or thinner pancakes.

Fold in banana. Test pan for heat. Drops of water should bounce all over it. Drop batter by tablespoonfuls on lightly greased 380°F (190°C) pan. When bubbles appear and edges begin to dry, turn to brown other side. Pan should not need to be greased again. Makes about 40 pancakes, 4 inch (10 cm) size.

Pictured below.

Note: Bananas may turn dark as the pancakes cool. This is natural and will not affect the taste. Do not freeze.

Overnight Oven French Toast

A real time-saver when you have a houseful of guests.
Serve with maple syrup.

Butter or hard margarine, melted	¼ cup	60 mL
Large eggs	7	7
Milk (see Note)	2 cups	450 mL
Granulated sugar	⅓ cup	75 mL
Ground nutmeg	¼ tsp.	1 mL
Ground cinnamon	¼ tsp.	1 mL
Salt	¼ tsp.	1 mL
Vanilla	1½ tsp.	7 mL
French bread loaf, cut into 1 inch (2.5 cm) slices	1	1
Icing (confectioner's) sugar, sprinkle		

Pour melted butter into bottom of baking sheet to coat.

Beat next 7 ingredients together well.

Dip both sides of each bread slice into egg mixture. Lay in baking sheet. Pour any remaining mixture over slices. Cover and refrigerate overnight. Can be frozen at this state. Uncover and bake in 450°F (230°C) oven on bottom rack for 20 to 25 minutes. Place on rack to cool.

Dust with icing sugar when warm. Serves 6 to 8.

Pictured below.

Note: Commercial eggnog can be substituted for milk for a richer flavor.

When bananas become too ripe to eat, peel and put them in a freezer bag. Or, peel and mash overripe bananas, then measure and freeze in 1 cup (250 mL) portions. Three medium bananas mashed equal approximately 1 cup (250 mL). Frozen bananas may darken when thawed but are not spoiled; in fact, their flavor is enhanced. Use in any recipe calling for mashed bananas.

Overnight Oven French Toast, page 76
Orange Marmalade, page 12
Banana Pancakes, page 76

Left: Eggs Lyonnaise   Top: Oven Apple Pancake   Right: Sausage Strata

Sausage Strata

A time-saver, as this is assembled the night before.

Bread slices, crusts removed	6	6
Grated sharp Cheddar cheese	2 cups	500 mL
Sausage meat	2 lbs.	900 g
Bread slices, crusts removed	6	6
Large eggs	8	8
Salt	1 tsp.	5 mL
Pepper	¼ tsp.	1 mL
Onion powder	½ tsp.	2 mL
Worcestershire sauce	1 tsp.	5 mL
Dry mustard powder	½ tsp.	2 mL
Milk	2⅔ cups	650 mL

Line bottom of greased 9 x 13 inch (22 x 33 cm) pan with first bread slices. Sprinkle with cheese.

Scramble-fry sausage meat. Drain off fat. Sprinkle meat over cheese.

Cover meat with remaining bread slices.

Beat eggs in bowl. Add remaining ingredients. Mix. Pour over bread. Cover. Refrigerate overnight. Bake, uncovered, in 350°F (175°C) oven for about 1 hour until set. Serves 10 to 12.

Pictured on this page.

Eggs Lyonnaise

An excellent quick breakfast. This is easily doubled or tripled.

Butter or hard margarine	2 tbsp.	30 mL
Chopped onion	3 tbsp.	50 mL
All-purpose flour	1 tbsp.	15 mL
Chopped parsley (or ½ tsp., 2 mL parsley flakes)	1 tbsp.	15 mL
Salt	¼ tsp.	1 mL
Pepper, sprinkle		
Milk	1 cup	250 mL
Hard-boiled eggs, sliced	4	4
Bread slices, toasted and buttered	4	4

Melt butter in saucepan. Add onion. Sauté until soft and golden.

Mix in flour, parsley, salt and pepper. Stir in milk until mixture boils and thickens.

Gently stir in egg slices.

Spoon over toast. Makes 4 servings.

Pictured above.

Oven Apple Pancake

Serve with maple syrup and sausages.

Butter or hard margarine	¼ cup	60 mL
Brown sugar, packed	⅓ cup	75 mL
Ground cinnamon, light sprinkle		
Apples, peeled, cored and sliced in wedges ¼ inch (6 mm) thick	2	2
Large eggs	3	3
Milk	¾ cup	175 mL
Salt	½ tsp.	2 mL
All-purpose flour	¾ cup	175 mL

Melt butter in 9 inch (22 cm) pie plate in 425°F (220°C) oven.

Stir brown sugar into melted butter. Sprinkle with cinnamon. Overlap apples in single layer. Cook in oven for 10 minutes.

Beat eggs with spoon in bowl. Add milk, salt and flour. Stir to moisten. Don't try to smooth out small lumps. Pour over apples. Return to oven. Bake for 20 to 25 minutes. Cut into wedges. Serves 4 to 6.

Pictured on this page.

Christmas
Cakes &
Puddings

Christmas Cakes & Puddings

Chronicled in literature and steeped in tradition, Christmas

cakes and puddings have been an honored part of the

holiday menu for generations. Indeed if any single dish

has come to represent Christmas, then surely it is the

Christmas pudding, followed closely by Christmas cake.

Their esteemed status need not be intimidating.

True, the ingredients for these special cakes

and puddings are a step removed from the everyday

but are readily available nonetheless.

Likewise, the preparation of Christmas cakes and

puddings is simple enough and the result is

well worth the time and effort.

1. **Plum Pudding,** page 81
2. **Pastel Hard Sauce,** page 86
3. **Steamed Chocolate Pudding,** page 83
4. **Light Fruitcake,** page 82

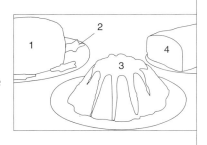

Steamed Fruit Pudding

An old-time suet pudding recipe for a light-colored and light-textured pudding. One of the best.

All-purpose flour	2 cups	500 mL
Brown sugar, packed	¾ cup	175 mL
Beef suet, ground	2 cups	500 mL
Ground cinnamon	2 tsp.	10 mL
Salt	1 tsp.	5 mL
Ground cloves	1 tsp.	5 mL
Baking soda	1 tsp.	5 mL
Cream of tartar	1 tsp.	5 mL
Large eggs, beaten	2	2
Milk	1¼ cups	300 mL
Sultana raisins	1 cup	250 mL
Golden raisins	½ cup	125 mL
Currants	1 cup	250 mL
Cut mixed peel, finely chopped or coarsely ground	¾ cup	175 mL

Mix first 10 ingredients in order given in large bowl.

Add next 4 ingredients. Mix in. Scrape into greased 8 cup (2 L) pudding container. Cover with double square greased foil, tying edges down with string. Place in steamer, with boiling water halfway up side. Steam, covered, for 4 hours adding more boiling water as needed to keep level up. Remove container from water. Let stand for ½ hour. Turn out of pan. Cool on rack. Wrap in foil or plastic. Will keep in refrigerator for weeks. Freezes well. To reheat, steam about 1½ hours or until hot and serve with Rum Sauce, page 87. May also be reheated, covered with plastic wrap, in microwave. Makes 1 pudding.

Pictured below and on page 23.

Steamed Fruit Pudding, page 80, with Rum Sauce, page 87

Plum Pudding

The crowning touch for Christmas dinner.

Dark raisins	2 cups	450 mL
Currants	1 cup	225 mL
Ground almonds	7/8 cup	200 mL
Chopped glazed cherries	1/2 cup	125 mL
Cut mixed peel	1/2 cup	125 mL
Glazed pineapple rings, chopped	4	4
Medium coconut	1/2 cup	125 mL
All-purpose flour	1/2 cup	125 mL
Chopped beef suet	1 cup	225 mL
Dry bread crumbs	1 1/2 cups	350 mL
Baking powder	2 tsp.	10 mL
Baking soda	1/2 tsp.	2 mL
Salt	1 tsp.	5 mL
Ground cinnamon	1 tsp.	5 mL
Ground nutmeg	1 tsp.	5 mL
Ground ginger	1/2 tsp.	2 mL
All-purpose flour	3/4 cup	175 mL
Large eggs	3	3
Milk	1 cup	250 mL

Measure first 8 ingredients in large bowl. Stir well to coat fruit with flour.

Add next 9 ingredients. Mix well.

Beat eggs in small mixing bowl until frothy. Stir in milk. Pour over fruit mixture. Stir well until moistened. Turn into greased 2 quart (2 L) pudding pan. Cover with double square greased foil, tying sides down with string. Place in steamer with boiling water 2/3 way up pudding pan. Steam, covered, for 3 hours adding more boiling water as needed to keep level up. Serve with Rum Sauce, page 87, or Pastel Hard Sauce, page 86. Serves 12 to 15.

Pictured on page 78.

White Fruitcake

White Fruitcake

Wonderfully moist. Full of color.

Light raisins	3 cups	675 mL
Cut mixed glazed fruit	2 cups	450 mL
Candied pineapple slices, cut up	6	6
Chopped orange peel	1/3 cup	75 mL
Chopped lemon peel	1/3 cup	75 mL
Green glazed cherries	1 cup	225 mL
Red glazed cherries	1 cup	225 mL
Whole blanched almonds	1 1/2 cups	350 mL
Pecan halves	1 1/2 cups	350 mL
All-purpose flour	1 cup	225 mL
Butter or hard margarine, softened	1 lb.	454 g
Granulated sugar	2 cups	450 mL
Large eggs	10	10
Grated rind of 1 lemon		
Juice of 1 lemon		
Almond flavoring	2 tsp.	10 mL
Vanilla flavoring	1 tsp.	5 mL
All-purpose flour	3 cups	675 mL
Salt	1 tsp.	5 mL
Baking powder	1 tsp.	5 mL

Line 3 greased 9 x 5 x 3 inch (22 x 12 x 7 cm) loaf pans with brown paper. Grease paper. Measure first 10 ingredients into large bowl. Stir to coat fruit with flour.

Cream butter and sugar in large mixing bowl. Beat in eggs, 1 at a time. Add remaining ingredients. Stir. Add fruit mixture. Stir. Divide among prepared pans. Bake in 275°F (140°C) oven for 2 to 2 1/2 hours until an inserted wooden pick comes out clean. Cool on rack. Remove from pans. Wrap in plastic to store for 2 to 3 weeks before freezing. Makes 3 cakes or 8 pounds (3.6 kg) total.

Pictured above and on page 23.

Light Fruitcake

A traditional Christmas cake with a little something for everyone.

Glazed cherries, halved	1 cup	250 mL
Glazed pineapple rings, chopped	6	6
Cut citron	½ cup	125 mL
Cut mixed peel	½ cup	125 mL
Light raisins	1 cup	250 mL
Slivered almonds	1½ cups	375 mL
Fine coconut	2½ cups	575 mL
Butter or hard margarine, softened	1 cup	250 mL
Granulated sugar	1½ cups	375 mL
Large eggs	6	6
Lemon juice, fresh or bottled	1½ tbsp.	25 mL
Rum flavoring	1 tbsp.	15 mL
Vanilla	1 tsp.	5 mL
Milk	½ cup	125 mL
All-purpose flour	4 cups	1 L
Baking powder	1 tsp.	5 mL
Baking soda	½ tsp.	2 mL
Salt	½ tsp.	2 mL

Line 2 greased 9 x 5 x 3 inch (22 x 12 x 7 cm) loaf pans with brown paper. Grease paper. Combine first 7 ingredients in large bowl. Stir well.

Cream butter and sugar in large bowl. Beat in eggs, 1 at a time. Add lemon juice, flavorings and milk. Mix.

Add remaining ingredients. Stir to moisten. Add fruit mixture. Stir well. Divide between prepared pans. Bake in 275°F (140°C) oven for 2¼ to 2½ hours until an inserted wooden pick comes out clean. Cool on rack. Remove from pans. Wrap in plastic to stand 2 to 3 weeks before freezing. Makes 2 cakes, 5½ pounds (2.5 kg) total.

Pictured on page 79.

Steamed Cranberry Pudding

Appearance and texture are excellent. Flavor is not too sweet.

Cranberries, fresh or frozen, halved	2 cups	500 mL
All-purpose flour	1⅓ cups	325 mL
Baking powder	½ tsp.	2 mL
Large egg	1	1
Mild molasses	¼ cup	60 mL
Golden corn syrup	¼ cup	60 mL
Vanilla	1 tsp.	5 mL
Baking soda	2 tsp.	10 mL
Hot water	⅓ cup	75 mL

Stir cranberries, flour and baking powder together in bowl.

Beat egg in mixing bowl. Beat in molasses, corn syrup and vanilla.

Dissolve baking soda in hot water in cup. Add to egg mixture. Mix. Add cranberry mixture. Stir to moisten. Turn into greased 8 cup (2 L) pudding pan. Cover with double square greased foil, tying sides down with string. Put in steamer with boiling water ⅔ up sides of pan. Cover. Steam for 1½ hours, adding more boiling water as needed to keep level up. Remove pan from water. Let stand ½ hour. Turn out of pan. Cool on rack. Wrap in plastic or foil. Freeze up to 2 months or keep in refrigerator 2 to 3 weeks. Reheat just before serving. Serve with Creamy Pudding Sauce, page 87. Serves 8 to 12.

Pictured below.

Steamed Cranberry Pudding, page 82 with Creamy Pudding Sauce, page 87

Orange Gumdrop Loaf

Orange Gumdrop Loaf

Nice and moist. Lots of orange throughout.

Gumdrop orange slices, cut up	1/3 lb.	150 g
Chopped dates	3/4 cup	175 mL
All-purpose flour	1/8 cup	30 mL
Butter or hard margarine, softened	1/2 cup	125 mL
Granulated sugar	3/4 cup	175 mL
Large eggs	2	2
All-purpose flour	1 3/4 cups	425 mL
Fine coconut	2/3 cup	150 mL
Baking soda	1/2 tsp.	2 mL
Chopped pecans	1/2 cup	125 mL
Salt	1/4 tsp.	1 mL
Prepared orange juice	1/2 cup	125 mL

Toss first 3 ingredients together in small bowl. Set aside.

Beat butter and sugar together in large bowl. Beat in eggs, 1 at a time.

Stir next 5 ingredients together in separate bowl. Add to egg mixture. Stir.

Stir in orange juice then fruit mixture. Pour into greased 9 x 5 x 3 inch (22 x 12 x 7 cm) loaf pan. Bake in 350°F (175°C) oven for about 75 minutes until an inserted wooden pick comes out clean. Cool on rack. Remove from pan. Wrap in plastic or foil. Freeze up to 2 months or store in refrigerator 2 to 3 weeks. Makes 1 loaf.

Pictured above.

Steamed Chocolate Pudding

A delightful change from the fruit steamed puddings. Good with either sauce.

Butter or hard margarine, softened	1/2 cup	125 mL
Granulated sugar	3/4 cup	175 mL
Large eggs	2	2
Vanilla	1 tsp.	5 mL
All-purpose flour	2 cups	500 mL
Baking powder	1 tbsp.	15 mL
Salt	1/4 tsp.	1 mL
Milk	1 cup	250 mL
Unsweetened chocolate baking squares, cut up	2 x 1 oz.	2 x 28 g
Brown Sugar Sauce:		
Brown sugar, packed	1 cup	250 mL
All-purpose flour	1/4 cup	60 mL
Salt	1/2 tsp.	2 mL
Water	2 cups	500 mL
Butter or hard margarine	1 tbsp.	15 mL
Vanilla	1 tsp.	5 mL

Cream butter and sugar in large bowl. Add eggs 1 at a time, beating well after each addition. Add vanilla. Mix.

Measure flour, baking powder and salt into separate bowl. Stir.

Add milk in 2 parts alternately with flour mixture in 3 parts, beginning and ending with flour.

Melt chocolate on low, stirring often. Stir into batter. Turn into greased 2 quart (2 L) pudding pan. Cover with double square greased foil, tying in place. Place in steamer with boiling water 2/3 up the side of pan. Cover steamer. Boil for 1 hour adding more boiling water as needed to keep level up. Makes 1 pudding.

Brown Sugar Sauce: Stir first 3 ingredients together in saucepan. Add water. Stir well. Heat and stir on medium until mixture boils and thickens.

Stir in butter and vanilla. Serve over Steamed Chocolate Pudding. Makes 2 1/2 cups (625 mL) sauce.

Pictured on page 78 and 79.

Chocolate Pudding Sauce

Prepare Brown Sugar Sauce, adding 2 tbsp. (30 mL) cocoa to dry ingredients. Complete as above.

Loaves are easier to slice the next day. They are also easier to slice if frozen and slightly thawed. Return the unsliced portion to freezer. Keep muffins and loaves in the freezer for no longer than 3 months for best texture and taste.

U se heavy-bottomed saucepans when making thick sauces to prevent scorching. Most sauces can be frozen, unless they contain eggs. Freeze in airtight container leaving 1 inch (2.5 cm) head space. Remove any ice crystals that may have formed.

Christmas Pudding Sauce

Beautiful caramel color with perfect blend of flavors. Serve with your favorite Christmas pudding.

Brown sugar, packed	½ cup	125 mL
Granulated sugar	½ cup	125 mL
Cornstarch	3 tbsp.	50 mL
Water	1 cup	250 mL
Butter or hard margarine	¼ cup	60 mL
Lemon juice, fresh or bottled	2 tbsp.	30 mL
Rum flavoring	1 tsp.	5 mL

Mix both sugars and cornstarch in saucepan.

Add water. Stir. Add butter, lemon juice and rum flavoring. Heat and stir until it boils and thickens. Makes 1⅔ cups (400 mL) sauce.

Pictured on page 85.

1. Creamy Pudding Sauce, page 87
2. Christmas Pudding Sauce, page 84
3. Rum Sauce, page 87
4. Carrot Pudding, page 86

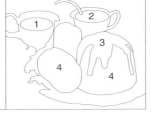

Pastel Hard Sauce

Try a variety of colors and shapes.
Make well in advance and store in fridge.
Layer between waxed paper.

Butter or hard margarine, softened	¼ cup	60 mL
Icing (confectioner's) sugar	1 cup	250 mL
Vanilla or brandy flavoring	1 tsp.	5 mL
Milk, for thinning		
Food coloring, if desired		

Beat butter, icing sugar and vanilla together. Add a bit of milk if needed, to make a touch softer. Work in food coloring with hands. Spread about ¼ inch (6 mm) thick on cookie sheet. Roll to smooth. Chill. Use cookie cutter to cut into Christmas trees, stars or balls. Remove with lifter. Soften scraps to room temperature. Repeat. Makes a scant 1 cup (250 mL) sauce.

Pictured on page 78.

Carrot Pudding

So moist, with a wonderful blend of flavors.

Grated carrot	1½ cups	375 mL
Chopped beef suet	1 cup	250 mL
All-purpose flour	2 cups	500 mL
Brown sugar, packed	1 cup	250 mL
Sultana raisins	1 cup	250 mL
Currants	1 cup	250 mL
Cut citron peel	1 cup	250 mL
Red or black currant jelly	½ cup	125 mL
Brandy flavoring	1 tsp.	5 mL
Ground ginger	1 tsp.	5 mL
Ground cinnamon	1 tsp.	5 mL
Baking powder	1 tsp.	5 mL
Baking soda	1 tsp.	5 mL
Ground allspice	½ tsp.	2 mL
Ground nutmeg	¼ tsp.	1 mL
Grated raw potato	1½ cups	375 mL

Combine first 7 ingredients in large bowl. Mix well.

Stir remaining 9 ingredients together in medium bowl. Add to first bowl. Stir well. Turn into greased 10 cup (2.5 L) pudding pan. Cover with double square greased foil, tying sides down with string. Put into steamer with boiling water ⅔ up sides of pan. Steam, covered, for 3 hours, adding more boiling water to keep level up. Cool. Remove from pan. Wrap in foil or plastic. Freeze for 2 months or store in refrigerator 2 to 3 weeks. Reheat just before serving. Serve with Rum Sauce, page 87. Serves 12 to 15.

Pictured on page 84 and 85.

For Gift Giving

Round Mini Loaves (Steamed Puddings)
Line bottoms of 3 greased 19 oz. (540 mL) cans with waxed paper. Divide pudding batter evenly among them. Top each with a glazed cherry placed in the center. Cover each can with double square greased foil, but first place foil over your fist to form a tent. Pudding tends to rise above the top of the can. Tie foil in place with string. Put all 3 cans into steamer or large pot (with bottom rack) with boiling water ⅔ way up sides of cans. Steam, covered, for 2¼ hours, adding more boiling water as needed to keep level up. Remove cans from steamer. While still warm, carefully loosen sides with table knife. Turn out onto rack to finish cooling. Wrap each pudding in plastic wrap and tie with decorative ribbon. Makes 3 small gift puddings.

Rectangular Mini Loaves (Fruitcakes)
Pour prepared fruitcake batter into 4 greased 2½ x 4 x 1 inch (6 x 10 x 2.5 cm) mini loaf pans. Bake in 350°F (175°C) oven for about 1 hour 15 minutes until an inserted wooden pick comes out clean. Cool on racks. Remove from pans. Wrap in plastic wrap and tie with decorative ribbon. Makes 4 mini gift loaves.

Christmas Cake

Nice hint of lemon. Not a heavy cake.

Raisins	2 cups	450 mL
Currants	2 cups	450 mL
Cut glazed mixed fruit	1 cup	225 mL
Glazed cherries, halved	1/2 cup	125 mL
Cut mixed peel	1/2 cup	125 mL
Chopped pecans or walnuts	1 cup	250 mL
Slivered almonds	3/4 cup	175 mL
All-purpose flour	1 cup	250 mL
Butter or hard margarine	1 cup	250 mL
Brown sugar, packed	1 cup	250 mL
Granulated sugar	1/4 cup	60 mL
Corn syrup	1/2 cup	125 mL
Large eggs	6	6
All-purpose flour	3 1/2 cups	875 mL
Baking powder	1 tsp.	5 mL
Ground cinnamon	1/2 tsp.	2 mL
Ground nutmeg	1/2 tsp.	2 mL
Ground allspice	1/2 tsp.	2 mL
Ground cloves	1/8 tsp.	0.5 mL
Apple juice	1 3/4 cups	425 mL
Grated rind of 1 lemon		
Juice of 1 lemon		
Brandy flavoring	1 tbsp.	15 mL

Line 2 greased 9 x 5 x 3 inch (22 x 12 x 7 cm) loaf pans with brown paper or 2 layers of waxed paper. Grease paper. Measure first 8 ingredients into large bowl. Stir well to mix in flour.

Cream butter and both sugars well in separate bowl. Beat in corn syrup. Add eggs, 1 at a time, beating well after each addition.

Measure next 6 ingredients into medium bowl. Stir well.

Combine apple juice, lemon rind, lemon juice and brandy flavoring in small bowl. Add flour mixture in 2 parts alternately with apple juice mixture in 2 parts. Add fruit mixture. Mix well. Divide between prepared pans. Bake in 300°F (150°C) oven for about 2 1/2 to 2 3/4 hours until an inserted wooden pick comes out clean. Let stand on rack to cool. Remove from pans. Wrap in plastic to store in cool place for 2 to 3 weeks before freezing for long-term storage. Makes 2 loaves, 8 pounds (3.6 kg) total.

Pictured on front cover.

Creamy Pudding Sauce

Serve with Steamed Cranberry Pudding, page 82.

Butter or hard margarine	1/2 cup	125 mL
All-purpose flour	2 tbsp.	30 mL
Evaporated skim milk (or light cream)	1 cup	250 mL
Granulated sugar	1 cup	250 mL
Vanilla	1 tsp.	5 mL
Salt	1/8 tsp.	0.5 mL

Melt butter in saucepan. Mix in flour.

Stir in milk. Heat and stir until it boils and thickens.

Add sugar, vanilla and salt. Stir to dissolve sugar. Makes 2 cups (500 mL) sauce.

Pictured on page 82 and on page 84.

Rum Sauce

Smooth and silky. Serve with Steamed Fruit Pudding, page 80 or Plum Pudding, page 81.

Butter or hard margarine	3 tbsp.	50 mL
All-purpose flour	3 tbsp.	50 mL
Salt	1/2 tsp.	2 mL
Water	1 1/2 cups	375 mL
Brown sugar, packed	3/4 cup	175 mL
Rum flavoring	1 tsp.	5 mL

Melt butter in saucepan. Mix in flour and salt.

Stir in water until it boils and thickens.

Add sugar and flavoring. Stir to dissolve sugar. Makes about 2 cups (500 mL) sauce.

Pictured on page 85.

Cookies & Confections

It's true that cookies come out of the oven year-round. But Christmas has a cookie collection all its own. That's when gingerbread men, shortbread and brightly-iced sugar cookies take shape by the dozen to be arranged on platters at home and beyond.

Likewise, confections are significant at this time of the year. Fudges, brittles and sweets by their very nature lend themselves to the holiday season because they look and taste great.

These holiday treats may be a bit more detailed than your usual efforts and definitely require

Use vegetable shortening or non-stick cooking spray rather than butter or margarine to grease baking sheets . This will help prevent burning. You may also line baking sheets with parchment paper. When reusing a baking sheet, be sure it has cooled before placing cookie dough on it. Leave 1 or 2 inches (2.5 or 5 cm) between each cookie.

a shopping list of ingredients specific to the season. But the reaction they get makes the extra effort worth it.

Far Left: Divinity Drops, page 95   Left: Jolly Fruit Drops, page 89

Cherry Winks

So easy to make. Freezes well, too. Nice combination of cherry and coconut flavors.

Butter or hard margarine, softened	½ cup	125 mL
Icing (confectioner's) sugar	1½ cups	375 mL
Fine coconut	1 cup	250 mL
Maraschino cherries, halved, dried on paper towel	20	20
Graham cracker crumbs	¼ cup	60 mL

Mix butter, icing sugar and coconut well. Form into a long tube to make it easier to mark off into 40 pieces.

Wrap each piece around a cherry half. Shape into a ball.

Roll each ball in graham crumbs. Store in covered container in refrigerator. Makes about 40 winks.

Pictured on page 89.

Top Center: Chocolate Snowballs, page 93   Bottom Center: Cherry Winks, page 88   Right: Whipped Shortbread, page 89

Whipped Shortbread

These melt in your mouth!

Butter, softened (do not use margarine)	1 cup	250 mL
Granulated sugar	½ cup	125 mL
All-purpose flour	1½ cups	375 mL
Cornstarch	¼ cup	60 mL

Cream butter and sugar in medium bowl. Beat until light and fluffy.

Add flour and cornstarch gradually while beating continuously. Beat until light. Drop by teaspoonfuls onto ungreased cookie sheet. Bake in 375°F (190°C) oven for 12 to 14 minutes. Makes 2½ dozen cookies.

Pictured above.

Jolly Fruit Drops

Batter will be thick but the result is nice and chewy. Colorful. Make ahead and freeze.

Butter or hard margarine, softened	1 cup	225 mL
Granulated sugar	½ cup	125 mL
Brown sugar, packed	½ cup	125 mL
Vanilla	1 tsp.	5 mL
Medium coconut	1 cup	225 mL
Chopped dates	½ cup	125 mL
Chopped red glazed cherries	¼ cup	60 mL
Chopped green glazed cherries	¼ cup	60 mL
Quick cooking rolled oats	2 cups	450 mL
All-purpose flour	1 cup	225 mL
Baking soda	½ tsp.	2 mL
Salt	½ tsp.	2 mL

Cream butter and both sugars in large bowl. Beat in vanilla.

Stir in coconut, dates and both cherries.

Add remaining ingredients. Mix. Drop by teaspoonfuls onto ungreased baking sheet. Bake in 350°F (175°C) oven for 12 to 15 minutes. Makes about 5 dozen cookies.

Pictured above.

Coffee Perks

Quick to make. Try different flavorings.
Stir into your evening coffee.

Dipping chocolate wafers (available at craft stores)	2 cups	450 mL
Oil-based liqueur flavoring (see Note)	1/8 tsp.	0.5 mL
Colored plastic spoons	18	18

Melt chocolate with liqueur flavoring in saucepan on lowest heat, or in top of double boiler over warm water, stirring often.

Dip ball of spoon in chocolate mixture. Hold above chocolate so drips run back in saucepan. Lay spoon on waxed paper on plate to harden. Dip 1 more time. When hardened, wrap in decorative cellophane and tie with pretty ribbons. Makes 18.

Pictured below.

Note: Available at some specialty kitchen stores.

Cookies being kept for several weeks or less can be stored at room temperature in an airtight container. For longer storage, keep in freezer up to 1 year. Cool cookies completely before packing. Use a separate container for each type of cookie. Crisp cookies will absorb moisture from softer cookies. When stacking cookies, place a layer of waxed paper or parchment paper between layers.

Merry Fruit Cookies

These yummy, attractive cookies make an ideal cookie exchange contribution.

Glazed cherries, quartered	2 cups	500 mL
Dark raisins	1 1/2 cups	375 mL
Red pineapple rings, cut up	4	4
Green pineapple rings, cut up	4	4
Chopped dates	1 cup	250 mL
All-purpose flour	1/2 cup	125 mL
Butter or hard margarine, softened	1 lb.	454 g
Granulated sugar	2 cups	450 mL
Large eggs	3	3
Vanilla	1 tsp.	5 mL
Almond flavoring	1/2 tsp.	2 mL
Baking powder	1 tsp.	5 mL
Baking soda	1 tsp.	5 mL
Ground cinnamon	1/2 tsp.	2 mL
All-purpose flour	4 1/2 cups	1 L

Place first 6 ingredients in medium bowl. Stir to coat fruit with flour.

Cream butter and sugar well in large bowl. Add eggs, 1 at a time, beating well after each addition. Add vanilla and almond flavoring.

Stir baking powder, baking soda and cinnamon into second amount of flour in separate bowl. Add fruit mixture. Stir. Add to batter. Stir until it is too difficult to mix. Work with your hands until flour is mixed in. Shape into 4 or 5 logs about 1 1/2 inches (4 cm) in diameter. Roll each log in waxed paper. Chill for 1 hour or longer. Cut in 1/4 inch (6 mm) slices. Arrange on greased baking sheet 1/2 inch (12 mm) apart. Bake in 375°F (190°C) oven for about 10 minutes until golden. Makes about 9 dozen cookies.

Pictured above.

Nutty Cherry Shortbread

Keep refrigerated. Slice and bake as you need them.

Butter, softened	1 lb.	454 g
Brown sugar, packed	2 cups	450 mL
All-purpose flour	3½ cups	800 mL
Cornstarch	½ cup	125 mL
Quartered glazed cherries	1 cup	250 mL
Ground or finely chopped almonds	1 cup	250 mL

Cream butter and sugar well in large bowl.

Add remaining ingredients. Work into butter mixture. Shape into 4 rolls about 1½ inches (4 cm) in diameter. Roll each roll in waxed paper. Chill. Cut in ¼ inch (6 mm) slices. Arrange on ungreased baking sheet about 1 inch (2.5 cm) apart. Bake in 400°F (205°C) oven for 6 to 7 minutes until edges show some browning. Makes 6 dozen cookies.

Pictured on page 99.

Cocoa Cookies

Let the kids help you make and decorate these.

Butter or hard margarine, softened	¼ cup	60 mL
Granulated sugar	1 cup	250 mL
Large egg	1	1
Milk	6 tbsp.	100 mL
Vanilla	½ tsp.	2 mL
All-purpose flour	2 cups	450 mL
Cocoa	½ cup	125 mL
Baking powder	1 tbsp.	15 mL
Salt	¼ tsp.	1 mL

Cream butter and sugar in medium bowl. Add egg. Beat well. Add milk and vanilla. Beat in.

Add flour, cocoa, baking powder and salt. Mix. Roll ¼ inch (0.5 cm) thick on lightly floured surface. Cut into 2 inch (5 cm) rounds or use Christmas cookie cutters. Arrange on greased cookie sheet. Bake in 400°F (205°C) oven for about 10 minutes. Makes about 4 dozen cookies.

Pictured below.

Spritz

The cream cheese keeps these cookies soft.

Butter or hard margarine, softened	1 cup	250 mL
Cream cheese, softened	4 oz.	125 g
Granulated sugar	1 cup	250 mL
Large eggs	2	2
Vanilla	1½ tsp.	7 mL
Salt	¼ tsp.	1 mL
All-purpose flour	3 cups	750 mL
Sugar, sprinkles, colored sugar, red and green glazed cherries		

Cream butter, cream cheese and sugar in large bowl. Beat in eggs 1 at a time. Add vanilla and salt. Beat.

Add flour. Work into batter. Fill cookie press and press your choice of design onto ungreased cookie sheet. Decorate. Bake in 400°F (205°C) oven for 10 to 12 minutes until set and edges are showing a hint of brown. Makes 6 to 7 dozen cookies.

Chocolate Spritz

Exchange 6 tbsp. (100 mL) of flour with 6 tbsp. (100 mL) cocoa.

Orange Spritz

Add 2 tsp. (10 mL) finely grated orange rind and ½ tsp. (2 mL) orange flavoring.

Chocolate Orange Spritz

Exchange 6 tbsp. (100 mL) flour with an equal amount of cocoa. Add 2 tsp. (10 mL) orange flavoring.

Pictured on this page and on page 22.

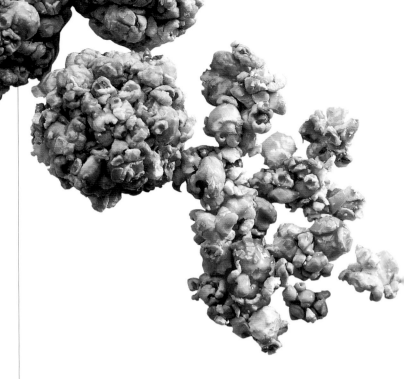

Flake Macaroons

Light and crunchy. Can be made ahead and frozen.

Egg whites (large), room temperature	2	2
Granulated sugar	1 cup	250 mL
Vanilla	1 tsp.	5 mL
Corn flakes	2 cups	500 mL
Chopped pecans or walnuts	½ cup	125 mL
Fancy flake coconut	1 cup	250 mL

Beat egg whites in small bowl until stiff. Transfer to large bowl.

Sprinkle ⅓ sugar over at a time, folding in after each addition. Fold in vanilla.

Fold in corn flakes, pecans and coconut. Form mounds of about 1 rounded teaspoon. Place about 1 inch (2.5 cm) apart onto greased baking sheet. Bake in 350°F (175°C) oven for about 15 minutes. Makes 24 cookies.

Pictured below.

Caramel Popcorn Balls

Toffee-like chewiness. Kids will love these.

Popped corn (pop about ½ cup, 125 mL)	14 cups	3.15 L
Granulated sugar	1 cup	250 mL
Boiling water	¾ cup	175 mL
Brown sugar, packed	½ cup	125 mL

Put popped corn into large bowl.

Heat granulated sugar, stirring continually, in heavy saucepan until sugar melts and turns golden brown in color.

Gradually add boiling water, stirring until spattering quits and caramel mixture dissolves.

Add brown sugar. Stir on medium-low heat until dissolved. Cook and stir until it reaches soft ball stage 238°F (116°C) on candy thermometer or until a small spoonful dropped in cold water forms a soft ball. Pour over popcorn. Stir well to coat. Shape into 2½ inch (6 cm) balls, using buttered hands. Wrap each ball in plastic wrap. Makes 50 balls.

Pictured above.

Caramel Popcorn

Do not shape into balls. Let mixture dry on cookie sheets. Break apart and store in airtight container.

Pictured above.

Popcorn Balls

Fun to make. Make it a second time but with green food coloring.

Popped corn (pop about ¼ cup, 60 mL)	8 cups	1.8 L
White miniature marshmallows	3 cups	675 mL
Butter or hard margarine	2 tbsp.	30 mL
Salt	¼ tsp.	1 mL
Red food coloring		

Place popped corn in large bowl.

Heat marshmallows, butter and salt in large heavy saucepan, stirring often, until marshmallows are melted.

Add food coloring by drops to make a pretty pink color. Pour over popcorn. Stir well to coat every piece. Brush palms of hands with butter or margarine. Shape mixture into 3 inch (7.5 cm) balls. Cool. Wrap each ball in plastic wrap. Makes 8 balls.

Pictured below.

Crunchy Popcorn Balls

Try these with strawberry jelly powder and red food coloring.

Popped corn (pop about ⅔ cup, 150 mL)	16 cups	3.6 L
Light corn syrup	1 cup	250 mL
Granulated sugar	½ cup	125 mL
Lime flavored gelatin (jelly powder)	3 oz.	85 g
Green food coloring, if desired		

Put popped corn into large bowl.

Heat and stir corn syrup and sugar in saucepan until it comes to a boil. Quit stirring. Let it reach a rolling boil (boils furiously). Remove from heat.

Stir in gelatin until it dissolves. Add a bit of green food coloring if you want a greener color. Pour over popcorn. Stir well to coat. Brush your hands with margarine. Shape into 2½ inch (6 cm) balls. Cool. Wrap each ball in plastic wrap. Makes 21 balls.

Pictured on this page.

Chocolate Snowballs

Very tender and fragile. A melt-in-your-mouth cookie.

Butter or hard margarine, softened	1¼ cups	300 mL
Granulated sugar	⅔ cup	150 mL
Vanilla	1½ tsp.	7 mL
All-purpose flour	2 cups	500 mL
Cocoa	½ cup	125 mL
Ground pecans (or walnuts)	1½ cups	350 mL
Icing (confectioner's) sugar	½ cup	125 mL

Cream butter, granulated sugar and vanilla together well.

Mix in flour, cocoa and pecans. Shape into 1 inch (2.5 cm) balls. Arrange on ungreased baking sheet. Bake in 350°F (175°C) oven for about 20 minutes.

When balls are cool enough to handle, roll them in icing sugar. Cool completely before storing. Makes 7 dozen snowballs.

Pictured on page 89.

Crunchy Popcorn Balls

Popcorn Balls

Alfajores

Alfajores

These alfa-HORE-ez are really different
and delicious, but take extra time.

Sweetened condensed milk	11 oz.	300 mL
Boiling water		
Cookies:		
Butter or hard margarine, softened	¹/₂ cup	125 mL
Granulated sugar	³/₄ cup	175 mL
Large egg	1	1
Egg yolk (large)	1	1
Finely grated lemon peel	1 tsp.	5 mL
Cornstarch	1¹/₄ cups	300 mL
All-purpose flour	³/₄ cup	175 mL
Baking powder	1 tsp.	5 mL
Caramelized sweetened condensed milk		
Thread coconut	¹/₂ cup	125 mL

Empty milk into 8 inch (20 cm) glass pie plate. Cover with foil. Put ¹/₄ inch (6 mm) hot water into 2 quart (2 L) shallow casserole. Set pie plate in water. Bake at 425°F (220°C) for about 1 hour 20 minutes to caramelize, replenishing water at halftime. Stir well until smooth.

Cookies: Cream butter and sugar in medium bowl. Beat in egg and egg yolk. Add lemon peel, cornstarch, flour and baking powder. Stir. Work with your hands until dough sticks together. Let dough rest for 15 minutes. Roll dough a scant ¹/₄ inch (6 mm) thick on floured surface. Cut into 1¹/₂ inch (4 cm) circles. Arrange on greased baking sheet. Bake in 325°F (160°C) oven for 10 to 15 minutes. They should be dry but not brown. Cool.

Sandwich 2 cookies together with a layer of caramelized condensed milk. Spread a thin layer of caramelized condensed milk around outside edge of alfajores. Roll edge in coconut. Makes 30 alfajores.

Pictured above.

Christmas Trees

"Plant" these trees in and around other cookies on your
cookie tray. But be prepared—they'll disappear quickly.

Butter or hard margarine	¹/₂ cup	125 mL
Icing (confectioner's) sugar	2 cups	450 mL
Milk	3 tbsp.	50 mL
Medium coconut	3 cups	675 mL
Vanilla or mint flavoring	¹/₂ tsp.	2 mL
Green food coloring		
White baking chocolate squares, cut up	4 × 1 oz.	4 × 28 g

Melt butter in large saucepan. Remove from heat. Stir in icing sugar and milk.

Mix in coconut and vanilla. Add enough food coloring to tint a pretty green. Shape into small balls about 1 inch (2.5 cm) in diameter. Squeeze top to form an upside down cone shape. Put on tray in refrigerator overnight, uncovered, to dry.

Melt chocolate in saucepan on lowest heat, stirring often. Dip tops of trees in chocolate to look like snow. Makes 30 "trees".

Pictured on page 105.

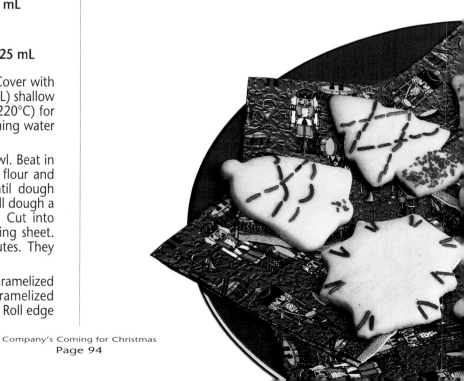

Sugar Cookies

Everyone's favorite. Make and freeze well ahead of time.

Butter or hard margarine, softened	¾ cup	175 mL
Granulated sugar	¾ cup	175 mL
Large egg	1	1
Vanilla	1 tsp.	5 mL
All-purpose flour	2 cups	450 mL
Baking soda	1 tsp.	5 mL
Cream of tartar	1 tsp.	5 mL
Cardamom (optional but good)	¼ tsp.	1 mL
Salt	¼ tsp.	1 mL

Cream butter and sugar in large bowl. Add egg and vanilla. Beat.

Mix remaining ingredients in separate bowl. Stir into batter. Roll out ⅛ inch (3 mm) thick on lightly floured surface. Cut into rounds or different shapes. Bake on greased cookie sheet in 350°F (175°C) oven for about 10 minutes. Cool. Decorate. Makes 7 dozen cookies.

Variation: For plain sugar cookies, sprinkle with granulated sugar before baking.

Variation: For decorated cookies, sprinkle with colored sugar or sprinkles before baking or decorate baked cookies with icing.

Pictured below and on page 22.

Sugar Cookies

Cookies are usually baked on the middle rack in the oven. However, if your cookies appear to be burning on the bottom, move them up one rack; if the tops are browning too much, move them down one rack. For delicate cookies (Whipped Shortbread, page 89) try stacking 2 cookie sheets together. When baking 2 sheets of cookies at the same time, put one on the middle rack to one side and one on the lower rack to the other side. Set your timer to switch them halfway through baking.

Divinity Drops

So white, with red and green flecks peeking through. Smooth melt-in-your-mouth texture.

Granulated sugar	3 cups	700 mL
White corn syrup	½ cup	125 mL
Hot water	¾ cup	175 mL
Salt	⅛ tsp.	0.5 mL
Egg whites (large), room temperature	2	2
Vanilla	1 tsp.	5 mL
Candied cherries, cut up, or finely chopped walnuts or pecans	½ cup	125 mL

Measure sugar, corn syrup, water and salt into 3 quart (3 L) heavy saucepan. Heat and stir constantly as you slowly bring it to a boil. Sugar should be dissolved before it starts to boil. Boil, without stirring, until candy thermometer reaches hard ball stage or until a small spoonful dropped in cold water forms a hard ball that is still pliable and plastic-like.

Meanwhile, beat egg whites in a large bowl until stiff. Pour hot syrup mixture in a thin stream over beaten egg whites, beating continually. Beat until fairly stiff and it loses its gloss. A small amount dropped on saucer should hold its shape.

Quickly stir in vanilla and cherries or walnuts. Work quickly with greased spoons and drop onto greased waxed paper. Makes 36 drops.

Pictured on page 88.

Christmas Fudge

A very pretty fudge—Christmas colors.
Freeze ahead. Keeps well in refrigerator.

Granulated sugar	3 cups	675 mL
Light cream	¾ cup	175 mL
Corn syrup	3 tbsp.	45 mL
Butter (do not use margarine)	1 tbsp.	15 mL
Vanilla	1 tsp.	5 mL
Almond flavoring	1 tsp.	5 mL
Chopped candied red cherries	¼ cup	60 mL
Chopped candied green cherries	¼ cup	60 mL
Chopped pecans	½ cup	125 mL
Sliced Brazil nuts	½ cup	125 mL
Chopped candied yellow pineapple	⅓ cup	75 mL

Put sugar, cream, syrup and butter into 3 quart (3 L) heavy saucepan. Heat on medium-low, stirring often, until it starts to boil. Boil gently, stirring occasionally to prevent sticking, until it reaches soft ball on candy thermometer or until a small spoonful forms a soft ball in cold water. Remove from heat. Remove thermometer. Let stand until crust forms on top but liquid is still warm, about 10 minutes. Beat until slightly thickened and a little lighter in color.

Add vanilla and almond flavoring. Beat with wooden spoon until it has lost its gloss.

Mix in remaining 5 ingredients quickly. Press with greased hands into 8 x 8 inch (20 x 20 cm) pan. Cool. Cuts into 36 pieces. Makes 2½ pounds (1.1 kg).

Pictured on page 97.

1. Condensed Fudge, page 96
2. Christmas Fudge, page 96
3. Special Chocolate Fudge, page 96

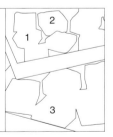

Special Chocolate Fudge

Sweet—like fudge should be!

Granulated sugar	3 cups	675 mL
Light cream	1 cup	225 mL
Unsweetened chocolate baking squares, cut up	3 x 1 oz.	3 x 28 g
Corn syrup	2 tbsp.	30 mL
Butter or hard margarine	2 tbsp.	30 mL
Salt	⅛ tsp.	0.5 mL
Vanilla	1 tsp.	5 mL
Chopped walnuts	¾ cup	175 mL

Combine first 6 ingredients in 3 quart (3 L) heavy saucepan. Heat and stir slowly until sugar is dissolved. Bring to a boil. Boil slowly until soft ball stage is reached on candy thermometer or until a small spoonful dropped in cold water forms a soft ball. Remove from heat. Remove thermometer. Let stand 40 minutes to cool slightly.

Add vanilla. Beat with wooden spoon until it loses its gloss and starts to thicken. Quickly add walnuts. Pour into greased 8 x 8 inch (20 x 20 cm) pan. Cool. Cuts into 36 pieces.

Pictured on page 97.

Condensed Fudge

Great brown sugar taste.

Sweetened condensed milk	11 oz.	300 mL
Brown sugar, packed	2 cups	450 mL
Granulated sugar	1 cup	225 mL
Milk	½ cup	125 mL
Butter or hard margarine	3 tbsp.	50 mL
Corn syrup	2 tbsp.	30 mL
Vanilla	1 tsp.	5 mL

Combine first 6 ingredients in 3 quart (3 L) saucepan. Heat on medium-low, stirring often as it comes to a boil. Boil, stirring occasionally to prevent sticking, until soft ball stage on candy thermometer or until a small spoonful dropped in cold water forms a soft ball. Remove from heat. Remove thermometer. Let stand 40 minutes.

Add vanilla. Beat with wooden spoon until it gets thick. Pour into greased 9 x 9 inch (22 x 22 cm) pan. Cool. Cuts into 36 pieces. Makes 2 pounds (900 g).

Pictured on page 97.

Top: Peanut Butter Treats
Center: Shortbread Squares

Right: Scotch Shortbread

Shortbread Squares

Crunchy and crisp.

Butter (do not use margarine)	½ lb.	225 g
All-purpose flour	2½ cups	575 mL
Granulated sugar	¾ cup	175 mL
Granulated sugar (plain or colored)	½ cup	125 mL

Melt butter in small saucepan.

Stir flour and first amount of sugar well in bowl. Add melted butter. Mix well. Pat out flat about ¼ inch (6 mm) thick on ungreased cookie sheet. Bake in 325°F (160°C) oven for about 25 minutes until golden.

Cut into squares while hot. Coat with remaining sugar. Makes 36 squares.

Pictured on this page.

Peanut Butter Treats

These no-bake treats freeze well. Very rich.

Butter or hard margarine	½ cup	125 mL
Smooth peanut butter	1 cup	250 mL
Graham cracker crumbs	1 cup	250 mL
Icing (confectioner's) sugar	2 cups	500 mL
Chopped walnuts	⅓ cup	75 mL
Icing:		
Semisweet chocolate chips	1 cup	250 mL
Butter or hard margarine	3 tbsp.	50 mL

Heat and stir butter and peanut butter in large saucepan until smooth.

Add graham crumbs, icing sugar and walnuts. Mix well. Press into ungreased 8 x 8 inch (20 x 20 cm) pan.

Icing: Heat and stir chocolate chips and butter in saucepan on low until smooth. Spread over top. Let stand until set. Cuts into 25 squares.

Pictured above.

Jean's Favorite

Scotch Shortbread

Perfect! Lightly golden squares with a dusting of icing sugar. Try the variation too.

Butter, softened (do not use margarine)	½ lb.	225 g
Icing (confectioner's) sugar	½ cup	125 mL
All-purpose flour	2 cups	450 mL
Baking powder	¼ tsp.	1 mL
Salt	⅛ tsp.	0.5 mL
Icing (confectioner's) sugar		

Cream butter and icing sugar in medium bowl.

Mix in flour, baking powder and salt. Press into 9 x 9 inch (22 x 22 cm) pan. Prick dough, using fork, every 2 inches (5 cm). Bake in 350°F (175°C) oven for about 30 minutes until golden.

Cut into squares while hot. Sprinkle with icing sugar. Store in airtight container. Makes 36 squares.

Variation: Press into large ceramic shortbread mold. Bake in 350°F (175°C) oven for about 30 minutes until golden. Unmold carefully when cool. Makes 1 large mold.

Pictured on this page.

Top: Beer Nuts, page 99
Center: Nutty Cherry Shortbread, page 91
Bottom: Chocolate Drop Cookies, page 99

Chocolate Drop Cookies

A soft, tasty cookie.

Butter or hard margarine	¹/₂ cup	125 mL
Unsweetened baking chocolate squares, cut up	2 × 1 oz.	2 × 28 g
Brown sugar, packed	1 cup	250 mL
Large egg	1	1
Milk	³/₄ cup	175 mL
Vanilla	1 tsp.	5 mL
All-purpose flour	2¹/₄ cups	500 mL
Baking soda	¹/₂ tsp.	2 mL
Topping:		
Semisweet baking chocolate squares, melted	2 × 1 oz.	2 × 28 g

Melt butter and chocolate in large saucepan over low heat, stirring often. Remove from heat.

Using spoon, beat in sugar, egg, milk and vanilla.

Stir flour and baking soda together. Add and stir to moisten. Drop by rounded teaspoonfuls onto greased cookie sheet about 1 inch (2.5 cm) apart. Bake in 350°F (175°C) oven for 8 to 10 minutes. Cool.

Topping: Drizzle with melted chocolate. Makes 4 dozen cookies.

Pictured above.

Beer Nuts

Nice, toasty flavor. Keep a good supply on hand.

Large peanuts, with skins	4 cups	1 L
Butter or hard margarine	¹/₂ cup	125 mL
Brown sugar, packed	1 cup	250 mL
Corn syrup	¹/₄ cup	60 mL
Salt	¹/₂ tsp.	2 mL
Baking soda	¹/₄ tsp.	1 mL

Place peanuts in shallow non-stick baking pan. Keep warm in 225°F (110°C) oven.

Combine butter, brown sugar, corn syrup and salt in saucepan. Cook to firm ball, 250°F (120°C), or until a small spoonful dropped in cold water retains a round shape when rolled between fingers. Remove from heat.

Stir in baking soda. Pour slowly over peanuts, stirring gently to coat. Return to 250°F (120°C) oven for about 1 hour. Stir every 15 minutes. Cool. Stir several times while cooling. Keep in airtight container. Makes 5 cups (1.25 L) nut mixture.

Pictured on this page.

Gingerbread Figures

A treat for little (or big) kids! Leave as is or glaze or decorate with icing and small candy silver balls.

Butter or hard margarine, softened	½ cup	125 mL
Granulated sugar	½ cup	125 mL
Fancy molasses	½ cup	125 mL
Egg yolk (large)	1	1
All-purpose flour	2 cups	500 mL
Baking powder	½ tsp.	2 mL
Baking soda	½ tsp.	2 mL
Ground cinnamon	1 tsp.	5 mL
Ground ginger	1 tsp.	5 mL
Ground cloves	½ tsp.	2 mL
Ground nutmeg	¼ tsp.	1 mL
Salt	¼ tsp.	1 mL
Frosting:		
Egg white, large	1	1
Icing (confectioner's) sugar	2 cups	500 mL

Cream butter, sugar, molasses and egg yolk together until light.

Add next 8 ingredients. Mix well. Wrap in plastic and chill at least 1 hour. Roll out. Cut into shapes with cookie cutters. Arrange on baking sheet. Bake in 350°F (175°C) oven for 10 to 15 minutes. Cool.

Frosting: Beat egg white with spoon in medium bowl. Beat in as much icing sugar as needed until icing will hold its shape. Ice cookies. Makes 12 to 16 gingerbread men cookies or a variety of other shapes.

Pictured below.

Gingerbread Lollipops

Shape ¼ to ⅓ cup (60 to 75 mL) dough into ball. Insert wooden stick. Place on greased cookie sheet. Press with bottom of tumbler to ¼ inch (6 mm) thick. Bake for 10 to 12 minutes. Cool.

Gingerbread Figures

Chocolate Oat Balls

*A no-bake confection. These can also be a
drop cookie, if desired.*

Butter or hard margarine	½ cup	125 mL
Granulated sugar	2 cups	500 mL
Milk	½ cup	125 mL
Quick cooking rolled oats	2 cups	500 mL
Cocoa	½ cup	125 mL
Vanilla	1 tsp.	5 mL
Toasted chopped pecans or walnuts (see Note)	1 cup	250 mL
Toasted finely chopped pecans or walnuts (see Note)	1 cup	250 mL

Heat butter, sugar and milk in saucepan, stirring often, until mixture comes to a simmer. Simmer 3 minutes. Remove from heat.

Add rolled oats, cocoa and vanilla. Stir well. Add first amount of pecans. Mix. Cool slightly. Shape into 1 inch (2.5 cm) balls.

Roll balls in remaining nuts. Store in airtight container. Makes 3 dozen cookies.

Pictured on page 104.

Note: To toast pecans or walnuts, spread on baking sheet. Bake in 350°F (175°C) oven for 5 to 8 minutes until "toasty" aroma.

Cherry Surprise

Very impressive and so easy to make. Freezes well.

Sweetened condensed milk	11 oz.	300 mL
Unsweetened chocolate baking squares, cut up	2 × 1 oz.	2 × 28 g
Graham wafer crumbs	2 cups	450 mL
Glazed cherries, red and green	32	32
Fine coconut	¾ cup	175 mL

Put milk and chocolate in top of double boiler. Cook over boiling water, stirring often, until thick, about 5 minutes.

Stir in graham crumbs. Chill for 1 hour.

Mold 1 tbsp. (15 mL) around each cherry.

Roll in coconut. Makes 32 confections.

Pictured on page 104.

Rum Balls

Rum Balls

*Always a favorite. Roll in chocolate sprinkles,
icing sugar or cocoa for variety.*

Vanilla wafer crumbs	3 cups	675 mL
Finely ground almonds or pecans	½ cup	125 mL
Cocoa	3 tbsp.	50 mL
Icing (confectioner's) sugar	1 cup	250 mL
Corn syrup	3 tbsp.	50 mL
Water	⅓ cup	75 mL
Rum flavoring	2 tsp.	10 mL
Icing (confectioner's) sugar	¼ cup	60 mL

Mix first 7 ingredients well in medium bowl. Shape into 1 inch (2.5 cm) balls.

Roll balls in remaining icing sugar. Store in covered container for several days before serving. Makes 36 balls.

Pictured above.

Taffy

Have a taffy pull party. Loads of fun!

Granulated sugar	2 cups	450 mL
Water	½ cup	125 mL
White vinegar	¼ cup	60 mL
Butter or hard margarine	2 tsp.	10 mL
Salt	⅛ tsp.	0.5 mL
Vanilla	1 tsp.	5 mL

Place sugar, water, vinegar, butter and salt in 3 quart (3 L) heavy saucepan. Heat and stir on medium until sugar dissolves. Bring to a boil. Boil, without stirring, until it reaches hard-ball stage 250°F (120°C) on candy thermometer. A teaspoonful dropped in some cold water will become hard. Remove from heat. Remove thermometer.

Stir in vanilla. Pour into buttered 9 × 13 inch (22 × 33 cm) pan to cool. When it has cooled enough to handle, divide among helpers. Pull with buttered fingertips. It will become much lighter in color. When it gets hard to pull, stretch into ropes about ½ to ¾ inch (12 to 18 mm) wide. Butter edges of scissors. Cut quickly into 1 inch (2.5 cm) lengths. Wrap each piece in waxed paper or plastic wrap. Makes about 100 pieces or 1¼ pounds (500 g).

Pictured below.

Breton Brittle

Fantastic people-pleaser. Quick and easy.

Dare Breton crackers (see Note)	28	28
Butter or hard margarine	1 cup	250 mL
Brown sugar, packed	1 cup	250 mL
Topping:		
Semisweet chocolate chips	1⅔ cups	400 mL
Finely chopped pecans or walnuts	⅓ cup	75 mL

Overlap crackers in foil-lined 9 × 13 inch (22 x 33 cm) pan so bottom is covered. Use 4 crackers across and 7 crackers lengthwise.

Stir butter and brown sugar together in saucepan until it comes to a boil. Pour carefully over crackers. Bake in 400°F (205°C) oven for 5 minutes.

Topping: Scatter chocolate chips over top. Let stand until soft. Spread to cover. Sprinkle with pecans. Cool. Store in refrigerator. Break or cut into pieces to serve. Makes 8 cups (2 L) brittle.

Pictured below.

Note: If Dare Breton crackers aren't available in your area, use thin round 2½ inch (6 cm) crackers (not soda) to line your pan.

Top Left: Peanut Brittle, page 103
Top Right: Almond Roca, page 103
Center: Breton Brittle, page 102
Bottom: Taffy, page 102

Almond Roca

Absolutely the best! Store in container in cool place—but keep handy.

Butter (do not use margarine)	1 lb.	454 g
Granulated sugar	2 cups	450 mL
Water	¼ cup	60 mL
Corn syrup	2 tbsp.	30 mL
Toasted, slivered almonds (see Note)	1⅓ cups	300 mL
Semisweet chocolate baking squares, cut up	4 × 1 oz.	4 × 28 g
Toasted, slivered almonds, finely chopped (see Note)	⅔ cup	150 mL
Semisweet baking chocolate squares, cut up	4 × 1 oz.	4 × 28 g

Melt butter in heavy saucepan over low heat. Add sugar. Stir to dissolve. Stir in water and corn syrup. Cook over low heat, stirring often but gently, until candy thermometer reads 290°F (142°C). Be patient. This will take 30 to 40 minutes. Remove from heat. Remove thermometer.

Add first amount of slivered almonds. Pour into greased 10 × 15 inch (25 × 30 cm) jelly roll pan about ¼ inch (6 mm) deep. Let cool.

Melt first amount of chocolate squares in saucepan over lowest heat, stirring often. Cool until you can hold your hand on saucepan but pan feels hot. Spread over candy.

Sprinkle with ½ remaining chopped almonds. Wait until chocolate hardens. Cover with waxed paper. Place another pan over top. Invert. Melt second amount of chocolate squares in saucepan over lowest heat. Cool until you can hold your hand on saucepan but pan feels hot. Spread over candy. Sprinkle with remaining chopped almonds. Allow to harden. Break into pieces to serve and to store. Makes 2 1/2 pounds (1.2 kg).

Pictured on page 102.

Note: To toast almonds, spread on baking sheet. Bake in 350°F (175°C) oven for 5 to 8 minutes until lightly browned.

Peanut Brittle

Include a box of this in your out-of-town parcels.

Granulated sugar	1½ cups	350 mL
Water	⅓ cup	75 mL
White corn syrup	⅔ cup	150 mL
Spanish peanuts	2 cups	450 mL
Butter (do not use margarine)	2 tbsp.	30 mL
Vanilla	1 tsp.	5 mL
Baking soda	2 tsp.	10 mL

Measure first 3 ingredients into heavy 3 quart (3 L) saucepan. Heat and stir until sugar dissolves and it starts to boil. Boil without stirring until it reaches soft-ball stage on candy thermometer or until a small spoonful dropped in cold water forms a soft ball.

Add peanuts and butter. Stir frequently until it reaches hard-crack or until a small spoonful dropped in cold water separates into threads and are hard and brittle and break between your fingers. Remove from heat. Grease baking sheet.

Add vanilla and baking soda. Work quickly and stir into mixture. It will foam. Immediately pour onto greased baking sheet. Spread evenly using greased pancake turner or spoon. Cool completely. Break into pieces. Makes 1½ pounds (680 g).

Pictured on page 102.

Butterscotches

Let the kids make these. Make as either a drop cookie or a rolled ball.

Granulated sugar	1½ cups	350mL
Butter or hard margarine	½ cup	125 mL
Evaporated milk (small can)	⅔ cup	150 mL
Butterscotch chips	1 cup	250 mL
Quick cooking rolled oats	3½ cups	800 mL
Medium coconut	½ cup	125 mL

Stir sugar, butter and milk in saucepan. Heat stirring constantly while it comes to a boil and boils for 1 minute. Remove from heat.

Add butterscotch chips. Stir until melted.

Mix in rolled oats and coconut. Stir well. Cool for 5 to 10 minutes. Drop by rounded teaspoonfuls onto waxed paper. Chill until firm. Makes about 6 dozen.

Pictured on page 104.

Dipped Vanillas

These are so pretty on a tray of mixed cookies. Freeze ahead.

Butter	½ cup	125 mL
Ground almonds	½ cup	125 mL
Granulated sugar	¼ cup	60 mL
Vanilla	1 tsp.	5 mL
All-purpose flour	1 cup	250 mL
Cornstarch	2 tbsp.	30 mL
Dip:		
Semisweet chocolate baking squares, cut up	2 × 1 oz.	2 × 28 g
Grated paraffin wax	2 tbsp.	30 mL

Cream butter, almonds, sugar and vanilla in mixing bowl.

Mix in flour and cornstarch. Shape into 1 inch (2.5 cm) balls. Roll each ball into a crescent shape. Place on greased baking sheet. Bake in 375°F (190°C) oven for 8 to 10 minutes. Cool.

Dip: Melt chocolate and wax in saucepan on lowest heat, stirring often. Dip top sides of crescents or 1 or both ends. Place on waxed paper to harden. Makes 30.

Pictured on page 104.

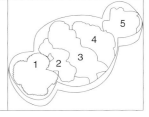

Desserts

Desserts

Special meals call for special desserts. You'll find the perfect finale for any of your holiday meals in this selection of squares, cakes and fancy desserts.

You can't go wrong with squares when it comes time for dessert. The variety is endless and they look and taste good.

Keep the pieces small for more variety on the plate. For easier cutting and serving, line the baking pan with foil. That makes it easier to lift the squares out for cutting.

If you think you will be serving a lot of squares during the season, cool and cut before freezing. That lets you scoop out the number you need without having to defrost the entire pan.

Cakes are another versatile and attractive choice. Some can be frozen and iced when defrosted. Depending on the icing, some cakes can be frosted ahead of time. Just be sure to use toothpicks to keep the wrap away from the icing.

Angel food and some kinds of tube cakes slice better when slightly frozen, while some other cakes cut better when defrosted a bit.

If you're looking for something different and a bit fun, try a fancy dessert. These whimsical concoctions will delight your guests to no end.

A fitting end is what you're looking for and that's what you get with these tempting dessert recipes.

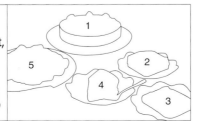

Strawberry Cream Dessert
Very strawberry! A pretty ending to a meal.

Crust:		
Butter or hard margarine	½ cup	125 mL
Graham cracker crumbs	2 cups	500 mL
Brown sugar, packed	¼ cup	60 mL
Filling:		
Frozen strawberries in syrup, thawed, syrup reserved	15 oz.	425 g
Reserved strawberry syrup		
Strawberry-flavored gelatin (jelly powder)	3 oz.	85 g
Granulated sugar	½ cup	125 mL
Lemon juice, fresh or bottled	2 tbsp.	30 mL
Whipping cream (or 1 envelope topping)	1 cup	250 mL
Topping:		
Whipping cream (or 1 envelope topping)	1 cup	250 mL
Granulated sugar	2 tsp.	10 mL
Vanilla	½ tsp.	2 mL
Reserved crumbs	½ cup	125 mL

Crust: Melt butter in saucepan. Stir in graham crumbs and sugar. Reserve ½ cup (125 mL) for topping. Press remaining crumbs in ungreased 9 x 9 inch (22 x 22 cm) pan. Bake in 350°F (175°C) oven for 10 minutes. Cool.

Filling: Strain strawberries. Reserve syrup.

Pour reserved syrup into saucepan over medium heat. Stir gelatin into hot syrup to dissolve.

Stir in sugar and lemon juice. Cool. Add strawberries. Stir. Chill, stirring and scraping down sides often, until it starts to thicken.

Beat cream in small bowl until stiff. Fold into strawberry mixture. Pour over crust. Chill.

Topping: Beat cream, sugar and vanilla in small bowl until stiff. Spread over all. Sprinkle with reserved crumbs. Chill. Cuts into 9 or 12 pieces.

Pictured on page 107.

Profiteroles

You've seen them on restaurant menus—but these are chocolate! Make pro-FIT-er-ohls at home.

Cream Puffs:

Hot water	1 cup	250 mL
Butter or hard margarine	½ cup	125 mL
Semisweet chocolate baking square, cut up	1 × 1 oz.	1 × 28 g
Salt	½ tsp.	2 mL
All-purpose flour	1 cup	250 mL
Granulated sugar	1 tbsp.	15 mL
Large eggs	4	4

Chocolate Filling:

Instant chocolate pudding powder, 4 serving size	1	1
Milk	1 cup	250 mL
Whipping cream (or 1 envelope topping)	1 cup	250 mL

Chocolate Glaze:

Semisweet chocolate baking squares, cut up	2 × 1 oz.	2 × 28 g
Milk	2 tbsp.	30 mL
Corn syrup	1 tbsp.	15 mL
Vanilla	¼ tsp.	1 mL

Cream Puffs: Combine first 4 ingredients in medium saucepan. Stir often over medium heat as mixture comes to a boil.

Add flour and sugar all at once. Cook and stir until it forms a ball of dough that won't stick to edge of saucepan. Remove from heat.

Add eggs 1 at a time, beating well after each addition. Divide dough into 4 equal portions. Spoon onto greased baking sheet getting 12 from each portion. Bake in 450°F (230°C) oven for 10 minutes. Reduce heat to 350°F (175°C). Bake about 5 minutes more until risen and browned. Cool.

Chocolate Filling: Beat pudding and milk together until smooth.

Beat cream until stiff. Fold into pudding. Cut tops not quite off puffs. Spoon in filling. Place on platter in shape of a bunch of grapes.

Chocolate Glaze: Combine all ingredients in saucepan. Heat and stir on medium-low until smooth. Drizzle over puffs. Makes 48. Serves 6 each to 8 guests.

Pictured on page 106.

Chocolate Truffle

Pure ecstacy!

Crust:

Butter or hard margarine	¼ cup	60 mL
Chocolate wafer crumbs	1¼ cups	300 mL
Granulated sugar	1 tbsp.	15 mL

Filling:

Butter or hard margarine	1 cup	250 mL
Semisweet chocolate chips	3 cups	750 mL
Large eggs, room temperature	5	5
Vanilla	1 tsp.	5 mL

Chocolate Glaze:

Semisweet chocolate chips	½ cup	125 mL
Evaporated milk or whipping cream	3 tbsp.	50 mL

Topping:

Whipping cream (or 1 envelope topping)	1 cup	250 mL
Granulated sugar	2 tsp.	10 mL
Vanilla	½ tsp.	2 mL
Cocoa, or grated chocolate, for dusting		

Crust: Melt butter in medium saucepan. Stir in crumbs and sugar. Press into bottom of ungreased 8 inch (20 cm) springform pan. Set pan on a piece of foil. Press foil up all around to prevent water leaking into pan. Set pan in roaster or other wide pan.

Filling: Melt butter in large saucepan on low. Add chocolate chips. Stir often until they melt. Pour into medium bowl.

Add eggs 1 at a time, beating well after each addition. Mix in vanilla. Pour over crust in pan. Pour boiling water in roaster about ½ to ⅔ up side of springform pan. Bake in 425°F (220°C) oven for about 15 minutes until outer edge is set. Center will still be soft. Lift springform out of water and place on rack. Cool. Chill for at least 4 hours. Remove sides of springform pan.

Chocolate Glaze: Melt chocolate chips with milk in small saucepan on low. Stir often until smooth. Pour on top of filling. Smooth to glaze top and sides. Let stand a few minutes to dry before adding topping.

Topping: Beat cream, sugar and vanilla in small mixing bowl until stiff. Drop in puff balls around outside edge of cake.

Dust puffs with cocoa or sprinkle with grated chocolate. Chill until ready to serve. Serves 8 to 12.

Pictured on page 106.

Buttermilk Cake   Luscious Chocolate Cake

Luscious Chocolate Cake

"This is to die for," it has been said.

Chocolate cake mix, 2 layer size	1	1
Instant chocolate pudding powder, 4 serving size	1	1
Large eggs	4	4
Cooking oil	½ cup	125 mL
Warm water	½ cup	125 mL
Sour cream	1 cup	250 mL
Semisweet chocolate chips	1½ cups	375 mL
Chocolate Glaze:		
Semisweet chocolate chips	½ cup	125 mL
Butter or hard margarine	1 tbsp.	15 mL

Combine first 6 ingredients in large bowl. Beat on low to moisten, scraping down sides 2 or 3 times. Beat on medium for 2 minutes.

Stir in chocolate chips. Turn into greased and floured 12 cup (2.7 L) bundt pan. Bake in 350°F (175°C) oven for 50 to 60 minutes until an inserted wooden pick comes out clean. Let stand for 20 minutes. Invert onto plate or rack to cool.

Chocolate Glaze: Melt chocolate chips and butter in saucepan over low heat, stirring often. Remove from heat. Spread over top of cake allowing some to run down sides. Makes 1 cake.

Pictured above.

Buttermilk Cake

Nice large cake. Freezes well. Very moist.

Butter or hard margarine, softened	1 cup	250 mL
Granulated sugar	3 cups	675 mL
Egg yolks (large)	5	5
Vanilla	1 tsp.	5 mL
Salt	⅛ tsp.	0.5 mL
Buttermilk, fresh or reconstituted from powder	1 cup	250 mL
Baking soda	¾ tsp.	4 mL
All-purpose flour	3 cups	750 mL
Egg whites (large), room temperature	5	5

Cream butter and sugar well in large bowl. Add egg yolks, 1 at a time, beating well after each. Stir in vanilla and salt.

Measure buttermilk into separate bowl. Stir in baking soda.

Add flour in 3 parts alternately with buttermilk in 2 parts, beginning and ending with flour.

Beat egg whites until stiff. Fold into batter. Turn into greased (bottom only) 10 inch (25 cm) angel food pan. Bake in 325°F (160°C) oven for about 1 hour. There will be tiny cracks in top. Cool completely in pan before removing. Makes 1 cake.

Pictured on this page.

Prune Cake

Nice spicy flavor but not strong. This will be a winner.

Cooking oil	½ cup	125 mL
Granulated sugar	1 cup	250 mL
Large eggs	2	2
Stewed, pitted and chopped prunes, drained, juice reserved	⅔ cup	150 mL
All-purpose flour	1½ cups	375 mL
Baking powder	½ tsp.	2 mL
Baking soda	½ tsp.	2 mL
Salt	½ tsp.	2 mL
Ground cinnamon	½ tsp.	2 mL
Ground nutmeg	½ tsp.	2 mL
Ground allspice	½ tsp.	2 mL
Sour milk (or 2 tsp. 10 mL, white vinegar plus milk, stand 5 minutes)	⅔ cup	150 mL
Prune Icing:		
Icing (confectioner's) sugar	3 cups	750 mL
Butter or hard margarine, softened	6 tbsp.	100 mL
Reserved prune juice	¼ cup	60 mL
Vanilla	½ tsp.	2 mL

Beat cooking oil, sugar and 1 egg together in large bowl. Beat in second egg. Add prunes and stir with spoon.

Stir next 7 ingredients in separate bowl.

Add flour mixture in 3 parts alternately with sour milk in 2 parts beginning and ending with flour. Divide between 2 greased 8 inch (20 cm) round layer pans. Bake in 350°F (175°C) oven for about 25 minutes. An inserted wooden pick should come out clean. Cool. Remove from pans.

Prune Icing: Beat all ingredients in medium bowl on low to moisten. Beat on medium, adding more juice or icing sugar if needed to make proper spreading consistency. Makes about 1½ cups (375 mL), enough to fill and ice Prune Cake. Makes 1 cake.

Pictured on page 106.

Chocolate Crêpes

Put dessert under wraps.

Large eggs	3	3
Milk	1 cup	250 mL
Water	½ cup	125 mL
All-purpose flour	1¼ cups	300 mL
Granulated sugar	¼ cup	60 mL
Cocoa	2 tbsp.	30 mL
Cooking oil	2 tbsp.	30 mL
Rum flavoring (optional)	½ tsp.	2 mL
Filling:		
Cottage cheese	2 cups	500 mL
Icing (confectioner's) sugar	⅔ cup	150 mL
Topping:		
Frozen raspberries (or strawberries), in syrup	15 oz.	425 g

Beat eggs in mixing bowl until frothy. Add remaining ingredients. Beat until smooth. Add a bit more milk if too thick. Spoon 2 tbsp. (30 mL) batter into hot greased crêpe pan or use crêpe pan that dips into batter. Tip pan quickly so batter covers bottom. When underside is brown, remove crêpe to plate. Repeat. Makes about 24 crêpes.

Filling: Beat cottage cheese and icing sugar in small bowl until quite smooth. Place 1½ tbsp. (25 mL) down center of each crêpe. Fold sides over.

Topping: Spoon raspberries with juice across center of folded crêpes.

Pictured below.

Chocolate Crêpes

Bread Pudding

Everyone will love the taste. Raisins can be substituted for the currants, if preferred. Serve with cream.

Evaporated skim milk	13½ oz.	385 mL
Milk	¼ cup	60 mL
Raisin bread slices, cut bite size	5	5
Butter or hard margarine	2 tbsp.	30 mL
Large eggs, beaten	2	2
Brown sugar, packed	⅔ cup	150 mL
Salt	½ tsp.	2 mL
Vanilla	1 tsp.	5 mL
Currants	½ cup	125 mL
Ground cinnamon	¼ tsp.	1 mL

Heat both milks in heavy saucepan until steaming. Remove from heat.

Add bread and butter.

Beat eggs in small bowl. Add brown sugar, salt and vanilla. Stir in currants and cinnamon. Pour into milk mixture. Stir well. Turn into greased 1 quart (1 L) casserole. Bake, uncovered, in 350°F (175°C) oven for 40 to 45 minutes until set. Serves 6.

Pictured below.

Bread Pudding

Angel Mint Roll

The roll can be frozen in the towel in a plastic bag, then thawed and filled the day of serving.

Angel food cake mix	1	1
Icing (confectioner's) sugar	¼ cup	60 mL
Filling:		
Milk	½ cup	125 mL
Large marshmallows	36	36
Whipping cream (or 2 envelopes topping)	2 cups	500 mL
Crème De Menthe, green	⅓ cup	75 mL
Chocolate crumbs	¼ cup	60 mL
Coating:		
Whipping cream (or 2 envelopes topping)	2 cups	500 mL
Granulated sugar	2 tbsp.	30 mL
Vanilla	1 tsp.	5 mL

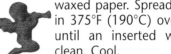

Prepare cake mix according to package directions. Line greased 10 × 15 inch (25 × 38 cm) jelly roll pan with waxed paper. Spread cake batter in pan. Bake in 375°F (190°C) oven for about 20 minutes until an inserted wooden pick comes out clean. Cool.

Turn out onto tea towel that has been well sprinkled with icing sugar. Carefully peel off waxed paper. Roll up with towel, starting from short side.

Filling: Heat, stirring often, milk and marshmallows in large saucepan until marshmallows melt. Cool thoroughly.

Beat whipping cream in large bowl until stiff. Add Crème De Menthe. Fold into cooled marshmallow mixture. Chill until fairly thick. Unroll angel cake. Spread with filling.

Sprinkle with chocolate crumbs. Roll up without towel.

Coating: Beat whipping cream, sugar and vanilla until stiff. Spread over roll covering sides, top and ends. Cuts into 12 slices.

Pictured on page 113.

Angel Mint Roll, page 112   Chocolate Roulade Yule Log, page 113

Chocolate Roulade Yule Log

A delicate roll.

Egg whites (large), room temperature	6	6
Cream of tartar	½ tsp.	2 mL
Egg yolks (large)	6	6
Granulated sugar	1 cup	250 mL
Cocoa	⅓ cup	75 mL
Vanilla	1 tsp.	5 mL
Salt, just a pinch		
Cocoa, sprinkle		
Filling:		
Whipping cream	2 cups	500 mL
Cocoa	½ cup	125 mL
Granulated sugar	½ cup	125 mL
Chocolate or coffee liqueur	¼ cup	60 mL
Large marshmallow	1	1
Pecan halves	6	6

Line greased 10 x 15 inch (25 x 38 cm) jelly roll pan with waxed paper. Beat egg whites in large bowl until soft peaks form. Add cream of tartar. Beat until stiff.

Using same beaters beat egg yolks, sugar, cocoa, vanilla and salt in medium bowl for about 2 minutes until mixed and color has lightened. Fold in egg whites. Spread in prepared pan. Bake in 350°F (175°C) oven for 15 to 20 minutes until an inserted wooden pick comes out clean.

Sift cocoa over a tea towel. Turn out cake onto cocoa. Peel off waxed paper. Cut crusty edges off log. Begin at shorter side. Roll both towel and cake together, continuing to dust with cocoa. Cool. When cool, unroll and spread with filling.

Filling: Beat cream, cocoa, sugar and liqueur in small bowl until thick.

Unroll cake. Spread with ½ filling. Roll up again without the towel. Chill. Spread outside with remaining filling, using large marshmallow to form "knot" on "log". Place pecan halves at random. Cuts into 12 slices.

Pictured above.

Cookies 'N Cake

*The kids will love this even without the icing
and chocolate drizzle.*

White cake mix, 2 layer size	1	1
Cooking oil	½ cup	125 mL
Large eggs	4	4
Water	1 cup	250 mL
Coarsely crushed cream filled chocolate cookies	1 cup	250 mL
Icing:		
Icing (confectioner's) sugar	1 cup	250 mL
Butter or hard margarine, softened	2 tbsp.	30 mL
Water	1½ tbsp.	25 mL
Vanilla	½ tsp.	2 mL
Unsweetened baking chocolate square, cut up, melted	1 × 1 oz.	1 × 28 g

Place cake mix, cooking oil, eggs and water into large bowl. Beat on low to moisten. Beat on medium for 2 minutes until smooth.

Carefully stir in crushed cookies. Turn into greased and floured 12 cup (2.7 L) bundt pan. Bake in 350°F (175°C) oven for about 45 to 55 minutes until an inserted wooden pick comes out clean. Cool. Turn out onto rack.

Icing: Stir all 4 ingredients together vigorously. Add more or less icing sugar or water to make a little softer than a spreading consistency. Spoon over cake allowing some to run down sides.

Drizzle chocolate over icing. Makes 1 cake.

Pictured on page 115.

Sherry Trifle

*Be sure and use a see-through dish or special trifle bowl.
The layers are so eye-catching.*

White cake mix, 2 layer size	1	1
Raspberry jam	½ cup	125 mL
Custard:		
Milk	2⅔ cups	650 mL
Custard powder	¼ cup	60 mL
Granulated sugar	¼ cup	60 mL
Milk	⅓ cup	75 mL
Vanilla	¾ tsp.	4 mL
Sherry (or alcohol-free sherry)	⅓ cup	75 mL
Reserved raspberry syrup		
Frozen raspberries in syrup, thawed, syrup reserved	15 oz.	425 g
Whipped Cream:		
Whipping cream (or 1 envelope topping)	1 cup	250 mL
Granulated sugar	1 tbsp.	15 mL
Vanilla	½ tsp.	2 mL

Maraschino cherries, for garnish

Make cake mix according to directions on box, using two 8 inch (20 cm) round cake pans. Cool completely. Slice cake layers in half horizontally to make 2 thin layers each. Spread 2 layers with ¼ cup (60 mL) jam each. Cut all 4 layers into cubes.

Custard: Heat first amount of milk in heavy saucepan until it simmers.

Stir custard powder and sugar together well in small bowl. Mix in remaining milk and vanilla. Stir slowly into hot milk until mixture boils and thickens. Cool completely.

Mix sherry and reserved raspberry syrup in small bowl.

Spread ½ the cake cubes in bottom of 2 quart (2 L) glass bowl. Pour ½ the sherry mixture over the cubes. Sprinkle with ½ the raspberries. Spread ½ custard over raspberries. Repeat with remaining cubes, sherry mixture, raspberries and custard. Chill until cold.

Whipped Cream: Beat cream, sugar and vanilla in small bowl until stiff. Spread over top layer of custard.

Garnish with cherries. Serves 6 to 8.

Pictured on page 115.

Left: Sherry Trifle, page 114
Right: Cookies 'N Cake, page 114

Pineapple Cake

Refreshing taste. Ice with Fluffy Frosting, page 122, and sprinkle with crushed rock candy.

Butter or hard margarine, softened	½ cup	125 mL
Granulated sugar	1½ cups	375 mL
Egg yolks, large	3	3
Crushed pineapple, with juice to measure	1 cup	250 mL
Vanilla	1½ tsp.	7 mL
Water	¼ cup	60 mL
Salt	½ tsp.	2 mL
Cake flour, sift before measuring	2½ cups	575 mL
Baking powder	1 tbsp.	15 mL
Egg whites (large), room temperature	3	3

Cream butter and sugar well in large bowl. Beat in egg yolks.

Add pineapple, juice, vanilla, water and salt. Stir to mix.

Add flour and baking powder. Stir slowly until moistened.

Beat egg whites with clean beater until stiff. Fold into cake batter. Turn into 2 greased 8 inch (20 cm) round layer pans. Bake in 350°F (175°C) oven for about 30 to 35 minutes. An inserted wooden pick should come out clean. Cool. Makes 1 cake.

Pictured below.

Pineapple Cake, page 116 with Fluffy Frosting, page 122

Creamy Chilled Dessert

Nice and creamy with a thick nutty shortbread crust.

Bottom Layer:		
All-purpose flour	2 cups	500 mL
Granulated sugar	⅓ cup	75 mL
Butter or hard margarine	1 cup	250 mL
Chopped pecans or walnuts	½ cup	125 mL
Second Layer:		
Cream cheese, softened	8 oz.	250 g
Icing (confectioner's) sugar	1 cup	250 mL
Vanilla	1½ tsp.	7 mL
Envelope dessert topping (to make 1½ cups, 375 mL)	1	1
Third Layer:		
Instant vanilla pudding powder, 6 serving size	1	1
Milk	2 cups	450 mL
Topping:		
Whipping cream (or 2 envelopes topping)	2 cups	500 mL
Granulated sugar	2 tbsp.	30 mL
Vanilla	2 tsp.	10 mL

Bottom Layer: Mix flour and sugar in medium bowl. Cut in butter until mixture is crumbly.

Add pecans. Stir. Pack into 9 x 13 inch (22 x 33 cm) pan. Bake in 350°F (175°C) oven for about 15 minutes. Cool.

Second Layer: Beat cream cheese, icing sugar and vanilla until smooth.

Prepare dessert topping as directed on envelope. Fold into cream cheese mixture. Spread over bottom layer.

Third Layer: Empty pudding mix into small bowl. Beat in milk for about 1½ minutes until smooth. Pour over second layer.

Topping: Beat whipping cream, sugar and vanilla until stiff. Spread over all. Chill. Cuts into 15 to 18 pieces.

Pictured on page 119.

Variation: Use frozen strawberries (or raspberries) in syrup, thawed, instead of whipped cream topping. Spoon over dessert.

Chocolate Cheesecake

Chocolate Cheesecake

A luscious, rich dessert.

Chocolate Cracker Crust:

Butter or hard margarine	6 tbsp.	100 mL
Graham cracker crumbs	1½ cups	375 mL
Cocoa	3 tbsp.	50 mL
Granulated sugar	3 tbsp.	50 mL

Filling:

Unsweetened chocolate baking squares, cut up	2 × 1 oz.	2 × 28 g
Semisweet chocolate baking squares, cut up	3 × 1 oz.	3 × 28 g
Cream cheese, softened	3 × 8 oz.	3 × 250 g
Granulated sugar	1¼ cups	300 mL
Large eggs	4	4
Sour cream	½ cup	125 mL
Vanilla	1 tsp.	5 mL
Rum flavoring	1 tsp.	5 mL

Chocolate Cracker Crust: Melt butter in medium saucepan. Stir in graham crumbs, cocoa and sugar. Press in bottom of ungreased 9 inch (22 cm) springform pan. Bake in 350°F (175°C) oven for 10 minutes.

Filling: Melt both chocolates in heavy saucepan over lowest heat, stirring often as it melts. Remove from heat.

Beat cream cheese and sugar in bowl until smooth. Add chocolate. Beat.

Add eggs 1 at a time beating slowly after each addition just to mix. Mix in sour cream, vanilla and rum flavoring slowly to mix. Pour over chocolate crust. Bake in 300°F (150°C) oven for about 50 minutes until set. Center will wobble a bit when jiggled. Place pan on wire rack. Run knife around top edge to allow cake to settle evenly. Cool. Chill, uncovered, overnight for best flavor. Serves 12.

Pictured above.

Coconut Cream Delight

Not too sweet. Crumb layer has a nice "toasty" flavor.
A real delight!

Bottom Layer:		
All-purpose flour	1 cup	250 mL
Fine coconut	1 cup	250 mL
Brown sugar, packed	1/4 cup	60 mL
Butter or hard margarine	1/2 cup	125 mL
Filling:		
Milk	2 1/4 cups	500 mL
Granulated sugar	1/2 cup	125 mL
All-purpose flour	1/2 cup	125 mL
Salt	1/4 tsp.	1 mL
Coconut flavoring	2 tsp.	10 mL
Large eggs	2	2
Flake coconut	1 cup	225 mL
Topping:		
Whipping cream (or 1 envelope topping)	1 cup	250 mL
Granulated sugar	2 tsp.	10 mL
Vanilla	1/2 tsp.	2 mL
Reserved crumbs	1/4 cup	60 mL

Bottom Layer: Mix all 4 ingredients together until crumbly. Spread in jelly roll pan. Bake in 400°F (205°C) oven for about 5 to 10 minutes until lightly browned. Reserve 1/4 cup (60 mL) for topping. Press remaining crumbs into ungreased 9 x 9 inch (22 x 22 cm) pan.

Filling: Heat milk in heavy saucepan.

Stir sugar, flour and salt in bowl. Add flavoring and eggs. Stir well. Beat with spoon. Stir into hot milk until it boils and thickens. Remove from heat.

Stir in coconut. Pour over bottom layer. Cool.

Topping: Beat cream, sugar and vanilla in small bowl until stiff. Spread over cooled filling.

Sprinkle with reserved crumbs. Chill. Cuts into 9 to 12 pieces.

Pictured on page 119.

For a graham crumb crust that cuts nicely and doesn't crumble, mix the butter and crumbs together thoroughly and then pack the crumbs very well using the tips of your fingers or the bottom of a glass.

Raspberry Dessert

Try various combinations of strawberry or raspberry gelatin and frozen strawberries or raspberries. All are delicious!

Graham Crust:		
Butter or hard margarine	1/2 cup	125 mL
Graham cracker crumbs	2 cups	500 mL
Brown sugar, packed	1/4 cup	60 mL
Second Layer:		
Cream cheese, softened	8 oz.	250 g
Icing (confectioner's) sugar	1/2 cup	125 mL
Vanilla	1 tsp.	5 mL
Salt	1/2 tsp.	2 mL
Third Layer:		
Boiling water	1 1/4 cups	275 mL
Strawberry flavored gelatin (jelly powder)	6 oz.	170 g
Granulated sugar	1/4 cup	60 mL
Frozen raspberries in syrup, thawed	15 oz.	425 g
Lemon juice, fresh or bottled	1 tsp.	5 mL
Top Layer:		
Whipping cream (or 2 envelopes topping)	2 cups	500 mL
Icing (confectioner's) sugar	1/4 cup	60 mL
Vanilla	1 tsp.	5 mL

Graham Crust: Melt butter in saucepan. Stir in graham crumbs and brown sugar. Reserve 1/2 cup (125 mL) for topping. Pack remaining mixture into ungreased 9 x 13 inch (22 x 33 cm) pan. Bake in 350°F (175°C) oven for 10 minutes. Cool.

Second Layer: Beat cream cheese, icing sugar, vanilla and salt in small bowl until smooth. Spread over cooled graham crust.

Third Layer: Pour boiling water into separate small bowl. Add gelatin powder and sugar. Stir until dissolved.

Add raspberries in syrup and lemon juice. Stir. Chill, stirring and scraping down sides of bowl every 10 minutes until it shows definite signs of thickening. Pour over cream cheese layer. Chill until set.

Top Layer: Beat cream, icing sugar and vanilla in small bowl until mixture holds stiff peaks. Smooth over red layer. Sprinkle with reserved crumbs. Chill. Cuts into 15 pieces.

Pictured on page 119.

Glimmering Slice

This looks spectacular.

Graham Crust:

Butter or hard margarine	½ cup	125 mL
Graham cracker crumbs	2 cups	500 mL
Brown sugar, packed	¼ cup	60 mL

Second Layer:

Unflavored gelatin	1 x ¼ oz.	1 x 7 g
Cold water	¼ cup	60 mL
Cold water	½ cup	125 mL
Lemon juice, fresh or bottled	½ cup	125 mL
Sweetened condensed milk (or 14 oz., 398 mL)	11 oz.	300 mL

Third Layer:

Raspberry flavored gelatin (jelly powder)	2 x 3 oz.	2 x 85 g
Boiling water	3 cups	675 mL

Graham Crust: Melt butter in saucepan. Stir in graham crumbs and sugar. Pack into ungreased 9 x 13 inch (22 x 33 cm) pan. Bake in 350°F (175°C) oven for 10 minutes. Cool.

Second Layer: Sprinkle gelatin over first amount of cold water in small saucepan. Let stand 1 minute. Heat and stir on medium-low to dissolve. Remove from heat.

Combine second amount of cold water, lemon juice and condensed milk in small bowl. Add dissolved gelatin mixture. Beat well. Smooth over graham crust.

Third Layer: Pour raspberry gelatin into small bowl. Add water. Stir until gelatin dissolves. Cool by placing bowl in cold water in sink. Stir as it cools. Chill in refrigerator, stirring and scraping down sides often with spatula, until it begins to thicken. Pour over second layer. Chill. Cuts into 15 pieces.

Pictured below.

Left: Coconut Cream Delight, page 118   Top Center: Creamy Chilled Dessert, page 116   Bottom Center: Glimmering Slice, page 119   Right: Raspberry Dessert, page 118

Date Cake

Rich and delicious. Very moist. Freezes well.

Chopped dates	1½ cups	375 mL
Baking soda	1½ tsp.	7 mL
Boiling water	1½ cups	375 mL
Butter or hard margarine, softened	¾ cup	175 mL
Brown sugar, packed	1 cup	250 mL
Granulated sugar	½ cup	125 mL
Large eggs	2	2
Vanilla	1 tsp.	5 mL
All-purpose flour	2½ cups	625 mL
Baking powder	1½ tsp.	7 mL
Salt	½ tsp.	2 mL
Topping:		
Butter or hard margarine	⅓ cup	75 mL
Brown sugar, packed	1 cup	250 mL
Cream or milk	3 tbsp.	50 mL
Fine coconut	1 cup	250 mL

Put dates into small bowl. Add baking soda. Pour boiling water over top. Cool.

Cream butter and both sugars in large bowl. Beat in eggs and vanilla.

Stir flour, baking powder and salt together. Add flour mixture in 3 parts alternately with date mixture in 2 parts beginning and ending with flour. Turn into greased 9 x 13 inch (22 x 33 cm) pan. Bake in 325°F (160°C) oven for 40 to 50 minutes until an inserted wooden pick comes out clean.

Topping: Measure butter, brown sugar and cream into saucepan. Heat and stir until it comes to a full rolling boil. Remove from heat.

Add coconut. Stir. Spoon over cake as soon as it is done. Broil until golden brown, 2 to 3 minutes. Makes 1 cake.

Pictured on page 121.

Dream Cake, page 120

Dream Cake

Festive square.

Bottom Layer:		
All-purpose flour	1½ cups	375 mL
Brown sugar, packed	¾ cup	175 mL
Butter or hard margarine	¾ cup	175 mL
Top Layer:		
Sweetened condensed milk	11 oz.	300 mL
Vanilla	½ tsp.	2 mL
Chopped walnuts	½ cup	125 mL
Chopped glazed cherries	⅓ cup	75 mL
Medium coconut	1½ cups	375 mL

Bottom Layer: Mix flour and sugar well. Cut in butter until crumbly. Pack into ungreased 9 x 13 inch (22 x 33 cm) pan. Bake in 350°F (175°C) oven for about 10 minutes until golden.

Top Layer: Stir all 5 ingredients together in bowl. Spoon dabs here and there over bottom layer. Spread. Bake in 350°F (175°C) oven for about 25 to 30 minutes until set and golden color. Cool. Cuts into 54 squares.

Pictured above.

Date Cake, page 120

Velvet Fruit Torte

Very smooth. Pears are a nice change. Drizzle with chocolate just before serving if desired.

First Layer:

All-purpose flour	1 cup	250 mL
Granulated sugar	¼ cup	60 mL
Butter or hard margarine	½ cup	125 mL
Chopped pecans or walnuts	½ cup	125 mL

Second Layer:

Cream cheese, softened	8 oz.	250 g
Large egg	1	1
Granulated sugar	½ cup	75 mL
Vanilla	½ tsp.	2 mL

Third Layer:

Canned pears, drained, cut in wedges	14 oz.	398 mL
Cinnamon, sprinkle		

First Layer: Mix flour and sugar. Cut in margarine until mixture resembles small crumbs. Add pecans. Press well into ungreased 9 x 9 inch (22 x 22 cm) pan. Bake in 350°F (175°C) oven for 12 minutes. Set aside.

Second Layer: Beat cream cheese, egg, sugar and vanilla in small mixing bowl until smooth. Spread over first layer.

Third Layer: Arrange pear wedges on top of second layer. Sprinkle with cinnamon. Bake in 350°F (175°C) oven for 35 to 40 minutes until set. Cool completely. Serves 9 to 12.

Pictured on page 107.

Pudding Brownies

Instant pudding adds the flavor.

Butter or hard margarine, softened	6 tbsp.	100 mL
Granulated sugar	⅔ cup	150 mL
Large eggs	2	2
Vanilla	1 tsp.	5 mL
All-purpose flour	½ cup	125 mL
Instant chocolate pudding powder, 4 serving size	1	1
Chopped walnuts	½ cup	125 mL

Cream butter and sugar in medium bowl. Beat in eggs 1 at a time. Add vanilla. Mix.

Add flour, pudding powder and walnuts. Stir until moistened. Spread in greased 8 x 8 inch (20 x 20 cm) pan. Bake in 350°F (175°F) oven for about 30 minutes until a wooden pick inserted in center comes out clean but moist. Cuts into 25 squares.

Pictured on page 125.

Fluffy Frosting

A glossy white finish.

Egg white (large), room temperature	1	1
Salt	⅛ tsp.	0.5 mL
Granulated sugar	2 tbsp.	30 mL
White corn syrup	⅓ cup	75 mL
Vanilla	½ tsp.	2 mL

Beat egg white and salt in small mixing bowl until frothy.

Add sugar gradually while beating until smooth and glossy.

Drizzle corn syrup in as you continue to beat. Beat until icing will stand in very stiff peaks.

Fold in vanilla. Makes 2 cups (500 mL) frosting.

Pictured on page 116.

Frozen Fast Forward

A hint of vanilla. This can be made and frozen well in advance.

Crust:		
Butter or hard margarine	6 tbsp.	100 mL
Graham cracker crumbs	1⅓ cups	325 mL
Filling:		
Vanilla instant pudding powder, 4 serving size	1	1
Milk	⅔ cup	150 mL
Butter pecan ice cream, slightly softened	4 cups	1 L
Whipping cream (or 1 envelope topping)	1 cup	250 mL
Topping:		
Skor or Heath candy bars, finely crushed or ground	2 x 1½ oz.	2 x 38 g

Crust: Melt butter in saucepan. Stir in graham crumbs. Pack into ungreased 10 inch (25 cm) springform pan. Chill.

Filling: Beat pudding powder with milk in large bowl until smooth.

Fold in ice cream.

Beat cream in small bowl until stiff. Fold into pudding mixture. Pour over crust.

Topping: Sprinkle with crushed candy bars. Freeze. Remove from freezer about 15 minutes before serving. Cuts into 12 wedges.

Pictured on page 123.

Maple Nut Sauce

Quick to make. Store in refrigerator up to three weeks. Serve over ice cream.

Sweetened condensed milk	11 oz.	300 mL
Chopped pecans or walnuts	2 tbsp.	30 mL
Maple flavoring	½ tsp.	2 mL

Stir milk, pecans and maple flavoring together in bowl. Makes 1½ cups (375 mL).

Pictured on page 125.

Frozen Fast Forward, page 122

Candy Cake

Easy. Delicious. Light texture.

All-purpose flour	2 cups	500 mL
Brown sugar, packed	2 cups	500 mL
Butter or hard margarine	½ cup	125 mL
Large egg, beaten	1	1
Milk	1 cup	250 mL
Baking soda	1 tsp.	5 mL
Salt	½ tsp.	2 mL
Vanilla	1 tsp.	5 mL

Topping:

Reserved crumbs	1 cup	250 mL
Skor or Heath bars, (39 g size), crumbled in blender	4	4

Mix flour and brown sugar in medium bowl. Cut in butter until crumbly. Measure out 1 cup (225 mL) and reserve.

Add egg, milk, baking soda, salt and vanilla to remaining crumb mixture. Beat well. Turn into greased 9 x 13 inch (22 x 33 cm) pan.

Topping: Stir reserved crumbs and Skor crumbs together. Sprinkle over cake batter. Bake in 350°F (175°C) oven for about 30 minutes until an inserted wooden pick comes out clean. Serve warm or cool. Makes 1 cake.

Pictured on page 125.

Six Layer Squares

Very quick to assemble. Freezes well. Great taste!

Butter or hard margarine	½ cup	125 mL
Graham cracker crumbs	1 cup	225 mL
Semisweet chocolate chips	1 cup	225 mL
Butterscotch chips	1 cup	225 mL
Flake coconut	1 cup	225 mL
Sweetened condensed milk	11 oz.	300 mL

Melt butter in 9 x 13 inch (22 x 33 cm) pan over low heat.

Sprinkle next 4 ingredients over butter in order given.

Heat condensed milk on low in small saucepan until just warm. Pour evenly over top. Bake in 350°F (175°C) oven for about 30 minutes. Cool. Cuts into 54 squares.

Pictured on page 125.

Maraschino Chocolate Cake

Rich chocolate flavor with moist texture.

Butter or hard margarine, softened	½ cup	125 mL
Granulated sugar	1 cup	250 mL
Large egg	1	1
Vanilla	1 tsp.	5 mL
Almond flavoring	½ tsp.	2 mL
Syrup, from 8 oz. (224 g) bottle of maraschino cherries	½ cup	125 mL
Unsweetened baking chocolate squares, cut up	2 x 1 oz.	2 x 28 g
All-purpose flour	2 cups	500 mL
Baking soda	1 tsp.	5 mL
Salt	¼ tsp.	1 mL
Buttermilk (fresh or reconstituted from powder)	1 cup	250 mL
Maraschino cherries, from 8 oz. (224 g) bottle, halved	¾ cup	175 mL
Chopped walnuts	½ cup	125 mL

Cream butter and sugar well in large bowl. Beat in egg, vanilla and almond flavoring. Mix in cherry syrup.

Heat chocolate in saucepan on low, stirring often, until smooth. Beat into batter.

Stir flour, baking soda and salt together in separate bowl.

Add flour in 3 additions alternately with buttermilk in 2 additions beginning and ending with flour.

Add cherries and walnuts. Mix in. Turn into greased 9 x 13 inch (22 x 33 cm) pan. Bake in 350°F (175 °C) oven for about 55 minutes until an inserted wooden pick comes out clean. Cool. Ice with Chocolate Icing, this page. Makes 1 cake.

Pictured below.

Maraschino Chocolate Cake with Chocolate Icing

Chocolate Icing

Rich chocolate brown. Satin-like appearance. Delicious.

Icing (confectioner's) sugar)	2 cups	500 mL
Cocoa	⅓ cup	75 mL
Butter or hard margarine, softened	¼ cup	60 mL
Water	3 tbsp.	50 mL
Vanilla	1 tsp.	5 mL

Beat all ingredients together in mixing bowl until smooth, adding more water or icing sugar as needed for proper spreading consistency. Makes about 1¼ cups (300 mL).

Pictured on this page.

Pineapple Squares

Meringue-like top. Do not freeze.

Bottom Layer:		
Butter or hard margarine, softened	½ cup	125 mL
Granulated sugar	½ cup	125 mL
All-purpose flour	1½ cups	375 mL
Baking powder	1 tsp.	5 mL
Salt	¼ tsp.	1 mL
Crushed pineapple, drained	14 oz.	398 mL
Top Layer:		
Large eggs	2	2
Granulated sugar	1 cup	250 mL
Medium coconut	1 cup	250 mL
Butter or hard margarine, melted	1 tbsp.	15 mL

Bottom Layer: Mix all 5 ingredients well in small bowl. Press firmly into ungreased 9 x 9 inch (22 x 22 cm) pan.

Scatter pineapple over top as evenly as you can.

Top Layer: Beat eggs in small bowl until smooth. Beat in sugar.

Stir in coconut and butter. Spread over pineapple. Bake in 350°F (175°C) oven for 30 to 40 minutes. Cut while warm. Cuts into 36 squares.

Pictured on page 127.

Top Left: Candy Cake, page 123
Bottom Left: Six Layer Squares, page 123

Center: Pudding Brownies, page 122

Top Right: Maple Nut Sauce, page 122
Bottom Right: Bees Knees Squares, page 125

Bees Knees Squares

Good eye appeal. Make ahead and freeze.

Butter or hard margarine, softened	1 cup	250 mL
Honey	1/3 cup	75 mL
Vanilla	1 tsp.	5 mL
Quick cooking rolled oats	1 1/2 cups	375 mL
All-purpose flour	1 1/2 cups	375 mL
Salt	1/2 tsp.	2 mL
Butterscotch chips	1 cup	250 mL
Slivered almonds	1/2 cup	125 mL
Honey	2 tbsp.	30 mL

Beat butter, first amount of honey and vanilla in mixing bowl until smooth.

Stir in rolled oats, flour and salt. Add butterscotch chips. Stir. Spread in greased 9 x 13 inch (22 x 33 cm) pan.

Sprinkle with almonds. Push down to make them stick.

Heat remaining honey slightly until it is runny. Brush or dab over surface. Bake in 350°F (175°C) oven for 25 to 30 minutes until golden browned. Cool before cutting into 54 squares.

Pictured above.

Chocolate Date Squares

Yummy combination of flavors.

Large egg	1	1
Butter or hard margarine, melted	¼ cup	60 mL
Granulated sugar	¼ cup	60 mL
Brown sugar	2 tbsp.	30 mL
Salt	⅛ tsp.	0.5 mL
All-purpose flour	⅔ cup	150 mL
Baking soda	½ tsp.	2 mL
Milk	¼ cup	60 mL
Prepared orange juice	¼ cup	60 mL
Chopped walnuts	½ cup	125 mL
Semisweet chocolate chips	½ cup	125 mL
Chopped dates	½ cup	125 mL
Icing:		
Icing (confectioner's) sugar	1 cup	250 mL
Butter or margarine, softened	2 tbsp.	30 mL
Prepared orange juice	1½ tbsp.	25 mL
Dry orange rind	¼ tsp.	1 mL

Beat egg well in large bowl.

Add next 6 ingredients. Mix.

Add next 5 ingredients. Stir well. Turn into greased 8 x 8 inch (20 x 20 cm) pan. Bake in 350°F (175°C) oven for about 25 minutes until an inserted wooden pick comes out clean. Cool.

Icing: Mix all ingredients in small bowl adding more or less orange juice to make spreading consistency. Spread over cooled squares. Let stand to firm icing a bit. Cuts into 36 squares.

Pictured on page 127.

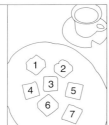

Cinnanut Squares

Cinnamon flavor comes through.

Bottom Layer:		
Butter or hard margarine, softened	½ cup	125 mL
Granulated sugar	½ cup	125 mL
Brown sugar, packed	¼ cup	60 mL
Large egg	1	1
All-purpose flour	1¼ cups	300 mL
Salt	½ tsp.	2 mL
Baking soda	½ tsp.	2 mL
Coarsely crushed corn flakes	1 cup	250 mL
Filling:		
Butter or hard margarine, softened	¼ cup	60 mL
Brown sugar, packed	½ cup	125 mL
Corn syrup	2 tbsp.	30 mL
Ground cinnamon	1 tsp.	5 mL
Chopped dates	½ cup	125 mL
Chopped walnuts	½ cup	125 mL

Bottom Layer: Mix butter, both sugars and egg in bowl.

Add flour, salt and baking soda. Stir well. Mix in corn flakes. Spread ½ in greased 8 x 8 inch (20 x 20 cm) pan.

Filling: Mix butter, sugar, syrup and cinnamon well in bowl.

Add dates and walnuts. Spread over layer in pan. Sprinkle with second ½ corn flake mixture. Bake in 350° (175°C) oven for about 30 minutes. Cuts into 25 squares.

Pictured on page 127.

Chewy Chip Squares

Nice and chewy—just like its name! Drizzle with melted chocolate to dress it up.

Graham cracker crumbs	1½ cups	350 mL
Semisweet chocolate chips	1 cup	225 mL
Butterscotch chips	1 cup	225 mL
Chopped walnuts	1 cup	225 mL
Sweetened condensed milk	11 oz.	300 mL

Measure all ingredients in bowl. Stir together well. Turn into greased 9 x 9 inch (22 x 22 cm) pan. Smooth with back of greased spoon. Bake in 350°F (175°C) oven for 30 to 35 minutes. Cool for 45 minutes. Cuts into 36 squares.

Pictured on page 127.

Almond Flake Squares

Almond Flake Squares
Decadent. Sweet, buttery and nutty.

Miniature marshmallows	9 oz.	250 g
Butter or hard margarine	½ cup	125 mL
Vanilla	1 tsp.	5 mL
Medium coconut	1 cup	250 mL
Flaked almonds, toasted (bake in 350°F, 175°C oven for about 5 minutes)	1 cup	250 mL
Corn flakes	5 cups	1.25 L
Reserved flaked almonds	¼ cup	60 mL

Heat and stir marshmallows, butter and vanilla in large saucepan until melted. Remove from heat.

Stir in coconut, ¾ cup (175 mL) almonds and corn flakes. Press lightly into greased 9 x 9 inch (22 x 22 cm) pan.

Sprinkle with reserved almonds. Press down slightly so they will stick. Cool. Cuts into 36 squares.

Pictured above.

Orange Chocolate Squares
Shortbread-type crust. A slightly chewy square.
An all-round winner!

Bottom Layer:		
All-purpose flour	2 cups	500 mL
Brown sugar, packed	½ cup	125 mL
Butter or hard margarine, softened	1 cup	250 mL
Second Layer:		
Large eggs	4	4
Grated rind of 2 oranges		
Juice from 2 oranges to equal	⅓ cup	75 mL
Granulated sugar	1 cup	250 mL
All-purpose flour	¼ cup	60 mL
Baking powder	1 tsp.	5 mL
Drizzle:		
Semisweet chocolate chips	½ cup	125 mL

Bottom Layer: Mix all ingredients together in bowl until crumbly. Pack in 9 x 13 inch (22 x 33 cm) ungreased pan. Bake in 350°F (175°C) oven for 15 to 20 minutes until golden.

Second Layer: Beat eggs in medium bowl until blended. Add orange rind, orange juice, sugar, flour, and baking powder. Mix. Pour over bottom layer. Bake in 325°F (160°C) oven for about 25 minutes until firm.

Drizzle: Melt and stir chocolate chips in small saucepan over lowest heat until smooth. Drizzle over top. Cool. Cuts into 54 squares.

Pictured on page 127.

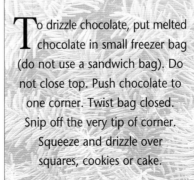

To drizzle chocolate, put melted chocolate in small freezer bag (do not use a sandwich bag). Do not close top. Push chocolate to one corner. Twist bag closed. Snip off the very tip of corner. Squeeze and drizzle over squares, cookies or cake.

Coconut Squares

The sides rise higher on these—but every bite is delicious nonetheless.

Butter or hard margarine	½ cup	125 mL
Brown sugar, packed	2 cups	500 mL
Large eggs	2	2
Vanilla	2 tsp.	10 mL
All-purpose flour	1 cup	250 mL
Baking powder	2 tsp.	10 mL
Salt	1 tsp.	5 mL
Flaked coconut	1½ cups	375 mL
Chopped walnuts	½ cup	125 mL

Melt butter in large saucepan. Stir in brown sugar. Beat in eggs and vanilla.

Stir flour, baking powder and salt together in bowl. Add to saucepan. Mix.

Stir in coconut and walnuts. Turn into greased 9 x 13 inch (22 x 33 cm) pan. Bake in 350°F (175°C) oven for 25 to 30 minutes. Cuts into 54 squares.

Pictured on page 127.

Back To Square One

Rich and gooey! Strong peanut flavor with an underlying sweetness.

Butter or hard margarine	6 tbsp.	100 mL
Creamy peanut butter	½ cup	125 mL
Brown sugar, packed	½ cup	125 mL
Corn syrup	½ cup	125 mL
Crisp rice cereal	2 cups	500 mL
Ground peanuts	1 cup	250 mL
Semisweet chocolate chips	1 cup	250 mL
Creamy peanut butter	⅓ cup	75 mL

Put butter, first amount of peanut butter, brown sugar and syrup into saucepan. Heat and stir until smooth.

Add cereal and peanuts. Mix. Pack into greased 9 x 9 inch (22 x 22 cm) pan.

Combine chocolate chips with last amount of peanut butter in saucepan. Heat, stirring often, on lowest heat until smooth. Spread over cereal mixture in pan. Chill. Cuts into 36 squares.

Pictured on page 127.

Jean's Favorite

Turtle Oat Squares

Chocolate and caramel go together nicely.

Butter or hard margarine	1 cup	250 mL
Vanilla	½ tsp.	2 mL
Quick cooking rolled oats	2 cups	500 mL
All-purpose flour	2 cups	500 mL
Brown sugar, packed	½ cup	125 mL
Baking soda	1 tsp.	5 mL
Salt	½ tsp.	2 mL
Semisweet chocolate chips	1 cup	250 mL
Caramel sundae topping	1½ cups	375 mL
All-purpose flour	¼ cup	60 mL

Melt butter with vanilla in large saucepan.

Add next 5 ingredients. Stir well. Press ⅔ in ungreased 9 x 13 inch (22 x 33 cm) pan.

Sprinkle with chocolate chips.

Stir caramel sundae topping and last amount of flour together. Drizzle over chocolate chips. Sprinkle with remaining ⅓ rolled oat mixture. Bake in 350°F (175°C) oven for about 25 minutes until golden brown. Cool. Cuts into 54 squares.

Pictured below.

Turtle Oat Squares

Main Courses

The Christmas season spans several weeks, yielding a host of opportunities for you and yours to get together to celebrate this special time of the year. What better place to gather than around the dinner table to visit and catch up with one another!

And that in turn calls for a special meal—one that is a little out of the ordinary but still suited to the majority, and a change from the traditional turkey fare that dominates the menu at Christmas.

Whether they're old favorites with a different twist or entirely new to you, our main course selections will make your holiday meals noteworthy.

Cajun Spareribs

Hot and tasty. There is lots of extra sauce to serve over rice.

Pork spareribs, cut short	3 lbs.	1.35 kg
Brown sugar, packed	½ cup	125 mL
All-purpose flour	1 tbsp.	15 mL
Dry mustard powder	1 tbsp.	15 mL
Chili powder	1 tsp.	5 mL
Salt	1 tsp.	5 mL
Pepper	1 tsp.	5 mL
Water	1 cup	250 mL
Ketchup	½ cup	125 mL
Worcestershire sauce	2 tsp.	10 mL
Hot pepper sauce	⅛ tsp.	0.5 mL
Large onion, sliced	1	1
Green pepper, seeded and chopped	1	1

Cut ribs into sections of about 3 ribs each. Place in 3 quart (3 L) casserole or small roaster.

Stir next 6 ingredients in medium bowl.

Add next 4 ingredients. Mix. Pour over ribs. Cover. Bake in 325°F (160°C) oven for 1 hour.

Scatter onion and green pepper over top. Cover. Cook in 300°F (150°C) oven for 1½ hours. Serves 4 to 6.

Pictured on page 139.

Stuffed Crown Roast Of Pork

So elegant—and showy! Choose your own combination of colors for the decorative "crowns". Apple in stuffing adds a delicate tartness.

Salt	2 tsp.	10 mL
Pepper	½ tsp.	2 mL
Worcestershire sauce	½ tsp.	2 mL
Garlic powder	¼ tsp.	1 mL
Rib roast, 16 ribs (about 7 lbs., 3.2 kg)	1	1
Stuffing:		
Margarine (butter browns too fast)	6 tbsp.	100 mL
Finely chopped onion	1 cup	250 mL
Finely chopped celery	½ cup	125 mL
Dry bread crumbs	6 cups	1.5 L
Medium cooking apples (McIntosh are good), peeled, cored and diced	2 cups	500 mL
Poultry seasoning	2 tsp.	10 mL
Salt	1 tsp.	5 mL
Pepper	¼ tsp.	1 mL
Parsley flakes	1 tbsp.	15 mL
Apple juice	1½ cups	375 mL

Combine salt, pepper, Worcestershire sauce and garlic powder in small bowl. Rub into sides of meat. Place in roaster, bone ends down. Cover. Roast in 325°F (160°C) oven for 2 hours. Prepare stuffing while roast is cooking.

Stuffing: Melt margarine in frying pan. Add onion and celery. Sauté until soft. Turn into large bowl, including all remaining margarine.

Add next 6 ingredients. Toss together well.

Add 1 cup (250 mL) of the apple juice. Stir well. Add the rest if needed so stuffing will hold together when squeezed lightly. Remove roast from oven. Turn so rib ends are up. Make a sleeve out of foil and push into center of roast. Fill with stuffing. Cover stuffing with foil. Place leftover stuffing in small greased casserole. Return roast and small casserole to oven. Continue roasting until thermometer reaches 170°F (78°C). This will take about 1½ hours more. Make Gravy, page 133, using ½ recipe. Serves 8.

Pictured on page 131.

1. **Stuffed Crown Roast Of Pork, page 130**
2. **Waldorf Spinach Toss, page 158**
3. **Carrot Medley, page 171**
4. **Festive Scalloped Potatoes, page 171**

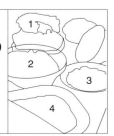

Turkey Au Gratin

A quick and easy casserole for leftover turkey.

Canned asparagus pieces, drained	12 oz.	341 mL
Cooked turkey, cut up	2 cups	500 mL
Cheese Sauce:		
Butter or hard margarine	2 tbsp.	30 mL
All-purpose flour	2 tbsp.	30 mL
Salt	1/4 tsp.	1 mL
Milk	3/4 cup	175 mL
Grated medium or sharp Cheddar cheese	1/2 cup	125 mL
Condensed cream of chicken soup	10 oz.	284 mL
Topping		
Butter or hard margarine	1 tbsp.	15 mL
Dry bread crumbs	1/3 cup	75 mL
Grated medium or sharp Cheddar cheese	2 tbsp.	30 mL

Arrange asparagus in bottom of greased 1½ quart (1.5 L) casserole. Spread turkey over top.

Cheese Sauce: Melt butter in saucepan. Mix in flour and salt. Stir in milk until it boils and thickens.

Add cheese. Stir to melt.

Add soup. Stir until smooth. Pour over turkey.

Topping: Melt butter in saucepan. Stir in bread crumbs and cheese. Sprinkle over top. Bake, uncovered, in 350°F (175°C) oven for about 25 minutes until hot and browned. Serves 4 to 6.

Pictured on page 136.

Golden Glazed Ham

Easy preparation. Glaze glistens.

Fully cooked boneless ham	6 lbs.	2.7 kg
Apricot Glaze:		
Apricot Jam	1/2 cup	125 mL
Brown sugar, packed	1/2 cup	125 mL
Cider vinegar	1½ tbsp.	25 mL
Prepared mustard	1 tsp.	5 mL
Ground cloves	1/8 tsp.	0.5 mL

Bake ham in covered roaster in 325°F (150°C) oven for about 2½ hours. Internal temperature should be 130°F (55°C). Drain off juice.

Apricot Glaze: Mix all ingredients in small saucepan. Heat and stir until hot and mixed well. Brush over top and sides of ham. Continue to bake, uncovered, at 350°F (175°C) for about 15 minutes until glaze dries. Serves 12.

Pictured on page 141.

Tourtière

A traditional meat pie.

Lean ground pork	2 lbs.	900 g
Lean ground beef	1 lb.	454 g
Chopped onion	2 cups	500 mL
Salt	1 tbsp.	15 mL
Pepper	1/2 tsp.	2 mL
Poultry seasoning	1/4 tsp.	1 mL
Pickling spice, in tea ball or tied in bag	2 tsp.	10 mL
Water, to almost cover		
Pastry for 2 double crust pies, your own or a mix		

Combine first 7 ingredients in large saucepan. Add water until you can just see it coming up the edge. Heat, stirring often until mixture comes to a boil. Simmer for about 20 minutes. Drain liquid into separate container. Chill liquid and meat overnight. In the morning discard fat from top of liquid. Combine liquid with meat. Stir.

Roll ½ pastry and line 2, 9 inch (22 cm) pie plates. Spread 4 cups (1 L) meat mixture in each crust. Roll top crusts. Moisten edges with water. Put top crusts in place. Trim. Crimp to seal. Cut several slits in top crusts. Bake in 400°F (205°C) oven for about 50 minutes until browned. Makes 2 double crust pies.

Pictured on page 136.

Gravy

This recipe works for any meat gravy.

Pan drippings	¾ cup	175 mL
All-purpose flour	¾ cup	175 mL
Salt	1 tsp.	5 mL
Pepper	¼ tsp.	1 mL
Water, including remaining drippings, fat removed (see Note)	6 cups	1.5 L

Pour first amount of drippings into large saucepan. Mix in flour, salt and pepper. Stir in water until it boils and thickens. A whisk works well for this. If gravy is pale, add a bit of gravy browner. Taste for salt and pepper, adding more if needed. Makes 6½ cups (1.45 L).

Note: Vegetable water, drained from potatoes, Brussels sprouts, carrots or other vegetable may be used.

Spiced Apricots

Serve with Roast Goose, page 140 or Golden Glazed Ham, page 132.

Brown sugar, packed	¼ cup	60 mL
White vinegar	1 tbsp.	15 mL
Ground cinnamon	¼ tsp.	1 mL
Ground nutmeg	⅛ tsp.	0.5 mL
Ground ginger	⅛ tsp.	0.5 mL
Reserved apricot syrup	1 cup	250 mL
Canned apricots, drained, syrup reserved	2 × 14 oz.	2 × 398 mL

Place first 6 ingredients in saucepan. Heat, stirring often, until mixture simmers. Simmer 15 to 20 minutes.

Add apricots. Simmer an additional 5 to 10 minutes. Serve hot or cold. Makes 2½ cups (625 mL).

Pictured on page 141.

Turkey Fajitas

A fun way to use up leftover turkey.

Hard margarine (butter browns too fast)	1 tbsp.	15 mL
Large onion, thinly sliced	1	1
Red pepper, seeded and cut in strips	1	1
Green or yellow pepper, seeded and cut in strips	1	1
Butter or hard margarine	1 tbsp.	15 mL
Leftover cooked turkey, cut in strips	3 cups	750 mL
Salt, sprinkle		
Pepper, sprinkle		
Tomatoes, seeded and diced	1 cup	250 mL
Grated medium Cheddar cheese	1 cup	250 mL
Shredded lettuce, lightly packed	1 cup	250 mL
Sour cream	1 cup	250 mL
Salsa	1 cup	250 mL
Guacamole	1 cup	250 mL
Flour tortillas, 10 inch (25 cm), heated in covered bowl	8-10	8-10

Melt margarine in frying pan. Add onion and peppers. Stir-fry until lightly browned.

Melt butter in saucepan. Add turkey. Sprinkle with salt and pepper. Cover. Heat, stirring as little as possible so turkey doesn't break up.

Put next 6 ingredients in separate bowls.

To prepare for eating, lay 1 tortilla on plate. Place some onion-pepper mixture down center. Add some turkey strips, then whatever you would like of the 6 garnishes. Fold tortilla over mixture. Makes 8 to 10 fajitas.

Pictured below.

Turkey Fajitas, page 133
Veal Birds, page 135

Chicken Provençale

Chicken Provençale

Colorful. Pleasing to the eye.

Cooking oil	1 tbsp.	15 mL
Chicken pieces, skin removed	3 lbs.	1.3 kg
Salt, sprinkle		
Pepper, sprinkle		
Red or green pepper seeded, cut in strips	1	1
Sliced onion	1 cup	250 mL
Garlic clove, minced (or ¼ tsp., 1 mL, garlic powder)	1	1
Sliced fresh mushrooms	2 cups	500 mL
Medium tomatoes, peeled, seeded and diced	2	2
Whole oregano	1 tsp.	5 mL
Salt, sprinkle		
Pepper, sprinkle		
White wine (or alcohol-free wine), optional	½ cup	125 mL
Cornstarch	3 tbsp.	50 mL
Water	¼ cup	60 mL

Heat cooking oil in frying pan. Add chicken. Brown both sides well. Transfer to small roaster. Cover. Bake 15 minutes in 350°F (175°C) oven while preparing vegetables.

Sauté green pepper, onion and garlic in frying pan for 3 minutes, adding more cooking oil if needed.

Add mushrooms, Continue to stir-fry until vegetables are soft.

Dip tomatoes in boiling water for about 2 minutes. Peel under cold running water. Dice and add to vegetables. Add oregano, second amounts of salt and pepper and white wine. Spoon over chicken. Continue to cook, covered, for 35 to 45 minutes until chicken is cooked. Remove chicken and vegetables from roaster.

Stir cornstarch in water. Add to liquid in bottom of roaster. Heat, stirring, until thickened. Return chicken and vegetables to roaster. Stir gently but thoroughly. Serves 4 to 6.

Pictured on this page.

Chicken In Gravy

Serve with rice or potatoes as there is lots of gravy.

All-purpose flour	⅔ cup	150 mL
Salt	2 tsp.	10 mL
Pepper	½ tsp.	2 mL
Seasoned salt	1 tsp.	5 mL
Dry mustard powder	¼ tsp.	1 mL
Paprika	2 tsp.	10 mL
Chicken parts	4 lbs.	1.8 kg
Buttermilk, fresh or reconstituted from powder	1 cup	250 mL
Hard margarine (butter browns too fast)	¼ cup	60 mL
Gravy:		
All-purpose flour	6 tbsp.	100 mL
Salt	1 tsp.	5 mL
Pepper	¼ tsp.	1 mL
Hard margarine (butter browns too fast)	1-5 tbsp.	15-75 mL
Water	5 cups	1.25 L

Mix first 6 ingredients in paper bag.

Dip chicken in buttermilk. Shake in seasoned flour to coat.

Heat margarine in frying pan. Add chicken. Fry quickly to brown both sides. Place in small roaster or large casserole.

Gravy: Add flour, salt and pepper to frying pan. Mix in. Add margarine as needed to mix. Stir in water until it boils and thickens. It will be thin but will thicken as chicken cooks. Taste to see if more salt needs to be added. Pour over chicken. Cover. Bake in 350°F (175°C) oven for 1 to 1½ hours until very tender. Serves 6.

Pictured on page 137.

Tamale Casserole

Great for the buffet table.

Boiling water	3¾ cups	925 mL
Salt	1½ tsp.	7 mL
Cornmeal	1 cup	250 mL
Chopped pitted ripe olives	1 cup	250 mL
Hard margarine (butter browns too fast)	2 tbsp.	30 mL
Chopped onion	1 cup	250 mL
Medium green pepper, seeded and chopped	1	1
Lean ground beef	1 lb.	454 g
Salt	1 tsp.	5 mL
Canned tomatoes, broken up	14 oz.	398 mL
Chili powder	2 tsp.	10 mL
Cayenne pepper	¼ tsp.	1 mL

Pour boiling water and salt into saucepan. Slowly stir cornmeal into boiling liquid. Cook, stirring continually, for 5 minutes.

Add olives. Stir.

Melt margarine in frying pan. Add onion, green pepper, ground beef and salt. Sauté until lightly browned and meat is no longer pink.

Add tomatoes, chili powder and cayenne pepper. Stir. Spread ½ cornmeal mixture in greased 3 quart (3 L) casserole. Spread meat mixture over top. Spread second ½ cornmeal mixture over meat. Bake, uncovered, in 350°F (175°C) oven for about 30 minutes until hot and lightly browned. Serves 6 to 8.

Pictured on page 137.

Beef Roast In Gravy

So easy to prepare. You can visit with guests while it's cooking.

Boneless rolled beef roast, sirloin tip, rump, chuck	4½ lbs.	2 kg
Envelope dry onion soup mix	1 × 1¼ oz.	1 × 38 g
Condensed cream of mushroom soup	10 oz.	284 mL

Place roast beef on foil in small roaster.

Stir onion soup mix into soup in bowl. Spoon over meat. Fold foil over top. Cover with roaster lid. Cook in 300°F (150°C) oven for 4 to 4½ hours depending on the degree of doneness you want. Serves 8 to 10.

Pictured on page 137.

Veal Birds

Make and freeze ahead of time. Freeze pan drippings separately. Make gravy just before serving. Slice birds 1 inch thick.

Veal steak, cut into 6 to 8 pieces, pounded thin	2 lbs.	900 g
Salt	1½ tsp.	7 mL
Pepper	¼ tsp.	1 mL
Ground thyme	¼ tsp.	1 mL
Stuffing:		
Large egg	1	1
Beef bouillon powder	1 tsp.	5 mL
Dry bread crumbs	1½ cups	375 mL
Poultry seasoning	½ tsp.	2 mL
Salt	¼ tsp.	1 mL
Pepper	⅛ tsp.	0.5 mL
Onion powder	¼ tsp.	1 mL
Water, to moisten		
Hard margarine (butter browns too fast)	3 tbsp.	50 mL
Hot water	½ cup	125 mL
Beef bouillon powder	1 tsp.	5 mL
White wine	½ cup	125 mL
Gravy:		
Cornstarch	1 tbsp.	15 mL
Water	3 tbsp.	50 mL

Lay veal pieces on counter.

Mix salt, pepper and thyme together in small bowl. Sprinkle over meat.

Stuffing: Beat egg in small bowl. Stir in next 6 ingredients. Add water to moisten until mixture holds together when squeezed in your hand. Divide among veal pieces. Roll up and tie in bundles with string.

Heat margarine in frying pan on medium. Add veal bundles. Brown well on all sides. Place in 2 quart (2 L) casserole.

Stir hot water, second amount of bouillon powder and white wine together in frying pan that veal was cooked in. Scrape up any brown bits from pan. Pour over veal. Cover. Bake in 325°F (160°C) oven for 1½ hours until tender. Remove to serving platter. Keep warm.

Gravy: Mix cornstarch and water together in small cup. Slowly stir into pan juices left in casserole. Heat and stir until thickened. Makes about 1 cup of gravy. Remove string from veal. Pour gravy over veal birds on platter. Serves 6 to 8.

Pictured on page 133.

Fancy Macaroni

A new twist to macaroni and cheese.

Elbow macaroni	1 cup	250 mL
Boiling water	2 qts.	2 L
Cooking oil	1 tsp.	5 mL
Salt	1 tsp.	5 mL
Large onion, grated	1	1
Grated sharp Cheddar cheese	1 cup	250 mL
Chopped pimiento	2½ tbsp.	37 mL
Egg yolks (large)	3	3
Green pepper, seeded and chopped	1	1
Parsley flakes	1 tsp.	5 mL
Butter or hard margarine, melted	¼ cup	60 mL
Salt	1 tsp.	5 mL
Milk	1½ cups	375 mL
Dry bread crumbs	½ cup	125 mL
Egg whites (large), room temperature	3	3

Cook macaroni in large uncovered saucepan in boiling water, cooking oil and salt for 5 to 7 minutes until tender but firm. Drain. Return macaroni to saucepan.

Stir in next 10 ingredients in order given.

Beat egg whites in bowl until stiff. Fold into mixture. Turn into greased 2 quart (2 L) casserole. Place in larger container and surround casserole with hot water. Bake, uncovered, in 350°F (175°C) oven for about 45 minutes. Serves 6 to 8.

Pictured on page 136 and 137.

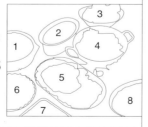

Lazy Ravioli

A little more preparation time needed,
but it's worth it! Serves a crowd.

Fusilli twists	12 oz.	375 g
Boiling water	3 qts.	3 L
Cooking oil	1 tbsp.	15 mL
Salt	1 tbsp.	15 mL
Hard margarine (butter browns too fast)	1 tbsp.	15 mL
Lean ground beef	1½ lbs.	680 g
Spaghetti sauce	14 oz.	398 mL
Tomato sauce	7½ oz.	213 mL
Tomato paste	5½ oz.	156 mL
Chopped onion	2 cups	500 mL
Canned sliced mushrooms, drained	10 oz.	284 mL
Frozen chopped spinach, thawed and squeezed dry	10 oz.	300 g
Granulated sugar	2 tsp.	10 mL
Salt	1 tsp.	5 mL
Pepper	¼ tsp.	1 mL
Garlic powder	¼ tsp.	1 mL
Sour cream	1 cup	250 mL
Grated medium or sharp Cheddar cheese	2 cups	500 mL
Grated mozzarella cheese	2 cups	500 mL

Cook fusilli in boiling water, cooking oil and salt in large uncovered pot for 8 to 10 minutes until tender but firm. Drain. Rinse with cold water. Drain.

 Melt margarine in frying pan. Scramble-fry ground beef until no pink remains in meat. Transfer to Dutch oven.

Add next 10 ingredients to Dutch oven. Heat, stirring often, for about 20 minutes until onion is tender. Assemble in small ungreased roaster or 5 quart (5 L) casserole.

Assemble in layers:
1. ½ fusilli in bottom
2. ½ meat sauce
3. all sour cream
4. ½ Cheddar
5. ½ fusilli
6. ½ meat sauce
7. ½ Cheddar
8. all mozzarella

Cover. Bake in 350°F (175°C) oven for 45 minutes. Remove cover. Bake another 15 minutes until cheese is melted and browns slightly. Serves 12.

Pictured on page 136.

Roast Turkey

Always a welcome tradition whether served on
Christmas Eve, Christmas Day or New Year's Day.

Young turkey, pan ready	15 lbs.	6.8 kg
Onion chunks or stuffing		

To Roast Unstuffed: Put 2 or 3 onion chunks in cavity. Tie string around body holding wings close to sides. Tie legs to tail. Place on rack in roaster. Cover with lid or foil. (To cook uncovered, rub skin with butter. You will need to baste a few times.) Roast in 400°F (205°C) oven for 30 minutes. Reduce heat to 325°F (160°C). Cook for about 5 hours, basting occasionally, until a thermometer inserted in thigh reads 190°F (95°C). Meat should show signs of pulling away from bone. Drumstick meat should feel soft when pressed. Leg should move and twist easily. To brown, remove cover for 20 to 30 minutes.

To Roast Stuffed: Stuff front and back cavities loosely. Tie string around body to hold wings close to sides. Skewer skin together to hold stuffing in place. Tie legs to tail. Cook as above, allowing an extra half hour to cook. When thermometer is inserted into center of stuffing it should read 165°F (75°C).

Remove bird and rack to platter. Remove stuffing to bowl and keep covered. Cover turkey while you make gravy. It will be easier to carve meat after it stands 30 minutes. Serves 12.

Pictured on front cover.

Left: Seafood Lasagne, page 145   Top Right: Showy Meatloaf, page 139   Bottom Right: Cajun Spareribs, page 130

Showy Meatloaf

The name says it all. So pretty when it's sliced.

Lean ground beef	2 lbs.	900 g
Large eggs	2	2
Fresh bread slices, blended to coarse crumbs	2	2
Ketchup	1/4 cup	60 mL
Milk	1/4 cup	60 mL
Salt	1 1/2 tsp.	7 mL
Pepper	1/4 tsp.	1 mL
Whole oregano	1 tsp.	5 mL
Onion powder	1/2 tsp.	2 mL
Thin slices of cooked ham	6	6
Frozen spinach, thawed and squeezed dry	10 oz.	300 g
Salt	1 tsp.	5 mL
Mozzarella cheese slices, cut in half diagonally	3	3

Place first 9 ingredients in large bowl. Mix well. Pat out on sheet of foil to 10 x 12 inch (25 x 30 cm) size.

Lay ham slices on top, keeping 1 inch (2.5 cm) in from edges. Spread spinach over ham. Sprinkle with second amount of salt. Roll up starting from long end, removing foil as you roll. Carefully transfer to baking sheet with sides. Pat in sides to smooth them. Bake in 350°F (175°C) oven for 1 1/4 hours.

Arrange cheese triangles over top. Return to oven for 1 to 2 minutes until cheese starts to melt. Cut into slices to serve. Serves 6 to 8.

Pictured above.

The secret to making a meatloaf that will slice nicely is threefold: first mix it well with your hands, pack it very well into the pan and let the cooked meatloaf stand at least 10 to 15 minutes before cutting.

Roast Goose

A nice change from turkey.

Potato Stuffing:

Medium potatoes, peeled and quartered	3	3
Boiling water		
Milk	1 cup	250 mL
Hard margarine	¼ cup	60 mL
Chopped onion	1¼ cups	300 mL
Chopped celery	½ cup	125 mL
Croutons (tiny)	5 cups	1.25 L
Parsley flakes	2 tsp.	10 mL
Sage, or poultry seasoning	1½ tsp.	7 mL
Salt	1 tsp.	5 mL
Pepper	¼ tsp.	1 mL
Goose	10 lbs.	4.5 kg

Potato Stuffing: Cook potatoes in boiling water until tender. Drain. Mash well.

Add milk. Mash. Mixture will be runny.

Melt margarine in frying pan. Add onion and celery. Sauté until soft. Turn into large container. Add mashed potato.

Add croutons, parsley, sage, salt and pepper. Toss well. Let stand for about 30 minutes so croutons can absorb moisture. If not moist enough, some water can be added.

Stuff goose. Skewer shut. Tie wings to body and legs to tail. Roast, covered, in 450°F (230°C) oven for 20 minutes. Reduce heat. Continue to roast in 350°F (175°C) oven for 3½ to 4 hours until very tender. Meat thermometer, inserted in breast area, should read 190°F (87°C). To brown, remove cover for about 10 minutes at the end of cooking. Serves 6 to 8.

Gravy:

Fat drippings from pan	½ cup	125 mL
All-purpose flour	½ cup	125 mL
Salt	½ tsp.	2 mL
Pepper	⅛ tsp.	0.5 mL
Pan drippings, without fat, plus water	4 cups	1 L
Gravy browner, if needed		

Stir fat, flour, salt and pepper in large saucepan. Mix in pan drippings and water until mixture boils and thickens. Add a bit of gravy browner if needed to make a rich brown. Taste for salt and pepper, adding more if needed. Makes 4 cups (1 L).

Pictured on this page.

Roast Goose, page 140   Potato Rolls, page 59

Turkey Wizard

Garnish with sliced almonds just before baking.
Uses leftover turkey.

Chopped onion	1½ cups	375 mL
Bacon slices, diced	8	8
All-purpose flour	2 tbsp.	30 mL
Curry powder, or to taste	1 tbsp.	15 mL
Water	1 cup	250 mL
Orange marmalade (or apricot jam)	¼ cup	60 mL
Ketchup	2 tbsp.	30 mL
White vinegar	1½ tbsp.	25 mL
Beef bouillon powder	2 tsp.	10 mL
Salt	½ tsp.	2 mL
Pepper	½ tsp.	2 mL
Leftover cooked turkey chunks	4 cups	1 L

Fry onion and bacon in frying pan until onion is soft and bacon is cooked.

Mix in flour and curry powder. Add water. Stir until it boils and thickens.

Add marmalade, ketchup, vinegar, bouillon powder, salt and pepper. Stir.

Place turkey in ungreased 3 quart (3 L) casserole. Pour onion mixture over top. Bake, uncovered, in 350°F (175°C) oven for 30 to 40 minutes until hot and bubbly. Serves 6.

Pictured on page 143.

Sausage Rice Casserole, page 145   Spiced Apricots, page 133   Golden Glazed Ham, page 132

Sausage Stuffing

A more substantial filling than the
traditional bread stuffing.

Pork sausage meat	1 lb.	454 g
Chopped onion	1 cup	250 mL
Chopped celery	1 cup	250 mL
Parsley flakes	1 tbsp.	15 mL
Poultry seasoning	1 tbsp.	15 mL
Salt	1½ tsp.	7 mL
Pepper	½ tsp.	2 mL
Dry bread crumbs and cubes	8 cups	1.8 L

Water, if needed

Scramble-fry sausage meat, onion and celery until meat is no longer pink, onion is clear and celery is soft.

Measure parsley, poultry seasoning, salt, pepper and bread crumbs into large bowl. Mix well. Add sausage meat, onion and celery.

Add water if needed so that when you squeeze a handful lightly it holds together. Makes enough stuffing for a 12 to 14 pound (5.4 to 6.3 kg) bird.

Pictured on front cover.

Swiss Steak

Excellent dish for company. Prepare ahead and
leave in fridge ready to bake.

Round steak	2 lbs.	900 g
All-purpose flour	½ cup	125 mL
Salt	2 tsp.	10 mL
Pepper	½ tsp.	2 mL
Cooking oil	3 tbsp.	50 mL
Chopped onion	2 cups	500 mL
Canned tomatoes, broken up	14 oz.	398 mL

Cut steak into serving size pieces. Place on waxed paper.

Mix flour, salt and pepper in bowl. Sprinkle over steak. Pound as much as possible into steak on both sides.

Heat cooking oil in frying pan. Brown steak on both sides. Transfer to small roaster. Add onions to frying pan. If needed, add a bit more cooking oil. Fry onions until browned. Spread over meat.

Add tomatoes. Cover. Bake in 350°F (175°C) oven for about 1½ hours or until tender. Serves 6 to 8.

Pictured on page 143.

Chicken Breasts Florentine

A very attractive dish. Nice for a sit-down dinner party.

Sour cream	½ cup	125 mL
Plain yogurt	½ cup	125 mL
Dry mustard powder	1½ tsp.	7 mL
Dill weed	½ tsp.	2 mL
Dry bread crumbs	1½ cups	375 mL
Boneless chicken breast halves, skin removed	8	8

Florentine Sauce:		
Butter or hard margarine	¼ cup	60 mL
All-purpose flour	¼ cup	60 mL
Salt	1 tsp.	5 mL
Pepper	¼ tsp.	1 mL
Onion powder	¼ tsp.	1 mL
Chicken bouillon powder	1 tsp.	5 mL
Dill weed	2 tsp.	10 mL
Ground nutmeg	¼ tsp.	1 mL
Milk	3 cups	675 mL
Frozen chopped spinach, thawed, squeezed dry	10 oz.	300 g
Grated Havarti or Muenster cheese	1 cup	250 mL

Mix first 4 ingredients in small bowl.

Place bread crumbs in another small bowl.

Dip chicken in sour cream mixture, then in bread crumbs. Arrange on greased baking sheet. Bake in 375°F (190°C) oven for 35 to 45 minutes until tender, turning chicken at half time.

Florentine Sauce: Melt butter in saucepan. Mix in next 7 ingredients. Stir in milk and spinach until mixture boils. Simmer gently, stirring often, for about 3 minutes.

Stir in cheese to melt. Place chicken breasts on platter or individual plates. Spoon sauce over top. Makes 8 servings.

Pictured below.

Chicken Breasts Florentine

Cauliflower Ham Bake

Cauliflower Ham Bake

Sharp cheddar taste complements the ham and cauliflower.

Medium cauliflower, broken in florets	4 cups	1 L
Boiling water, to cover		
Cubed cooked ham	2 cups	500 mL
Canned sliced mushrooms, drained	10 oz.	284 mL
Butter or hard margarine	2 tbsp.	30 mL
All-purpose flour	2 tbsp.	30 mL
Salt	½ tsp.	2 mL
Milk	1 cup	250 mL
Cubed sharp Cheddar cheese	1 cup	250 mL
Sour cream	½ cup	125 mL
Fine dry bread crumbs	1 tbsp.	15 mL

Cook cauliflower in boiling water until tender-crisp. Drain. Put into bowl.

Add ham and mushrooms to cauliflower. Mix well.

Melt butter in saucepan. Mix in flour and salt. Stir in milk until it boils and thickens.

Add cheese. Stir until melted. Add sour cream. Stir until smooth. Put ham and vegetable mixture into ungreased 3 quart (3 L) casserole. Pour sauce over top.

Sprinkle with crumbs. Bake, uncovered, in 350°F (175°C) oven for 30 to 40 minutes until heated through. Serves 6.

Pictured above.

Coquilles St. Jacques Casserole

Serve with a salad and vegetable or use for a buffet.

Boiling water	½ cup	125 mL
Sauterne wine (or alcohol-free white wine)	½ cup	125 mL
Salt	½ tsp.	2 mL
Cayenne pepper, just a pinch		
Scallops, halved or quartered if large	1 lb.	454 g
Butter or hard margarine	2 tbsp.	30 mL
Sliced fresh mushrooms	1 cup	250 mL
Finely chopped onion	½ cup	125 mL
All-purpose flour	¼ cup	60 mL
Finely grated lemon rind	½ tsp.	2 mL
Garlic powder	½ tsp.	2 mL
Reserved liquid from scallops		
Egg yolk (large)	1	1
Whipping cream	½ cup	125 mL
Chopped fresh parsley (or ½ tsp., 2 mL, parsley flakes)	1 tbsp.	15 mL
Pasta:		
Tiny shell pasta	1 cup	250 mL
Boiling water	2 qts.	2 L
Salt	1½ tsp.	7 mL
Cooking oil	1 tbsp.	15 mL
Topping:		
Butter or hard margarine	1 tbsp.	15 mL
Dry bread crumbs	½ cup	125 mL
Grated Parmesan cheese	2 tbsp.	30 mL
Chopped fresh parsley (or ½ tsp., 2 mL, parsley flakes)	1 tbsp.	15 mL

Combine first 5 ingredients in frying pan. Bring to a boil. Cover. Boil slowly for 3 to 5 minutes until scallops are opaque. Use slotted spoon to remove scallops to small bowl. Pour liquid into cup and reserve.

Melt butter in frying pan. Add mushrooms and onion. Sauté until soft.

Mix in flour, lemon rind and garlic. Stir in reserved liquid until mixture boils and thickens.

Mix egg yolk, cream and first amount of parsley in large bowl. Stir well. Stir into mushroom mixture. Cook and stir for 3 minutes. Add scallop mixture. Stir.

Pasta: Combine pasta, boiling water, salt and cooking oil in saucepan. Cook, covered, for about 15 minutes until tender. Drain. Add to scallop mixture. Stir. Put into 2 quart (2 L) ungreased casserole.

Topping: Melt butter in saucepan. Stir in bread crumbs, cheese and second amount of parsley. Sprinkle over top. Bake, uncovered, in 400°F (205°C) oven until browned and heated through, about 15 minutes. Serves 4 to 6.

Pictured below.

Top Left: Turkey Wizard, page 140
Top Right: Coquilles St. Jacques Casserole, page 143
Bottom Left: Seafood Deluxe, page 144
Bottom Right: Swiss Steak, page 141

Seafood Deluxe

Mustard adds a nice zip.

Sauce:		
Butter or hard margarine	1/4 cup	60 mL
All-purpose flour	1/4 cup	60 mL
Salt	1 tsp.	5 mL
Pepper	1/4 tsp.	1 mL
Evaporated skim milk	13 1/2 oz.	385 mL
Milk	1/4 cup	60 mL
Worcestershire sauce	1 tsp.	5 mL
Prepared mustard	1 tsp.	5 mL
Onion powder	1/4 tsp.	1 mL
Grated medium or sharp Cheddar cheese	1/2 cup	125 mL
Scallops, halved if large	1 lb.	454 g
Boiling water	2 cups	500 mL
Canned crabmeat, drained, membrane removed	4 oz.	113 g
Topping:		
Butter or hard margarine	2 tsp.	10 mL
Dry bread crumbs	1/4 cup	60 mL
Dried parsley flakes	1 tsp.	5 mL
Grated medium or sharp Cheddar cheese	2 tbsp.	30 mL

Sauce: Melt butter in saucepan. Mix in flour, salt and pepper. Stir in both milks, Worcestershire sauce, mustard and onion powder. Heat and stir until mixture boils and thickens.

Stir in cheese until melted. Set aside.

Combine scallops and boiling water in saucepan. Cook, covered, for about 5 minutes until opaque. Drain. Add to sauce.

Add crabmeat. Stir. Turn into ungreased 2 quart (2 L) casserole.

Topping: Melt butter in saucepan. Stir in crumbs and parsley flakes. Sprinkle over top.

Scatter cheese over bread crumbs. Bake, uncovered, in 350°F (175°C) oven for about 25 minutes until hot. Serves 4.

Pictured on page 143.

Triple Seafood Noodles

Great combination of seafood, wine and basil.

Medium egg noodles	3/4 lb.	375 g
Boiling water	4 qts.	4 L
Cooking oil	1 tbsp.	15 mL
Salt	1 tbsp.	15 mL
Hard margarine (butter browns too fast)	3 tbsp.	50 mL
Sliced fresh mushrooms	4 cups	1 L
Sliced green onion	1/4 cup	60 mL
Canned tomatoes, broken up, drained, reserve juice	14 oz.	398 mL
Sweet basil	2 tsp.	10 mL
Chicken bouillon powder	2 tsp.	10 mL
Beef bouillon powder	1 tsp.	5 mL
Parsley flakes	1 tsp.	5 mL
Garlic powder	1/2 tsp.	2 mL
White wine (or alcohol-free wine)	1/4 cup	60 mL
Butter or hard margarine	3 tbsp.	50 mL
Canned lobster, drained, cut up	5 oz.	142 g
Canned shrimp, rinsed and drained	4 oz.	113 g
Canned crabmeat, drained, membrane removed	4.2 oz.	120 g

Cook noodles in boiling water, cooking oil and salt in large uncovered pot about 5 to 7 minutes until tender but firm. Drain.

Melt margarine in frying pan. Add mushrooms and green onion. Sauté until soft. This is easier to do in 2 batches.

Put next 7 ingredients into Dutch oven. Heat, stirring often, until mixture boils. Simmer for 2 to 3 minutes.

Melt butter in frying pan. Add lobster, shrimp and crabmeat. Sauté until hot. Add to tomato mixture. Add noodles. Toss. Serves 8 to 10.

Pictured below.

Triple Seafood Noodles

Sausage Rice Casserole

*Have this ready to serve when the gang gets back
from skiing, skating or tobogganing.*

Long grain rice	1 cup	250 mL
Chopped onion	1 cup	250 mL
Salt	½ tsp.	2 mL
Boiling water	2 cups	500 mL
Sausage meat	1 lb.	454 g
Condensed cream of tomato soup	10 oz.	284 mL
Milk or water (use can to measure)	10 oz.	284 mL
Grated medium or sharp Cheddar cheese	1 cup	250 mL

Cook rice and onion in salt and boiling water for about 20 minutes until tender and water is absorbed.

Shape sausage meat into 1 inch (2.5 cm) balls. Flatten each ball into a tiny patty. Fry, browning both sides, until no pink remains in meat.

Whisk soup and milk together in bowl until smooth. Layer ½ the rice in bottom of 2 quart (2 L) ungreased casserole. Pour ½ soup mixture over rice. Add second ½ rice. Cover in single layer, with sausage patties. Pour remaining ½ soup mixture over patties.

Sprinkle with cheese. Bake in 350°F (175°C) oven for 35 to 45 minutes until bubbly hot. Serves 4 to 6.

Pictured on page 141.

Seafood Lasagne

*Fussy but fabulous. Assemble the day before,
cover and refrigerate. Bake just before serving.*

Lasagne noodles	8	8
Boiling water	4 qts.	4 L
Cooking oil	1 tbsp.	15 mL
Salt	1 tbsp.	15 mL
Butter or hard margarine	2 tbsp.	30 mL
Chopped onion	1 cup	250 mL
Chopped celery	¼ cup	60 mL
Cream cheese, softened, cut up	8 oz.	250 g
Creamed cottage cheese	1½ cups	375 mL
Large egg	1	1
Grated Parmesan cheese	2 tbsp.	30 mL
Dried basil	2 tsp.	10 mL
Salt	½ tsp.	2 mL
Pepper	⅛ tsp.	0.5 mL
Butter or hard margarine	¼ cup	60 mL
All-purpose flour	¼ cup	60 mL
Salt	½-1 tsp.	2-5 mL
Pepper	⅛-¼ tsp.	0.5-1 mL
Milk	2 cups	500 mL
Cooked shrimp, shelled and deveined (or 2 x 4 oz., 2 x 113 g cans)	1 cup	250 g
Canned crabmeat, drained, membrane removed	2 x 4 oz.	2 x 113 g
White wine (or alcohol-free wine)	⅓ cup	75 mL
Grated Parmesan cheese	¼ cup	60 mL
Grated medium or sharp Cheddar cheese	1 cup	250 mL

Cook lasagne noodles in boiling water, cooking oil and first amount of salt in large uncovered pot for 14 to 16 minutes until tender but firm. Drain.

Melt first amount of butter in frying pan. Add onion and celery. Sauté until soft.

Stir in cream cheese until it melts.

Mix in cottage cheese, egg, first amount of Parmesan cheese, basil, second amount of salt and first amount of pepper.

Melt second amount of butter in saucepan. Mix in flour, third amount of salt and second amount of pepper. Stir in milk until it boils and thickens.

Add shrimp, crabmeat and wine to milk sauce. Stir.

To assemble, layer as follows in greased 9 x 13 inch (22 x 33 cm) pan: 1. Layer of 4 noodles
        2. All cottage cheese mixture (see Note)
        3. Layer of 4 noodles
        4. All seafood mixture (see Note)
        5. Parmesan cheese

Bake, uncovered, in 375°F (190°C) oven for about 45 minutes. Sprinkle with Cheddar cheese. Return to oven for 3 to 4 minutes until it melts. Let stand 10 minutes before cutting into 12 pieces. Serves 8.

Pictured on page 139.

Note: Layers 2 and 4 may each be made up of ½ cottage cheese mixture and ½ seafood mixture rather than using all of each mixture for each layer.

Pies & Tarts

Fragrant Mince Pie, page 152, and chewy
Butter Tarts, page 149, are longtime Christmas favorites
and so of course they are included here.

But there are many more kinds of dessert pies that would do
justice to your holiday meals. Bi-Layer Pumpkin Pie, page 150,
Black Russian Pie, page 151, Cranberry Pear Pie, page 148,
and Frozen Peanut Butter Pie, page 148 are among the
intriguing selections for you to choose from.

Tips for making pastry are included, along with recipes
for crusts and fillings that let you go the traditional route
or take a new direction. Try one or the other or
both—your guests will love it!

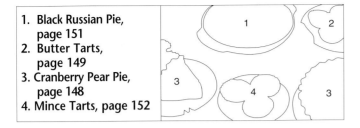

Cranberry Pear Pie

Try this with either the pastry topping or crumb topping.
Both are excellent.

Canned pears, drained and sliced, (see Note)	4 × 14 oz.	4 × 398 mL
Cranberries, halved	1 cup	250 mL
Granulated sugar	3/4 cup	175 mL
All-purpose flour	3 tbsp.	50 mL
Pastry for 2 crust pie, your own or a mix	1	1
Granulated sugar, sprinkle	1/4-1/2 tsp.	1-2 mL

Crumb Topping:

All-purpose flour	2/3 cup	150 mL
Brown sugar, packed	6 tbsp.	100 mL
Butter or hard margarine	6 tbsp.	100 mL
Ground cinnamon	1/2 tsp.	2 mL
Salt	1/4 tsp.	1 mL

Stir first 4 ingredients in bowl.

Roll out pastry and line 9 inch (22 cm) pie plate. Fill with fruit mixture.

Pastry Topping: Roll out top crust. Dampen edges of crust in pie plate. Cover with second crust. Trim and crimp to seal. Cut slits in top crust or make decorative cutouts.

Sprinkle with sugar.

Crumb Topping: Mix all ingredients together until crumbly. Sprinkle over fruit.

To cook either pastry-topped or crumb-topped pie, bake in 400°F (205°C) oven on bottom shelf for 15 minutes. Lower heat to 350°F (175°C). Continue to bake for about 30 to 40 minutes. Cool. Makes 1 pie.

Pictured on page 146 and on page 147.

Note: To use fresh pears, peel and slice 5 pears to make 4 cups (1 L). Use 1/3 cup (75 mL) flour instead of 1/4 cup (60 mL).

Frozen Peanut Butter Pie

For the peanut butter lover. This freezes well,
so you can make ahead.

Crust:

Butter or hard margarine	1/3 cup	75 mL
Chocolate wafer crumbs	1 1/4 cups	300 mL
Ground or finely chopped peanuts	1/3 cup	75 mL
Granulated sugar	1/4 cup	60 mL

Filling:

Egg whites (large), room temperature	2	2
Granulated sugar	1/2 cup	125 mL
Cream cheese, softened	8 oz.	250 g
Granulated sugar	1/4 cup	60 mL
Egg yolks (large)	2	2
Creamy peanut butter	1 cup	250 mL
Vanilla	1 tsp.	5 mL
Whipping cream (or 1 envelope topping)	1 cup	250 mL
Granulated sugar	2 tsp.	10 mL
Vanilla	1/2 tsp.	2 mL
Ground or finely chopped peanuts	2 tbsp.	30 mL
Chocolate, grated or curls, for garnish	2 tbsp.	30 mL

Crust: Melt butter in saucepan. Stir in chocolate crumbs, peanuts and sugar. Press into bottom and sides of 9 inch (22 cm) pie plate. Bake in 350°F (175°C) oven for 10 minutes. Cool.

Filling: Beat egg whites in small bowl until soft peaks form. Gradually beat in first amount of sugar until stiff.

Using same beaters, beat cream cheese, second amount of sugar and egg yolks in separate bowl until smooth. Add peanut butter and vanilla. Beat until mixed. Dough will be quite stiff. Fold in egg whites.

Beat whipping cream, sugar and vanilla until stiff. Fold into peanut butter mixture. Turn into prepared crust. Freeze.

To serve, let pie stand at room temperature for about 35 minutes. Sprinkle with peanuts and chocolate. Makes 1 pie.

Pictured on page 149.

Cranberry Cheese Pie

Cranberry tartness with a sweet cream cheese filling. Crunchy topping.

Crust:

Pastry for 10 inch (25 cm) pie shell, your own or a mix	1	1

First Filling Layer:

Cream cheese, softened	8 oz.	250 g
Large egg	1	1
Icing (confectioner's) sugar	½ cup	125 mL
Sweetened condensed milk	11 oz.	300 mL
Lemon juice, fresh or bottled	¼ cup	60 mL

Second Filling Layer:

Cornstarch	2 tbsp.	30 mL
Canned whole cranberry sauce	14 oz.	398 mL

Topping:

All-purpose flour	⅔ cup	150 mL
Brown sugar, packed	⅓ cup	75 mL
Cinnamon	¼ tsp.	1 mL
Salt	¼ tsp.	1 mL
Butter or hard margarine	¼ cup	60 mL
Chopped pecans or walnuts (optional)	½ cup	125 mL

Crust: Roll out pie shell and line 10 inch (25 cm) pie plate. If you don't have a 10 inch (25 cm) pie plate, use a 9 inch (22 cm) and a 4 or 5 inch (10 or 13 cm) size. If you choose to put all the filling in a 9 inch (22 cm) pie plate, place it on a baking sheet to catch any boil-overs.

First Filling Layer: Beat cream cheese, egg and icing sugar in medium bowl until smooth. Add condensed milk and lemon juice. Beat. Spread in bottom of pie shell.

Second Filling Layer: Stir cornstarch into cranberry sauce in small bowl. Spoon over first filling.

Topping: Mix flour, sugar, cinnamon and salt in bowl. Cut in butter until mixture is crumbly.

Stir in pecans. Sprinkle over second filling layer. Bake in 375°F (190°C) oven for 45 to 55 minutes until set and lightly browned. Lay a piece of foil over pie if topping is getting too brown. Makes 1 pie.

Pictured on page 151.

Butter Tarts

Gooey but not runny. Great and always lots of takers. Freezes well.

Brown sugar, packed	½ cup	125 mL
Corn syrup	½ cup	125 mL
Butter or hard margarine, softened	3 tbsp.	50 mL
Large egg	1	1
Raisins or currants	½ cup	125 mL
Medium or fine coconut	2 tbsp.	30 mL
Finely chopped pecans	2 tbsp.	30 mL
Vinegar	1½ tsp.	7 mL
Salt, just a pinch		
Unbaked pastry tart shells, your own or store bought, (or 24 miniature shells)	12	12

Cream brown sugar, syrup and butter well in medium bowl.

Add next 6 ingredients. Stir well.

Divide among pastry shells. Bake in 375°F (190°C) oven for about 20 minutes for regular size and 10 to 15 minutes for miniature size. Makes 12 large or 24 tiny tarts.

Pictured on page 147.

Top: Frozen Peanut Butter Pie, page 148   Bottom: Bi-Layer Pumpkin Pie, page 150

Bi-Layer Pumpkin Pie

A delicious change from the ordinary.

Graham Crust:

Butter or hard margarine	1/3 cup	75 mL
Graham cracker crumbs	1 1/4 cups	300 mL
Granulated sugar	2 tbsp.	30 mL

First Filling Layer:

Cream cheese, softened	4 oz.	125 g
Milk	1 tbsp.	15 mL
Granulated sugar	1 tbsp.	15 mL
Frozen whipped topping, thawed	1 1/2 cups	325 mL

Second Filling Layer:

Instant vanilla pudding powders, 4 serving size each	2	2
Milk	1 cup	250 mL
Canned pumpkin, without spice	14 oz.	398 mL
Ground cinnamon	1 tsp.	5 mL
Ground ginger	1/2 tsp.	2 mL
Ground cloves	1/4 tsp.	1 mL

Topping:

Frozen whipped topping, thawed	2 cups	500 mL

Graham Crust: Melt butter in saucepan. Stir in graham crumbs and sugar. Press firmly into bottom and sides of 9 inch (22 cm) pie plate.

First Filling Layer: Beat cream cheese, milk and sugar in bowl until smooth.

Fold in whipped topping. Spread in pie shell.

Second Filling Layer: Beat pudding powders and milk together in bowl until smooth.

Add pumpkin and spices. Stir well. Pour over first layer. Chill.

Topping: Spread whipped topping over all. Chill. Makes 1 pie.

Pictured on page 149.

Date Pie

Sweet date flavor. Cut meringue with hot wet knife.

Chopped dates	2 cups	450 mL
Water	1 cup	225 mL
Granulated sugar	1/4 cup	60 mL
Milk	1 cup	225 mL
Cornstarch	2 tbsp.	30 mL
Egg yolks (large)	3	3
Vanilla	1 tsp.	5 mL
Baked 9 inch (22 cm) deep dish pie shell, your own pastry or frozen	1	1

Meringue:

Egg whites (large)	3	3
Cream of tartar	1/4 tsp.	1 mL
Granulated sugar	6 tbsp.	100 mL

Cook dates, water and sugar slowly in saucepan about 10 minutes until dates are mushy and water has almost disappeared.

Mix milk and cornstarch. Stir into date mixture until it boils and thickens.

Beat egg yolks and vanilla with fork in small bowl. Stir in a few spoonfuls of hot mixture then stir it back into saucepan.

Pour into pie shell. Cool slightly.

Meringue: Beat egg whites and cream of tartar on medium speed until soft peaks form. Continue to beat while adding sugar gradually. Beat until stiff peaks form. Spoon over filling, sealing to crust all around edge. Bake in 375°F (190°C) oven for about 10 minutes until nicely browned. Makes 1 pie.

Pictured on page 151.

Pastry, whether for a filled or unfilled pie shell, should be chilled before rolling. This helps to minimize shrinking. Always wrap dough in plastic wrap if not using immediately.

Top Center: Peachy Prune Pie, page 151   Bottom Center: Date Pie, page 150   Right: Cranberry Cheese Pie, page 149

Peachy Prune Pie

Lovely color combination.

Granulated sugar	1 cup	250 mL
All-purpose flour	3 tbsp.	50 mL
Reserved syrup from peaches	¹/₂ cup	125 mL
Lemon juice, fresh or bottled	¹/₄ cup	60 mL
Large egg, beaten	1	1
Pitted quartered prunes	1 cup	250 mL
Canned peach slices, drained syrup reserved	2 × 14 oz.	2 × 398 mL
Pastry for a 2 crust pie, your own or a mix	1	1
Granulated sugar	¹/₄ tsp.	1 mL

Stir first amount of sugar and flour together well in saucepan. Mix in syrup, lemon juice, beaten egg and prunes. Heat and stir until mixture boils and thickens. Cool. Set saucepan in cold water, stirring frequently to hasten cooling.

Add peaches. Stir.

Roll out pastry and line 9 inch (22 cm) pie plate. Pour filling into pie shell. Roll out second layer. Dampen edge of bottom crust. Top with second crust. Trim. Crimp to seal. Cut slits in top or make decorative cutouts.

Sprinkle with sugar. Bake in 400°F (205°C) oven for about 35 minutes until browned. Makes 1 pie.

Pictured above.

Black Russian Pie

Totally decadent. Oh so smooth.

Chocolate Graham Crust:		
Butter or hard margarine	¹/₃ cup	75 mL
Graham cracker crumbs	1¹/₄ cups	300 mL
Granulated sugar	3 tbsp.	50 mL
Cocoa	2 tbsp.	30 mL
Filling:		
Large marshmallows	24	24
Milk	¹/₂ cup	125 mL
Salt	¹/₄ tsp.	1 mL
Kahlua liqueur	¹/₃ cup	75 mL
Whipping cream (or 1 envelope topping)	1 cup	250 mL

Reserved crumb mixture
Chocolate-covered coffee beans, for garnish

Chocolate Graham Crust: Melt butter in saucepan. Stir in graham crumbs, sugar and cocoa. Reserve ¹/₃ cup (75 mL). Press remainder in bottom and sides of 9 inch (22 cm) pie plate. Bake in 350°F (175°C) oven for 10 minutes. Cool.

Filling: Put marshmallows, milk and salt in large saucepan. Heat, stirring often, until melted and smooth. Chill until it mounds. Stir in Kahlua.

Beat cream in small bowl until stiff. Fold into marshmallow mixture. Turn into cooled pie shell.

Garnish with reserved crumb mixture and coffee beans. Makes 1 pie.

Pictured on page 146 and 147.

Mock Black Bottom Pie

Add red or green food coloring to cream cheese filling for more layered effect.

Graham Cracker Crust:

Butter or hard margarine	⅓ cup	75 mL
Graham cracker crumbs	1¼ cups	300 mL
Granulated sugar	2 tbsp.	30 mL

Black Bottom:

Instant chocolate pudding, 6 serving size	1	1
Milk	1½ cups	350 mL

Filling:

Cream cheese	8 oz.	250 g
Icing (confectioner's) sugar	1 cup	250 mL
Frozen whipped topping, thawed	2 cups	500 mL

Topping:

Frozen whipped topping, thawed	2 cups	500 mL
Chocolate curls or trimettes		

Graham Cracker Crust: Melt butter in saucepan. Stir in graham crumbs and sugar. Press in bottom and sides of 9 inch (22 cm) pie plate. Bake in 350°F (175°C) oven for 10 minutes. Cool.

Black Bottom: Beat pudding powder and milk together in bowl for about 1½ minutes until smooth. Pour into cooled crust.

Filling: Beat cream cheese and icing sugar in bowl until smooth. Chill to firm.

Fold in first amount of frozen topping. Spread over firmed black bottom.

Topping: Spread second amount of frozen topping over filling. Garnish with chocolate curls. Makes 1 pie.

Pictured below.

Mock Black Bottom Pie

Mincemeat

Use to make pies or tarts. Enough to make 4 pies.

Ground beef or pork suet	1 cup	250 mL
Peeled and cored chopped apples	6 cups	1.5 L
Apple juice	1 cup	250 mL
Raisins	2 cups	500 mL
Currants	2 cups	500 mL
Cut candied citron	2 cups	500 mL
Lemons, juice and grated rind	3	3
Brown sugar, packed	4 cups	1 L
Granulated sugar	1 cup	250 mL
Ground cinnamon	4 tsp.	20 mL
Ground allspice	2 tsp.	10 mL
Ground nutmeg	1 tsp.	5 mL
Ground cloves	½ tsp.	2 mL
Brandy or rum flavoring, optional	1 tbsp.	15 mL

Combine first 13 ingredients in large saucepan. Heat, stirring often until mixture comes to a simmer. Simmer, stirring often, for 30 minutes.

Stir in brandy if desired. Cool. Freeze in cartons or store in refrigerator for several months. Makes 8 cups (2 L).

Mince Pie

Always a Christmas favorite.

Filling:

Mincemeat, see recipe above	2 cups	450 mL
Applesauce	¾ cup	175 mL
Minute tapioca	1½ tbsp.	25 mL

Crust:

Pastry for 2 crust pie, your own or a mix	1	1
Granulated sugar	¼-½ tsp.	1-2 mL

Filling: Stir first 3 ingredients together in bowl.

Crust: Roll out pie crust on lightly floured surface. Line 9 inch (22 cm) pie plate. Turn filling into pie shell. Roll out second crust. Dampen edge of first crust. Top with second crust. Trim. Crimp to seal. Cut slits in top.

Sprinkle with sugar. Bake in 400°F (205°C) oven for 30 to 35 minutes until browned. Makes 1 pie.

Mince Tarts

Spoon filling from Mince Pie, above, into 36 tart shells. Filling is especially nice in tarts if run through blender first. Bake at 400°F (205°C) for 20 minutes. Makes 36 tarts.

Pictured on page 146 and 147.

Chocolate Chiffon Pie

This is so velvety. Great flavor.

Unflavored gelatin	1 × ¼ oz.	1 × 7 g
Water	½ cup	125 mL
Milk	1 cup	250 mL
Granulated sugar	⅓ cup	75 mL
Cocoa	½ cup	125 mL
All-purpose flour	2 tbsp.	30 mL
Salt	¼ tsp.	1 mL
Egg yolks (large)	4	4
Vanilla	1 tsp.	5 mL
Egg whites (large), room temperature	4	4
Cream of tartar	½ tsp.	2 mL
Granulated sugar	⅔ cup	150 mL
Baked 9 inch (22 cm) pie shell	1	1
Grated chocolate, for garnish		

Sprinkle gelatin over water in medium saucepan. Let stand 1 minute.

Add milk. Heat, stirring often, on medium until gelatin is dissolved and mixture starts to boil.

Mix next 6 ingredients together in small bowl. Add a little hot mixture and stir until smooth. Pour into mixture in saucepan. Stir until it boils and thickens. Cool.

Beat egg whites and cream of tartar in mixing bowl until soft peaks form. Add sugar gradually as you continue beating until stiff.

Make sure filling will pile nicely before adding egg white mixture. Fold egg whites into chilled filling. Turn into baked pie shell. Chill at least 4 hours before cutting. Makes 1 pie.

Pictured below.

Nutty Mousse Pie

Creamy rich flavor. May be prepared the day before.

Chocolate Crust:		
Butter or hard margarine	⅓ cup	75 mL
Chocolate wafer crumbs	1¼ cups	275 mL
Filling:		
Large marshmallows	30	30
Milk	½ cup	125 mL
Semisweet chocolate chips	1 cup	250 mL
Brown sugar, packed	⅓ cup	75 mL
Whipping cream (or 1 envelope topping)	1 cup	250 mL
Topping:		
Chopped pecans	⅓ cup	75 mL

Chocolate Crust: Melt butter in saucepan. Stir in wafer crumbs. Press into 9 inch (22 cm) pie plate. Bake in 350°F (175°C) oven for 10 minutes. Cool.

Filling: Combine all 4 ingredients in large saucepan. Heat on medium-low, stirring often until melted and smooth. Chill, stirring and scraping down sides of bowl often, until mixture resembles a thick paste. It should pile and hold its shape a while before becoming smooth.

Beat cream in small bowl until stiff. Fold into thickened mixture. Turn into pie shell.

Topping: Sprinkle pecans over pie filling. Chill. Makes 1 pie.

Pictured below.

Chocolate Chiffon Pie

Nutty Mousse Pie

Cranberry Mold

Fruit Salad Mold

Salads

Salads are such a tasty way to add color and variety to the table at Christmas. This selection of molded and tossed salads (with accompanying dressings) offers you several ways to accomplish this.

Presentation means so much, so take the time to arrange your salad attractively and add a little festive touch wherever possible—maybe a poinsettia decoration on top, or a few nuts or candies.

Consider the color and texture of the salad you choose. The appropriate choice laid out attractively in a holiday dimension will have everyone coming back for more!

Fruit Salad Mold

The color is outstanding! This velvety-smooth salad can work as a main course accompaniment or as a refreshing dessert.

Raspberry flavored gelatin (jelly powder)	2 × 3 oz.	2 × 85 g
Boiling water	2 cups	500 mL
Raspberry sherbet	2 cups	500 mL
Filling:		
Canned pineapple chunks, well drained	14 oz.	398 mL
Canned mandarin oranges, well drained	10 oz.	284 mL
Flaked coconut	1 cup	250 mL
Miniature marshmallows	1 cup	250 mL
Sour cream	1 cup	250 mL

Stir gelatin into boiling water in medium bowl until dissolved. Cool 5 minutes. Add sherbet. Mix in until no streaks appear. Pour into 6 cup (1.5 L) ring mold. Chill for several hours.

Filling: Combine all 5 ingredients in bowl. Stir well. Unmold salad ring onto plate. Spoon fruit mixture into center. Serves 10 to 12.

Pictured on this page.

Variation: Lime-flavored gelatin and sherbet may be used instead of raspberry to have a green colored salad.

Cranberry Mold

Soft mauve-pink color with flecks of red. This will receive a round of applause.

Unflavored gelatin	2 × ¼ oz.	2 × 7 g
Water	½ cup	125 mL
Water	½ cup	125 mL
Canned whole cranberry sauce	14 oz.	398 mL
Crushed pineapple, drained	14 oz.	398 mL
Sour cream	1 cup	250 mL
Icing (confectioner's) sugar	⅓ cup	75 mL

Sprinkle gelatin over first amount of water in small saucepan. Let stand 1 minute. Heat and stir until dissolved.

Add second amount of water. Pour into medium bowl.

Stir in remaining ingredients. Chill, stirring and scraping down sides often, until it shows signs of thickening. Pour into 6 cup (1.5 L) mold. Chill. Serves 8.

Pictured above and on front cover.

Green Pepper Salad

Tomato Shrimp Aspic

Glossy red with celery and shrimp peeking through.

Tomato juice	2½ cups	625 mL
Bay leaf	½	½
Onion powder	½ tsp.	2 mL
Unflavored gelatin	2 x ¼ oz.	2 x 7 g
Cold water	½ cup	125 mL
Granulated sugar	3 tbsp.	50 mL
Salt	¾ tsp.	4 mL
Paprika, generous measure	¼ tsp.	1 mL
Chopped celery	¾ cup	175 mL
Canned small shrimp, rinsed and drained	4 oz.	113 g

Put tomato juice, ½ bay leaf and onion powder in saucepan. Heat. Simmer 5 minutes. Discard bay leaf.

Sprinkle gelatin over water in small saucepan. Let stand 1 minute. Heat and stir to dissolve. Add to tomato juice.

Stir in sugar, salt and paprika until sugar dissolves. Chill, stirring and scraping down sides often until mixture shows signs of thickening.

Fold in celery and shrimp. Turn into 3 cup (750 mL) mold. Chill until firm. Serves 6 to 8.

Pictured below.

Molded salads can be made the day before. Spray the pan with non-stick cooking spray for easier removal. Rub plate with wet hand before unmolding salad so that you can center it. When removing, hold plate against mold, lift both together on end and shake gently. This allows air to enter at edge and loosen salad.

Green Pepper Salad

This two-tone salad is so festive! Its refreshing flavor works well with turkey, beef or in a buffet.

Lime-flavored gelatin (jelly powder)	3 oz.	85 g
Boiling water	1 cup	250 mL
Lime-flavored gelatin (jelly powder)	3 oz.	85 g
Boiling water	1 cup	250 mL
Cold water	¾ cup	175 mL
Salad dressing (or mayonnaise)	½ cup	125 mL
White vinegar	1 tsp.	5 mL
Finely chopped green pepper	1 cup	250 mL
Finely chopped celery	½ cup	125 mL
Creamed cottage cheese	1 cup	250 mL

Stir first gelatin into first amount of boiling water in medium bowl until dissolved. Chill, stirring and scraping down sides often, until it shows signs of thickening.

As soon as first gelatin goes in the refrigerator, stir second gelatin into second amount of boiling water in another medium bowl until dissolved. Add cold water. Stir. Chill, stirring and scraping down sides often, until it shows signs of thickening.

To first gelatin, whisk in salad dressing and vinegar. Add green pepper, celery and cottage cheese. Stir. Turn into 6 cup (1.5 L) mold. Chill. When second gelatin is beginning to thicken, pour over top of first gelatin in mold. Chill. Serves 8 to 10.

Pictured above.

Tomato Shrimp Aspic

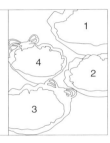

Special Coleslaw

This is a nice brunch or buffet salad. Bright, colorful and great taste.

Grated cabbage, packed	2 cups	500 mL
Crushed pineapple, drained, juice reserved	½ cup	125 mL
Miniature marshmallows	50	50
Slivered or sliced almonds	½ cup	125 mL
Medium coconut	½ cup	125 mL
Salad dressing (or mayonnaise)	½ cup	125 mL
Reserved juice, enough to thin		
Cayenne pepper, just a pinch		

Combine first 5 ingredients in bowl.

Mix salad dressing, reserved juice if needed and cayenne pepper in separate bowl. Pour as much over salad as needed. Toss well to mix. Serves 6.

Pictured on page 157.

Fruity Coleslaw

A nice variation of traditional coleslaw. The dressing is excellent.

Grated cabbage, packed	3 cups	750 mL
Red apples, unpeeled, cored and finely diced	2	2
Chopped walnuts	½ cup	125 mL
Salad dressing (or mayonnaise)	½ cup	125 mL
Milk	1 tbsp.	15 mL
Onion powder	¼ tsp.	1 mL
Paprika	¼ tsp.	1 mL
Granulated sugar	1 tsp.	5 mL

Put cabbage, apple and walnuts into large bowl.

Mix in remaining ingredients in small bowl. Add to cabbage mixture. Stir. Makes 4 cups (1 L).

Pictured on page 159.

Citrus Salad

A very attractive individual salad. The dressing is a pretty pink color.

Lettuce cups	4	4
Pineapple slices	4	4
Oranges, peeled and sectioned	2	2
Grapefruit, peeled and sectioned	1	1
Maraschino cherries for garnish		
Cranberry Dressing:		
Cranberry jelly	½ cup	125 mL
Salad dressing (or mayonnaise)	½ cup	125 mL

Place 1 lettuce cup on each salad plate. Lay pineapple slice on each cup. Arrange, starting from one side on top of pineapple, 1 orange section, 1 grapefruit section, 1 orange section, 1 grapefruit section and 1 orange section.

Place cherry slices here and there to decorate.

Cranberry Dressing: Whisk both ingredients together. Serve on the side or spoon over top just before serving. Serves 4.

Pictured on page 158.

Cottage Salad

This colorful salad will go nicely with a casserole supper or a quiche brunch.

Head of lettuce, cut or torn	1	1
Medium carrots, grated	2	2
Medium tomatoes, cut, seeded and diced, drained well	2	2
Thinly sliced celery	1 cup	250 mL
Continental Dressing:		
White vinegar	2 tbsp.	30 mL
Cooking oil	1 tbsp.	15 mL
Water	1 tbsp.	15 mL
Prepared mustard	½ tsp.	2 mL
Salt	½ tsp.	2 mL
Pepper, just a pinch		
Granulated sugar	½-1 tsp.	2-5 mL
Paprika	¼ tsp.	1 mL
Creamed cottage cheese	1 cup	250 mL

Combine first 4 ingredients in large bowl.

Continental Dressing: Whisk first 8 ingredients together in small bowl. Cover and keep chilled until ready to serve salad.

Just before serving salad, add cottage cheese to greens. Toss. Add dressing. Toss lightly. Serves 6 to 8.

Pictured on page 159.

Sauerkraut Salad

Flavor is excellent and color is showy.
Best when served the next day.

Canned sauerkraut, drained	28 oz.	796 mL
Chopped celery	1 cup	250 mL
Chopped onion	½ cup	125 mL
Grated carrot	½ cup	125 mL
Chopped red or green pepper	½ cup	125 mL
Pimiento slivers	2 tbsp.	30 mL
Granulated sugar	1 cup	250 mL
White vinegar	½ cup	125 mL

Combine first 6 ingredients in bowl.

Heat and stir sugar and vinegar in saucepan until it comes to a boil. Remove from heat. Cool to lukewarm. Pour over vegetables. Cover. Chill overnight. Makes 5 cups (1.25 L) salad.

Pictured on page 159.

Waldorf Spinach Toss

Take two old favorites and combine for a new holiday salad.

Pecan pieces, lightly toasted	¾ cup	175 mL
Red apple, with peel, cored and sliced in thin wedges	1	1
Orange, peeled (white pith removed), halved and thinly sliced	1	1
Red onion, thinly sliced and separated	½ cup	125 mL
Spinach bunches, torn bite size	2 × 10 oz.	2 × 285 g
Dressing:		
Reserved toasted pecan pieces	¼ cup	60 mL
Granulated sugar	½ cup	125 mL
Dry mustard	1 tsp.	5 mL
Hot pepper sauce	⅛ tsp.	0.5 mL
White vinegar	½ cup	125 mL
Cooking oil	½ cup	125 mL

Toast pecans in 350°F (175 °C) oven for 5 to 8 minutes until lightly browned. Reserve ¼ cup (75 mL) for dressing. Place pecans, apple, orange, onion and spinach in large salad bowl.

Dressing: Combine reserved pecans, sugar, mustard, hot pepper sauce, vinegar and cooking oil in blender. Blend for 2 minutes until smooth. Pour over spinach mixture and toss to coat salad. Serves 6 to 8.

Pictured on page 131.

Colorful Tossed Salad

As the name says, lots of color. Dressing is very tasty.

Parmesan Dressing:		
Salad dressing (or mayonnaise)	½ cup	125 mL
Grated Parmesan cheese	¼ cup	60 mL
Milk	3 tbsp.	50 mL
Granulated sugar	1 tsp.	5 mL
Dill weed	1 tsp.	5 mL
Lemon pepper	1 tsp.	5 mL
Onion powder	¼ tsp.	1 mL
Salad:		
Medium head of lettuce, cut up	1	1
Radishes, thinly sliced	6-8	6-8
Green onions, thinly sliced	3-5	3-5
Diced medium or sharp Cheddar cheese	½ cup	125 mL
Medium tomatoes, halved, seeded and diced	2	2

Parmesan Dressing: Stir all ingredients well in jar. Chill until needed. Makes ⅔ cup (150 mL) dressing.

Salad: Combine first 4 ingredients in large bowl. Chill until needed.

Put tomato into small separate bowl. When ready to serve, drain tomato and add to lettuce mixture. Add dressing as needed. Toss to coat. Serves 8 to 10.

Pictured on page 157.

Citrus Salad, page 156

Sauerkraut Salad, page 158   Cottage Salad, page 156   Fruity Coleslaw, page 156

Turkey Salad

Great for Boxing Day.

Cooked turkey	4 cups	1 L
Seedless grapes, halved	1 cup	250 mL
Sliced celery	1 cup	250 mL
Canned mandarin oranges, drained	10 oz.	284 mL
Toasted slivered almonds	½ cup	125 mL
Diced apple, with peel	1 cup	250 mL
Chopped peeled cucumber	1 cup	250 mL
Bean sprouts, large handful		
Dressing:		
Salad dressing (or mayonnaise)	½ cup	125 mL
White vinegar	2 tbsp.	30 mL
Frozen concentrated orange juice	1 tbsp.	15 mL
Granulated sugar	1 tbsp.	15 mL
Salt	½ tsp.	2 mL
Onion powder	¼ tsp.	1 mL

Put first 8 ingredients into large bowl.

Dressing: Stir all ingredients together well. Add as much as needed to salad. Toss well. Makes ¾ cup (175 mL) dressing. Salad serves 6 to 8.

Pictured on page 157.

Fruit And Cheese Salad

Blue cheese sneaks into this salad for a nice sharp flavor. Dressing is a malty-creamy color.

Medium head of iceberg lettuce, cut or torn	1	1
Small zucchini with peel, sliced thinly	2	2
Oranges, peeled, sectioned and cut into 3 pieces each	2	2
Grapefruit, peeled, sectioned and cut into 4 pieces each	1	1
Tiny cauliflower florets	2 cups	500 mL
Crumbled blue cheese	½ cup	125 mL
Sour Cream Dressing:		
Sour cream	1 cup	250 mL
Balsamic vinegar	2 tbsp.	30 mL

Combine all 6 ingredients in large bowl. Cover and chill until needed.

Sour Cream Dressing: Mix sour cream with balsamic vinegar. Pour over salad and toss or serve on the side. Salad serves 8 to 10.

Pictured on page 157.

Soups

If there's a forgotten item on the holiday menu it's likely soup, and that shouldn't be. Soups have a presence of their own, from the clear broths that accompany the higher-profile dishes at dinner to the chunky chowders, cream soups and bisques full-bodied enough to be a meal by themselves.

Discover the possibilities of this underestimated component and give soups their due. Appreciate their potential and they will return the favor in their own way.

Top: Smooth Bean Soup, page 164
Left Center: Broccoli Soup, page 160
Right Center: Tomato Consommé, page 161
Bottom: Corn Chowder, page 160

Corn Chowder
Creamy, rich and thick.

Diced potatoes	3 cups	750 mL
Chopped celery	1 cup	250 mL
Grated carrots	1 cup	250 mL
Chopped onion	1 cup	250 mL
Water	2 cups	500 mL
Bacon slices, diced	4	4
All-purpose flour	1/4 cup	60 mL
Milk	2 1/4 cups	500 mL
Evaporated skim milk (or light cream)	13 1/2 oz.	385 mL
Cream-style corn	14 oz.	398 mL
Salt	1 tsp.	5 mL
Pepper	1/2 tsp.	2 mL
Cayenne pepper, optional	1/2 tsp.	2 mL

Cover and cook potato, celery, carrot and onion in water in large saucepan until tender. Do not drain.

Fry bacon in frying pan.

Mix flour in with bacon. Stir in both milks until mixture boils and thickens. Add to potato mixture.

Add corn, salt, pepper and cayenne pepper. Stir and heat through. Makes 10 cups (2.5 L) chowder.

Pictured on this page.

Broccoli Soup
Perfect after an outdoor winter activity.

Head of broccoli, finely cut	1	1
Medium onion, finely chopped	1	1
Butter or hard margarine	1 tbsp.	15 mL
Salt	3/4 tsp.	4 mL
Pepper	1/8 tsp.	0.5 mL
Water, to just cover		
Canned evaporated milk	13 1/2 oz.	385 mL
Parsley flakes	1 tsp.	5 mL

Put broccoli, onion, butter, salt and pepper in saucepan. Add water. Bring to a boil. Boil until vegetables are tender.

Add milk and parsley. Return to a boil. Boil, slowly for 15 minutes. Taste for salt and pepper, adding more if needed. Makes 3 1/2 cups (800 mL) soup.

Pictured above.

Note: if your want a smooth soup, run through blender before adding milk and parsley flakes.

Variation: Add 3 to 4 strips of cooked, crumbled bacon or add 4 oz. (125 g) Velveeta cheese. Try adding both bacon and cheese for a pleasant change.

Onion Soup

This always hits the spot! Nice beefy broth.

Thin sirloin steak, diced	1 lb.	454 g
Water	9 cups	2.25 L
Chopped celery	1 cup	250 mL
Thinly sliced narrow carrots	2 cups	500 mL
Diced potato	2 cups	500 mL
Bay leaf	1	1
Whole garlic cloves	2	2
Salt	2 tsp.	10 mL
Pepper	½ tsp.	2 mL
Beef bouillon powder	3 tbsp.	50 mL
Sliced onion	4 cups	1 L
French bread slices, toasted	10	10
Grated mozzarella cheese	1 cup	250 mL

Combine steak and water in large saucepan. Bring to a boil. Boil slowly for 15 minutes.

Add next 9 ingredients. Return to a boil. Simmer for about 1 hour until vegetables are tender. Discard bay leaf. Ladle into oven-proof soup bowls.

Lay a slice of toast on top of each bowl, cutting to fit if necessary. Sprinkle heavily with cheese. Bake in 450°F (230°C) oven to melt and brown cheese. If bowls aren't oven-proof, melt and brown cheese on toast slices placed on a baking sheet then transfer to bowls. Makes 10 cups (2.5 L) soup.

Pictured on page 165.

Tomato Consommé

A smooth beginning to a holiday meal.

Beef bouillon cubes	3	3
Boiling water	3 cups	675 mL
Tomato juice	6 cups	1.35 L
Lemon juice, fresh or bottled	1 tbsp.	15 mL
Soy sauce	1 tbsp.	15 mL
Worcestershire sauce	2 tsp.	10 mL
Onion powder	2 tsp.	10 mL
Granulated sugar	1½ tsp.	7 mL
Chopped chives, for garnish		

Dissolve bouillon cubes in boiling water in saucepan.

Add next 6 ingredients. Bring to a boil.

Ladle into 8 soup bowls. Garnish with chives. Makes 9 cups (2.25 L) consommé.

Pictured on page 160.

Carrot Cauliflower Soup

Lovely orange color. Very thick. Freezes well.

Medium potato, diced	1	1
Medium carrots, diced	4	4
Chopped onion	1 cup	250 mL
Small head of cauliflower, cut up	1	1
Water	2 cups	500 mL
Water	2 cups	500 mL
Chicken bouillon powder	4 tsp.	20 mL
Beef bouillon powder	1 tsp.	5 mL
Prepared mustard	1 tsp.	5 mL
Ground nutmeg	½ tsp.	2 mL
Salt	1 tsp.	5 mL
Pepper	¼ tsp.	1 mL
Grated medium Cheddar cheese	1 cup	250 mL
Sherry (or alcohol-free sherry)	3 tbsp.	50 mL

Combine first 5 ingredients in saucepan. Cook until vegetables are done. Do not drain. Remove from heat.

Stir in next 8 ingredients. Pour into large bowl. In 3 or 4 batches, purée in food processor or blender. Return to saucepan.

Add sherry. Heat until very hot. Makes generous 7 cups (1.75 L) soup.

Pictured below.

Carrot Cauliflower Soup

Hearty Scallop Chowder

Nice chunky chowder. Easily doubled.

Water	2 cups	500 mL
Chicken bouillon cubes	2	2
Diced potatoes	3 cups	750 mL
Chopped onion	1 cup	250 mL
Diced carrot	½ cup	125 mL
Diced celery	1 cup	250 mL
Small bay leaf	1	1
Salt	½ tsp.	2 mL
Pepper	¼ tsp.	1 mL
Ground thyme	¼ tsp.	1 mL
Butter or hard margarine	4 tsp.	25 mL
Fresh mushrooms, sliced	½ lb.	225 g
Scallops, fresh or frozen, cut in half or smaller	½ lb.	225 g
Dry white wine (or apple juice)	2 tbsp.	30 mL
Cream (the heavier the better)	1 cup	250 mL

Put first 10 ingredients into large saucepan. Simmer, stirring often, to dissolve bouillon cubes and cook vegetables. Remove bay leaf. Cool a bit and run mixture through blender. Set aside in saucepan.

Combine butter and mushrooms in frying pan. Sauté until mushrooms are beginning to brown.

Add scallops and wine. Cover and steam fry about 1 minute, stirring 2 or 3 times. Add to puréed vegetables.

Stir in cream. Heat but don't boil. Garnish with parsley or chives. Makes about 6 cups (1.5 L) chowder.

Pictured on page 163.

Scallop Bisque

Thick creamy soup. Serve with crackers.

Butter or hard margarine	6 tbsp.	100 mL
Leeks, chopped (white part)	2	2
All-purpose flour	¼ cup	60 mL
Salt	¼ tsp.	1 mL
Pepper	⅛ tsp.	0.5 mL
Chicken bouillon powder	2 tsp.	10 mL
Boiling water	2 cups	500 mL
Milk	2 cups	500 mL
Tomato sauce	7½ oz.	213 mL
Scallops, fresh or frozen, cut up	1 lb.	454 g
Whipping cream	1 cup	250 mL

Put butter into frying pan. Add leeks and sauté about 5 minutes.

Mix in flour, salt, pepper and bouillon powder. Stir in water until mixture boils and thickens.

Add milk, tomato sauce and scallops. Return to boil. Simmer for 5 minutes to cook scallops.

Add cream. Process in blender until smooth. Heat and serve. Makes about 8 cups (2 L) bisque.

Pictured on page 163.

Shrimp Chowder

Chunky, rich and thick. Nice combination of shrimp and cheese. Light orange in color.

Chopped onion	2 cups	500 mL
Butter or hard margarine	3 tbsp.	50 mL
Diced potato	3 cups	750 mL
Water	1¼ cups	300 mL
Salt	½ tsp.	2 mL
Pepper	⅛ tsp.	0.5 mL
Milk	1 cup	250 mL
Velveeta cheese, cut up	8 oz.	250 g
Canned broken shrimp, drained	2 × 4 oz.	2 × 113 g

Sauté onion in butter in large saucepan until soft.

Add potato, water, salt and pepper. Cover and cook until potato is tender. Do not drain. Mash about half the potatoes.

Add milk and cheese. Heat slowly, stirring often to melt cheese.

Add shrimp. Keep just below boiling to blend flavors. Makes 6 cups (1.5 L) chowder.

Pictured on page 163.

Tomato Cream Soup

Quick and easy.

Hard margarine (butter browns too fast)	2 tbsp.	30 mL
Chopped onion	1 cup	250 mL
Canned condensed tomato soup	2 × 10 oz.	2 × 284 mL
Soup cans of milk	2 × 10 oz.	2 × 284 mL
Cream cheese, diced	4 oz.	125 g

Melt margarine in large saucepan. Add onion. Sauté until soft.

Add soup, milk and cheese. Heat and stir to blend flavors and melt cheese. Makes 6 cups (1.5 L) soup.

Pictured on page 163.

Smooth Bean Soup

Looks can be deceiving. Wonderful flavor!

Dried navy beans	2 cups	500 mL
Water, to cover		
Meaty ham bone	1	1
Water	4 cups	1 L
Chopped carrot	3/4 cup	175 mL
Chopped celery	1/2 cup	125 mL
Chopped onion	1 cup	250 mL
Medium potatoes, cut up	3	3
Salt	1 tsp.	5 mL
Pepper	1/8 tsp.	0.5 mL
Lettuce, cut up, packed	3 cups	750 mL
Whipping cream	1 cup	250 mL

Put beans into bowl. Pour first amount of water over top to come 2 to 3 inches (5 to 8 cm) above beans. Let soak overnight.

Drain beans. Put beans into large saucepan or Dutch oven. Add next 8 ingredients. Cook slowly, stirring often for 2 hours.

Run bean mixture, along with lettuce, through blender. Return to saucepan.

Add cream. Heat through, without boiling. Makes 9 cups (2.25 L) soup.

Pictured on page 160.

Lobster Chowder Feed

Start a Christmas Eve tradition. Serves a large group—but be prepared for seconds. Good with Drop Cheese Biscuits, page 61.

Butter or hard margarine	1/2 cup	125 mL
Chopped onion	3 cups	750 mL
Diced celery	2 cups	500 mL
Small green peppers, seeded and diced	2	2
All-purpose flour	1/2 cup	125 mL
Boiling water	4 cups	1 L
Diced potato	5 cups	1.25 L
Salt	3 1/2 tsp.	17 mL
Pepper	1/2 tsp.	2 mL
Butter or hard margarine	1/4 cup	60 mL
Frozen cans of lobster, thawed	2 × 11 1/2 oz.	2 × 320 g
Boiling water	1 cup	250 mL
Scallops, halved if large	1 lb.	454 g
Haddock fillets, cut bite size	2 lbs.	900 g
Canned evaporated milk	2 × 13 1/2 oz.	2 × 385 mL
Homogenized milk	3 cups	750 mL

Melt first amount of butter in frying pan. Add onion, celery and green pepper. Sauté until tender.

Sprinkle flour over vegetables. Mix in well.

Put first amount of boiling water, diced potato, salt and pepper in large heavy Dutch oven. Stir. Cover. Cook until potatoes are tender-crisp. Add flour mixture.

Melt second amount of butter in frying pan. Add lobster. Sauté just long enough for the red color from the lobster to go into the butter. Add to potato mixture.

In separate small saucepan, put second amount of boiling water and scallops. Cook for 3 to 5 minutes until opaque. Do not drain. Set aside. Add to potato mixture.

Add haddock to potato mixture. Cook until fish turns white and flakes or falls apart.

Add both milks. Heat, stirring occasionally, until hot. Watch closely so it does not boil. Makes 6 quarts (6 L) chowder.

Pictured on page 163.

Minestrone, page 165   Tomato Cabbage Soup, page 165   Onion Soup, page 161

Tomato Cabbage Soup

This will be a big hit with cabbage or soup lovers!
Serve before a main course entrée or for lunch.

Margarine (butter browns too fast)	2 tbsp.	30 mL
Chopped onion	1½ cups	375 mL
Chopped celery	⅔ cup	150 mL
Canned tomatoes, broken up	2 × 14 oz.	2 × 398 mL
Coarsely grated cabbage, packed	6 cups	1.5 L
Thinly sliced carrots	1½ cups	375 mL
Chili sauce	¼ cup	60 mL
Granulated sugar	2 tsp.	10 mL
Salt	2 tsp.	10 mL
Pepper	½ tsp.	2 mL
Water	8 cups	2 L
Beef bouillon powder	2 tbsp.	30 mL
Whole oregano	¼ tsp.	1 mL
Sweet basil	¼ tsp.	1 mL

Melt margarine in Dutch oven. Add onion and celery. Sauté until soft.

Add remaining ingredients. Bring to a boil, stirring often. Cover. Boil slowly until vegetables are tender. Makes 13 cups (3.25 L) soup.

Pictured above.

Minestrone

Perfect for a cold winter evening. Serve with salad and buns.

Cooking oil	2 tbsp.	30 mL
Lean ground beef	1 lb.	454 g
Chopped onion	1½ cups	375 mL
Chopped celery	1 cup	250 mL
Boiling water	6 cups	1.5 L
Beef bouillon powder	3 tbsp.	50 mL
Canned tomatoes, broken up	3 × 14 oz.	3 × 398 mL
Grated cabbage, packed	2 cups	500 mL
Thinly sliced narrow carrot	¾ cup	175 mL
Parsley flakes	1 tbsp.	15 mL
Salt	1 tsp.	5 mL
Pepper	¼ tsp.	1 mL
Garlic powder	¼ tsp.	1 mL
Elbow macaroni	1 cup	250 mL
Canned red kidney beans, with juice	14 oz.	398 mL

Grated Parmesan cheese

Heat cooking oil in frying pan. Scramble-fry ground beef, onion and celery until no pink remains in beef and vegetables are soft. Put into large saucepan or Dutch oven.

Mix boiling water and bouillon powder. Add to pot.

Add next 7 ingredients to pot. Bring to a boil, stirring occasionally. Boil slowly for 15 minutes.

Stir in macaroni. Boil for 10 minutes more.

Add kidney beans. Stir. Boil until macaroni is tender, about 5 minutes.

Sprinkle each serving with Parmesan cheese. Makes 12 cups (3 L) soup.

Pictured above.

Vegetables

Holiday dinners need vegetables to accompany the main dishes. Familiar is fine but how about giving those basic veggies a slightly new shape?

These recipes incorporate that little something—a dressing, a topping, an extra ingredient or two—that turns the expected into a memorable taste experience.

Many of these vegetable recipes are for casserole-type dishes which can be prepared ahead of time—another plus on the big day.

Make the ordinary extraordinary when it comes to vegetables this holiday season.

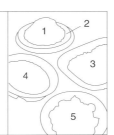

Stewed Tomato Casserole

Christmas colors—red and green. Extra easy, extra good!

Small zucchini with peel, sliced	2	2
Boiling water, to cover		
Canned stewed tomatoes	2 x 14 oz.	2 x 398 mL
Onion flakes	1 tbsp.	15 mL
Granulated sugar	½ tsp.	2 mL
Salt	⅛ tsp.	0.5 mL
Pepper, light sprinkle		
Hot pepper sauce drops	4	4
Dry bread crumbs	½ cup	125 mL
Butter or hard margarine	½ cup	125 mL
Fresh bread crumbs	1¼ cups	300 mL

Combine zucchini and boiling water in large saucepan. Bring to a boil. Boil 1 minute. Drain.

Combine next 7 ingredients in bowl.

Melt butter in saucepan. Stir in bread crumbs. Cover bottom of 2 quart (2 L) greased casserole with ½ crumb mixture. Add layer of ½ zucchini, layer of ½ tomato mixture then the remaining ½ zucchini and ½ tomato mixture. Top with second ½ crumbs. Bake, uncovered, in 350°F (175°C) oven until hot and browned. Serves 6 to 8.

Pictured on page 167.

Honey Glazed Onions

A quick addition to the dinner table.

Small white pearl onions, peeled	2 lbs.	900 g
Boiling salted water		
Butter or hard margarine	3 tbsp.	50 mL
Honey	3 tbsp.	50 mL
Salt, sprinkle		
Pepper, sprinkle		
Cornstarch	2 tsp.	10 mL
Water	1 tbsp.	15 mL

Cook onions in about 2 inches (5 cm) boiling water until tender. Drain.

Stir butter and honey together in small bowl to mix well. Add to onions. Heat and stir slowly until glazed. Sprinkle with salt and pepper. Stir. Remove onions.

Mix cornstarch in water. Stir into remaining liquid to thicken. Return onions to saucepan. Stir. Serves 6 to 8.

Pictured on page 167.

Cauliflower Au Gratin

The cheese sauce has a nice nip to it. Cut in wedges to serve.

Large head of cauliflower, left whole, leaves removed	2 lbs.	900 g
Boiling salted water		
Cheese Sauce:		
Butter or hard margarine	3 tbsp.	50 mL
All-purpose flour	3 tbsp.	50 mL
Salt	½ tsp.	2 mL
Paprika	¼ tsp.	1 mL
Cayenne pepper, just a pinch		
Milk	2 cups	500 mL
Grated sharp Cheddar cheese	1 cup	250 mL

Cook cauliflower in large saucepan in about 2 inches (5 cm) boiling salted water until tender. Drain.

Cheese Sauce: Melt butter in saucepan. Mix in flour, salt, paprika and cayenne. Stir in milk until it boils and thickens.

Add cheese. Stir until it melts. Place whole cauliflower in serving bowl. Pour cheese sauce over top. Serves 6 to 8.

Pictured on page 167.

Dressed Peas

Serve this as a hot or cold vegetable. Either way the basil and mustard flavors are just right with the peas.

Dressing:		
Water	¼ cup	60 mL
Cornstarch	1 tsp.	5 mL
Red wine vinegar	2 tbsp.	30 mL
Granulated sugar	1 tsp.	5 mL
Sweet basil	1 tsp.	5 mL
Prepared mustard	1 tsp.	5 mL
Salt	¼ tsp.	1 mL
Pepper, just a pinch		
Nutmeg, just a pinch		
Frozen peas	2¼ lbs.	1 kg

Dressing: Measure first 9 ingredients in saucepan. Heat and stir until it boils and thickens slightly.

Cook peas according to directions on package. Drain. Add dressing to warm peas just before serving. Stir. Serves 12.

Pictured on page 167.

Sauced Broccoli

Nice contrast in color between sauce and broccoli.

Broccoli heads, cut up	2-3	2-3
Boiling water		
Poppy Seed Sauce:		
Sour cream	1½ cups	375 mL
Granulated sugar	2 tsp.	10 mL
Chopped chives	1 tsp.	5 mL
Poppy seed	1 tsp.	5 mL
Salt	¼ tsp.	1 mL
Pepper	⅛ tsp.	0.5 mL

Cook broccoli in boiling water until tender-crisp. Drain.

Poppy Seed Sauce: Mix all ingredients. Heat and stir until very warm. Pour over broccoli. Serves 6 to 8.

Pictured on front cover.

Hasselback Potatoes

Hasselback Potatoes

A new look to baked potatoes. Serve with sour cream and chives.

Smooth oval medium baking potatoes, unpeeled	8	8
Butter or hard margarine, softened	2 tbsp.	30 mL
Salt, generous sprinkle (see Note)		
Pepper, light sprinkle		

Place 1 potato on tablespoon. Set on counter. Make cuts ¼ inch (6 mm) apart from top almost to bottom. Tablespoon should keep knife from reaching bottom of potato. Set potatoes cut side up in greased 9 x 13 inch (22 x 33 cm) pan. Pat tops dry with paper towel.

Brush potatoes with butter. Sprinkle with salt and pepper. Bake, uncovered, in 450°F (230°C) oven for about 40 minutes until tender when pierced with tip of sharp knife. Brush again with butter at half time. Serves 8.

Pictured above.

Note: Sprinkle with seasoned salt for a zippier flavor.

Squash Casserole

Squash Casserole

Beautiful golden yellow color. Pecan Topping is attractive for festive occasions or use the Butter Topping.

Acorn squash	4	4
Squash pulp, approximately	8 cups	2 L
Butter or hard margarine	1/4 cup	60 mL
Large eggs	2	2
Salt	1 1/2 tsp.	7 mL
Pecan Topping:		
Butter or hard margarine	1/4 cup	60 mL
Brown sugar, packed	1/2 cup	125 mL
All-purpose flour	1/4 cup	60 mL
Chopped pecans	1/2 cup	125 mL
Butter Topping:		
Butter or hard margarine	2 tbsp.	30 mL
Salt, sprinkle		
Pepper, sprinkle		

Cut squash in half lengthwise. Discard seeds. Place cut side down on greased baking sheet with sides. Bake, uncovered, in 350°F (175°C) oven for about 50 minutes until tender. Cool until you can handle. Scoop out pulp into saucepan.

Mash pulp with butter, eggs, and salt using fork for coarser texture or food processor for smoother texture. Turn into 3 quart (3 L) ungreased casserole.

Pecan Topping: For a special topping melt butter in saucepan. Stir in sugar, flour and pecans. Sprinkle over top. Bake, uncovered, in 350°F (175°C) oven for about 30 minutes. Serves 16.

Pictured above.

Butter Topping: Simple but good. Make indentations with back of tablespoon all over surface. Put dab of butter in each one. Sprinkle whole surface with salt and pepper. Bake as in Pecan Topping. Serves 16.

Tomato Bean Dish

The red and green colors make this particularly festive. Best made the day of serving.

Frozen green beans, cooked and drained	6 cups	1.5 L
Medium tomatoes, chopped	6	6
Grated medium or sharp Cheddar cheese	2 cups	500 mL
Topping:		
Large eggs	4	4
Milk	1 cup	250 mL
Biscuit mix	1 cup	250 mL
Salt	1 tsp.	5 mL
Cayenne pepper	1/2 tsp.	2 mL
Sweet basil	1 tsp.	5 mL

Spread green beans in layer in ungreased 9 × 13 inch (22 × 33 cm) pan. Layer tomatoes over top. Sprinkle with cheese.

Beat eggs in mixing bowl. Add milk, biscuit mix, salt, cayenne and basil. Beat. Pour over cheese. Bake, uncovered, in 350°F (175°C) oven for about 50 minutes until browned and heated through. Serves 10 to 12.

Pictured below.

Tomato Bean Dish

Broccoli Casserole

Broccoli Casserole

*The green broccoli and red pimiento make this
a showy Christmas casserole.*

Frozen chopped broccoli	3 × 10 oz.	3 × 300 g
Salt	1/2 tsp.	2 mL
Boiling water		
Condensed cream of	10 oz.	284 mL
mushroom soup		
Grated sharp Cheddar cheese	1 cup	250 mL
Salad dressing (or mayonnaise)	1/4 cup	60 mL
Chopped pimiento	2 tbsp.	30 mL
Topping:		
Butter or hard margarine	2 tbsp.	30 mL
Cracker crumbs	1/2 cup	125 mL

Cook broccoli in salted boiling water until tender-crisp.
Drain well. Transfer to 2 quart (2 L) ungreased casserole.

In separate bowl stir soup, cheese, salad dressing and
pimiento. Pour over broccoli.

Topping: Melt butter in small saucepan. Stir in cracker
crumbs. Sprinkle over top. Bake, uncovered, in 350°F
(175°C) oven for 30 to 40 minutes until browned and
bubbly hot. Serves 8 to 10.

Pictured above.

Sweet Potato Bake

*Assemble the night before but do not bake. Marshmallow
topping is added during last few minutes of baking.*

Quick cooking rolled oats	1/2 cup	125 mL
All-purpose flour	1/2 cup	125 mL
Brown sugar, packed	1/2 cup	125 mL
Ground cinnamon	1 tsp.	5 mL
Butter or hard margarine	6 tbsp.	100 mL
Sweet potatoes drained and	2 × 19 oz.	2 × 540 mL
cubed (see Note)		
Cranberries, fresh or frozen,	2 cups	500 mL
coarsely chopped		
Reserved crumb mixture	1 cup	250 mL
Miniature marshmallows	2 cups	500 mL

Place first 5 ingredients in bowl. Stir to mix well. Measure
out 1 cup (250 mL) and reserve for cranberry mixture.

In large bowl, combine sweet potato, cranberries and
crumb mix. Toss well. Turn into ungreased 1 1/2 quart
(1.5 L) casserole. Sprinkle with remaining crumbs. Bake,
uncovered, in 350°F (175°C) oven for 30 minutes.

Cover with single layer of marshmallows. Bake for 10 to
12 minutes until lightly browned. Serves 8 to 10.

Pictured below.

Note: Two large fresh sweet potatoes may be substituted
for canned. Cook in boiling water until just tender.

Sweet Potato Bake

Festive Scalloped Potatoes

Red onion makes a colorful contrast.

Medium potatoes, thinly sliced	8	8
Medium red or white onion, thinly sliced in rings	1	1
Sauce:		
Butter or hard margarine	½ cup	125 mL
All-purpose flour	½ cup	125 mL
Salt	2 tsp.	10 mL
Pepper	½ tsp.	2 mL
Paprika	½ tsp.	2 mL
Milk	4½ cups	1.1 L

Paprika, generous sprinkle

Place potato slices in 1 container and onion slices in another.

Sauce: Melt butter in saucepan. Mix in flour, salt, pepper and paprika. Stir in milk until it boils and thickens. To assemble, layer ½ potatoes, then ½ onion in greased 3 quart (3 L) casserole. Pour ½ sauce over top. Layer second ½ potatoes and onion followed by second ½ sauce.

Sprinkle with paprika. Bake, covered, in 350°F (175°C) oven for about 1 hour until tender. Remove cover for last 10 minutes. Serves 8 to 10.

Pictured on page 131.

Carrot Medley

Slightly dressier carrots. Use for sit-down dinner or buffet.

Margarine (butter browns too fast)	2 tbsp.	30 mL
Coarsely chopped onion	2 cups	500 mL
Sliced fresh mushrooms, (1 lb., 454 g)	4 cups	1 L
Carrots, cut in thick slices	2 lbs.	900 g
Chicken bouillon powder	2 tsp.	10 mL
Water	1 cup	250 mL

Melt margarine in frying pan. Add onion. Sauté until soft. Remove to bowl.

Add mushrooms to frying pan along with more margarine if needed. Sauté until soft. Add to onions.

Put carrot, bouillon powder and water in large saucepan. Bring to a simmer. Simmer, covered, until tender-crisp. Add onion and mushroom mixture. Simmer until tender. Serves 8.

Pictured on page 131.

Zucchini Casserole

Delicious casserole for formal or informal entertaining.

Medium zucchini with peel, sliced	4	4
Boiling salted water		
Hard margarine (butter browns too fast)	6 tbsp.	100 mL
Chopped onion	1 cup	250 mL
Grated carrot	½ cup	125 mL
Top of stove stuffing mix and envelope seasoning	1½ cups	375 mL
Condensed cream of mushroom soup	10 oz.	284 mL
Sour cream (or plain yogurt)	½ cup	125 mL
Hard margarine (butter browns too fast)	2 tbsp.	30 mL
Remaining stuffing mix		

Boil zucchini in boiling salted water for 8 to 10 minutes until tender. Drain.

Melt first amount of margarine in frying pan. Add onion and carrot. Sauté until soft. Transfer to large bowl.

Mix stuffing and seasoning in separate bowl. Measure out 1½ cups (375 mL). Reserve remainder for topping.

Add mushroom soup, sour cream and stuffing mix to onion mixture. Stir well. Add zucchini. Stir lightly. Turn into ungreased 2 quart (2 L) casserole.

Keep onions in cold storage or in the refrigerator. A cold onion produces few, if any tears! For a milder flavor, soak Spanish and purple onions in cold water for ½ hour before serving.

Melt second amount of margarine in frying pan. Add remaining stuffing mix. Sauté until browned. Sprinkle over casserole. Bake in 350°F (175°C) oven for 30 to 40 minutes. Serves 6 to 8.

Pictured on page 167.

Table Centerpieces, Decorations & Settings

A brightly-lit tree in the living room and outside the front door. Pine boughs along the staircase and around the doorways. A Christmas village on a table in the corner. Christmas is a time for decorating the house inside and out.

The dinner table is no exception. While the menu is important, so is the atmosphere, and that's where candles, wreaths, sprigs of holly, silver garlands and other Yuletide decorations add so much.

A well-appointed table is a delight at any time of year, but especially at Christmas. Polish the silver and get out the best china and linen. Decorate with a flourish. It's worth the extra effort because you're creating memories.

Centerpieces

"Wrap-Up" Your Table Centerpiece

You will need:

1	Piece of styrofoam or board 10" × 30" × ½ " (25 cm × 75 cm × 1.5 cm)
1	Piece of plain broadcloth material 18" × 36" (45 cm × 90 cm) This can either complement the tablecloth or blend in with it.
9 to 14	Small empty boxes of varying shapes and sizes We used 13.
4 to 5	Rolls of coordinated Christmas wrapping paper We used 4 different wraps—2 solid foil and 2 patterned foil.
4 to 5	Rolls of coordinated Christmas ribbon We used 2 wired and 2 non-wired.
4 to 5	Christmas picks Picks are available at craft stores in a variety of colors and styles; choose a color that accents, blends or matches a secondary color.
4 to 5	Pieces of short garland or fir boughs
	Hot glue gun

Base:

1. Center styrofoam on material.
2. Starting on one long side, pull edge of material over base. Put dabs of glue on styrofoam about ¼" (1 cm) in under material. Press material down over glue spots.
3. Repeat on second long side, pulling taut.
4. For ends, fold material in at sides then pull up and over end. Repeat gluing process.
5. Repeat on other end to form smooth and tightly-wrapped finish.

Presents:

1. Wrap half the boxes with at least one of each of the papers, gluing rather than taping. (Do not choose the ribbons yet.)
2. Begin arranging the boxes on the base, keeping in mind that your highest point should be near the center. (Do not begin to glue yet.)
3. Once the central boxes have been established, choose additional boxes that will create a pleasing extension to both ends. Wrap these boxes in the papers that work best to balance the color and design.
4. Choose your ribbons for each box to create additional color effect and balance of color. (Do not do bows yet.) Glue ribbons to paper, rather than tying or taping.
5. Beginning with the boxes that are touching the base, put dabs of glue just in from each corner on the underside of the box and press it into its "spot" on the base. When those boxes are in place, continue gluing the other boxes into place on top of the other ones. Where one box leans against another, put just one dab of glue where they touch.
6. Make bows from the various ribbons and glue into place on each box. Use narrower ribbon to gather loops of wider ribbon together to form bow. The wired ribbon forms wonderful bows.

Finishing Touches:

Glue pieces of garland or boughs at various spots around the base of the boxes making sure they overhang slightly.

Stand back and take a look at the centerpiece from both sides. Determine the locations for the Christmas picks. Tuck and glue them into the little "caves" that show, as well as glue them under the ends of one or two boxes.

Your table is now ready to greet family and friends this festive season.

Create a special effect for your holiday table with the Wrap-Up Centerpiece. Its size, shape, color and theme possibilities are endless — limited only by your imagination.

Here are a few suggestions to get you started.

For Family/Young Children
Choose red and green wrappings that have a Santa Claus/reindeer theme. Finish with candy canes and holly.

For A Country Christmas Buffet Or Brunch
Cover the boxes with gingham material in various colors. Decorate with burlap, wool strands, cinnamon sticks, dried flower and eucalyptus.

For An Elegant Dinner
Go formal with gold, lace, netted ribbons and balls, or try a combination of silver and winter white.

Festive Ribbon Centerpiece

You will need:

1 Piece of gold, red or green metallic mesh ribbon 72" (2 m) length, 6" (15 cm) wide

1 Piece of thin, pliable wire, 12" (31 cm) length

1 Piece of red or green felt, 1/2" x 3" (12 mm x 7.5 cm) length

1 Pine cone, large
Leave natural, or spray lightly with gold, or glue glitter to some of the edges.

2 Sprigs of plastic greenery

2 Picks (berries and/or small poinsettias)

1 Christmas pick (small gift package or ball and ribbon)
Picks are available at craft stores in a variety of colors and styles; choose a color that accents, blends or matches a secondary color.

Hot glue gun

To Assemble:

1. Fold ribbon back and forth, starting in middle, under itself two times increasing length of each fold, to form bow shape. Leave enough on one side to form tail and to cut off 10" (25 cm) as tail for other side (see Figure 1).

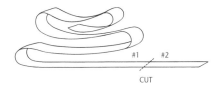

Figure 1

2. Take the 10" (25 cm) piece and place underneath the other side so both sides have a tail (see Figure 2).

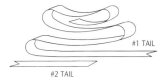

Figure 2

3. Thread wire up and down through the center of all layers and pull loosely to form bow shape. Bring ends of wire around bow and twist together underneath. Thread wire ends through ribbon so they don't show (see Figure 3).

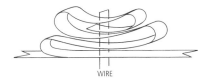

Figure 3

4. Glue felt piece to bottom center of ribbon, covering the wire.

5. Arrange pine cone and greenery on the top side in the middle of the ribbon. Pine cone should be in center with enough greenery around to offset it. Don't glue yet.

6. Arrange the berries, holly, poinsettias, etc. on top of the greenery, so that the centerpiece looks pleasing from all sides.

7. Once everything is placed as you like it, carefully remove the layers and start gluing. Start with the greenery, then the pine cone, then the picks.

8. Cut the ribbon tails in a "V" shape and fluff up the ribbon.

Variation:

Make this centerpiece on a smaller scale, using narrower ribbon, smaller pine cones, etc.

Decorations

Large Wreath Candleholder

You will need:

1	Circle of corrugated cardboard, 10" (25.5 cm) diameter
1	Circle of red or green felt, 5" (12.5 cm) diameter.
1	Straight pin
50-60	Pine cones, various sizes Leave natural or create a glittery look by spray painting a few gold or glue glitter on the tips of some cones.
1	Candle, 6" (15 cm) tall; 3" (7.5 cm) diameter
10-12	Unshelled walnuts, pecans, hazelnuts, almonds, or Brazil nuts, All of one kind or a combination
	Plastic greenery or silk poinsettias (optional)
	Spray varnish, gloss or matte
1	Red, green or gold ribbon, 42" (107 cm) length. Should be wide enough to cover the thickness of the cardboard.
	Hot glue gun

To Assemble:

1. Mark the center of the cardboard circle by drawing 5 intersecting lines across the diameter of the circle. Where they meet will be the center.

2. Glue the felt circle onto the center of the cardboard. To help keep felt centered on the cardboard, first push a pin up from the bottom, through the cardboard and then push felt down over pin. Glue down in spots.

3. The pattern created on your wreath will depend on the size of your pine cones. Glue one row of pine cones around the outside of the circle with bottoms facing out. Make sure they come to the edge of the cardboard or just slightly over.

4. Glue another row of cones to the inside of the first layer—this time with the tops facing out.

5. Push the candle onto pin to hold in center.

6. Using more pine cones, fill in the area left free between the candle and the two rows of glued pine cones. These cones should be snug against the candle but still allow the candle to be removed and inserted easily. (Be careful not to glue the cones to the candle.)

7. Fill in any holes or spaces with small pine cones and nuts.

8. Remove candle and pin. Spray wreath with a thin coat of varnish, gloss or matte, depending on what look you want. Make sure to spray from the inside of the circle out, so all surfaces are covered. Let dry and spray once more if needed.

9. Tie the ribbon around the circle of cardboard, ending with a bow. Put a small dot of glue on the knot to hold in place.

10. Stand back and take a good look at your wreath. If there are any spaces that look empty, fill with a few pieces of greenery or silk poinsettias.

Small Wreath Candleholder

You will need:

1	Circle of corrugated cardboard, 3½" (9 cm) diameter
1	Circle of red or green felt, approximately 1.5" (4 cm) diameter
1	Straight pin
1	Taper candle, 4½" (11.5 cm) tall
3	Pine cones, medium Leave natural, or spray lightly with gold, or glue glitter to some of the edges.
12-14	Pine cones, small
	Spray varnish, gloss or matte
1	Red, green or gold ribbon, 20" (50 cm) length Wide enough to cover the thickness of the cardboard
	Hot glue gun

To Assemble:

1. Mark the center of the cardboard circle by drawing 5 intersecting lines across the diameter of circle. Where the lines meet will be the center.

2. Glue the felt circle onto the center of the cardboard. To help keep felt centered on the cardboard, first push a pin up from bottom, through the cardboard and then push felt down over pin. Glue down in spots.

3. Push the candle onto pin to hold in center.

4. Before gluing any cones, arrange a pattern of cones around the candle to see which looks best. Place the 3 medium cones against the candle to create a holder. (It is important to use cones that can hold the candle upright.) Place a row of small cones around the outside of circle, being careful to come to edge of cardboard or just slightly over. When you are satisfied with the arrangement, remove cones and glue to cardboard circle, being careful not to glue cones to candle.

5. Check for spaces. Glue small cones in place to cover any spaces. (If you can't find cones small enough, cut the tips off less-than-perfect larger cones.)

6. Remove the candle. The pin may be left in to help hold the candle firmly, or remove if you like. Spray the wreath with varnish. Make sure all surfaces are covered with a thin coat. Let dry. Spray again if needed.

7. Tie the ribbon around the cardboard circle, ending with a bow. Put a small dot of glue on knot to hold in place.

Small Wreath Candleholder

Large Wreath Candleholder

Yuletide Log Candleholder

You will need:

1   Birch log, 10" to 12" (25 cm to 31 cm) length, split in half lengthwise

6   Felt circles, 1" (2.5 cm) diameter

1   Small bag of moss
If you gather your own, dry in 140°, (65°C) oven for 1 hour to kill bacteria.

1   Taper candle, 12" (31 cm) length

2   Christmas picks (with small presents, balls or cones) to match candle
Picks are available at craft stores.

3   Sprigs of plastic greenery

10-12   Pine cones, small

2-4   Picks (berries and/or small poinsettias)

Hot glue gun

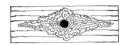

Use your imagination when making your Yuletide Log. Choose colors to match your Christmas color scheme. Choose logs of different sizes. Use straight taper candles or spiral candles, or make 2 or 3 holes in the log for a candelabra effect.

To Assemble:

1. Drill a hole in the center of birch log, the diameter of the candle.

2. Glue the felt circles to bottom of the log to prevent scratching table surface.

3. Glue the moss to the log, starting from the top, outside of log down to middle, bottom. Continue around log. When you look down onto top of log, the moss should be in a diamond shape. (see Figure 1)

Figure 1

TOP VIEW

4. Put the candle in the hole; if loose, put dab of glue at bottom of hole to hold the candle upright.

5. Pull apart the greenery sprigs. Glue pieces on top of the moss, keeping to diamond shape.

6. Cut long stems from the two Christmas picks. Place just off center on each side of the candle on the long part of log. Glue in place close to the candle, but do not glue to candle.

7. Fill in spaces with small cones, balls, berries or poinsettias. The overall shape, when looking from the side, should form a triangle, with the two Christmas picks and candle forming the tip. (see Figure 2)

Figure 2

"Wrap-Up" Napkin Holder

You will need (for 1 napkin holder):

1   Wired ribbon, 2" (5 cm) wide, 30" (75 cm) length
    Ribbon should be the same pattern (or be solid) on both sides

1   Piece gold cord, 8" (20 cm) length

1   Christmas pick
    Picks are availble at craft stores in a variety of colors and styles.

    Hot glue gun

To Assemble:

1. Fold ribbon in half crosswise. Form loop 2½" (6.25 cm) in diameter from folded end. Tie tightly with gold cord. (See Figure 1).

Figure 1

2. To make bow, form loop at knot 6½" (16 cm), using ribbon 1. Hold ribbon in place between fingers, and repeat with ribbon 2. Tie ends of gold cord around bow. Make a knot.

3. Glue Christmas pick to knot in center of bow.

4. Open out loop that will hold napkin. Open out 2 loops to form bow.

5. Repeat steps 1 through 4 for as many napkin holders as you need.

"Wrap-Up" Place Cards

You will need (for 1 place card):

1   Tiny box, rectangular
    Use a matchbox, raisin box or jewelry box.

1   Piece of wrapping paper, approximately 2½ times the size of the box.

1   Ribbon, solid-colored, 2 inch (5 cm) wide, circumference of box crosswise plus ½" (6 mm).

    Hot glue gun

    Gold ink pen

To Assemble:

1. Wrap box, having seam of paper meet on underside of box, horizontally. Glue sparingly. Fold side flaps down, to make points. Fold points down on underside of box.

2. Place center point of ribbon on center point of top side of box, keeping ribbon horizontal. Fold ends of ribbon around sides of box to underside and glue sparingly. (Note: Ribbon will hold flaps of wrapping paper in place.)

3. On top side of box, write or print the guest's name on the solid portion of ribbon. Let dry 2 minutes before using.

4. Repeat steps 1 through 3 for as many place cards as you need.

Variation:

Use a different size and shape of tiny box for each guest or a different pattern or color of wrapping paper for each guest.

Buffet "Mitten"

You will need (for 1 mitten):

1 Piece of brown paper (or other heavier paper), approximately 6" x 8"(15 cm x 20 cm)

Pencil

Ruler

Scissors

1 Piece of black felt (or other color), approximately 9" x 12" (23 cm x 30 cm)

Tailor's chalk or colored pencil
Use contrasting color to felt.

Pinking shears

Sewing machine

1 Piece silver cord, 8" (20 cm) length

Hot glue gun

1 Tiny pine cone, sprayed silver, or silver jingle bell

To Assemble:

1. To enlarge pattern, draw a rectangle 4" x 5" (10 x 12.5 cm) on brown paper. Mark into 1 inch (2.5 cm) squares. Using Figure 1, transfer pattern to brown paper grid, matching lines within each square. Cut out pattern.

2. Using tailor's chalk, trace pattern twice onto felt. Cut out with pinking shears.

3. Place mitts together, matching edges. Sew together, using 1/8" (3 mm) seam allowance, along outer edge from Point A to Point B.

4. Tie cord into a bow.

5. Glue bow onto mitten at Point C. (Be sure and glue bow on same side of each mitten.)

6. Glue pine cone or bell to middle of bow.

7. Fray ends of corded ribbon.

8. Repeat steps 2 through 7 for as many "mittens" as you need.

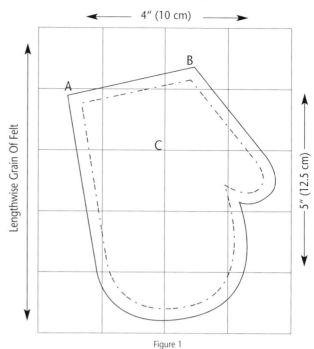

1 Square = 1 inch (2.5 cm)

4" (10 cm)

Lengthwise Grain Of Felt

5" (12.5 cm)

Figure 1

Santa Napkin Holder

You will need (for 1 napkin holder):

1   Piece of brown paper (or other heavier paper), approximately 10" × 10" (25 cm × 25 cm)

    Pencil

    Ruler

    Pair of scissors

1   Piece of felt in each of red, flesh-tone or light pink, black, and white

    Tailor's chalk or colored pencil
    Use contrasting color to felt.

    Hot glue gun

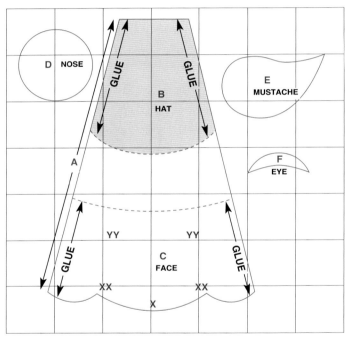

1 Square = 1 inch (2.5 cm)

Figure 1

To Assemble:

1. To enlarge pattern: Draw a square 7" × 7" (18 cm × 18 cm) on brown paper. Mark into 1 inch (2.5 cm) squares. Using Figure 1, transfer patterns to brown paper grid, matching lines within each square. Cut out patterns.

2. Using tailor's chalk, trace pattern A, B and D onto red felt, pattern C onto flesh-toned felt, pattern E onto white felt and pattern F onto black felt. Cut out.

3. Glue hat (pattern B) onto background (pattern A) matching top and sides as shown. Note: Glue only side edges together.

4. Glue nose (pattern D) onto face (pattern C) at X. Note: Glue only top half of nose; rest will hang below face.

5. Glue both mustaches (pattern E) onto face (pattern C) at XX, slightly overlapping onto nose (pattern D).

6. Glue both eyes (pattern F) onto face (pattern C) at YY.

7. To use: fold white paper napkin in thirds forming a triangle/diamond shape. Starting at the bottom, push the long point of the napkin up behind face and continue up behind hat to form the point of the hat and Santa's "beard".

8. Repeat steps 2 through 7 for as many napkin holders as you need.

Settings

Buffet Dinner

Guests should be able to move easily around the buffet table and to serve themselves in a logical order. Traffic should flow toward the seating area. The buffet table can be positioned in several places in the dining room depending on your space and number of guests. The most common arrangement is in the center of the room, allowing traffic to flow comfortably around the table using either the one-line or two-line layout. If more space is needed, the table can be placed against a wall with the food line moving in one direction.

Against-The-Wall Buffet

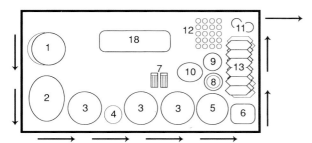

One Line Buffet

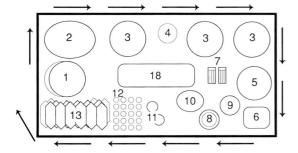

Two Line Buffet

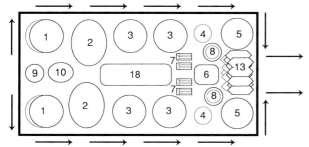

1. Plates
2. Meat
3. Vegetable
4. Gravy
5. Salad (Tossed)
6. Salad (Jellied)
7. Salt, Pepper
8. Condiments
9. Butter
10. Dinner Rolls
11. Water, Milk
12. Glasses
13. Napkins, Cutlery
14. Coffee/Tea
15. Dessert
16. Spoons
17. Mints
18. Centerpiece
19. Cups, Saucers
20. Cream, Sugar

Sit-Down Dinner

Make your table the center of attraction. Put extra thought into colors by coordinating your centerpiece, dishes and linens. Neat and orderly settings will make any table look inviting. Plates and cutlery should be 1 inch (2.5 cm) in from the edge of the table. Too much cutlery on a table can be overwhelming and look cluttered. Set only the cutlery needed.

Basic setting.

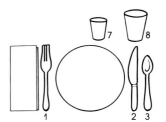

Setting for main course and dessert. This works if salad is served along with the main course.

Setting for salad course and main course. Teaspoon can be used for a spoon-eaten dessert or dessert forks can be brought in on dessert plates.

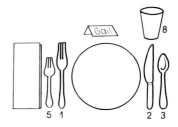

Setting for soup, salad, main course and dessert. To serve salad after the main course, move salad fork to the right of dinner fork.

1. Dinner Fork
2. Dinner Knife
3. Teaspoon
4. Dessert Fork
5. Salad Fork
6. Soup Spoon
7. Juice Glass
8. Water Glass
9. Wine Glass
10. Butter Knife

Measurement Tables

Throughout this book measurements are

given in Conventional and Metric measure.

To compensate for differences between

the two measurements due to rounding,

a full metric measure is not always used.

The cup used is the standard 8 fluid ounce.

Temperature is given in degrees Fahrenheit and Celsius.

Baking pan measurements are in inches

and centimetres as well as quarts and litres.

An exact metric conversion is given below

as well as the working equivalent (Standard Measure).

Oven temperatures

Fahrenheit (°F)	Celsius (°C)
175°	80°
200°	95°
225°	110°
250°	120°
275°	140°
300°	150°
325°	160°
350°	175°
375°	190°
400°	205°
425°	220°
450°	230°
475°	240°
500°	260°

Pans

Conventional Inches	Metric Centimetres
8x8 inch	20x20 cm
9x9 inch	22x22 cm
9x13 inch	22x33 cm
10x15 inch	25x38 cm
11x17 inch	28x43 cm
8x2 inch round	20x5 cm
9x2 inch round	22x5 cm
10x4$^1/_2$ inch tube	25x11 cm
8x4x3 inch loaf	20x10x7 cm
9x5x3 inch loaf	22x12x7 cm

Spoons

Conventional Measure	Metric Exact Conversion Millilitre (mL)	Metric Standard Measure Millilitre (mL)
$^1/_8$ teaspoon (tsp.)	0.6 mL	0.5 mL
$^1/_4$ teaspoon (tsp.)	1.2 mL	1 mL
$^1/_2$ teaspoon (tsp.)	2.4 mL	2 mL
1 teaspoon (tsp.)	4.7 mL	5 mL
2 teaspoons (tsp.)	9.4 mL	10 mL
1 tablespoon (tbsp.)	14.2 mL	15 mL

Cups

$^1/_4$ cup (4 tbsp.)	56.8 mL	50 mL
$^1/_3$ cup (5$^1/_3$ tbsp.)	75.6 mL	75 mL
$^1/_2$ cup (8 tbsp.)	113.7 mL	125 mL
$^2/_3$ cup (10$^2/_3$ tbsp.)	151.2 mL	150 mL
$^3/_4$ cup (12 tbsp.)	170.5 mL	175 mL
1 cup (16 tbsp.)	227.3 mL	250 mL
4$^1/_2$ cups	1022.9 mL	1000 mL (1 L)

Dry measurements

Conventional Measure Ounces (oz.)	Metric Exact Conversion Grams (g)	Metric Standard Measure Grams (g)
1 oz.	28.3 g	30 g
2 oz.	56.7 g	55 g
3 oz.	85.0 g	85 g
4 oz.	113.4 g	125 g
5 oz.	141.7 g	140 g
6 oz.	170.1 g	170 g
7 oz.	198.4 g	200 g
8 oz.	226.8 g	250 g
16 oz.	453.6 g	500 g
32 oz.	907.2 g	1000 g (1 kg)

Casseroles (Canada & Britain)

Standard Size Casserole	Exact Metric Measure
1 qt. (5 cups)	1.13 L
1$^1/_2$ qts. (7$^1/_2$ cups)	1.69 L
2 qts. (10 cups)	2.25 L
2$^1/_2$ qts. (12$^1/_2$ cups)	2.81 L
3 qts. (15 cups)	3.38 L
4 qts. (20 cups)	4.5 L
5 qts. (25 cups)	5.63 L

Casseroles (United States)

Standard Size Casserole	Exact Metric Measure
1 qt. (4 cups)	900 mL
1$^1/_2$ qts. (6 cups)	1.35 L
2 qts. (8 cups)	1.8 L
2$^1/_2$ qts. (10 cups)	2.25 L
3 qts. (12 cups)	2.7 L
4 qts. (16 cups)	3.6 L
5 qts. (20 cups)	4.5 L

Index

A

Company's Coming®
Home for the Holidays

All New Festive Recipes by Jean Paré

Home for the Holidays

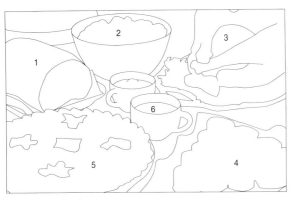

Pictured on divider:

Pictured at left:

Top: Peanut Butter Bites, page 88
Centre: Grasshopper Squares, page 86
Centre Right: Rum And Butter Balls, page 84
Bottom Left: Ambrosia Orange Cookies, page 85

Home for the Holidays was created thanks to the dedicated efforts of the people and organizations listed below.

COMPANY'S COMING PUBLISHING LIMITED

Author	Jean Paré
President	Grant Lovig
Production Manager	Derrick Sorochan
Design Director	Jaclyn Draker
Publishing Coordinator	Shelly Willsey

The Recipe Factory

Research & Development Manager	Nora Prokop
Editor	Laurel Hoffmann
Editorial Assistant	Rendi Dennis
Associate Editor	Sarah Campbell
Copywriter	Debbie Dixon
Proofreaders	Audrey Dahl
	Connie Townsend
	Audrey Whitson
Food Editor	Lynda Elsenheimer
Associate Food Editor	Suzanne Hartman
Researcher	Sheila Hradoway
Test Kitchen Supervisor	Jessica Pon
Test Kitchen Staff	Lori Bateman
	James Bullock
	Ellen Bunjevac
	Janice Ciesielski
	Sandra Clydesdale
	Pat Yukes
Photographer	Stephe Tate Photo
Assistant Photographer	John McDougall
Photo Editor	Sherri Cunningham
Food Stylists	Allison Dosman
	Leah Duperreault
Prep Kitchen Coordinator	Audrey Smetaniuk
Prep Kitchen Staff	Cathy Anderson
	Dana Royer
Prop Stylists	Paula Bertamini
	Snezana Ferenac
Nutrition Analyst	Margaret Ng, B.Sc., M.A., R.D.

Our special thanks to the following businesses for providing extensive props for photography.

Anchor Hocking Canada	Michael's The Arts And Crafts Store
Bernardin Ltd.	Pfaltzgraff Canada
Browne & Co. Ltd.	Pyrex® Serveware
Canhome Global	Regal Greetings & Gifts
Cherison Enterprises Inc.	Sears Canada
Corningware®	Stokes
Dansk Gifts	The Bay
Linens 'N Things	Wiltshire®

Table of Contents

Foreword

I just love Christmas! It's always been my favourite time of the year. The season to celebrate the spirit of giving, strengthen family ties and renew old friendships. It's a time to be thankful for all we hold dear.

There seems to be something magical about the holiday season that touches us all. And where does this enchantment come from? Well, certainly, there's magic in the wonderful traditions and folklore that surround the season. Many of the customs I grew up with are familiar favourites: decorating the Christmas tree, waiting for Santa Claus and attending church and school concerts. I even remember finding a lump of coal in my stocking on one or two occasions (along with some candy, because Santa was forgiving!).

We love to recreate some of our own favourite childhood memories by passing on these ageless traditions to our children and grandchildren. As you might imagine, in my family, cooking became a special and important tradition begun by my mother. Her energy was limitless as she bustled in the kitchen on Christmas Day, enthusiastically preparing not just one but two feasts for us to enjoy at lunch and dinner. While she cooked, Dad would take the rest of us down to our store to pick out toys, groceries and candy. Once our arms were laden with food and gifts, we drove a few miles out of town to visit a family who couldn't afford to celebrate Christmas. We followed this tradition of goodwill for many years.

Yes, Christmas is a special time to remember. It's also a busy time. Indeed, more often than not, I notice that as the days count down, everyone seems more rushed. There are cards to write, gifts to buy and holiday activities to plan—and of course, family and guests to feed. This book holds a wonderful collection of recipes for any holiday occasion and also features fun crafts, as well as party and decorating ideas the whole family will enjoy. With the turn of every page, you will find interesting ways to help make your Christmas season memorable.

Maybe you would like to spend more time with family. Start a new tradition—make a day out of decorating your tree, your home and even your yard. Invite neighbours, family and friends to join in the celebration and be sure to include some of the ideas from our section on hosting a **Tree-Trimming Party.**

Create wonderful memories for your children with the craft projects in our **Christmas is for Kids** section. Their energy is boundless this time of year, and busy hands can help to pass the time. Christmas only happens once a year, so why not take the time to make a gingerbread log cabin? Children love to create such delicious decorations, and even adults will find it entertaining.

Maybe your idea of the Christmas spirit includes a gesture of goodwill to others. Think about a family food drive or spending an evening knocking on a few neighbourhood doors to say "Merry Christmas." We've included some simple home-cooked gifts you can take along with you in **Gifts for the Host.**

As Christmas Day grows nearer, most of us begin planning the evening feast. If the family has decided to congregate at your home for a traditional Christmas dinner, that probably means you need to cook a turkey. You'll find inspiration in our section **Know Your Turkey** dedicated to this traditional main course—from selecting, to thawing, cooking and carving the perfect turkey. When the feast is over and the guests have left, you'll find inspiration to cook yet again with some delicious and economical leftover recipe ideas.

But Christmas is also a time to explore new ways to celebrate with family and friends, and maybe even create a few traditions of your own. Think about creating your own special tradition by including a few of the global flavours in your Christmas menu. You'll find an excellent selection of recipe ideas in **International Buffet.**

Not everyone celebrates the holiday season in the same way, so we've assembled a variety of menus to suit any get-together from small quiet evenings to larger festive parties.

Finally, the tree is brought down and the last ornament packed away, but the magic lives on in precious Christmas memories—a reminder of the warmth and love that surrounds the season. I'm especially proud to see that some of the special traditions that I grew up with are now those of my children and grandchildren. It's my hope that you will also find something special inside *Home for the Holidays* that will make your own celebrations memorable.

From everyone here at Company's Coming to you and your loved ones, we wish you all the best of the holiday season. Have a Merry Christmas!

Jean Paré

Each recipe has been analyzed using the most up-to-date version of the Canadian Nutrient File from Health Canada, which is based on the United States Department of Agriculture (USDA) Nutrient Data Base. If more that one ingredient is listed (such as "hard margarine or butter"), then the first ingredient is used in the analysis. Where an ingredient reads "sprinkle", "optional", or "for garnish", it is not included as part of the nutrition information.

Margaret Ng, B.Sc. (Hon), M.A.
Registered Dietitian

Tree-Trimming Party

Bring the holiday season to life with an invitation for family
and friends to join in this fun Christmas tradition.
Include a handicraft project in your celebrations
to make it an event to remember!

Cookie Hangers

The idea of cookie hangers has been around for a number of years. Create a theme with certain shapes or colours.
Personalize them with the names of your family and friends (see page 192). Use your imagination!
Or invite a group over to help make your tree hangers—it would be nice to let each guest take one home too.
Have a batch of Butter Cookie Dough (below) and Gingerbread Cookie Dough (below) already chilling.

BUTTER COOKIE DOUGH

Shortening, softened	1/2 cup	125 mL
Butter (not margarine), softened	1/2 cup	125 mL
Finely grated lemon peel	2 tsp.	10 mL
Granulated sugar	2 cups	500 mL
Egg whites (large)	4	4
Container of lemon (or plain) yogurt	4 1/2 oz.	125 mL
All-purpose flour	5 1/2 cups	1.4 L
Baking powder	1 tsp.	5 mL
Baking soda	1 tsp.	5 mL
Salt	1/2 tsp.	2 mL

Large straw, for making hole

Butter Cookie Dough: Beat shortening, butter and lemon peel together in large bowl. Gradually beat in sugar. Add egg whites. Beat well. Beat in yogurt on lowest speed until combined.

Combine next 4 ingredients in separate large bowl. Add to butter mixture. Stir until just moistened and forms a ball. Divide dough into 4 portions. Cover each portion with plastic wrap. Chill for at least 3 hours.

Roll out 1 portion of dough on lightly floured surface to 1/4 inch (6 mm) thickness. Cut out desired shapes using cookie cutters. Arrange on greased cookie sheets. Make hole near top of each cookie, using straw. Repeat with remaining portions of dough. Bake in 350°F (175°C) oven for about 8 minutes until edges are just golden. Let stand on cookie sheets for 5 minutes before removing to wire racks to cool.

GINGERBREAD COOKIE DOUGH

Hard margarine (or butter), softened	3/4 cup	175 mL
Granulated sugar	1/2 cup	125 mL
Brown sugar, packed	1/2 cup	125 mL
Large egg	1	1
Fancy (mild) molasses	1 cup	250 mL
White vinegar	2 tbsp.	30 mL
All-purpose flour	5 cups	1.25 L
Ground ginger	2 tsp.	10 mL
Ground cinnamon	1 tsp.	5 mL
Baking soda	1 1/2 tsp.	7 mL
Salt	3/4 tsp.	4 mL
Ground cloves	1/4 tsp.	1 mL
Ground allspice	1/4 tsp.	1 mL
Ground nutmeg	1/4 tsp.	1 mL

Large straw, for making hole

Gingerbread Cookie Dough: Cream margarine and both sugars together in large bowl. Beat in egg. Add molasses and vinegar. Beat well.

Stir next 8 ingredients together in medium bowl. Add to molasses mixture. Mix until well combined. Divide dough into 4 portions. Cover each portion with plastic wrap. Chill for at least 3 hours.

Roll out 1 portion of dough on lightly floured surface to 1/4 inch (6 mm) thickness. Cut out desired shapes using cookie cutters. Arrange, 1 inch (2.5 cm) apart, on ungreased cookie sheets. Make hole near top of each cookie, using straw. Repeat with remaining portions of dough. Bake in 375°F (190°C) oven for about 10 minutes until firm and edges are browned. Let stand on cookie sheets for 5 minutes before removing to wire racks to cool.

TO DECORATE:
Edible coloured glitter (optional)
Coloured fine sugar (optional)
Royal Icing, page 19 (optional)
Gold and silver dragées (optional)
Ribbon (or string), cut into 8 inch (20 cm) lengths

Sprinkle glitter and/or fine sugar on cookies while still warm. Decorate cooled cookies with icing and dragées. Thread ribbons through holes in cookies. Tie to make loops. Each recipe makes about thirty-six 3 inch (7.5 cm) cookie hangers.

Pictured on page 12/13.

Spiced Apple Potpourri Balls

*Poh-puh-REE can also be used in a bowl
by itself as a room fragrance.*

Medium apples, with peel, cut in half, cored and very thinly sliced	2	2
Lemon juice	1/4 cup	60 mL
Medium oranges, quartered lengthwise, seeded and thinly sliced	3	3
Sprigs of fresh rosemary	5	5
Strips of lemon zest	1/2 cup	125 mL
Whole green cardamom	1/4 cup	60 mL
Whole cloves	1/4 cup	60 mL
Whole allspice	1/4 cup	60 mL
Coarsely chopped cinnamon bark	1 cup	250 mL
Strips of Christmas fabric (optional), for potpourri in a bowl		
Clear acrylic balls (3 inch, 7.5 cm, size), with vent holes	6	6
Ribbons (8 inch, 20 cm, each, in length)	6	6
Christmas decorations, for top of ball	6	6
Glue gun		

Toss apple slices and lemon juice together in medium bowl. Drain. Arrange in single layer on lightly greased baking sheet. Arrange orange slices in single layer on separate lightly greased baking sheet. Bake in 200°F (95°C) oven, with door ajar, for 1 1/2 hours, switching positions of pans at halftime. Turn oven off. Close door. Let stand for several hours until completely dry. Cool.

Spread rosemary and lemon zest on separate ungreasd baking sheet. Bake in 200°F (95°C) oven for 30 minutes. Turn over. Bake, with door slightly ajar, for 8 minutes until dry. Spread on paper towel to cool. Remove and discard stems from rosemary.

Combine next 4 ingredients in large bowl. Add apple, orange, rosemary and lemon zest. Toss. Add fabric only if using potpourri in a bowl for room fragrance. Makes 8 cups (2 L) potpourri.

Place 3/4 cup (175 mL) potpourri in bottom half of 1 acrylic ball. Put ball together. Thread 1 length of ribbon through loop on top. Tie. Glue 1 decoration around loop. Repeat with remaining supplies. Makes 6 balls.

Pictured on page 13.

Cone Ornament

*Decorate these ornaments with colours complementary
to the scheme of other decorations on your tree.*

6 styrofoam balls (2 inch, 5 cm, size)
6 sugar ice cream cones
Small paring knife

Glue gun
6 Christmas decorations

12 ribbons (8 inch, 20 cm, length, each)

Shape styrofoam ball so bottom fits just below rim of cone.

Glue decorations onto round side of ball. Gently set into cone to check placement. Glue shaped end of ball into cone.

Glue 1 end of each of 2 pieces of ribbon to either side of cone. Tie in bow. Repeat with remaining supplies. Makes 6 ornaments.

Pictured on page 12.

Heart And Fruit Garland

*Make more garlands and tie together
to make longer garland.*

Fishing line (3 – 3 1/2 foot, 0.9 – 1.07 m, length)
1 long sewing needle
4 grapevine mini heart wicker decorations
6 kumquats
12 fresh cranberries

Knot fishing line at 1 end. Thread other end through needle. Thread through 1 heart, 1 kumquat, 4 cranberries, 1 kumquat. Repeat pattern, ending with heart. Knot other end of fishing line. Makes one 3 foot (0.9 m) long garland.

Pictured above and on page 12/13.

Candy Icicle Garland

*Make more garlands and tie together
to make longer garland.*

3 tbsp. (50 mL) pure white rolled fondant

Icing (confectioner's) sugar, for dusting
Wooden pick (or small straw)

Hole punch
24 pieces of wrapped candy
3 – 3 1/2 feet (0.9 – 1.07 m) white pearl string
   (1/8 inch, 3 mm, size)

Keep fondant in resealable plastic bag to prevent drying out. Divide into nine 1 tsp. (5 mL) portions. Roll each portion into ball.

To make icicles: Place 1 ball on working surface lightly dusted with icing sugar. Roll into 4 inch (10 cm) rope, making 1 end pointed. Twist rope around wooden pick. Remove pick. Poke hole in thick end of rope using wooden pick. Hole needs to be big enough for pearl string. Lay flat. Repeat with remaining balls of fondant. Let stand for at least 1 day to dry completely.

Punch hole through wrapping at both ends of candy. Knot 1 end of pearl string, making a loop to hang on tree. Thread other end through 1 icicle, then through 3 wrapped candies. Repeat pattern, ending with icicle. Knot other end of pearl string, making a loop to hang on tree. Makes one 3 foot (0.9 m) long garland.

Pictured on page 12/13.

Photo Legend next page:

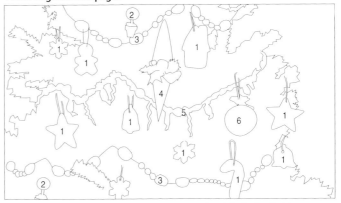

1. Cookie Hangers, page 9
2. Candy Cane Topiary, page 14
3. Heart And Fruit Garland, this page
4. Cone Ornament, page 10

5. Candy Icicle Garland, this page
6. Spiced Apple Potpourri Balls,
   page 10

Candy Cane Topiary

These trendy little decorations are easy to make.

12 styrofoam balls (1 inch, 2.5 cm, size)
6 terra cotta pots (1 inch, 2.5 cm, size)
6 cinnamon sticks (4 inch, 10 cm, each, in length)
6 paper clips
Glue gun

18 miniature candy canes, broken into small pieces
6 ribbons (6 inch, 15 cm, length, each)

Glue 1 styrofoam ball into pot. Gently push 1 cinnamon stick into middle of ball. Push second styrofoam ball onto top of cinnamon stick. Straighten paper clip at 1 end, leaving hook at other end. Push and glue straight end into top of second ball.

Divide and glue candy pieces onto both styrofoam balls. Tie ribbon into bow around rim of pot. Glue to secure. Repeat with remaining supplies. Makes 6 topiaries.

Pictured on page 12.

Sugared Snowflakes

Crispy, sweet and colourful. Hang on the Christmas tree or from the ceiling to enjoy their delicate prettiness, or pile on a plate for munching. They will last for years if handled and packed carefully.

Small flour tortillas (6 inch, 15 cm, size)	10	10
Water		
Foil		
Scissors		
Sharp knife		
Cooking oil	1 tbsp.	15 mL
Coloured fine sugar (available at grocery stores in cake decoration section; wider variety of colours and brands at craft stores)	2 tbsp.	30 mL
Gold thread (or ribbon)		

Wet each tortilla by running hand under water and then rubbing over surface of tortilla. Stack. Tightly cover with foil. Heat in 350°F (175°C) oven for 10 minutes. Keep tortillas covered with damp cloth and keep warm to maintain pliability.

Fold tortilla in half. Fold in half again. Cut out decorative edge along curved side, using scissors. Make small cut-outs along straight edges.

Cut out designs in area between straight edges, using tip of knife. Open tortilla.

Brush both sides of tortilla with cooking oil. Place on baking sheet. Repeat with remaining tortillas, arranging in single layer on baking sheets. Bake on centre rack in 350°F (175°C) oven for 10 to 15 minutes, turning at halftime, until crisp and golden. Sprinkle sugar over tortillas. Tie gold thread through 1 hole of each snowflake. Makes 10 snowflakes.

Christmas is for Kids

Children are so excited during this magical time of year.
Why not focus that energy on some fun crafts
to keep them busy? These projects can be
adapted to suit almost any age group.

Gingerbread Log Cabin

"Deep in the woods you will find a log cabin.
It is the home of the friendly woodcutter and his family..."

BASE
Foamcore board (20 × 24 inches, 50 × 60 cm)
Piece of heavy-duty aluminum foil (22 × 26 inches,
   55 × 65 cm)
Masking tape

LOG CABIN
Piece of brown paper (or other heavier paper),
   18 × 24 inch (45 × 60 cm) size
Scissors
Gingerbread Cookie Dough, page 9
Sharp knife

5 recipes of Royal Icing (white), about 10 cups (2.5 L),
   page 19

ASSORTED CANDY FOR DECORATING CABIN
50 candy sticks, 2 different patterns, for roof
24 square pink candies, for edges of roof
12 round Christmas candies, for peak of roof
15 cinnamon sticks, for corners of house, chimney and
   above door
156 chocolate sticks with mint filling (such as Ovation),
   for walls and chimney
2 miniature candy canes, for inside and outside of door
1 mint patty, placed above door as wreath
1 foil-covered Santa, to stick out chimney

SUGAR POND
Piece of parchment paper
   (10 × 10 inches, 25 × 25 cm)

Granulated sugar	1/2 cup	125 mL
Water	2 tbsp.	30 mL

3 – 4 drops of blue food colouring
20 stone-shaped candies

TREES
3 – 4 drops of green food colouring
2 regular-sized pointed ice cream cones
2 miniature pointed ice cream cones

PATH/FENCE
2 cups (500 mL) hard candies (such as Jolly
   Rancher), coarsely chopped
72 small pretzels

Base: Cover board with foil. Tape underneath to secure.

To enlarge pattern: Mark brown paper into 1 inch
(2.5 cm) squares. Transfer pattern to grid, matching lines
within each square. Cut out patterns.

Log Cabin: Roll out 1/3 of dough on lightly floured surface
to 1/4 inch (6 mm) thickness. Lay front wall pattern on top.
Cut out, using tip of knife. Carefully transfer to lightly
greased baking sheet. Repeat using remaining dough
and patterns. Place smaller patterns on separate lightly
greased baking sheet. Bake in 375°F (190°C) oven for 8 to
10 minutes for larger pieces and 5 to 7 minutes for smaller
pieces until edges are beginning to brown. Let stand on
baking sheets for 10 minutes before removing to wire racks
to cool completely.

LOG CABIN PATTERN

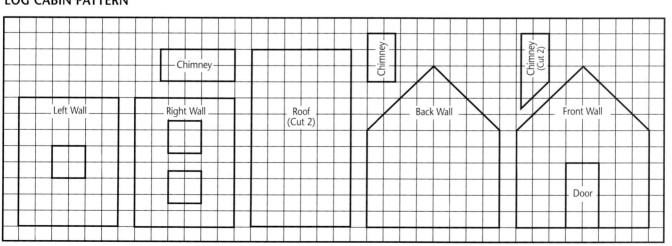

Left Wall — Right Wall — Chimney — Roof (Cut 2) — Chimney — Back Wall — Chimney (Cut 2) — Front Wall — Door

41 inches (103 cm)

14 inches (25 cm)

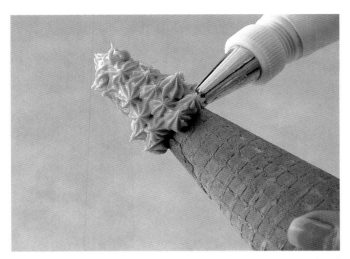

Spread 3 cups (750 mL) icing over base. Keep slightly uneven to look like snow. Cover remaining icing with damp cloth until ready to use. Stand front wall in desired position on base. Generously spread icing up and down side edges. Place side walls in place. Hold for 1 minute to "glue." Add back wall in similar manner. Once all walls are up, allow icing to dry completely before assembling roof. Assemble roof and chimney in same manner, following photo on page 19, allowing icing to dry completely before decorating. This will use about 1 cup (250 mL) icing.

Trees: Colour 1 cup (250 mL) icing with green food colouring. Pipe stars around ice cream cones. "Glue" trees around yard.

Decorate cabin with assorted candy. "Glue" in place with dabs of icing. This will use about 1 1/2 cups (375 mL) icing.

Sugar Pond: Place parchment paper on baking sheet. Put remaining 3 ingredients into small saucepan. Stir. Bring to a boil on medium-high, stirring occasionally. Boil, without stirring, until mixture reaches hard crack stage (300 to 310°F, 150 – 154°C) on candy thermometer or until small amount dropped into very cold water separates into hard, brittle threads. Sugar should not brown. Remove from heat. Pour onto parchment paper to form pond-like circle. Let stand until set. "Glue" pond in front yard, off to one side. "Glue" stone-shaped candies around edge of pond.

Path: Press chopped hard candies into icing from front edge of base in winding pattern leading up to front door. Any remaining candy pieces can be "glued" randomly onto trees.

Fence: "Glue" pretzels around outside of base and along both sides of path, alternating 1 up and 1 down.

Royal Icing

Use to decorate Cookie Hangers, page 9, and to construct the Gingerbread Log Cabin, page 17, and Good-To-Eat Popcorn Tree, page 21.

Icing (confectioner's) sugar	4 1/3 cups	1.1 L
Liquid albumen (such as Simply Egg Whites)	6 1/2 tbsp.	107 mL
Cream of tartar, just a pinch		

Sift icing sugar into medium bowl. Add albumen and cream of tartar. Beat until smooth and thickened. Add more icing sugar, 1 tsp. (5 mL) at a time, if necessary, until desired consistency. Cover with plastic wrap or damp cloth until ready to use. Makes 2 cups (500 mL).

Pipe remaining icing around edge of roof to look like icicles.

Jigsaw Puzzle Cookies

These are lots of fun with just one child or a whole gang. Vary the degree of difficulty depending on the age of the children.

Butter Cookie Dough, page 9

EGG YOLK PAINT

Egg yolks (large)	4	4
Water	1 tsp.	5 mL
Food colouring (paste is best for more vibrant colours)		
Sharp knife		

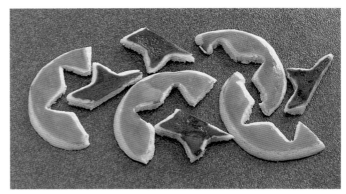

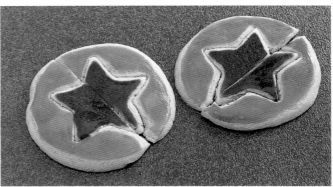

Roll out 3 inch (7.5 cm) ball of dough on lightly floured surface to 1/4 inch (6 mm) thickness. Cut out desired shapes.

Transfer shapes to greased cookie sheet. Cut dough with 1 or 2 cookie cutters.

Egg Yolk Paint: Combine egg yolks and water in small dish using fork. Divide into several very small bowls. Add different food colouring to each bowl. Paint onto dough using fine brush. Use knife to cut shapes into puzzle pieces. Do not separate. Bake in 350°F (175°C) oven for 5 minutes. Remove from oven. Re-cut lines using tip of knife. Bake for 3 to 4 minutes until edges are barely browned. Remove to wire racks to cool completely.

Place cookies on solid work surface. Gently cut or break apart. Mix pieces up and have fun putting cookies back together!

Good-To-Eat Popcorn Tree

Decorate with a variety of different candies. Smaller individual trees can be made for children to decorate.

Stiff paper (16 × 16 inch, 40 × 40 cm, size)
Scotch tape
Waxed paper (16 × 16 inch, 40 × 40 cm, size)

Popped corn (about 1/3 cup, 75 mL, unpopped)	8 cups	2 L
Colourful fruit loops-type cereal	8 cups	2 L
Hard margarine (or butter)	1/2 cup	125 mL
Bag of miniature white marshmallows	14 oz.	400 g
Vanilla	2 tsp.	10 mL

Shoestring licorice, for decorating
Assorted candies, for decorating
Royal Icing, page 19

Fold stiff paper to make cone shape with 8 inch (20 cm) base. Tape along seam. Trim base to sit flat. (Cone should be about 14 inches, 35 cm, high.) Generously grease 1 side of waxed paper. Fold, greased side in, to make cone shape with 8 inch (20 cm) base. Tape along seam. Fit inside stiff paper cone.

Mix popped corn and cereal in extra-large bowl.

Melt margarine in large saucepan on medium-low. Add marshmallows. Stir until coated with margarine. Heat, stirring frequently to prevent scorching, until most marshmallows are melted. Remove from heat.

Add vanilla. Stir until smooth. Pour over popcorn mixture. Stir to coat.

"Glue" licorice and candies on tree using icing.

Spoon popcorn mixture into cone, packing lightly, but well, as you go. Let stand upright on flat surface until cool. Remove stiff paper cone. Peel off waxed paper cone.

Gifts for the Host

You'll be rewarded with smiles of delight
when you hand these tasty morsels to your host.

Nutty Pecan Logs

This impressive homemade candy has a nougat centre coated with caramel and nuts. You'll need strong arms to make these! Easy but pricey.

Jar of marshmallow crème	7 oz.	200 g
Vanilla	1 tsp.	5 mL
Almond flavouring	1/4 tsp.	1 mL
Icing (confectioner's) sugar	3 cups	750 mL
COATING		
Caramels (about 10 oz., 285 g)	40	40
Water	2 tbsp.	30 mL
Finely chopped pecans	1 1/2 cups	375 mL

Mix marshmallow crème, vanilla and almond flavouring in large bowl.

Add icing sugar, 1 cup (250 mL) at a time, until all sugar is absorbed and mixture is very thick and firm. Divide into 6 equal portions. Shape each portion into log, 1 inch (2.5 cm) in diameter. Arrange on ungreased baking sheets. Set in freezer.

Coating: Combine caramels and water in heavy medium saucepan. Heat on medium-low, stirring often, until smooth. Roll each log in caramel mixture until coated.

Immediately roll each log in pecans. Cover with plastic wrap or foil. Store in airtight container at room temperature for up to 4 weeks. For longer storage, cover with plastic wrap and freeze. Makes 6 logs, each cutting into about 10 slices, for a total of 60 slices.

1 slice: 74 Calories; 2.5 g Total Fat; 13 mg Sodium; 1 g Protein; 13 g Carbohydrate; trace Dietary Fibre

Pictured on page 24/25.

Test your candy thermometer before each use. Bring cold water to a boil. Candy thermometer should read 212°F (100°C) at sea level. Adjust recipe temperature up or down based on test results. For example, if your thermometer reads 206°F (97°C), subtract 6°F (43°C) from each temperature called for in recipe.

Candied Nuts

Nuts with sugar and spice in a thin fudge coating.

Granulated sugar	1 cup	250 mL
Milk	6 tbsp.	100 mL
Ground cinnamon	1 tsp.	5 mL
Mixed nuts (toasted, optional)	3 cups	750 mL
Vanilla	1/2 tsp.	2 mL

Combine sugar, milk and cinnamon in small heavy saucepan. Heat and stir until boiling. Cook on medium, without stirring, until mixture reaches firm ball stage (242° to 248°F, 117° to 120°C) on candy thermometer or until small amount dropped into very cold water forms a firm but pliable ball.

Stir nuts and vanilla into sugar mixture. Pour onto buttered baking sheet. Separate nuts using fork. Serve warm or cool. Store in airtight container for up to 1 week at room temperature. For longer storage, cover with plastic wrap and freeze. Makes 4 1/2 cups (1.1 L).

1/4 cup (60 mL): 184 Calories; 12 g Total Fat; 5 mg Sodium; 4 g Protein; 17 g Carbohydrate; 1 g Dietary Fibre

Pictured on page 25.

Photo Legend next page:

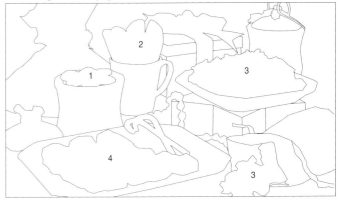

1. Chocolate-Coated Mint Patties, page 26
2. Mandarin Chocolate Biscotti, page 26
3. Candied Nuts, above
4. Nutty Pecan Logs, this page

Season's Greetings

~ Peace on Earth Good will

Chocolate-Coated Mint Patties

*Just as good as the store-bought patties,
but better because you made them at home!*

All-purpose flour	3 1/2 tbsp.	57 mL
Milk	6 tbsp.	100 mL
Icing (confectioner's) sugar	3 cups	750 mL
Peppermint flavouring	3/4 tsp.	4 mL
Milk (or dark) chocolate melting wafers (about 9 oz., 255 g)	1 1/3 cups	325 mL

Mix flour and milk in small saucepan until smooth. Heat and stir on medium until boiling and very thick. Remove from heat.

Add icing sugar and peppermint flavouring. Mix well. Let stand for 5 minutes. Turn out onto surface dusted with icing sugar. Knead until smooth, adding more icing sugar as necessary, until no longer sticky. Divide into 2 equal portions. Shape each portion into log, 1 inch (2.5 cm) in diameter. Cover with plastic wrap. Let stand at room temperature overnight. Cut into 1/4 inch (6 mm) slices, re-shaping as necessary. Place on ungreased baking sheets. Let stand, uncovered, for about 1 hour, turning at halftime, until dry.

Heat chocolate in small glass bowl over simmering water in small saucepan, stirring occasionally, until just melted. Dip patties into chocolate (see Tip, below), allowing excess to drip back into bowl. Place on foil or waxed paper-lined baking sheets. Make small swirl on top while chocolate is still soft if desired. Let stand at room temperature until firm. Makes about 5 dozen mint patties.

1 mint patty: 49 Calories; 1.3 g Total Fat; 4 mg Sodium; trace Protein; 9 g Carbohydrate; trace Dietary Fibre

Pictured on page 24.

For best results when dipping candies into chocolate, be sure the candy is at room temperature. Place candy on a fork or other similar utensil and lower candy into chocolate to cover completely. Lift, allowing excess chocolate to drip back into bowl.

Mandarin Chocolate Biscotti

Little bits of chocolate and orange peel are visible in these great dunkers in hot coffee.

Hard margarine (or butter), softened	1/2 cup	125 mL
Granulated sugar	1 cup	250 mL
Large eggs	3	3
Egg yolk (large)	1	1
Vanilla	1 tsp.	5 mL
All-purpose flour	4 cups	1 L
Baking powder	2 1/2 tsp.	12 mL
Salt	1/4 tsp.	1 mL
Large seedless mandarin oranges, peel reserved	2	2
Finely chopped reserved mandarin orange peel, white pith scraped off	1 1/2 tbsp.	25 mL
Milk chocolate candy bar, coarsely chopped (about 2/3 cup, 150 mL)	1	1
Egg white (large)	1	1
Water	1 tsp.	5 mL
Granulated sugar	1 tbsp.	15 mL

Cream margarine and first amount of sugar together in large bowl. Beat in eggs, egg yolk and vanilla.

Combine flour, baking powder and salt in medium bowl. Stir into egg mixture until thoroughly combined.

Separate oranges into sections. Cut each section into 3 or 4 pieces, reserving any juice. You should have about 1 cup (250 mL) orange pieces with juice. Mix into dough. Add orange peel and chocolate. Mix well. Turn dough out onto well-floured surface. Divide into 2 equal portions. Shape each portion into oval-shaped log, 1 inch (2.5 cm) in diameter and 11 inches (28 cm) long. Arrange 1 1/2 to 2 inches (3.8 to 5 cm) apart on large ungreased baking sheet.

Combine egg white and water in small bowl. Brush over logs. Sprinkle second amount of sugar over top. Bake in 375°F (190°C) oven for 30 minutes until lightly browned. Let stand on baking sheet for 1 hour until cool. Diagonally cut each log into 1/2 inch (12 mm) slices. Lay slices flat on same baking sheet. Bake in 325°F (160°C) oven for 30 to 35 minutes, turning slices over at halftime, until crisp. Remove to wire racks to cool completely. Makes about 32 biscotti.

1 biscotti: 144 Calories; 4.8 g Total Fat; 94 mg Sodium; 3 g Protein; 23 g Carbohydrate; 1 g Dietary Fibre

Pictured on page 24.

Cranberry Mango Chutney

Deep red colour and chunky texture to this beautiful and festive gift. Serve with Cranberry Scones, page 64.

Can of sliced mango in syrup, chopped	14 oz.	398 mL
Bag of fresh (or frozen, thawed) cranberries	12 oz.	340 g
Chopped red pepper	1 cup	250 mL
Chopped onion	1 cup	250 mL
Brown sugar, packed	2/3 cup	150 mL
Dark raisins	1/2 cup	125 mL
Apple cider vinegar	1/4 cup	60 mL
Grated gingerroot (or 3/4 tsp., 4 mL, ground ginger)	1 tbsp.	15 mL
Yellow mustard seed	1 tsp.	5 mL
Dried crushed chilies	3/4 tsp.	4 mL
Ground coriander	1/2 tsp.	2 mL
Salt	1 tsp.	5 mL
Freshly ground pepper	1/4 tsp.	1 mL
Strip of lemon peel (4 inch, 10 cm, length)	1	1

Combine all 14 ingredients in large pot or Dutch oven. Bring to a boil on medium. Reduce heat to medium-low. Simmer, uncovered, for 50 to 60 minutes until thickened. Remove and discard lemon peel. Store in refrigerator for up to 4 weeks. Makes about 4 cups (1 L).

2 tbsp. (30 mL): 40 Calories; 0.1 g Total Fat; 75 mg Sodium; trace Protein; 10 g Carbohydrate; 1 g Dietary Fibre

Pictured on this page and on page 67.

Quick Rumtopf

Instead of taking months to make using fresh fruit, this only takes one week. Delicious to serve over ice cream or cake.

Can of sliced peaches in syrup, drained and syrup reserved, diced	14 oz.	398 mL
Can of sliced mango in syrup, drained and syrup reserved, diced	14 oz.	398 mL
Cans of mandarin orange segments (10 oz., 284 mL, each), drained and juice reserved	2	2
Can of pineapple tidbits, drained and juice reserved	19 oz.	540 mL
Dried cherries (see Note)	2 cups	500 mL
Amber rum	1 cup	250 mL
Reserved syrup and fruit juice	3 3/4 cups	925 mL
Granulated sugar	2 cups	500 mL

Combine peach, mango, orange, pineapple and cherries in large bowl. Spoon into large pitcher.

Pour rum over fruit mixture.

Stir reserved syrup, reserved fruit juice and sugar together in large saucepan. Heat, stirring occasionally, until boiling. Gently boil, uncovered, for 10 minutes. Cool for 1 hour. Pour over fruit mixture. Cover. Store in refrigerator for 1 week to blend flavours and up to 5 weeks. Makes about 9 cups (2.25 L).

1/2 cup (125 mL): 222 Calories; 0.7 g Total Fat; 4 mg Sodium; 1 g Protein; 48 g Carbohydrate; 2 g Dietary Fibre

Pictured below.

Note: Don't be disappointed when cherries and other fruit lose their colour. They still lend their flavour to the finished product.

Centre: Quick Rumtopf, this page
Bottom Left: Cranberry Mango Chutney, this page

Italian Panettone

Pronounced pan-uh-TOH-nee. Rich, fruit-filled and pine nut-studded sweet bread. Although traditionally done in a round dome shape, this can be baked in coffee cans or deep round pans. Very festive when glazed and decorated.

Milk	2 cups	500 mL
Butter (not margarine), cut into chunks	1/2 cup	125 mL
Large eggs	4	4
Granulated sugar	2/3 cup	150 mL
Finely grated orange peel	2 tsp.	10 mL
Aniseed, crushed (optional)	1 1/2 tsp.	7 mL
Salt	1 tsp.	5 mL
All-purpose flour	2 cups	500 mL
Instant yeast	1 tbsp.	15 mL
All-purpose flour	4 1/2–5 cups	1.1–1.25 L
Mixed glazed fruit, diced	2/3 cup	150 mL
Sultana raisins	1/2 cup	125 mL
Pine nuts, toasted (see Tip, page 100)	1/3 cup	75 mL
Sliced almonds, toasted (see Tip, page 100)	1/3 cup	75 mL
Large egg	1	1
Milk	1 tsp.	5 mL
GLAZE (optional)		
Lemon juice	1 tbsp.	15 mL
Icing (confectioner's) sugar	1/2–2/3 cup	125–150 mL

Red and/or green glazed cherries, for garnish
Almonds, for garnish

Heat first amount of milk and butter in small saucepan until butter is melted and mixture is hot. Remove from heat.

Beat first amount of eggs, granulated sugar, orange peel, aniseed and salt together in large bowl. Slowly whisk in hot milk mixture. Temperature of egg mixture should feel very warm but not hot.

Combine first amount of flour and yeast in small bowl. Mix into egg mixture until smooth.

Add second amount of flour, 1 cup (250 mL) at a time, stirring well and working in with hands, until sticky ball forms. Turn out onto floured surface. Knead dough, adding small amounts of remaining flour as necessary, until soft dough forms. Place dough in greased bowl, turning once to grease top. Cover with greased waxed paper and tea towel. Let stand in oven with light on and door closed for about 1 hour until doubled in bulk. Punch dough down. Turn out onto greased surface. Press or roll dough out to large rectangle.

Sprinkle with mixed fruit, raisins, pine nuts and almonds. Roll up, jelly roll-style. Knead, greasing work surface with cooking oil as dough becomes tacky, until fruit and nuts are well distributed and dough is elastic and no longer sticky. Divide into 2 portions. Form each portion into round shape. Place on greased baking sheet. Cover with greased waxed paper and tea towels. Let stand in oven with light on and door closed for about 45 minutes until doubled in size.

Beat second amounts of egg and milk together in small cup using fork. Brush over tops of loaves. Bake in 350°F (175°C) oven for 45 to 50 minutes until golden brown and hollow sounding when tapped.

Glaze: Measure lemon juice into small bowl. Stir in icing sugar, 1 tbsp. (15 mL) at a time, adding more icing sugar or lemon juice, until barely pourable consistency. Drizzle over top centre of panettone, allowing some to run down sides.

Garnish with cherries and almonds when glaze has stopped moving but before becoming dry. Makes 2 loaves, each cutting into about 20 slices, for a total of about 40 slices.

1 slice: 158 Calories; 4.6 g Total Fat; 102 mg Sodium; 4 g Protein; 25 g Carbohydrate; 1 g Dietary Fibre

Pictured on page 29.

Variation: Form each portion into balls. Put into well-greased 2 1/4 lb. (1 kg) coffee can.

Italian Panettone, this page

Know Your Turkey

A golden turkey, roasted to tender perfection, is an
established tradition at many Yuletide feasts. Here are
a few guidelines on how to truss, thaw, cook and carve
the perfect Christmas turkey. Recipes for stuffing
and next-day turkey delights are included.

Trussing the Turkey

Over the years, cooks have developed various ways to truss (or tie up) the turkey so that the legs and wings stay tucked into the sides, preventing overcooking and drying out. Is there a right way and a wrong way? We don't believe so, but, if you are going to carve your turkey at the table (see page 33), we'd like to recommend this method. Place cleaned bird on cutting board. Loosely stuff cavities in body and neck with stuffing if desired.

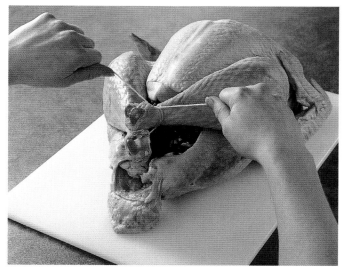

Loop centre of butcher's string (18 inches, 45 cm, long) 1 1/2 times around each leg. Bring string together and tie to secure.

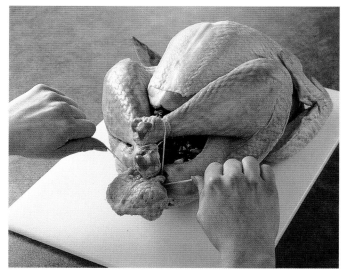

Bring ends down under tail. Tie to secure. Trim excess string.

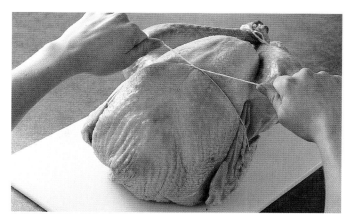

Turn turkey around. Work separate piece of string (30 inches, 75 cm, long) under turkey. Bring ends of string up and over turkey. Tie across breast to secure wings. Trim any excess string.

TURKEY COOKING GUIDE			
Oven temperature at 350°F (175°C)			
Weight		Unstuffed	Stuffed
6 – 8 lbs.	2.7 – 3.5 kg	2 1/4 – 3 1/4 hrs.	3 – 3 1/2 hrs.
8 – 10 lbs.	3.5 – 4.5 kg	2 3/4 – 3 hrs.	3 1/4 – 3 1/2 hrs.
10 – 12 lbs.	4.5 – 5.4 kg	3 – 3 1/2 hrs.	3 3/4 – 4 1/2 hrs.
12 – 16 lbs.	5.4 – 7 kg	3 3/4 – 4 3/4 hrs.	4 – 5 1/4 hrs.
16 – 22 lbs.	7 – 10 kg	4 1/2 – 5 1/4 hrs.	5 – 6 1/2 hrs.

❋ For unstuffed turkey — Use a meat thermometer to ensure that breast meat reaches an internal temperature of 185°F (85°C) and thigh meat reaches an internal temperature of 170°F (77°C).

❋ For stuffed turkey — Use a meat thermometer to ensure that breast meat reaches an internal temperature of 185°F (85°C) and thigh meat reaches an internal temperature of 180°F (82°C).

❋ If turkey is stuffed, temperature of stuffing should reach 165°F (74°C).

❋ Juices should run clear, leg should move easily and no pink should remain in meat.

❋ Cooking time can be affected by the starting temperature of the turkey, size of the turkey, size of oven, type of roasting pan, covered or uncovered, lid or foil cover, etc. but the times noted above should be a reasonable guideline. A fresh turkey that has never been frozen will take a bit longer than a frozen, thawed turkey. A meat thermometer reading is the best assurance of doneness.

TO STUFF OR NOT TO STUFF:

The question of whether or not to stuff the turkey is often asked these days. Food safety information indicates that the stuffing must be put into the cavity of the turkey just before cooking and removed immediately after the turkey is taken from the oven. We have provided two options: Wild Rice And Herb Stuffing, below, that is cooked separately in a casserole dish in the oven or can be cooked inside the cavity of the turkey, and Spicy Sausage And Bread Stuffing, page 149, that is cooked in a slow cooker.

Wild Rice And Herb Stuffing

Chewy with great nutty flavour.
Wonderful aroma of sage and other herbs.

Cans of condensed chicken broth (10 oz., 284 mL, each)	2	2
Water	2 cups	500 mL
Wild rice	1 1/2 cups	375 mL
Chopped onion	1 cup	250 mL
Chopped celery	1 cup	250 mL
Diced red pepper	2/3 cup	150 mL
Diced fresh mushrooms	1 cup	250 mL
Hard margarine (or butter)	1/4 cup	60 mL
Coarse dry bread crumbs	1 cup	250 mL
Pine nuts, chopped	1/2 cup	125 mL
Chopped fresh parsley (or 1 1/2 tsp., 7 mL, flakes)	2 tbsp.	30 mL
Chopped fresh mint leaves (or 1 1/2 tsp., 7 mL, dried)	2 tbsp.	30 mL
Chopped fresh thyme (or 1 1/2 tsp., 7 mL, dried)	2 tbsp.	30 mL
Chopped fresh sage (or 3/4 tsp., 4 mL, dried)	1 tbsp.	15 mL
Salt	1/2 tsp.	2 mL
Pepper	1/4 tsp.	1 mL

Bring broth and water to a boil in large saucepan.

Add rice. Stir. Cover. Bring to a boil on medium. Reduce heat to medium-low. Simmer for about 45 minutes until rice has just popped but is still slightly firm. Turn into large bowl.

Sauté onion, celery, red pepper and mushrooms in margarine in large frying pan for about 5 minutes until onion is soft.

Add remaining 8 ingredients. Stir until well combined. Add to rice. Stir. Transfer stuffing to well-greased 3 quart (3 L) baking dish. Cover. Bake in 350°F (175°C) oven for 30 to 60 minutes until heated through. Makes 8 cups (2 L).

1/2 cup (125 mL): 160 Calories; 6.7 g Total Fat; 416 mg Sodium; 7 g Protein; 20 g Carbohydrate; 2 g Dietary Fibre

Pictured on front cover and on this page.

Carving the Turkey

EQUIPMENT:
❋ A good quality carving knife is essential. An electric knife works well, but does not have the precision or control that a carving knife will have when guided by your hand. Be sure that the blade is sharp.

❋ Having a carving fork in the opposite hand helps to steady the turkey as you carve and to lift slices to serving platter.

❋ Always work on a clean cutting board, preferably one that has grooves to catch drippings.

BEFORE CARVING:
❋ Remove turkey from oven and roasting pan and let stand on cutting board for 10 to 15 minutes before carving.

❋ If turkey is stuffed, remove stuffing immediately and put into serving bowl after turkey is taken from oven. Keep warm.

CARVING AT THE TABLE:

Remove turkey from cutting board to platter. Remove strings. Have small cutting board at table beside platter to cut leg/thigh meat. Depending on number of guests, some people carve only from one side of turkey first and, if necessary, turn platter and work from other side.

Slice through skin, between leg and body, down to leg joint. Pull leg slightly away from body. Cut through joint closest to body. Cut meat from thigh and leg, making slices roughly parallel to bone. Remove tough tendons from leg meat.

Starting at 1 end of breast, cut off thin slices of meat. A slightly diagonal slant to the knife will give larger slices. Once you have sliced down to the bone, change angle of cut to remove more meat further down breast.

CARVING IN THE KITCHEN:

Follow same steps for removing and slicing leg.

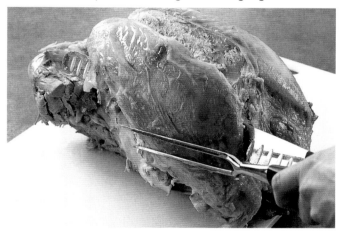

For breast meat, slice down along breastbone following the rib cage. Remove the entire breast from the body of the turkey and place on cutting board.

Make horizontal cut just above wing, slicing through just to bone of rib cage.

Slice breast across the grain into thin slices. Place on platter.

Turkey Fricassee

An elegant way to serve leftover turkey!
Serve in puff pastry patty shells.

Finely chopped onion	1/2 cup	125 mL
Finely chopped celery	1/2 cup	125 mL
Garlic cloves, minced (or 1/2 tsp., 2 mL, powder)	2	2
Hard margarine (or butter)	3 tbsp.	50 mL
All-purpose flour	2 tbsp.	30 mL
Milk	1 1/4 cups	300 mL
Chopped cooked turkey	1 1/2 cups	375 mL
Frozen peas	1 cup	250 mL
Jar of pimiento, drained and finely diced	2 oz.	57 mL
Chicken bouillon powder	2 tsp.	10 mL
Parsley flakes	1 1/2 tsp.	7 mL
Salt	1/2 tsp.	2 mL
Pepper	1/4 – 1/2 tsp.	1 – 2 mL

Sauté onion, celery and garlic in margarine in large saucepan until onion is soft.

Sprinkle flour over onion mixture. Stir well. Add milk. Heat and stir until boiling and thickened.

Add next 7 ingredients. Stir. Bring to a boil. Reduce heat. Simmer, uncovered, for about 3 minutes, stirring often, until peas are tender. Makes 2 3/4 cups (675 mL).

1/4 cup (60 mL): 174 Calories; 7.7 g Total Fat; 227 mg Sodium; 15 g Protein; 11 g Carbohydrate; 2 g Dietary Fibre

Pictured on page 35.

Honey Mustard Turkey Salad

A crunchy and hearty salad with a sweet dressing.

HONEY MUSTARD DRESSING

Finely chopped red onion	1/4 cup	60 mL
Red wine vinegar	1/4 cup	60 mL
Lemon juice	1/4 cup	60 mL
Dijon mustard	1/4 cup	60 mL
Liquid honey	1/4 cup	60 mL
Cooking oil	2 tbsp.	30 mL
Dill weed	1 tsp.	5 mL
Salt	1/2 tsp.	2 mL
Pepper	1/4 tsp.	1 mL
Chopped cooked turkey	4 cups	1 L
Shredded savoy cabbage	1 1/2 cups	375 mL
Sliced celery	1 cup	250 mL
Seedless red grapes, halved	25	25
Baby greens lettuce	3 1/2 cups	875 mL

Small bunches of red grapes, for garnish

Honey Mustard Dressing: Stir first 9 ingredients together in small bowl. Makes 1 1/4 cups (300 mL) dressing.

Combine turkey, cabbage, celery and halved grapes in large bowl. Drizzle dressing over salad. Toss to coat.

Arrange lettuce on serving platter or on individual salad plates. Top with turkey mixture.

Garnish with grape bunches. Makes 7 cups (1.75 L).

1 cup (250 mL): 246 Calories; 7.1 g Total Fat; 382 mg Sodium; 27 g Protein; 20 g Carbohydrate; 1 g Dietary Fibre

Pictured on page 35.

Top Right: Turkey Mixed Bean Soup, page 161
Centre & Centre Left: Turkey Fricassee, this page
Top Left & Bottom Right: Honey Mustard Turkey Salad, above

Top Left: Turkey Cristo Sandwich, page 161   Centre: Hot Turkey Sandwich, below   Top Right: Fresh Tomato Relish, page 93

Hot Turkey Sandwich

A meal unto itself—just add some vegetables or a salad.
Toast the bread for a crispier sandwich.

Cold leftover gravy	2 tbsp.	30 mL
White bread slice	1	1
Leftover Spicy Sausage And Bread Stuffing, page 149 (or other leftover stuffing)	3 tbsp.	50 mL
Sliced cooked turkey, to cover	2 oz.	57 g
Whole cranberry sauce, mashed	2 tbsp.	30 mL
White bread slice	1	1
Leftover gravy, thinned with a little hot water, if necessary	1/4 cup	60 mL
Pepper, sprinkle		

Spread first amount of gravy over first bread slice. Place on microwave-safe plate.

Scatter stuffing over gravy. Lay turkey over stuffing. Carefully spread cranberry sauce over turkey. Cover. Microwave on medium (50%) for 2 minutes, turning plate at halftime if microwave doesn't have turntable.

Lay second bread slice over cranberry sauce. Pour second amount of gravy over bread slice. Microwave, uncovered, on medium (50%) for 1 minute. Sprinkle pepper over top. Let stand for 1 minute. Makes 1 sandwich.

1 sandwich: 409 Calories; 11.3 g Total Fat; 1045 mg Sodium; 26 g Protein; 50 g Carbohydrate; 2 g Dietary Fibre

Pictured above.

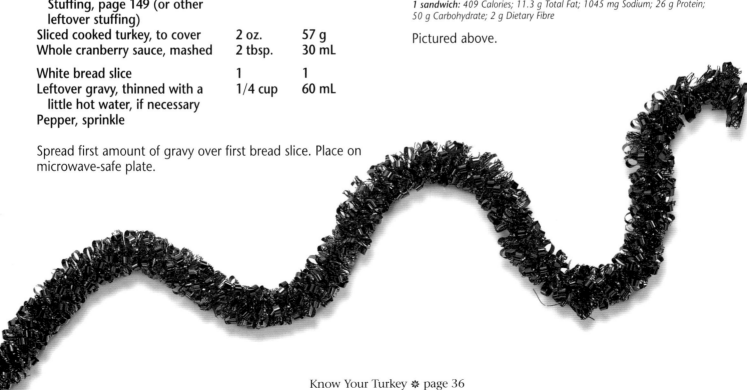

Turkey Salad Wraps, below

Turkey Salad Wraps

A good way to use all the bits of turkey that seem to get bypassed for larger pieces.

Whole cranberry sauce	2/3 cup	150 mL
Salad dressing (or mayonnaise)	1/3 cup	75 mL
Large spinach (or flour) tortillas (about 10 inches, 25 cm), see Tip, this page	5	5
Large iceberg lettuce leaves	5	5
Slivered (or diced) cooked turkey	2 cups	500 mL
Medium tomato, seeded and diced	1	1
Ground rosemary	1/8 tsp.	0.5 mL
Dried sweet basil, crushed	1/8 tsp.	0.5 mL
Salt	1/4 tsp.	1 mL
Pepper, sprinkle		

Combine cranberry sauce and salad dressing in small bowl. Spread about 3 tbsp. (50 mL) down centre of each tortilla.

Lay 1 lettuce leaf over top of each cranberry mixture.

Toss remaining 6 ingredients together in medium bowl. Spoon about 1/2 cup (125 mL) down centre of each lettuce leaf. Fold 1 end of tortilla over filling and fold in sides, leaving top end open. Makes 5 wraps.

1 wrap: 375 Calories; 12.8 g Total Fat; 478 mg Sodium; 22 g Protein; 42 g Carbohydrate; 2 g Dietary Fibre

Pictured above.

To make folding tortillas easier, sprinkle some water onto each tortilla. Stack damp tortillas on foil. Enclose. Heat in 350°F (175°C) oven for about 20 minutes until warm or microwave tortillas individually, unwrapped, on high (100%) for 20 seconds.

Menu Suggestions

Large or small, mellow or festive, the Christmas season plays host

to a medley of social activities. These menu ideas are just some

of the ways you can mix and match recipes for

any occasion—the possibilities are endless.

Family Lunch

Spinach And Olive Braid, page 76

Burger Strata, page 80

Cream Of Mushroom Soup, page 156

Greek Pea Salad, page 138

Spice Coffee Cake, page 77

Late Night Supper

Rich Chicken Stew, page 127

Sautéed Sprouts, page 146

Eggnog Chantilly, page 103

or

Blackened Chicken Caesar Salad, page 138

Orange Couscous With Sultanas, page 150

Eggnog Fondue, page 102

Holiday Open House

Refreshing Cranberry Tonic, page 57

Hot Tea Wassail, page 60

Feta Spinach Mushroom Caps, page 43

Crab Wrap 'N' Roll, page 44

Candied Nuts, page 23

Chocolate-Coated Mint Patties, page 26

Butter Crunch, page 83

Chocolate Almond Cookies, page 84

Butterscotch Cookies, page 88

Caramel Nut Squares, page 91

Italian Panettone, page 28

Stuffed Ham Casserole, page 126

In From Outdoors

By-The-Fire Hot Chocolate, page 59

Warm Spiced Cranberry, page 60

Scotch Broth, page 154

Sweet Potato Biscuits, page 65

Rice Pudding, page 174

Celebrate-The-Holidays Teen Party

Fruit Slush, page 58

Spicy Sticky-Finger Wings, page 50

Holiday Whirls, page 50

Creamed Tahini Dip, page 54
(with fresh vegetables)

Butter Crunch, page 83

Butterscotch Cookies, page 88

Peanut Butter Bites, page 88

Toasted Popcorn Snack, page 91

Romantic Dinner

Two-Toned Buns, page 65

Shrimp Marinara Sauce, page 118

Ginger Honey-Glazed Beans, page 146

Eggnog Chantilly, page 103

Finger Food Party

Rush Eggnog, page 56

Maple And Rye Gravlax, page 48

Old-Fashioned Bran Bread, page 71

Honey Mustard Sauce, page 92

Mustard Ranch Drumettes, page 50

Cocktail Shrimp-On-A-Pineapple, page 48

Grape Cheese Wreath, page 51

Gorgonzola Cheese Dip, page 54
(with fresh vegetables)

Spiced Plum Sauce, page 55

Spring Rolls, page 167

Toasted Popcorn Snack, 91

Kid's Sleepover Brunch

Refreshing Cranberry Tonic, page 57

Doctored Oatmeal Porridge, page 75

The Big Breakfast, page 81

Two-Toned Buns, page 65

Snowed-In Supper

Caramel Cider Tea, page 59

Holiday Whirls, page 50

Barley And Rice Pilaf, page 141

Paprika Stew With Zucchini Biscuits, page 119

Butterscotch Cookies, page 88

Pear And Ginger Pie, page 130

Trim-The-Tree Treats

Rush Eggnog, page 56

Fruit Slush, page 58

Ricotta And Jalapeño Tarts, page 44

Crab Wrap 'N' Roll, page 44

Mustard Ranch Drumettes, page 50

Grasshopper Squares, page 86

Peanut Butter Bites, page 88

Ragged Chocolate Drops, page 89

Norwegiean Almond Pastry, page 174

Progressive Supper

Organize a holiday progressive supper with friends or neighbours. Start with cocktails and appetizers at the first house, salad and bread at the second stop, the main course at the next, and dessert and coffee at the last. It's an easy way to share the cooking, plus you get to see everyone's holiday decorations!

Hot Tea Wassail, page 60

Spicy Sticky-Finger Wings, page 50

Mexican Christmas Salad, page 168

Christmas Bread, page 72

Cajun Chicken, page 111

Pineapple Fluff Cake, page 104

Quiet Christmas Eve

Refreshing Cranberry Tonic, page 57

Cornmeal Muffins, page 64

Creamy Seafood Sauce, page 117

Rice Pudding, page 174

Make-Ahead Christmas Morning

Rush Eggnog, page 56

Peanut Butter Dip, page 54
(with fresh fruit)

Breakfast Trifle, page 73

Blueberry Streusel French Toast, page 77

Cranberry Scones, page 64

Christmas Day Wrap-Up

Hot Mushroom Dip, page 51

Oriental Candied Pork, page 45

Horseradish Dipping Sauce, page 54

Rum And Butter Balls, page 84

Piña Colada Squares, page 82

Chocolate Raspberry Biscotti, page 106
(with coffee)

New Year's Eve Dinner

Candy Cane Bread, page 70

Cranberry Scones, page 64

Slaw Special, page 137

Stuffed Turkey Breast, page 121

Hot Carrot Ring, page 146

Broccoli With Lemon Cheese Sauce, page 142

Varenyky With Onion Butter, page 170

Pumpkin Chiffon Pie, page 130

Recipes

Celebrate the holiday season in style
with this festive collection of recipes.
Create some imaginative showpieces, such as the
Cocktail Shrimp-On-A-Pineapple, page 48,
or Candy Cane Bread, page 70, and uncover
some ideas for dressing up buffet trays
and punch bowls.

Appetizers

Feta Spinach Mushroom Caps

*A very nice one-bite appetizer. Have them on hand
in the freezer for unexpected company.
Serve on a bed of shredded carrots.*

Finely chopped onion	1/2 cup	125 mL
Garlic clove, minced (or 1/4 tsp., 1 mL, powder), optional	1	1
Hard margarine (or butter)	2 tsp.	10 mL
Box of frozen spinach, thawed, squeezed dry and finely chopped	10 oz.	300 g
Seasoned salt	1 tsp.	5 mL
Pepper, heavy sprinkle		
Crumbled feta cheese	1 cup	250 mL
Parsley flakes	1 tsp.	5 mL
Dried sweet basil	1/4 tsp.	1 mL
Dried whole oregano	1/4 tsp.	1 mL
Fresh medium mushrooms (about 1 lb., 454 g), cleaned and stems removed	40	40

Sauté onion and garlic in margarine in frying pan for about
3 minutes until onion is soft.

Add spinach, seasoned salt and pepper. Sauté for 3 to
4 minutes until spinach is tender. Drain. Turn into medium
bowl. Cool completely.

Add cheese, parsley flakes, basil and oregano. Stir.

Pack about 2 tsp. (10 mL) filling in each mushroom cap.
Arrange on ungreased baking sheet. Bake, uncovered, in
450°F (230°C) oven for 6 to 8 minutes until hot. To cook
from frozen, bake for about 10 minutes until heated
through. Makes 40 mushroom caps.

*1 mushroom cap: 19 Calories; 1.2 g Total Fat; 82 mg Sodium; 1 g Protein;
1 g Carbohydrate; trace Dietary Fibre*

Pictured on page 47.

Whole heated or partially cooked mushrooms will
unavoidably "weep" a bit, so arrange on a bed
of lettuce or shredded carrot to make a more attractive
presentation for company.

Outer Ring: Ricotta And Jalapeño Tarts, below

Centre: Crab Wrap 'N' Roll, below

Ricotta And Jalapeño Tarts

A delicious little tart that invites your guests to stick around for the rest of the meal.

Jalapeño pepper, seeded and diced (see Note)	1	1
Sliced green onion	2 tbsp.	30 mL
Finely grated carrot	2 tbsp.	30 mL
Cooking oil	2 tsp.	10 mL
Salt	1/2 tsp.	2 mL
Dried whole oregano, crushed	1/4 tsp.	1 mL
Ricotta cheese	1 cup	250 mL
Large egg, fork-beaten	1	1
Unbaked mini-tart shells (or line small tart pans with your own pastry)	20	20

Sauté jalapeño pepper, green onion and carrot in cooking oil in frying pan for 2 to 3 minutes until soft.

Stir in salt and oregano. Cool.

Stir in cheese and egg. Divide among tart shells. Bake in 400°F (205°C) oven for 12 to 15 minutes until pastry is golden and filling is set. Serve warm. Makes 20 tarts.

1 tart: 75 Calories; 5.1 g Total Fat; 122 mg Sodium; 2 g Protein; 5 g Carbohydrate; trace Dietary Fibre

Pictured above.

Note: Wear gloves when chopping jalapeño peppers and avoid touching your eyes.

Crab Wrap 'N' Roll

These pretty spirals are a confetti of colours.

Can of crabmeat, drained, cartilage removed, flaked	4 1/4 oz.	120 g
Green onion, thinly sliced	1	1
Small roma (plum) tomato, seeded, finely diced and drained	1	1
Finely diced red pepper	2 tbsp.	30 mL
Cream cheese, softened	2 tbsp.	30 mL
Mayonnaise (not salad dressing)	2 tsp.	10 mL
Creamed horseradish	1/2 tsp.	2 mL
Celery seed	1/8 tsp.	0.5 mL
Salt, sprinkle		
Pepper, sprinkle		
Large red and/or green flour tortillas (about 10 inches, 25 cm), see Tip, page 37	2	2

Combine first 10 ingredients in medium bowl. Makes 1 1/3 cups (325 mL) filling.

Spread 1/2 of filling over each tortilla to within 1/2 inch (12 mm) of edge. Roll up tightly. Cover with plastic wrap. Twist ends to seal well. Chill overnight. Trim and discard 1 inch (2.5 cm) from each end. Cut each roll into 1 inch (2.5 cm) slices. Makes 2 rolls, each cutting into 8 slices, for a total of 16 slices.

1 slice: 35 Calories; 1.6 g Total Fat; 83 mg Sodium; 2 g Protein; 3 g Carbohydrate; trace Dietary Fibre

Pictured above.

Itty-Bitty Crab Bits

The curry paste in these appetizers leaves a pleasant warmth in the back of the throat. Serve with plain yogurt to cool the palate! This recipe works best, and is quite fast, in a food processor. Mince the ingredients very fine if doing by hand. Serve with Creamed Tahini Dip, page 54.

White bread slice, torn into several pieces	1	1
Fresh parsley sprig, cut into 3 pieces	1	1
Finely grated gingerroot (or 1/4 tsp., 1 mL, ground ginger)	1 tsp.	5 mL
Green onion, cut into several pieces	1	1
Flake coconut	2 tbsp.	30 mL
Salt	1/2 tsp.	2 mL
Freshly ground pepper, sprinkle		
Can of crabmeat, drained and cartilage removed	4 1/4 oz.	120 g
Large egg, fork-beaten	1	1
Green curry paste	2 – 3 tsp.	10 – 15 mL
Lemon juice	1 1/2 tsp.	7 mL
COATING		
Medium coconut	3 tbsp.	50 mL
Finely crushed soda crackers (3 to 4)	3 tbsp.	50 mL

Cooking oil, for deep-frying

Put first 7 ingredients into food processor. Pulse with on/off motion 3 to 4 times until coarsely chopped. Process for about 5 seconds until finely chopped.

Add crab, egg, curry paste and lemon juice. Pulse with on/off motion several times until evenly moistened. Shape into 3/4 inch (2 cm) balls.

Coating: Combine coconut and cracker crumbs in small bowl. Roll crab balls in coconut mixture to coat completely.

Deep-fry, in about 3 batches, in hot (375°F, 190°C) cooking oil for about 1 minute until golden. Place on paper towel to drain. Makes about 24 crab bits.

1 crab bit: 41 Calories; 3.6 g Total Fat; 95 mg Sodium; 1 g Protein; 1 g Carbohydrate; trace Dietary Fibre

Pictured on page 47.

To Make Ahead: Prepare crab bits and freeze. To reheat from frozen, do not thaw. Place on greased baking sheet. Bake in 350°F (175°C) oven for about 10 minutes until hot.

Oriental Candied Pork

Slices of meat with a chewy coating and tender inside. Serve with Spiced Plum Sauce, page 55.

MARINADE		
Soy sauce	1/4 cup	60 mL
Brown sugar, packed	1/4 cup	60 mL
Hoisin sauce	3 tbsp.	50 mL
Liquid honey	2 tbsp.	30 mL
Apple cider vinegar	2 tbsp.	30 mL
Garlic clove, minced (or 1/4 tsp., 1 mL, powder)	1	1
Red food colouring	1 tsp.	5 mL
Pork tenderloin	1 lb.	454 g
Water		

Marinade: Combine first 7 ingredients in small saucepan. Bring to a boil, stirring constantly, until brown sugar is dissolved. Pour into shallow glass dish. Cool.

Add pork to marinade. Turn to coat. Cover. Marinate in refrigerator overnight, or for up to 24 hours, turning once. Remove pork, reserving marinade. Pour marinade into medium saucepan. Bring to a boil. Heat and stir for 3 minutes.

Place pork on rack in roasting pan containing about 1/2 inch (12 mm) water. Roast in 275°F (140°C) oven for 2 hours, adding more water if needed. Generously brush pork several times with marinade. Cool before cutting into 1/4 inch (6 mm) slices. Makes about 40 slices.

1 slice: 30 Calories; 0.7 g Total Fat; 164 mg Sodium; 3 g Protein; 3 g Carbohydrate; trace Dietary Fibre

Pictured on page 53.

Photo Legend next page:

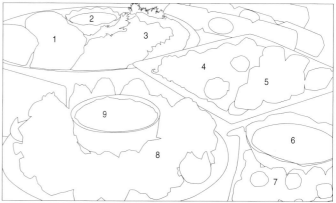

1. Old-Fashioned Bran Bread, page 71
2. Honey Mustard Sauce, page 92
3. Maple And Rye Gravlax, page 48
4. Feta Spinach Mushroom Caps, page 43
5. Holiday Whirls, page 50
6. Creamed Tahini Dip, page 54
7. Itty-Bitty Crab Bits, this page
8. Mustard Ranch Drumettes, page 50
9. Gorgonzola Cheese Dip, page 54

Maple And Rye Gravlax

Traditionally a Scandinavian delicacy of raw salmon cured in sugar mixture. Canadianized here with maple flavouring and rye whiskey. Requires 3 days curing time, so plan ahead. Serve very thinly sliced with Old-Fashioned Bran Bread, page 71, and Honey Mustard Sauce, page 92.

Fresh salmon fillet, with skin, blotted dry	1 1/2 lbs.	680 g
Cheesecloth, enough to wrap salmon in double thickness		
Rye whiskey	3 tbsp.	50 mL
Coarse sea salt	3 tbsp.	50 mL
Brown sugar, packed	3 tbsp.	50 mL
Maple flavouring	1 tsp.	5 mL
Pepper	1/4 tsp.	1 mL
Fresh dill sprigs, to cover		
Fresh rosemary sprigs, to cover		

Lay salmon, skin-side down, on cheesecloth.

Drizzle whiskey over top of salmon. Sprinkle with sea salt.

Stir brown sugar, maple flavouring and pepper together in small cup until evenly coloured. Spread over sea salt.

Layer dill and rosemary sprigs over top. Wrap cheesecloth around salmon. Set, skin side-down, in shallow glass dish. Lay sheet of plastic wrap over cheesecloth. Do not seal. Place 3 unopened 28 oz. (796 mL) cans in pan that will fit inside glass dish. Place weighted pan on top of salmon. Chill, without turning, for 3 days. Unwrap cheesecloth. Remove dill and rosemary sprigs. Very thinly slice salmon across grain on diagonal removing fish from skin. Tightly cover any uncut gravlax with plastic wrap. Chill for up to 5 days. Serves 6.

1 serving: 250 Calories; 12.3 g Total Fat; 3605 mg Sodium; 23 g Protein; 7 g Carbohydrate; trace Dietary Fibre

Pictured on page 46.

Cocktail Shrimp-On-A-Pineapple

A spectacular way to present shrimp at a gathering.

SEAFOOD SAUCE

Chili sauce	1/4 cup	60 mL
Ketchup	1/2 cup	125 mL
White vinegar	1 tsp.	5 mL
Granulated sugar	1 tsp.	5 mL
Prepared horseradish	3/4 tsp.	4 mL
Onion powder	1/8 tsp.	0.5 mL
Garlic powder	1/8 tsp.	0.5 mL
Salt	1/8 tsp.	0.5 mL
Water	2 cups	500 mL
White (or alcohol-free) wine	1/2 cup	125 mL
Bay leaves	2	2
Chopped celery, with leaves	1/4 cup	60 mL
Raw medium shrimp (about 1 1/2 lbs.,680 g), peeled and deveined, tails left intact	50	50
Ice water		

PINEAPPLE HOLDER

Whole large pineapple (about 4 inches, 10 cm, in diameter)	1	1
Cocktail (or wooden or plastic) picks (4 inch, 10 cm, lengths)	50	50

Seafood Sauce: Combine first 8 ingredients in small bowl. Chill. Makes 3/4 cup (175 mL) sauce.

Combine water, wine, bay leaves and celery in large saucepan. Bring to a boil.

Add shrimp. Stir. Cover. Cook for 3 minutes until shrimp are pink and curled. Remove shrimp. Immerse shrimp in ice water until cold. Add more ice as needed to chill well. Drain. Blot dry. Discard liquid.

Pineapple Holder: Wash outside of pineapple and leaves under running water. Drain and pat dry. Cut thin slice from bottom to allow pineapple to sit flat. Using ruler and felt marker, measure and mark 5 lengthwise wedges, about 2 1/4 inches (5.6 cm) across, leaving about 3/4 inch (2 cm) in between each wedge. Cut each wedge at a 45° angle, slicing right to core. Remove cut out pineapple wedges (see Line Drawing, below). From bird's eye viewpoint, pineapple should resemble star shape. Slice off and discard outer skin from wedges. Cut pineapple into at least 50 bite-size pieces.

Thread 1 pineapple piece and 1 shrimp onto each cocktail pick. Poke about 10 filled picks into each wedge, shrimp-side out, filling in all empty spaces. Chill. Serve with Seafood Sauce. Makes 50 appetizers.

1 appetizer: 23 Calories; 0.3 g Total Fat; 76 mg Sodium; 3 g Protein; 2 g Carbohydrate; trace Dietary Fibre

Pictured on this page.

TRADITIONAL SHRIMP COCKTAIL: To present as a first course, arrange 6 shrimp per person on crushed ice in individual seafood cocktail glasses. If you don't have seafood cocktail glasses, make bed of lettuce on individual plates. Arrange about 6 shrimp per plate on top of lettuce and drizzle with Seafood Sauce. Serves 8.

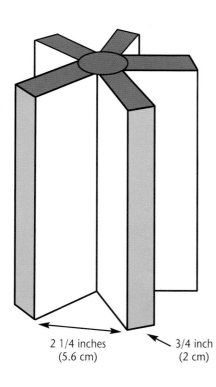

2 1/4 inches
(5.6 cm)   3/4 inch
                  (2 cm)

Cocktail Shrimp-On-A-Pineapple, page 48

Spicy Sticky-Finger Wings

Have plenty of napkins handy when you serve these yummy appetizers. Serve with Horseradish Dipping Sauce, page 54.

Chili sauce	2/3 cup	150 mL
Liquid honey	1/3 cup	75 mL
Indonesian sweet soy sauce	1/4 cup	60 mL
Prepared mustard	1 tbsp.	15 mL
Hot pepper sauce	1 tsp.	5 mL
Garlic powder	1/4 tsp.	1 mL
Whole chicken wings (about 18), split in half, tips discarded	3 lbs.	1.4 kg

Combine first 6 ingredients in small bowl.

Place chicken in shallow dish. Pour marinade over chicken. Stir to coat. Cover. Marinate in refrigerator for several hours or overnight, stirring several times. Turn out wings and marinade onto greased foil-lined 11 x 17 inch (28 x 43 cm) baking sheet. Arrange in single layer. Bake, uncovered, in 450°F (230°C) oven for 15 minutes. Stir and turn wings to coat with marinade. Bake for 10 minutes. Stir. Bake for about 10 minutes until completely coated with sticky sauce. Makes 36 wings.

1 wing: 64 Calories; 3.3 g Total Fat; 153 mg Sodium; 4 g Protein; 5 g Carbohydrate; trace Dietary Fibre

Pictured on page 52.

Mustard Ranch Drumettes

Great taste with just a hint of mustard.
Use a hot, spicy mustard for more intense flavour.
Serve with Gorgonzola Cheese Dip, page 54.

Ranch dressing	1 cup	250 mL
Grainy mustard	1/4 cup	60 mL
Mustard powder	1 tsp.	5 mL
Chicken drumettes (or whole wings, split in half, tips discarded)	3 lbs.	1.4 kg
Fine dry bread crumbs	1 1/3 cups	325 mL

Combine first 3 ingredients in small bowl.

Place chicken in shallow dish. Pour marinade over chicken. Stir to coat. Cover. Marinate in refrigerator for several hours or overnight, stirring several times. Remove chicken. Discard marinade.

Roll chicken in bread crumbs until completely coated. Arrange in single layer on greased foil-lined baking sheet. Bake, uncovered, in 425°F (220°C) oven for 15 minutes. Turn over. Bake for about 15 minutes until brown and crispy. Makes 24 drumettes or 36 wing pieces.

1 drumette: 149 Calories; 10.9 g Total Fat; 206 mg Sodium; 7 g Protein; 6 g Carbohydrate; trace Dietary Fibre

Pictured on page 46/47.

Holiday Whirls

These appetizers have the festive colours of red, white and green. Serve on a bed of mint leaves.

Block of cream cheese, softened	8 oz.	250 g
Crumbled feta cheese (about 8 oz., 225 g), room temperature	1 3/4 cups	425 mL
Chopped dried cranberries	1 cup	250 mL
Finely chopped fresh mint leaves (or green onion)	1/4 cup	60 mL
Large spinach tortillas (about 10 inches, 25 cm), see Tip, page 37	5	5

Cream both cheeses together in medium bowl until well mixed. Stir in cranberries and mint.

Spread about 1/2 cup (125 mL) cheese mixture on each tortilla to within 1/2 inch (12 mm) of edge. Roll up tightly, jelly roll-style. Cover each roll securely with plastic wrap. Chill for several hours or overnight. Trim and discard about 1 inch (2.5 cm) from ends of each roll. Cut each roll on diagonal into 1 inch (2.5 cm) slices. Makes 5 rolls, each cutting into 8 slices, for a total of 40 pieces.

1 piece: 65 Calories; 4 g Total Fat; 121 mg Sodium; 2 g Protein; 5 g Carbohydrate; 1 g Dietary Fibre

Pictured on page 47.

Grape Cheese Wreath

So pretty on a buffet table! Mild green peppercorn flavour with a slight sweet orange accent. Serve on buttery crackers with wedges of apple and other fruits.

WREATH

Block of cream cheese, softened	8 oz.	250 g
Whole green peppercorns in brine, drained, slightly crushed	2 tsp.	10 mL
Rounds of Brie cheese (4 oz., 125 g, each), chilled and diced	2	2

FROSTING

Block of cream cheese, softened	4 oz.	125 g
Frozen concentrated orange juice, thawed	1 tbsp.	15 mL
Icing (confectioner's) sugar	1 tsp.	5 mL
Finely grated orange zest	1/2 tsp.	2 mL

GARNISHES

Red seedless grapes, halved, approximately	3	3
Chopped fresh parsley	1/4 cup	60 mL
Long piece of orange peel	1	1

Wreath: Beat cream cheese and peppercorns together in large bowl until fluffy.

Stir Brie cheese into cream cheese mixture. Beat for about 2 minutes until combined. Cover. Chill for several hours or overnight. Form into log about 1 1/2 inches (3.8 cm) in diameter. Join ends to form ring on serving plate. Flatten edges with knife if desired. Cover. Chill.

Frosting: Beat cream cheese, concentrated orange juice, icing sugar and orange zest together in small bowl until smooth. Spread on ring.

Garnishes: Decorate ring using grapes and parsley. Tie orange peel into bow and place on ring. Serves about 20.

1 serving: 111 Calories; 10.1 g Total Fat; 137 mg Sodium; 4 g Protein; 1 g Carbohydrate; trace Dietary Fibre

Pictured on page 53.

Hot Mushroom Dip

Hot and spicy from the cheese with a definite mushroom and onion presence. Great make-ahead appetizer. Can also be served cold but will become thicker.

Finely chopped onion	1 cup	250 mL
Garlic clove, minced (or 1/4 tsp., 1 mL, powder), optional	1	1
Chopped fresh white mushrooms	3 cups	750 mL
Hard margarine (or butter)	2 tbsp.	30 mL
Block of cream cheese, room temperature, cut into 8 pieces	8 oz.	250 g
Seasoned salt	1/2 tsp.	2 mL
Dill weed	1/2 tsp.	2 mL
Pepper, heavy sprinkle		
Mayonnaise (not salad dressing)	1/2 cup	125 mL
Grated Monterey Jack With Jalapeño cheese	1 1/2 cups	375 mL
Fresh mushroom slices, for garnish	7	7
Fresh chives (or sliced green onion), for garnish	1 tbsp.	15 mL

Sauté onion, garlic and first amount of mushrooms in margarine in large frying pan for about 10 minutes until liquid from mushrooms has evaporated and mushrooms are golden. Remove from heat.

Add next 4 ingredients. Stir until cream cheese is melted.

Add mayonnaise and Monterey Jack cheese. Mix well. Spread in shallow baking dish or glass pie plate.

Garnish with second amount of mushrooms and chives. Cover and chill for up to 2 days if desired. Bake in 350°F (175°C) oven for about 30 minutes until heated through. Makes 2 1/2 cups (625 mL).

2 tbsp. (30 mL): 131 Calories; 12.5 g Total Fat; 153 mg Sodium; 3 g Protein; 2 g Carbohydrate; trace Dietary Fibre

Pictured on page 52/53.

Buffet Platters

* Arrange items in relation to shape of plate or platter.
* Cut bite size or at least similar in size.
* As you fill the plate, maintain symmetrical balance, that is, repeat on one side what you did on the other.
* Alternate light and dark items for visual balance.
* Use paper napkins or doilies to add background colour.
* Garnish with parsley sprigs, fresh herbs, carrot/tomato roses or radish flowers.

Deli Platter

Thin slices of deli roast beef, rolled
Thin slices of Black Forest (or other) ham,
   rolled into cone shapes
Thin slices of peppered (or other) salami, folded into fan
Thin slices of farmer's sausage, rolled with thin slices
   of process Cheddar cheese
Thin slices of mozzarella cheese
Assortment of pickles and olives
Assortment of hard cheeses, cut into sticks

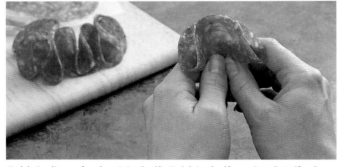

Fold 1 slice of salami in half. Fold in half again. Set 'fan' on platter with final fold up.

Pictured at right:

Top Left: Hot Mushroom Dip, page 51
Top Right: Spiced Plum Sauce, page 55,
   with Oriental Candied Pork, page 45
Bottom Left: Spicy Sticky-Finger Wings, page 50,
   with Horseradish Dipping Sauce, page 54
Bottom Right: Grape Cheese Wreath, page 51

Creamed Tahini Dip

A smooth dip with the distinctive taste of sesame seeds.
Good with Itty-Bitty Crab Bits, page 45.

Tahini	1/3 cup	75 mL
Indonesian sweet soy sauce	1 tbsp.	15 mL
Lemon juice	2 tsp.	10 mL
Whipping cream	3/4 cup	175 mL
Roasted sesame seeds	1/2 tsp.	2 mL

Combine tahini, soy sauce and lemon juice in small bowl.

Beat whipping cream in medium bowl until soft mounds form but don't stay in peaks.

Fold in tahini mixture and sesame seeds. Chill for at least 1 hour. Makes 1 1/2 cups (375 mL).

2 tbsp. (30 mL): 87 Calories; 8.5 g Total Fat; 52 mg Sodium; 2 g Protein; 2 g Carbohydrate; 1 g Dietary Fibre

Pictured on page 47.

Gorgonzola Cheese Dip

A creamy dip that is great with Mustard Ranch Drumettes, page 50, and vegetables.

Sour cream	1 cup	250 mL
Crumbled Gorgonzola cheese, softened	1/3 cup	75 mL
Block of cream cheese, softened, cut into 4 pieces	4 oz.	125 g
Dried chives	1 1/2 tsp.	7 mL
White vinegar	1 tsp.	5 mL
Prepared horseradish	1 tsp.	5 mL
Onion salt	3/4 tsp.	4 mL

Fresh chives, sliced, for garnish

Beat first 7 ingredients together in medium bowl until smooth and fluffy.

Garnish with chives. Makes about 1 1/2 cups (375 mL).

2 tbsp. (30 mL): 81 Calories; 7.3 g Total Fat; 163 mg Sodium; 2 g Protein; 2 g Carbohydrate; trace Dietary Fibre

Pictured on page 46.

Horseradish Dipping Sauce

A distinct tangy flavour in this dipping sauce.
Serve with meatballs, sausages, ham or
Spicy Sticky-Finger Wings, page 50.

Mayonnaise (not salad dressing)	1/4 cup	60 mL
Creamed horseradish	3 tbsp.	50 mL
Ketchup	2 tbsp.	30 mL
Prepared mustard	2 tsp.	10 mL
Worcestershire sauce	1/4 tsp.	1 mL

Combine all 5 ingredients in small bowl. Cover. Chill until ready to serve. Makes about 1/2 cup (125 mL).

2 tbsp. (30 mL): 117 Calories; 11.5 g Total Fat; 211 mg Sodium; 1 g Protein; 3 g Carbohydrate; trace Dietary Fibre

Pictured on page 52/53.

Peanut Butter Dip

Creamy smooth blend of peanut butter and orange flavours.
Good with fresh fruit, celery and peppers.

Smooth peanut butter	1/2 cup	125 mL
Prepared orange juice	3 tbsp.	50 mL
Corn syrup	1 1/2 tbsp.	25 mL
Frozen whipped topping, thawed	1 cup	250 mL

Stir first 3 ingredients together in small bowl until smooth.

Fold in whipped topping until blended well. Makes 1 1/3 cups (325 mL).

1 tbsp. (15 mL): 53 Calories; 4 g Total Fat; 31 mg Sodium; 2 g Protein; 3 g Carbohydrate; trace Dietary Fibre

Pictured on page 55.

To keep your bowl from moving while using an electric hand mixer, place a dampened, folded tea towel underneath.

Cranberry Cheese

A pretty and festive spread that can be molded to any shape you desire. Serve with crackers or melba toast.

Grated sharp white Cheddar cheese, room temperature	2 cups	500 mL
Block of cream cheese, room temperature	4 oz.	125 g
Dried cranberries, coarsely chopped	1/4 cup	60 mL

Beat Cheddar cheese and cream cheese together in medium bowl until smooth.

Mix in cranberries. Press into ungreased 1 1/2 cup (375 mL) mould or large cookie cutter, packing well to avoid air spaces. Cover with plastic wrap. Chill for at least 3 hours until firm. Loosen in mould. Invert onto serving plate. Serves 6 to 8.

1 serving: 242 Calories; 20.5 g Total Fat; 309 mg Sodium; 12 g Protein; 4 g Carbohydrate; 1 g Dietary Fibre

Pictured below.

Spiced Plum Sauce

This sauce has a nice heat that lingers and a slight honey sweetness. Serve with Oriental Candied Pork, page 45.

Can of prune plums in heavy syrup, pits removed	14 oz.	398 mL
Liquid honey	1/4 cup	60 mL
White vinegar	2 tbsp.	30 mL
Chili sauce	1 tbsp.	15 mL
Cornstarch	2 tsp.	10 mL
Dried crushed chilies	1/4 – 1/2 tsp.	1 – 2 mL

Measure all 6 ingredients into blender. Process until almost smooth. Pour into medium saucepan. Bring to a boil. Reduce heat to medium-low. Simmer, uncovered, for about 10 minutes, stirring occasionally, until thickened slightly. Cool. Makes 1 1/2 cups (375 mL).

2 tbsp. (30 mL): 51 Calories; 0.1 g Total Fat; 26 mg Sodium; trace Protein; 13 g Carbohydrate; trace Dietary Fibre

Pictured on page 53.

Left: Cranberry Cheese, this page
Right: Peanut Butter Dip, page 54

Beverages

Left: Rush Eggnog, below

Rush Eggnog

A quick and easy way to spruce up store-bought eggnog.

Eggnog	4 cups	1 L
Milk	2 cups	500 mL
Liquor of your choice (such as brandy, Irish whiskey or rum)	1/2 – 3/4 cup	125 –175 mL
Whipping cream	1 cup	250 mL

Measure eggnog, milk and liquor into punch bowl. Stir.

Beat whipping cream in medium bowl until stiff peaks form. Add to eggnog mixture. Stir gently. Chill until ready to serve. Makes 7 cups (1.75 L).

1 cup (250 mL): 331 Calories; 18 g Total Fat; 127 mg Sodium; 9 g Protein; 25 g Carbohydrate; 0 g Dietary Fibre

Pictured above.

Centre: Refreshing Cranberry Tonic, below

Right: Cool Coffee Nog, below

Refreshing Cranberry Tonic

This cool, tart drink will quench your thirst.
Float orange slices and whole cranberries in tonic.

Fresh (or frozen) cranberries, chopped	4 cups	1 L
Granulated sugar	2 cups	500 mL
Water	4 cups	1 L
Prepared orange juice	1 1/2 cups	375 mL
Lemon juice	1/2 cup	125 mL
Tonic water (or club soda or water)	6 cups	1.5 L

Combine cranberries, sugar and water in large pot or Dutch oven. Bring to a boil on medium-high, stirring occasionally. Reduce heat to medium-low. Simmer, uncovered, for about 10 minutes until cranberries are soft. Pour through fine sieve or double thickness of cheesecloth over large punch bowl. Discard solids.

Add remaining 3 ingredients. Stir gently. Chill until ready to serve. Makes 13 1/2 cups (3.4 L).

*1 cup (250 mL): 193 Calories; 0.1 g Total Fat; 6 mg Sodium; trace Protein;
50 g Carbohydrate; trace Dietary Fibre*

Pictured above.

Cool Coffee Nog

Pleasant, cool, creamy coffee flavour in this nog with a punch!
Serve with mint chocolate sticks.

Cold prepared strong coffee	4 cups	1 L
Coffee-flavoured liqueur (such as Kahlúa)	1/2 cup	125 mL
Chocolate-flavoured liqueur (such as Crème de Cacao)	1/4 cup	60 mL
Vanilla ice cream, softened	4 cups	1 L

Pour coffee into 2 quart (2 L) pitcher. Add both liqueurs and ice cream. Stir gently until smooth. Chill until ready to serve. Makes 6 2/3 cups (1.65 L).

*1 cup (250 mL): 272 Calories; 10.8 g Total Fat; 81 mg Sodium; 3 g Protein;
30 g Carbohydrate; 0 g Dietary Fibre*

Pictured above.

Variation: Omit vanilla ice cream. Use same amount of coffee or chocolate ice cream.

Variation: Omit chocolate-flavoured liqueur. Use same amount of orange-flavoured liqueur (such as Grand Marnier or Triple Sec).

Fruit Slush

Cloudy, lemon yellow, frozen slush with banana.
Very cold and refreshing. Serve with Ice Ring, this page.

Prepared orange juice	6 cups	1.5 L
Pineapple juice	3 cups	750 mL
Lemon juice	2/3 cup	150 mL
Granulated sugar	2 cups	500 mL
Small ripe bananas, puréed	4	4
Ginger ale	6 cups	1.5 L

Pour orange juice, pineapple juice and lemon juice into medium bowl. Add sugar. Stir until sugar is dissolved.

Add banana. Stir, using whisk, until combined well. Pour into airtight container. Freeze until firm.

Turn frozen mixture into large punch bowl at least 4 hours before serving. Add ginger ale just before serving. Stir. Makes 18 cups (4.5 L).

1 cup (250 mL): 205 Calories; 0.2 g Total Fat; 8 mg Sodium; 1 g Protein; 52 g Carbohydrate; 1 g Dietary Fibre

Pictured below.

Outside Ring: Fruit Slush, above   Centre: Ice Ring, this page

Ice Ring

A simple punch is transformed into a stunning show-stopper with this crystal creation of fruit and juice.
Use in Fruit Slush, this page.

Crushed ice	2 cups	500 mL
Seedless red grapes	2 cups	500 mL
Fresh cranberries	1 cup	250 mL
Sliced frozen mango	1/4 cup	60 mL
Star fruit, sliced	1	1
Fresh blueberries	1/4 cup	60 mL
Medium orange, sliced	1	1
Fruit punch	1 cup	250 mL
Mango juice	1 cup	250 mL

Put crushed ice into bottom of 12 cup (3 L) bundt pan. Arrange fruit on top of ice, sticking some star fruit and orange slices into ice to anchor fruit. Freeze, keeping level, for 1 hour.

Combine punch and juice in 2 cup (500 mL) liquid measure. Slowly pour juice mixture, in one spot, over fruit. To prevent fruit from floating, do not submerge fruit. Freeze, keeping level, for at least 8 hours. To unmold, run warm water over underside of bundt pan for a few seconds. Carefully remove ice ring. Gently place in prepared punch.

Left: By-The-Fire Hot Chocolate, below

Right: Caramel Cider Tea, below

By-The-Fire Hot Chocolate

Definite cinnamon flavour to this holiday hot chocolate.

Granulated sugar	1/2 cup	125 mL
Cocoa, sifted if lumpy	1/2 cup	125 mL
Milk (not skim)	6 cups	1.5 L
Cinnamon sticks (4 inch, 10 cm, lengths)	2	2
Large eggs	2	2
Vanilla	2 tsp.	10 mL

Miniature marshmallows, for garnish
Grated chocolate, for garnish

Combine sugar and cocoa in large saucepan. Slowly stir in milk. Add cinnamon sticks. Heat, uncovered, on medium for about 8 minutes, stirring occasionally, until steaming and very foamy.

Beat eggs and vanilla in small bowl using fork. Add 1/2 cup (125 mL) cocoa mixture to egg mixture. Stir. Remove and discard cinnamon sticks. Whisk egg mixture into cocoa mixture. Whisk vigorously for about 4 minutes until mixture is almost boiling and froth forms on top.

Ladle into mugs. Garnish with marshmallows and chocolate. Makes 6 cups (1.5 L).

1 cup (250 mL): 223 Calories; 5.5 g Total Fat; 152 mg Sodium; 12 g Protein; 35 g Carbohydrate; 2 g Dietary Fibre

Pictured above.

Caramel Cider Tea

Tea that tastes like apple pie—delicious and comforting.

Apple juice (or cider)	4 cups	1 L
Water	2 cups	500 mL
Brown sugar, packed	2 tbsp.	30 mL
Cinnamon stick (4 inch, 10 cm, length)	1	1
Orange pekoe tea bag	1	1
Whipped cream (or prepared dessert topping)	1 1/3 cups	325 mL
Thick caramel ice cream topping	3 tbsp.	50 mL
Ground cinnamon, sprinkle (optional)		
Cinnamon sticks (4 inch, 10 cm, lengths), optional	4	4

Heat apple juice, water, brown sugar and cinnamon stick in large saucepan until boiling. Remove from heat.

Add tea bag. Cover. Let steep for 5 minutes. Remove and discard tea bag and cinnamon stick. Ladle into 4 large mugs.

Top each with about 1/3 cup (75 mL) whipped cream.

Put ice cream topping into small resealable freezer bag. Cut tiny hole in 1 corner. Squeeze over whipped cream in zigzag pattern. Dust cinnamon over top. Add 1 cinnamon stick to each mug. Serves 4.

1 serving: 318 Calories; 13.8 g Total Fat; 88 mg Sodium; 1 g Protein; 50 g Carbohydrate; trace Dietary Fibre

Pictured above.

Cool Irish Coffee

A real treat. Dark mocha coffee with a white creamy layer on top. Sprinkle with edible brown glitter to dress up this drink.

Boiling water	2 tbsp.	30 mL
Instant coffee granules	2 tsp.	10 mL
Granulated sugar	1 tsp.	5 mL
Cold water	1 cup	250 mL
Vanilla ice cream	1/2 cup	125 mL
Irish whiskey	2 tbsp.	30 mL

Frozen whipped topping
(or whipped cream), optional

Stir boiling water into coffee granules in small bowl. Add sugar and cold water. Stir until sugar is dissolved.

Spoon ice cream into large mug. Add whiskey. Pour coffee mixture over ice cream mixture to fill mug. Makes 1 3/4 cups (425 mL).

Top with dollop of whipped topping. Serves 1.

1 serving: 230 Calories; 7.7 g Total Fat; 57 mg Sodium; 3 g Protein; 22 g Carbohydrate; 0 g Dietary Fibre

Pictured on page 61.

Variation: Omit cold water. Use 1 cup (250 mL) milk for a richer taste.

Warm Spiced Cranberry

Pretty amber colour with a rose hue. Not-too-sweet, fruity blend with a hint-of-cinnamon drink.

Cranberry cocktail	4 cups	1 L
Prepared orange juice	2 cups	500 mL
Lemon juice	1/2 cup	125 mL
Granulated sugar	1/4 cup	60 mL
Cinnamon sticks (4 inch, 10 cm, lengths)	2	2
Whole cloves	4	4
Ginger ale, room temperature	4 cups	1 L

Combine first 6 ingredients in large saucepan. Heat on low, stirring often, until simmering. Cover. Simmer for 15 minutes. Pour into warm punch bowl.

Add ginger ale. Stir. Makes about 10 cups (2.5 L).

1 cup (250 mL): 143 Calories; 0.1 g Total Fat; 10 mg Sodium; trace Protein; 36 g Carbohydrate; trace Dietary Fibre

Pictured on page 61.

Hot Tea Wassail

Pronounced WAHS-uhl. Norwegian for "be in good health." Made in the slow cooker. A nice blend of wine, tea, apple, lemon and spices.

Orange pekoe tea bags	4	4
Boiling water	6 cups	1.5 L
Large lemon, sliced 1/2 inch (12 mm) thick	1	1
Liquid honey	1/2 cup	125 mL
Dry red (or alcohol-free) wine	3 cups	750 mL
Cinnamon sticks (3 inch, 7.5 cm, lengths)	2	2
Small cooking apples (such as McIntosh), with skin, cored	3	3
Whole allspice	12	12
Whole cloves	12	12

Preheat slow cooker on Low until warm. Add tea bags. Pour boiling water over tea bags. Cover. Let steep for 10 minutes. Squeeze and discard tea bags.

Stir in lemon, honey, wine and cinnamon sticks.

Pierce skin on apples several times with tip of paring knife. Push allspice and cloves into slits in apples. Add to wine mixture. Cover. Heat on Low for 2 hours. Do not boil or may become bitter tasting. Strain and discard solids just before serving. Makes 9 3/4 cups (2.4 L).

1 cup (250 mL): 124 Calories; 0 g Total Fat; 7 mg Sodium; trace Protein; 20 g Carbohydrate; trace Dietary Fibre

Pictured on page 61.

Top: Cool Irish Coffee, this page
Left Centre: Hot Tea Wassail, above
Bottom Right: Warm Spiced Cranberry, this page

Cherry Muffins

Mild almond flavour with a cherry surprise in the middle.

Hard margarine (or butter), softened	6 tbsp.	100 mL
Brown sugar, packed	1/3 cup	75 mL
Granulated sugar	1/3 cup	75 mL
Large egg	1	1
Milk	7/8 cup	200 mL
Maraschino cherry syrup	2 tbsp.	30 mL
Vanilla	1 tsp.	5 mL
All-purpose flour	2 cups	500 mL
Baking powder	1 tbsp.	15 mL
Salt	1/2 tsp.	2 mL
Maraschino cherries, blotted dry	12	12
Chopped pecans	1/3 cup	75 mL

Cream margarine and both sugars together in large bowl. Beat in egg. Add milk, cherry syrup and vanilla. Beat until mixed.

Combine flour, baking powder and salt in medium bowl. Add to margarine mixture. Stir until just moistened. Fill greased muffin cups 3/4 full.

Press 1 cherry into centre of batter in each muffin cup. Sprinkle with pecans. Bake in 400°F (205°C) oven for about 18 minutes until wooden pick inserted in centre of muffin comes out clean. Let stand in pan for 5 minutes before turning out onto wire rack to cool. Makes 12 muffins.

1 muffin: 233 Calories; 9 g Total Fat; 281 mg Sodium; 4 g Protein; 35 g Carbohydrate; 1 g Dietary Fibre

Pictured on page 63.

Gingerbread Muffins

The taste of Christmas and the comfort of home all in one muffin. Serve warm with butter.

Hard margarine (or butter), softened	1/2 cup	125 mL
Granulated sugar	1/2 cup	125 mL
Large eggs	2	2
Fancy (mild) molasses	2/3 cup	150 mL
Milk	1/4 cup	60 mL
All-purpose flour	2 1/2 cups	625 mL
Baking soda	1 tsp.	5 mL
Baking powder	1 tsp.	5 mL
Ground ginger	1 1/2 tsp.	7 mL
Ground cinnamon	1 tsp.	5 mL
Salt	1/2 tsp.	2 mL
Ground cloves	1/4 tsp.	1 mL

Cream margarine and sugar together in large bowl. Beat in eggs, 1 at a time, beating well after each addition. Add molasses and milk. Beat until mixed.

Combine remaining 7 ingredients in medium bowl. Add to margarine mixture. Stir until just moistened. Fill greased muffin cups 3/4 full. Bake in 375°F (190°C) oven for about 20 minutes until wooden pick inserted in centre of muffin comes out clean. Let stand in pan for 5 minutes before turning out onto wire rack to cool. Makes 12 muffins.

1 muffin: 274 Calories; 9.3 g Total Fat; 352 mg Sodium; 4 g Protein; 44 g Carbohydrate; 1 g Dietary Fibre

Pictured below.

Top Centre & Bottom Left: Cherry Muffins, page 62
Top Right: Gingerbread Muffins, this page

Cornmeal Muffins

Slightly sweet, cheesy corn-flavoured muffins.

Cooking oil	1/4 cup	60 mL
Granulated sugar	1/4 cup	60 mL
Large egg	1	1
Milk	1 cup	250 mL
Sour cream	1/4 cup	60 mL
Grated sharp Cheddar cheese	3/4 cup	175 mL
Yellow cornmeal	1 cup	250 mL
All-purpose flour	3/4 cup	175 mL
Baking powder	1 tbsp.	15 mL
Salt	1/2 tsp.	2 mL

Beat cooking oil, sugar and egg together in medium bowl until smooth. Add milk and sour cream. Stir in cheese.

Combine cornmeal, flour, baking powder and salt in separate medium bowl. Add to milk mixture. Stir until just moistened. Fill greased muffin cups 3/4 full. Bake in 400°F (205°C) oven for about 18 minutes until wooden pick inserted in centre of muffin comes out clean. Let stand in pan for 5 minutes before removing to wire rack to cool. Makes 12 muffins.

1 muffin: 188 Calories; 9 g Total Fat; 257 mg Sodium; 5 g Protein; 22 g Carbohydrate; 1 g Dietary Fibre

Pictured on page 67.

Fruit Tea Loaf

Moist and fruity. Very nice flavour with a hint of tea.

Strong prepared tea	1 cup	250 mL
Granulated sugar	1 cup	250 mL
Raisins	1/2 cup	125 mL
Chopped mixed glazed fruit	1/2 cup	125 mL
Hard margarine (or butter)	1/4 cup	60 mL
Large eggs	2	2
Vanilla	1 tsp.	5 mL
All-purpose flour	2 1/4 cups	550 mL
Baking powder	2 tsp.	10 mL
Salt	1/2 tsp.	2 mL

Heat first 5 ingredients in large saucepan, stirring occasionally, until simmering. Simmer, uncovered, for 3 minutes. Cool until saucepan feels warm to touch.

Beat eggs and vanilla together in small cup using fork. Stir into fruit mixture.

Add flour, baking powder and salt. Mix until just moistened. Turn into greased 9 x 5 x 3 inch (22 x 12.5 x 7.5 cm) loaf pan. Bake in 350°F (175°C) oven for about 50 minutes until wooden pick inserted in centre comes out clean. Let stand in pan for 10 minutes before turning out onto wire rack to cool. Cuts into 18 slices.

1 slice: 170 Calories; 3.5 g Total Fat; 151 mg Sodium; 3 g Protein; 33 g Carbohydrate; 1 g Dietary Fibre

Pictured on page 66.

Cranberry Scones

These are the perfect Christmas scones. Serve hot with butter and jam or Cranberry Mango Chutney, page 27.

All-purpose flour	2 cups	500 mL
Granulated sugar	1/4 cup	60 mL
Baking powder	4 tsp.	20 mL
Salt	1/2 tsp.	2 mL
Large egg	1	1
Hard margarine (or butter), melted	6 tbsp.	100 mL
Milk	2/3 cup	150 mL
Dried cranberries	1 1/2 cups	375 mL
TOPPING		
Milk	1 tbsp.	15 mL
Granulated sugar	1 tbsp.	15 mL

Combine flour, sugar, baking powder and salt in large bowl. Make a well in centre.

Beat egg in small bowl until frothy. Add margarine and milk. Mix. Pour into well. Add cranberries. Stir until just moistened. Turn out onto well-floured surface. Knead 8 to 10 times. Divide into 2 equal portions. Pat each into 6 inch (15 cm) circle. Arrange on greased baking sheet.

Topping: Brush tops with milk. Sprinkle with sugar. Score each circle into 6 wedges. Bake in 425°F (220°C) oven for about 15 minutes until risen and lightly golden. Makes 12 scones.

1 scone: 195 Calories; 6.7 g Total Fat; 304 mg Sodium; 4 g Protein; 31 g Carbohydrate; 3 g Dietary Fibre

Pictured on page 66/67.

Sweet Potato Biscuits

So yummy, everybody will want to eat their vegetables.

All-purpose flour	3 1/2 cups	875 mL
Brown sugar, packed	1/4 cup	60 mL
Flaxseeds	4 tsp.	20 mL
Baking powder	4 tsp.	20 mL
Baking soda	1/2 tsp.	2 mL
Salt	1 tsp.	5 mL
Milk	1 cup	250 mL
White vinegar	1 tbsp.	15 mL
Can of sweet potatoes, drained and mashed	19 oz.	540 mL
Cooking oil	1/2 cup	125 mL

Combine first 6 ingredients in large bowl. Make a well in centre.

Combine milk and vinegar in medium bowl. Let stand for 5 minutes.

Add sweet potato and cooking oil to milk mixture. Mix. Pour into well. Stir until dough forms soft ball. Turn out onto lightly floured surface. Pat out to 1 inch (2.5 cm) thick. Cut into 2 1/2 inch (6.4 cm) circles. Arrange on greased baking sheet. Bake in 400°F (205°C) oven for about 20 minutes until risen and golden. Makes 16 biscuits.

1 biscuit: 216 Calories; 8 g Total Fat; 300 mg Sodium; 4 g Protein; 32 g Carbohydrate; 1 g Dietary Fibre

Pictured on page 66.

Two-Toned Buns

Serve these fun buns for the undecided on Christmas Day and wow your guests. Wonderful with Turkey Mixed Bean Soup, page 161.

Granulated sugar	1 tsp.	5 mL
Warm water	1/2 cup	125 mL
Active dry yeast	2 1/2 tsp.	12 mL
Granulated sugar	2 tbsp.	30 mL
Hard margarine (or butter), softened	2 tbsp.	30 mL
Salt	2 tsp.	10 mL
Warm milk	2 cups	500 mL
All-purpose flour	2 cups	500 mL
Whole wheat flour, approximately	2 cups	500 mL
All-purpose flour, approximately	2 cups	500 mL
Hard margarine (or butter), melted (optional)	1 tbsp.	15 mL

Stir first amount of sugar and warm water in large bowl until sugar is dissolved. Sprinkle yeast over top. Let stand for 10 minutes. Stir to dissolve yeast.

Add next 5 ingredients. Beat on low to moisten. Beat on high until smooth.

Divide batter equally between 2 medium bowls. Work whole wheat flour into 1 portion and second amount of all-purpose flour into other portion until dough forms a ball. Turn out each portion onto lightly floured surface. Knead until smooth and elastic. Place each portion in separate greased bowl, turning once to grease top. Cover with tea towels. Let stand in oven with light on and door closed for 1 to 1 1/2 hours until doubled in bulk. Punch dough down. Divide and shape dough into about 1 1/2 inch (3.8 cm) balls. Put 1 white and 1 whole wheat ball into each greased muffin cup. Cover with tea towels. Let stand in oven with light on and door closed for about 35 minutes until almost doubled in size. Bake in 400°F (205°C) oven for about 15 minutes until golden.

Brush tops with second amount of margarine. Makes 3 dozen buns.

1 bun: 93 Calories; 1.1 g Total Fat; 147 mg Sodium; 3 g Protein; 18 g Carbohydrate; 1 g Dietary Fibre

TWO-TONED BREAD TWISTS: Divide each portion into 18 pieces. Roll each piece into 8 inch (20 cm) long rope. Twist 1 all-purpose and 1 whole wheat rope together 5 or 6 times and pinch ends together tightly. Arrange about 3 inches (7.5 cm) apart on greased baking sheets. Cover with tea towels. Let stand in oven with light on and door closed for about 35 minutes until almost doubled in size. Bake in 400°F (205°C) oven for about 15 minutes until golden. Brush tops with second amount of margarine. Makes 18 bread twists.

Pictured on page 67.

Photo Legend next page:

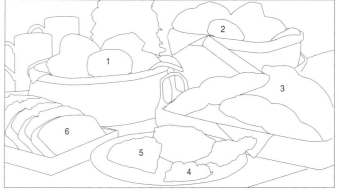

1. Sweet Potato Biscuits, this page
2. Cornmeal Muffins, page 64
3. Two-Toned Bread Twists, this page
4. Cranberry Mango Chutney, page 27
5. Cranberry Scones, page 64
6. Fruit Tea Loaf, page 64

Eggnog Candy Bread

Butter rum and eggnog flavours make for a wonderful aroma while this is baking and a wonderful taste when it's being eaten.

Cooking oil	1/3 cup	75 mL
Large eggs	2	2
Granulated sugar	2/3 cup	150 mL
Rum flavouring	2 tsp.	10 mL
Vanilla	1 tsp.	5 mL
Eggnog	1 cup	250 mL
All-purpose flour	2 1/4 cups	550 mL
Baking powder	2 tsp.	10 mL
Salt	1/2 tsp.	2 mL
Rolls of butter rum-flavoured doughnut-shaped hard candies (3/4 oz., 25 g, each)	2	2

Beat first 6 ingredients together well in large bowl.

Add flour, baking powder and salt. Stir until just moistened.

Put unwrapped hard candies into resealable plastic bag. Seal. Pound until candies are broken into small pieces. Reserve about 1/4 of candy pieces. Add remaining candy pieces to batter. Stir gently. Turn into greased 9 × 5 × 3 inch (22 × 12.5 × 7.5 cm) loaf pan. Sprinkle reserved candy pieces over top. Bake in 350°F (175°C) oven for 50 to 55 minutes until wooden pick inserted in centre comes out clean. Let stand in pan for 10 minutes before turning out onto wire rack to cool. Cuts into 18 slices.

1 slice: 168 Calories; 6.2 g Total Fat; 124 mg Sodium; 3 g Protein; 25 g Carbohydrate; 1 g Dietary Fibre

Pictured on page 69.

Mini Lemon Loaves

An attractive loaf that is very tasty.

Hard margarine (or butter), softened	6 tbsp.	100 mL
Granulated sugar	1 cup	250 mL
Large eggs	2	2
Milk	1 cup	250 mL
All-purpose flour	2 cups	500 mL
Baking powder	1 tsp.	5 mL
Baking soda	1/2 tsp.	2 mL
Salt	1/2 tsp.	2 mL
Finely grated lemon rind	2 tbsp.	30 mL
GLAZE		
Freshly squeezed lemon juice (about 1 medium)	1/3 cup	75 mL
Granulated sugar	3 tbsp.	50 mL

Left: Mini Lemon Loaves, this page

Cream margarine, sugar and 1 egg together in large bowl. Beat in second egg. Add milk. Beat until well mixed.

Add next 5 ingredients. Beat on low, or stir, until just moistened. Divide and turn into 4 greased 5 3/4 × 3 1/4 × 2 inch (14 × 8 × 5 cm) mini-loaf pans. Bake in 350°F (175°C) oven for about 30 minutes until wooden pick inserted in centre comes out clean. Poke holes all over top of hot loaves using wooden pick.

Glaze: Stir lemon juice and sugar together in small bowl. Drizzle glaze over warm loaves. Let loaves stand in pan for 10 minutes before removing to wire racks to cool. Makes 4 loaves, each cutting into 5 slices, for a total of 20 slices.

1 slice: 142 Calories; 4.2 g Total Fat; 164 mg Sodium; 2 g Protein; 24 g Carbohydrate; trace Dietary Fibre

Pictured above.

Variation: Bake in 9 × 5 × 3 inch (22 × 12.5 × 7.5 cm) loaf pan for about 1 hour until wooden pick inserted in centre comes out clean.

Centre: Cranberry Mint Loaf, below

Right: Eggnog Candy Bread, page 68

Cranberry Mint Loaf

A loaf with the traditional Christmas colours and an unusual, yet delicious, combination of flavours.

Fresh cranberries, coarsely chopped	1 cup	250 mL
Leaf-shaped spearmint gumdrops (about 20), diced (see Note)	1 cup	250 mL
All-purpose flour	1 tbsp.	15 mL
Hard margarine (or butter), softened	1/2 cup	125 mL
Granulated sugar	1 cup	250 mL
Large eggs	2	2
Mint flavouring	1/2 tsp.	2 mL
Finely grated lemon rind	2 tsp.	10 mL
All-purpose flour	2 cups	500 mL
Baking powder	1 tsp.	5 mL
Baking soda	1/2 tsp.	2 mL
Salt	1/4 tsp.	1 mL
Milk	2/3 cup	150 mL

Toss cranberries, gumdrops and first amount of flour together in small bowl until cranberries and gumdrops are coated. Set aside.

Cream margarine and sugar together in large bowl. Add eggs, 1 at a time, beating well after each addition. Beat in flavouring and lemon rind.

Combine next 4 ingredients in separate large bowl. Add to margarine mixture. Stir until just moistened. Batter will be very thick.

Stir in milk and cranberry mixture until just combined. Turn into greased 9 x 5 x 3 inch (22 x 12.5 x 7.5 cm) loaf pan. Bake in 350°F (175°C) oven for 1 to 1 1/4 hours until wooden pick inserted in centre comes out clean. Let stand in pan for 10 minutes before turning out onto wire rack to cool completely. Cuts into 18 slices.

1 slice: 205 Calories; 6.2 g Total Fat; 169 mg Sodium; 3 g Protein; 35 g Carbohydrate; 1 g Dietary Fibre

Pictured above.

Note: Gumdrops are easiest to cut with greased kitchen scissors or very sharp greased knife.

Candy Cane Bread

Such a pretty centrepiece for your brunch buffet.
Each cut slice shows off both fillings.

BREAD DOUGH

Very warm water	1 cup	250 mL
Granulated sugar	3 tbsp.	50 mL
Active dry yeast	1 1/2 tsp.	7 mL
Large egg	1	1
Hard margarine (or butter), softened	3 tbsp.	50 mL
Salt	1 tsp.	5 mL
All-purpose flour	1 cup	250 mL
All-purpose flour, approximately	2 1/3 cups	575 mL

POPPY SEED FILLING

Poppy seeds	1/4 cup	60 mL
Water	1/2 cup	125 mL
Slivered almonds	1/4 cup	60 mL
Liquid honey	2 tbsp.	30 mL
Hard margarine (or butter), melted	1 tbsp.	15 mL

ALMOND FILLING

Hard margarine (or butter), softened	1 tbsp.	15 mL
Granulated sugar	2 tbsp.	30 mL
Almond flavouring	1/4 tsp.	1 mL
Rice flour	1 tbsp.	15 mL
Salt, sprinkle		
Egg white (large)	1	1
Ground almonds	1/4 cup	60 mL
Drops of red food colouring (optional)	4 – 5	4 – 5
Green and red glazed cherries, finely chopped	1/2 cup	125 mL

Bread Dough: Stir warm water and sugar together in large bowl until sugar is dissolved. Sprinkle yeast over top. Let stand for 10 minutes. Stir to dissolve yeast.

Add next 4 ingredients. Beat on low until just moistened. Beat on medium for 2 minutes until thick and smooth.

Work in enough of second amount of flour until dough pulls away from sides of bowl. Turn out onto floured surface. Knead for 8 to 10 minutes until smooth and elastic. Place dough in large greased bowl, turning once to grease top. Cover with tea towel. Let stand in oven with light on and door closed for about 1 hour until doubled in bulk.

Poppy Seed Filling: Combine poppy seeds and water in small saucepan. Bring to a boil. Boil for 1 minute. Let stand for 30 minutes. Drain. Rinse. Drain well. Put poppy seeds into blender.

Add slivered almonds, honey and margarine. Process, scraping down sides as necessary, until poppy seeds are ground and almonds are chopped. Set aside.

Almond Filling: Beat first 6 ingredients together in small bowl until smooth.

Stir in ground almonds and food colouring until thick paste forms. Set aside.

To form bread: Punch dough down. Divide into 2 portions. Turn 1 portion out onto very lightly greased surface. Roll out to 6 x 26 inch (15 x 65 cm) rectangle about 1/4 inch (6 mm) thick. Repeat with second portion of dough.

Spread Poppy Seed Filling on 1 portion of dough to within 1/2 inch (12 mm) of edges. Spread Almond Filling on remaining portion of dough to within 1/2 inch (12 mm) of edges. Sprinkle cherries over Poppy Seed Filling. Roll up both rectangles tightly, jelly roll-style, from long sides. Dampen long edges. Pinch to seal.

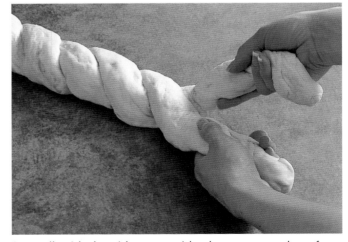

Lay rolls side by side, seam-side down, on work surface. Starting in the centre and working towards one end, gently lift 1 roll over and across other roll. Lift bottom roll over and across top roll. Repeat 4 or 5 times, creating tight, twisted effect, keeping seam side down as best you can. Repeat from centre to other end.

Turn 11 × 17 inch (28 × 43 cm) baking sheet upside down. Cover with sheet of greased foil. Carefully transfer dough onto foil. Curve top 1/3 of dough into hook of cane shape. Arrange remaining 2/3 of dough diagonally across baking sheet as straight and narrow as possible. Dampen ends. Pinch to seal. Tuck ends in and slightly underneath. Cover with tea towel. Let stand for 15 minutes. Cut a 2 inch (5 cm) slit into top of 1 twist of dough, following the direction of the twist, until several layers of filling are exposed. Repeat with other twists. Bake in 350°F (175°C) oven for 20 minutes until golden. Cool. Slice diagonally to serve. Cuts into about 18 slices.

1 slice: 192 Calories; 6.2 g Total Fat; 178 mg Sodium; 4 g Protein;
30 g Carbohydrate; 1 g Dietary Fibre

Variation: Pipe thin lines of Glaze, page 72, to emphasize the stripes on a candy cane.

Pictured below.

Candy Cane Bread, page 70

Old-Fashioned Bran Bread

Serve with Maple And Rye Gravlax, page 48.
Nice nutty-sweet flavour.

Water	1/2 cup	125 mL
Hard margarine (or butter)	1/4 cup	60 mL
Liquid honey	1/4 cup	60 mL
Salt	1 tsp.	5 mL
Large egg	1	1
Milk	1/2 cup	125 mL
Whole wheat flour	1 1/2 cups	375 mL
Instant yeast	1 tbsp.	15 mL
Natural wheat bran	1/3 cup	75 mL
Flaxseeds, toasted (see Tip, page 100)	1 tbsp.	15 mL
Roasted sunflower seeds	1 tbsp.	15 mL
All-purpose flour, approximately	2 cups	500 mL
Hard margarine (or butter), melted (optional)	4 tsp.	20 mL

Heat water, first amount of margarine, honey and salt in small saucepan until almost boiling and margarine is melted.

Whisk egg and milk together in large bowl. Gradually add hot water mixture while whisking. Temperature should still be very warm.

Stir whole wheat flour and yeast together in small bowl. Stir into milk mixture until smooth. Add bran, flax seeds and sunflower seeds. Stir.

Work in 1 1/2 cups (375 mL) all-purpose flour, 1/2 cup (125 mL) at a time, until soft dough forms and pulls away from sides of bowl. Turn out onto well-floured surface. Knead for 5 to 10 minutes, adding more all-purpose flour as needed, until smooth and elastic but still slightly tacky. Place dough in lightly greased bowl, turning once to grease top. Cover with tea towel. Let stand in oven with light on and door closed for 30 minutes until doubled in bulk. Divide dough into 4 portions. Put into 4 greased 5 3/4 × 3 1/4 × 2 inch (14 × 8 × 5 cm) mini-loaf pans or 4 greased 19 oz. (540 mL) tins. Cover with tea towel. Let stand in oven with light on and door closed for about 45 minutes until doubled in size or at top edge of loaf pans. Bake in 350°F (175°C) oven for about 25 minutes until hollow sounding when tapped. Turn out onto wire racks to cool.

Brush warm tops with second amount of margarine. Makes 4 loaves, each cutting into 10 slices, for a total of 40 slices.

1 slice: 67 Calories; 1.7 g Total Fat; 78 mg Sodium; 2 g Protein; 11 g Carbohydrate; 1 g Dietary Fibre

Pictured on page 46.

Christmas Bread, below

Christmas Bread

Fruit and glaze add sweetness to this moist golden bread.
Use Glaze for Candy Cane Bread, page 70.

Loaf of frozen white bread dough, thawed according to package directions	1	1
Currants (or raisins)	1/4 cup	60 mL
Maraschino cherries, drained and quartered	1/4 cup	60 mL
Cut mixed peel	1 tbsp.	15 mL
Ground cinnamon	1/4 tsp.	1 mL
Hard margarine (or butter), melted (optional)	1 tsp.	5 mL
GLAZE		
Icing (confectioner's) sugar	1/3 cup	75 mL
Water	1 1/4 tsp.	6 mL
Slivered almonds, toasted (see Tip, page 100), for garnish	2 tbsp.	30 mL

Roll out bread dough on lightly floured surface into rectangle, making short side the same length as loaf pan. Scatter currants, cherries and peel over bread dough. Sprinkle cinnamon over top. Roll up, jelly roll-style, beginning at short end. Put, seam-side down, into greased 9 x 5 x 3 inch (22 x 12.5 x 7.5 cm) loaf pan. Cover with tea towel. Let stand in oven with light on and door closed until doubled in size. Bake in 375°F (190°C) oven for about 30 minutes until golden. Turn out onto wire rack to cool.

Brush warm top with margarine. Cool.

Glaze: Mix icing sugar with just enough water until desired piping consistency. Makes about 2 tbsp. (30 mL) glaze. Pipe onto loaf.

Immediately sprinkle almonds over glaze. Cuts into 16 slices.

1 slice: 100 Calories; 1 g Total Fat; 153 mg Sodium; 2 g Protein; 20 g Carbohydrate; 1 g Dietary Fibre

Pictured on front cover and above.

Brunch & Lunch

Hot Fruit Compote

*A sweet blend of fruit flavours in this easy-to-prepare dessert.
Serve over Griddle Corn Cakes, page 81.*

Can of sliced peaches, drained	14 oz.	398 mL
Fresh (or frozen) blueberries	1 cup	250 mL
Large underripe banana, sliced	1	1
Can of whole cranberry sauce	14 oz.	398 mL
Minute tapioca	1 tbsp.	15 mL
Brown sugar, packed	1/4 cup	60 mL

Toss peaches, blueberries and banana together in ungreased
1 1/2 quart (1.5 L) casserole.

Combine cranberry sauce and tapioca in small bowl until
well mixed. Spread over fruit mixture.

Sprinkle with brown sugar. Bake, uncovered, in 350°F
(175°C) oven for about 40 minutes until bubbly. Serves 8.

*1 serving: 169 Calories; 0.3 g Total Fat; 22 mg Sodium; 1 g Protein;
43 g Carbohydrate; 2 g Dietary Fibre*

Pictured on page 79.

Breakfast Trifle

*Bread, dairy and fruit in this delicious breakfast trifle.
Good to eat and good for you. Make the night before
to serve for breakfast Christmas morning.*

Coarsely chopped blueberry muffins (or 6 whole grain blueberry cereal bars, coarsely chopped)	4 cups	1 L
Sliced fresh strawberries	1 1/3 cups	325 mL
Fresh blueberries	1 1/3 cups	325 mL
Sliced ripe kiwifruit	1 1/3 cups	325 mL
Seedless red grapes	11	11
Strawberry-flavoured yogurt	4 cups	1 L

Put 1/2 of muffin pieces into 2 1/2 quart (2.5 L) glass bowl.
Arrange 1/2 of strawberries, blueberries and kiwifruit in
attractive pattern over muffin pieces. Spoon 1/2 of yogurt
evenly over fruit. Cover with remaining muffin pieces.
Spoon remaining yogurt evenly over muffin pieces. Garnish
with remaining strawberries, blueberries, kiwifruit and
grapes in attractive pattern. Makes 8 cups (2 L).

*1 cup (250 mL): 251 Calories; 4.5 g Total Fat; 181 mg Sodium; 7 g Protein;
46 g Carbohydrate; 2 g Dietary Fibre*

Pictured on page 74.

Variation: Use your choice of muffins, fresh fruit and yogurt.

Top Left: Breakfast Trifle, page 73
Bottom Left: The Big Breakfast, page 81

Top Centre: Doctored Oatmeal Porridge, page 75
Bottom Right: Onion Cheese Pie, page 75

Onion And Potato Tart

This quiche is a very filling brunch dish.

Pastry for 2 crust pie, your own
  or a mix, chilled

Medium potatoes, cut into chunks (about 2 3/4 cups, 675 mL)	3	3
Water	1 cup	250 mL
Salt	1 tsp.	5 mL
Grated Gruyère cheese	1 1/4 cups	300 mL
Dried thyme	1/2 tsp.	2 mL
Coarsely chopped onion	4 1/2 cups	1.1 L
Hard margarine (or butter)	1 1/2 tbsp.	25 mL
Seasoned salt	1 tsp.	5 mL
Ground nutmeg	1/8 tsp.	0.5 mL
Pepper, generous sprinkle		
Large eggs	5	5
Milk (homogenized is best)	1 1/2 cups	375 mL

Roll out pastry to fit 10 inch (25 cm) glass pie plate. Line pie plate, with pastry overhanging edge about 1/2 inch (12 mm). Turn overhanging edge under until level with edge of pie plate. Lightly press down against pie plate.

Make decorative edge (see Pretty Pastry, page 134). Poke bottom and side of pie shell in several places using fork. Roll out scraps and make cut-outs with small canapé or cookie cutters. Place pie shell and cut-outs on baking sheet. Bake in 375°F (190°C) oven for 15 minutes. Remove pie crust from baking sheet. Bake cut-outs for additional 2 to 3 minutes until firm and golden.

Cook potato in water and salt in medium saucepan until soft. Drain. Cool. Break up potatoes with fork or pastry blender until size of large peas. Turn into crust. Do not pack down.

Sprinkle with cheese and thyme.

Sauté onion in margarine in large frying pan for about 15 minutes until soft. Reduce heat to low.

Sprinkle seasoned salt, nutmeg and pepper over onion. Cover. Cook for about 10 minutes, stirring occasionally, until onion is browned and very soft. Evenly sprinkle over cheese.

Beat eggs and milk together in small bowl using fork. Carefully pour over onion mixture. Gently shake to allow spaces to fill in. Arrange cut-outs decoratively over tart. Bake on bottom rack in oven for 55 to 60 minutes until set and crust is golden. Let stand on wire rack for 10 minutes to cool slightly. Cuts into 8 wedges.

1 wedge: 412 Calories; 23.3 g Total Fat; 507 mg Sodium; 14 g Protein; 37 g Carbohydrate; 2 g Dietary Fibre

Pictured on page 76.

Doctored Oatmeal Porridge

A good change from regular oatmeal with apple and cinnamon flavours. Serve with apple slices on top.

Apple juice	1 3/4 cups	425 mL
Quick-cooking rolled oats (not instant)	1 cup	250 mL
Medium cooking apple (such as McIntosh), peeled and grated	1	1
Ground cinnamon	1/2 tsp.	2 mL
Salt	1/8 tsp.	0.5 mL

Combine all 5 ingredients in medium saucepan. Bring to a boil, stirring often. Cook for 3 to 5 minutes until porridge is thickened and apple is tender. Makes 2 1/4 cups (550 mL).

2/3 cup (150 mL): 206 Calories; 2.4 g Total Fat; 97 mg Sodium; 5 g Protein; 43 g Carbohydrate; 4 g Dietary Fibre

Pictured on page 74.

Onion Cheese Pie

A simple hearty lunch. This quiche is for cheese lovers.

Grated Swiss cheese	1 cup	250 mL
Grated Gouda cheese	1 cup	250 mL
All-purpose flour	1 tbsp.	15 mL
Unbaked 9 inch (22 cm) pie shell	1	1
Large eggs	3	3
Skim evaporated milk	1 cup	250 mL
Salt	1/2 tsp.	2 mL
Pepper	1/8 tsp.	0.5 mL
Cayenne pepper	1/8 tsp.	0.5 mL
Thinly sliced onion rings, cut into quarters	2 cups	500 mL

Toss both cheeses and flour together in medium bowl. Sprinkle over bottom of pie shell.

Beat eggs in separate medium bowl until frothy. Add evaporated milk, salt, pepper and cayenne pepper. Beat. Pour over cheese mixture.

Scatter onion over egg mixture. Bake on bottom rack in 350°F (175°C) oven for about 45 minutes until knife inserted in centre comes out clean. Let stand in pie plate for 10 minutes before cutting. Cuts into 6 wedges.

1 wedge: 351 Calories; 20.4 g Total Fat; 636 mg Sodium; 19 g Protein; 23 g Carbohydrate; 1 g Dietary Fibre

Pictured on page 74.

Egg Roll With Shrimp

A delicious brunch dish for special guests or very pretty to present on a buffet table.

Large eggs	3	3
Salt	1/2 tsp.	2 mL
Creamed horseradish	2 tsp.	10 mL
Milk	2/3 cup	150 mL
All-purpose flour	1/3 cup	75 mL
Hard margarine (or butter)	1 tbsp.	15 mL
FILLING		
Green onions, sliced	2	2
Finely diced celery	1/4 cup	60 mL
Medium roma (plum) tomatoes, seeded and diced (about 2/3 cup, 150 mL)	2	2
Salt, sprinkle		
Pepper, sprinkle		
Grated mozzarella cheese	3/4 cup	175 mL
Small frozen shrimp (about 6 oz., 170 g), thawed and blotted dry	1 cup	250 mL
Spicy cocktail sauce	2 tbsp.	30 mL
Sharp Cheddar cheese, cut into 4 strips	2 oz.	57 g

Stir first 4 ingredients together in medium bowl until smooth. Add flour. Stir until smooth.

Melt margarine in bottom of greased 9 x 13 inch (22 x 33 cm) pan in 350°F (175°C) oven for about 2 minutes until sizzling. Pour egg mixture into pan. Bake, uncovered, for 25 to 30 minutes until set and lightly browned. Loosen edges by running spatula around sides of pan. Turn out onto baking sheet.

Filling: Immediately sprinkle green onion, celery and tomato over egg mixture. Season with salt, pepper, mozzarella cheese and shrimp.

Place small dabs of cocktail sauce randomly over shrimp. Roll up, jelly roll-style, from long side. Arrange seam-side down on same baking sheet. Lay Cheddar cheese on top of roll. Bake in 350°F (175°C) oven for 8 to 10 minutes until Cheddar cheese is melted. Cuts into 8 diagonal slices. Serves 4.

1 serving: 331 Calories; 18 g Total Fat; 749 mg Sodium; 25 g Protein; 17 g Carbohydrate; 1 g Dietary Fibre

Pictured on page 76.

Spinach And Olive Braid

Wonderful Mediterranean flavours of spinach, feta and olives in this stuffed bread. Makes a good lunch served with Greek Pea Salad, page 138.

FILLING

Garlic cloves, minced (or 1/2 tsp., 2 mL, powder)	2	2
Olive (or cooking) oil	2 tsp.	10 mL
Chopped fresh spinach, packed (about 3 oz., 85 g)	1 1/2 cups	375 mL
Water	1 tbsp.	15 mL
Fine dry bread crumbs	1 tbsp.	15 mL
Sour cream	2 tbsp.	30 mL
Kalamata olives, pits removed, finely chopped	7	7
Crumbled feta cheese (about 2 1/2 oz., 70 g)	1/2 cup	125 mL
Jar of pimiento, drained, finely diced	2 oz.	57 mL
Dried whole oregano	1/4 tsp.	1 mL
Salt	1/4 tsp.	1 mL
Lemon pepper	1/4 tsp.	1 mL
Loaf of frozen white bread dough, thawed according to package directions	1	1
Large egg, fork-beaten	1	1
Sea salt (optional)	1/4 tsp.	1 mL
Poppy seeds (optional)	1/4 tsp.	1 mL

Filling: Sauté garlic in olive oil in frying pan for about 1 minute until beginning to turn golden.

Add spinach and water. Stir. Cover. Cook on medium for 2 to 3 minutes until spinach is soft and wilted. Stir. Cook, uncovered, for 2 minutes, stirring occasionally, until liquid has evaporated. Remove from heat.

Sprinkle with bread crumbs. Stir. Cool slightly.

Add next 7 ingredients. Stir. Makes 3/4 cup (175 mL) filling.

Roll out bread dough on lightly floured surface into 8 x 16 inch (20 x 40 cm) rectangle. Spread filling down centre to within 2 inches (5 cm) of edge. Cut diagonal slashes about 1 1/2 inches (3.8 cm) wide down long edges of bread dough to within 1/4 inch (6 mm) of filling. Fold bread dough strips over centre, alternating sides to form braid pattern. Carefully transfer to lightly greased baking sheet. Cover with tea towel. Let stand in oven with light on and door closed for about 40 minutes until doubled in size.

Brush with egg. Sprinkle with sea salt and poppy seeds. Bake in 375°F (190°C) oven for 17 to 20 minutes until golden brown. Cuts into 10 pieces.

1 piece: 173 Calories; 5.6 g Total Fat; 440 mg Sodium; 6 g Protein; 24 g Carbohydrate; 1 g Dietary Fibre

Pictured below.

Top Left: Onion And Potato Tart, page 74   Top Right: Egg Roll With Shrimp, page 75   Bottom Right: Spinach And Olive Braid, above

Blueberry Streusel French Toast

The perfect make-ahead brunch dish. A sure hit with maple syrup or blueberry syrup drizzled on top.

Hard margarine (or butter)	1 tbsp.	15 mL
Thick bread slices (such as Texas Toast)	12	12
Large eggs	9	9
Milk	1 1/2 cups	375 mL
Granulated sugar	1 1/2 tbsp.	25 mL
Salt	1/4 tsp.	1 mL
Vanilla	1 tbsp.	15 mL
STREUSEL		
Quick-cooking rolled oats (not instant)	1 1/4 cups	300 mL
Brown sugar, packed	1/2 cup	125 mL
All-purpose flour	1/4 cup	60 mL
Finely grated lemon zest	1/2 tsp.	2 mL
Hard margarine (or butter)	1/3 cup	75 mL
Frozen (or fresh) blueberries	1 cup	250 mL

Grease 11 × 17 inch (28 × 43 cm) baking sheet with thick coating of margarine.

Arrange bread slices close to each other on baking sheet.

Beat next 5 ingredients together in large bowl. Pour over bread slices.

Streusel: Combine rolled oats, brown sugar, flour and lemon zest in medium bowl.

Cut in margarine until mixture is crumbly. Sprinkle over bread slices.

Sprinkle blueberries over streusel. Cover. Chill overnight. Remove cover. Bake in 450°F (230°C) oven for 30 minutes until topping is crisp and golden brown around edges. Makes 12 slices.

1 slice: 364 Calories; 13.1 g Total Fat; 460 mg Sodium; 12 g Protein; 49 g Carbohydrate; 3 g Dietary Fibre

Pictured on page 79.

To keep pancakes warm and moist, but not soggy, arrange, slightly overlapping, on large platter. Loosely cover with foil. Heat in 200°F (95°C) or less oven. To keep waffles warm and crisp or to reheat, place directly on oven rack or on wire rack in oven. Do not cover. Heat for no more than 15 minutes.

Spice Coffee Cake

A delicious cake with a dark swirl.
Drizzle Butterscotch Sauce, page 98, over cake.

Spice cake mix (2 layer size)	1	1
Instant butterscotch pudding powder (4 serving size)	1	1
Large eggs	3	3
Cooking oil	1/3 cup	75 mL
Water	1 cup	250 mL
Brown sugar, packed	1/3 cup	75 mL
Cocoa, sifted if lumpy	2 tbsp.	30 mL
All-purpose flour	2 tbsp.	30 mL
Ground cinnamon	1 tsp.	5 mL
Ground nutmeg	1/4 tsp.	1 mL
Ground cloves	1/8 tsp.	0.5 mL

Empty cake mix and pudding powder into large bowl. Add eggs, cooking oil and water. Beat on low until moistened. Beat on medium for 2 minutes. Turn into greased and floured 12 cup (3 L) bundt pan.

Stir remaining 6 ingredients together in small bowl. Sprinkle over cake mix mixture. Swirl with knife to create marble effect. Bake in 350°F (175°C) oven for about 1 hour until wooden pick inserted in centre comes out clean. Let stand in pan for 20 minutes before turning out onto wire rack to cool. Cuts into 16 wedges.

1 wedge: 247 Calories; 9.8 g Total Fat; 330 mg Sodium; 3 g Protein; 38 g Carbohydrate; trace Dietary Fibre

Pictured on page 78.

Photo Legend next page:

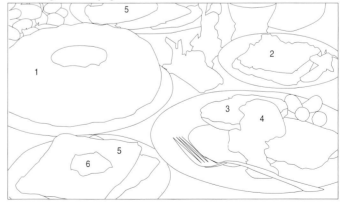

1. Spice Coffee Cake, above, with Butterscotch Sauce, page 98
2. Blueberry Streusel French Toast, this page
3. Griddle Corn Cakes, page 81
4. Hot Fruit Compote, page 73
5. Crab And Cheddar Waffles, page 81
6. Fresh Herb Sauce, page 92

Top: Seafood Focaccia Loaf, below   Bottom: Burger Strata, this page

Heat second amount of olive oil in same frying pan. Add shrimp and scallops. Stir-fry for 2 to 3 minutes until seafood is opaque and firm. Scatter over vegetable mixture.

Sprinkle olives and feta cheese over seafood mixture. Bake in 350°F (175°C) oven for 15 to 20 minutes until edges are crusty. Place top half of focaccia bread over seafood mixture. Gently press down. Serves 4 to 6.

1 serving: 406 Calories; 14 g Total Fat; 659 mg Sodium; 20 g Protein; 49 g Carbohydrate; 3 g Dietary Fibre

Pictured on this page.

Burger Strata

Tastes like a cheeseburger with extra cheese. Have this ready the day before to pop in the oven for lunch the next day.

Bread slices, crusts removed, lightly toasted	8	8
Lean ground beef	1 1/2 lbs.	680 g
Finely chopped onion	1 cup	250 mL
Finely chopped celery	1/3 cup	75 mL
Salt	1/2 tsp.	2 mL
Pepper	1/4 tsp.	1 mL
Grated medium Cheddar cheese	2 cups	500 mL
Bread slices, crusts removed, lightly toasted	8	8
Large eggs	4	4
Prepared mustard	2 tbsp.	30 mL
Milk	2 cups	500 mL
Grated medium Cheddar (or mozzarella) cheese	1 cup	250 mL

Arrange first amount of bread slices in single layer in greased 9 x 13 inch (22 x 33 cm) pan.

Scramble-fry ground beef, onion and celery in frying pan until beef is no longer pink. Drain. Sprinkle with salt and pepper. Mix. Layer over bread slices.

Sprinkle first amount of cheese over beef mixture. Cover with second amount of bread slices.

Beat eggs, mustard and milk together in medium bowl until frothy. Slowly pour onto bread slices. Cover. Chill overnight. Remove cover.

Sprinkle with second amount of cheese. Bake, uncovered, in 350°F (175°C) oven for about 45 minutes until set. Serves 8.

1 serving: 507 Calories; 27.2 g Total Fat; 833 mg Sodium; 36 g Protein; 29 g Carbohydrate; 1 g Dietary Fibre

Pictured on this page.

Seafood Focaccia Loaf

This very appetizing dish is full of flavour.

Herb focaccia bread (about 7 1/2 – 8 inch, 19 – 20 cm, round or 6 x 9 inch, 15 x 22 cm, rectangle)	1	1
Basil pesto	1/4 cup	60 mL
Garlic clove, minced (or 1/4 tsp., 1 mL, powder)	1	1
Diced onion	1/2 cup	125 mL
Diced green pepper	1/2 cup	125 mL
Diced fresh mushrooms	1/2 cup	125 mL
Olive (or cooking) oil	1 tsp.	5 mL
Olive (or cooking) oil	1 tsp.	5 mL
Frozen medium shrimp, thawed and blotted dry	4 oz.	113 g
Frozen small scallops, thawed and blotted dry	4 oz.	113 g
Diced ripe olives (or seasoned black Italian olives)	2 tbsp.	30 mL
Crumbled feta cheese	1/2 cup	125 mL

Cut focaccia bread in half horizontally to make 2 layers. Spread each cut side with pesto. Place, cut side up, on ungreased baking sheet.

Sauté garlic, onion, green pepper and mushrooms in first amount of olive oil in frying pan for 2 to 3 minutes until onion is soft. Spread over bottom half of focaccia bread.

Crab And Cheddar Waffles

Slightly sweet with nice flavour from the crab, cheese and onion. Serve with Fresh Herb Sauce, page 92.

All-purpose flour	1 1/4 cups	300 mL
Baking powder	2 tsp.	10 mL
Granulated sugar	1 1/2 tsp.	7 mL
Salt	1/2 tsp.	2 mL
Cayenne pepper (optional)	1/8 tsp.	0.5 mL
Grated sharp Cheddar cheese	1/2 cup	125 mL
Can of crabmeat, drained, cartilage removed, flaked	4 1/4 oz.	120 g
Finely sliced green onion	2 tbsp.	30 mL
Large egg, fork-beaten	1	1
Milk	1 1/4 cups	300 mL
Cooking oil	1/4 cup	60 mL

Sift first 5 ingredients into large bowl.

Add cheese, crab and green onion. Stir.

Combine egg, milk and cooking oil in small bowl. Add to flour mixture. Mix until just moistened. Do not overmix. Cook about 1/2 cup (125 mL) batter in hot waffle iron until golden. Repeat with remaining batter. Makes about 10 waffles.

1 waffle: 168 Calories; 8.9 g Total Fat; 330 mg Sodium; 7 g Protein; 15 g Carbohydrate; 1 g Dietary Fibre

Pictured on page 78/79.

The Big Breakfast

Not only big, this is no boring breakfast!

Bacon slices, diced (or Chorizo sausage, cut up or cocktail sausages)	1 lb.	454 g
Large eggs	12	12
Sliced fresh mushrooms	1 cup	250 mL
Grated sharp Cheddar cheese	3 cups	750 mL
Green onions, thinly sliced	3	3
Can of diced green chilies	4 oz.	113 g
Salt	1 tsp.	5 mL
Pepper	1/4 tsp.	1 mL
Whipping cream	1 cup	250 mL

Fry bacon in frying pan until crisp. Drain well. Cool.

Beat eggs in large bowl using fork. Stir in next 6 ingredients. Add bacon. Stir. Pour into greased 9 x 13 inch (22 x 33 cm) pan.

Slowly pour whipping cream over top. Cover and chill overnight or cook immediately. Bake, uncovered, in 350°F (175°C) oven for about 40 minutes until edges start to brown and knife inserted near centre comes out clean. Serves 10.

1 serving: 388 Calories; 32.3 g Total Fat; 750 mg Sodium; 21 g Protein; 3 g Carbohydrate; trace Dietary Fibre

Pictured on page 74.

Griddle Corn Cakes

Very nice sweet corn flavour to these filling cakes. Wonderful with Hot Fruit Compote, page 73.

All-purpose flour	1 cup	250 mL
Yellow cornmeal	1 cup	250 mL
Granulated sugar	1/4 cup	60 mL
Baking powder	4 tsp.	20 mL
Milk	1/4 cup	60 mL
Large eggs, fork-beaten	2	2
Can of cream-style corn	14 oz.	398 mL
Cooking oil	2 tbsp.	30 mL

Combine flour, cornmeal, sugar and baking powder in medium bowl.

Combine milk, eggs, corn and cooking oil in separate medium bowl. Add flour mixture to milk mixture. Stir until just moistened. Drop 1/4 cup (60 mL) batter onto hot lightly greased griddle or frying pan. Cook for 3 to 4 minutes per side until lightly browned. Makes 15 corn cakes.

1 corn cake: 131 Calories; 2.9 g Total Fat; 192 mg Sodium; 3 g Protein; 24 g Carbohydrate; 1 g Dietary Fibre

Pictured on page 79.

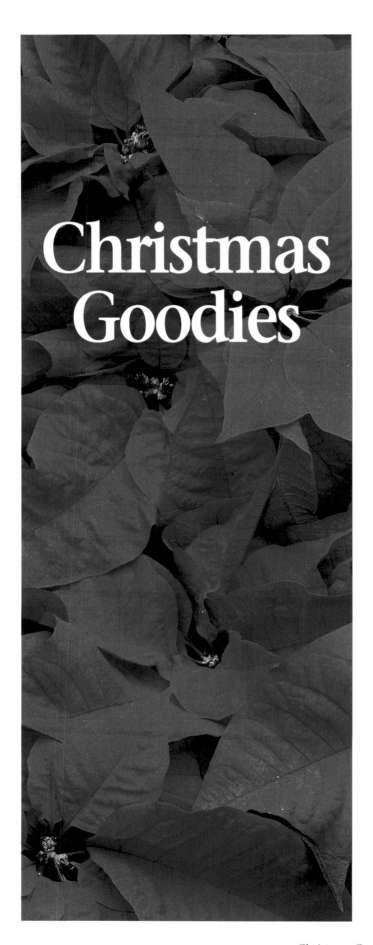

Christmas Goodies

Piña Colada Squares

Another great twist to Nanaimo bars. A nice blend of pineapple and coconut. These squares need to be kept chilled as they soften quickly.

BOTTOM LAYER		
Hard margarine (or butter), softened	1/2 cup	125 mL
Granulated sugar	1/4 cup	60 mL
Cocoa, sifted if lumpy	1/3 cup	75 mL
Large egg, fork-beaten	1	1
Milk	2 tbsp.	30 mL
Graham cracker crumbs	1 3/4 cups	425 mL
Chopped walnuts	1/2 cup	125 mL
Medium coconut	3/4 cup	175 mL
MIDDLE LAYER		
Hard margarine (or butter), softened	1/2 cup	125 mL
Icing (confectioner's) sugar	2 cups	500 mL
Crushed pineapple, very well drained	1/2 cup	125 mL
Coconut flavouring	3/4 tsp.	4 mL
TOP LAYER		
Semi-sweet chocolate chips	2/3 cup	150 mL
Hard margarine (or butter)	2 tbsp.	30 mL

Bottom Layer: Stir margarine, sugar and cocoa together in large saucepan on medium until margarine is melted. Add egg and milk. Heat and stir for a few moments until slightly thickened. Remove from heat.

Add graham crumbs, walnuts and coconut. Stir until well coated. Firmly press into ungreased 9 x 9 inch (22 x 22 cm) pan. Pan may be lined with foil for easy removal and cutting.

Middle Layer: Put all 4 ingredients into medium bowl. Mix well. Spread over first layer. Chill overnight until firm.

Top Layer: Heat and stir chocolate chips and margarine in small heavy saucepan on low until melted and smooth. Let stand until cool but still runny. Spread over second layer. Chill until ready to serve. Cuts into 36 squares.

1 square: 150 Calories; 10 g Total Fat; 100 mg Sodium; 1 g Protein; 15 g Carbohydrate; 1 g Dietary Fibre

Pictured on page 85.

White Chocolate Fudge Truffles

Fabulous! Sweet, rich and creamy truffles that are well worth the effort.

Granulated sugar	1 1/2 cups	375 mL
Evaporated milk (not skim)	1/2 cup	125 mL
White chocolate chips	1 cup	250 mL
Butter (not margarine), softened	1/3 cup	75 mL
Clear vanilla	2 tsp.	10 mL
Salt, just a pinch		
White chocolate melting wafers	1/2 cup	125 mL
Dark (or milk) chocolate melting wafers	1/2 cup	125 mL
Pink chocolate melting wafers	1/2 cup	125 mL

Combine sugar and evaporated milk in 3 quart (3 L) heavy saucepan. Heat and stir on medium for about 4 minutes until mixture comes to a rolling boil that cannot be stirred down. Reduce heat to medium-low to keep a hard boil without boiling over top of pan. Boil hard for 6 minutes, stirring occasionally. Remove from heat.

Combine chocolate chips, butter, vanilla and salt in small bowl. Add all at once to milk mixture. Beat with electric mixer in saucepan for about 8 minutes until tablespoonful will remain on surface rather than sink. Pour into greased 8 × 8 inch (20 × 20 cm) pan. Chill until cold. Drop by 1 1/2 tsp. (7 mL) onto cold waxed paper-lined baking sheet. If fudge becomes too soft to work with, chill until cold. Chill. Roll each portion into a smooth ball. Chill.

Heat melting wafers separately in small glass bowls over simmering water in small saucepan on low, stirring constantly, until smooth and melted. Remove from heat. Dip 1/3 of balls into white chocolate, allowing excess to drip back into bowl. Place on waxed paper-lined baking sheet. Repeat with remaining balls and dark and pink chocolate. Keep well chilled until completely set. Drizzle any remaining melted chocolate decoratively over truffles. Makes 47 truffles.

1 truffle: 82 Calories; 3.9 g Total Fat; 22 mg Sodium; 1 g Protein; 12 g Carbohydrate; trace Dietary Fibre

Pictured on this page.

To make truffles that are uniform in size, use a miniature ice cream scoop. If the truffles are not going to be dipped for a long period of time (i.e. until next day) cover well or place in an airtight container and chill to prevent drying out.

Top Centre: Butter Crunch, below
Centre Left, Right & Bottom: White Chocolate Fudge Truffles, this page

Butter Crunch

Thin, crunchy candy with a chocolate and nut covering. Easily breaks into pieces for gift giving.

Butter (not margarine)	1 cup	250 mL
Granulated sugar	1 cup	250 mL
Water	2 tbsp.	30 mL
Corn syrup	1 tbsp.	15 mL
Semi-sweet chocolate chips	1/2 cup	125 mL
Finely chopped pecans	1/2 cup	125 mL

Melt butter in heavy medium saucepan on medium-low. Add sugar. Stir until mixture begins to bubble.

Stir in water and corn syrup. Cook for about 35 minutes, stirring often but gently, until mixture reaches soft crack stage (270° to 290°F, 132° to 143°C) on candy thermometer or until small amount dropped into very cold water separates into hard, but pliable threads. Pour in thin layer on greased baking sheet. Let stand until cooled and hardened.

Heat chocolate chips in small heavy saucepan on lowest heat, stirring often, until just melted. Let stand until you can hold your hand on bottom of saucepan. Spread evenly over top of candy.

Sprinkle pecans over chocolate. Lightly press down with your hand. Makes about 1 lb. (454 g).

1 oz. (28 g): 212 Calories; 16.2 g Total Fat; 125 mg Sodium; 1 g Protein; 18 g Carbohydrate; 1 g Dietary Fibre

Pictured above.

Rum And Butter Balls

A delightfully decadent alternative to traditional rum balls!

Butter (or hard margarine), softened	1/4 cup	60 mL
Icing (confectioner's) sugar	1 3/4 cups	425 mL
Vanilla wafer crumbs	1 cup	250 mL
Water	2 tbsp.	30 mL
Rum flavouring	1/2 tsp.	2 mL
Butter flavouring	1/2 tsp.	2 mL
Finely chopped walnuts	1/2 cup	125 mL
Icing (confectioner's) sugar	1/3 cup	75 mL

Measure first 7 ingredients into large bowl. Mix well until stiff dough forms. Divide into 2 equal portions. Roll each portion into long rope. Cut each rope in half. Cut each half into 6 equal pieces. Roll each piece into ball.

Roll each ball in icing sugar. Makes 2 dozen balls.

1 ball: 93 Calories; 4.2 g Total Fat; 32 mg Sodium; 1 g Protein; 14 g Carbohydrate; trace Dietary Fibre

Pictured on page 3 and on page 87.

Chocolate Orange Treats

Pretty goodies that taste as good as they look.

Butterscotch chips	1 cup	250 mL
Semi-sweet chocolate chips	1 cup	250 mL
Skim evaporated milk	1/2 cup	125 mL
Graham cracker crumbs	2 cups	500 mL
Finely grated orange peel	2 tsp.	10 mL
Tiny Christmas-shaped decorating candies (optional)	1/2 cup	125 mL

Combine butterscotch and chocolate chips and evaporated milk in heavy medium saucepan. Heat on low, stirring often, until smooth.

Add graham crumbs and orange peel. Stir. Chill for at least 1 hour. Shape into 1 inch (2.5 cm) balls, using about 1 1/2 tsp. (7 mL) for each.

Roll in decorating candies. Makes 4 1/2 dozen balls.

1 ball: 46 Calories; 1.4 g Total Fat; 24 mg Sodium; 1 g Protein; 8 g Carbohydrate; trace Dietary Fibre

Pictured on page 85.

Chocolate Almond Cookies

Large soft and chewy cookies with lots of chocolate bits! Mix three kinds of chocolate for a variety of tastes. Great as a dipper in Eggnog Fondue, page 102.

Butter (not margarine), softened	1 1/2 cups	375 mL
Brown sugar, packed	2 cups	500 mL
Granulated sugar	1 cup	250 mL
Large eggs	4	4
Almond flavouring	2 tbsp.	30 mL
All-purpose flour	4 2/3 cups	1.15 L
Baking soda	2 tsp.	10 mL
Salt	2 tsp.	10 mL
Milk (or dark or white) chocolate candy bars (3 1/2 oz., 100 g, each), coarsely chopped	6	6
Slivered almonds, lightly toasted (see Tip, page 100)	1 cup	250 mL

Cream butter and both sugars together in large bowl. Beat in eggs, 1 at a time, beating well after each addition. Add almond flavouring. Beat.

Stir flour, baking soda and salt together in medium bowl. Add to butter mixture. Mix well until no dry flour remains.

Add chocolate and almonds. Stir. Drop 3 tbsp. (50 mL) batter, 3 to 4 inches (7.5 to 10 cm) apart, onto greased cookie sheet. Bake in 350°F (175°C) oven for 11 to 12 minutes until edges turn golden. Do not overbake. Cookies may still look slightly undercooked in centre. Let stand on sheet for 2 minutes before removing to wire racks to cool. Makes 3 1/2 dozen cookies.

1 cookie: 276 Calories; 13.7 g Total Fat; 268 mg Sodium; 3 g Protein; 36 g Carbohydrate; 1 g Dietary Fibre

Pictured on page 85 and on page 102.

To always have food on hand for unexpected guests, make your favourite freezable recipes and fill up your freezer. This is especially handy for casseroles, cookies, breads and squares.

Left: Piña Colada Squares, page 82   Top Centre: Chocolate Orange Treats, page 84   Right: Chocolate Almond Cookies, page 84

Ambrosia Orange Cookies

Lovely delicate orange flavour with hint of coconut.
Edible gold glitter fancies these cookies up for any occasion.

GLAZE

Prepared orange juice	3 tbsp.	50 mL
Icing (confectioner's) sugar	2 tbsp.	30 mL
Hard margarine (or butter), softened	1/4 cup	60 mL
Granulated sugar	2/3 cup	150 mL
Large egg	1	1
Prepared orange juice	2 tbsp.	30 mL
Finely grated orange rind	2 tsp.	10 mL
All-purpose flour	1 cup	250 mL
Baking soda	1/2 tsp.	2 mL
Salt	1/4 tsp.	1 mL
Medium coconut	1/2 cup	125 mL

Edible gold glitter (or coloured
  fine sugar), for garnish

Glaze: Stir first amount of orange juice and icing sugar together in small bowl until smooth. Set aside.

Cream margarine and sugar together in large bowl. Beat in egg, second amount of orange juice and rind.

Slowly mix in flour, baking soda, salt and coconut. Drop by rounded teaspoonfuls 2 inches (5 cm) apart on greased cookie sheet. Bake in 350°F (175°C) oven for about 10 minutes until edges turn golden. Let stand for 1 minute before removing to wire racks to cool.

Brush with glaze. Sprinkle with edible gold glitter. Makes 2 dozen cookies.

1 cookie: 80 Calories; 3.6 g Total Fat; 79 mg Sodium; 1 g Protein; 11 g Carbohydrate; trace Dietary Fibre

Pictured on page 2/3 and on page 86/87.

Grasshopper Squares

A pretty green mint layer sandwiched between chocolate cake and chocolate glaze layers.

BOTTOM LAYER

Hard margarine (or butter), softened	1/2 cup	125 mL
Brown sugar, packed	1 cup	250 mL
Large eggs	2	2
Vanilla	1/2 tsp.	2 mL
All-purpose flour	1/2 cup	125 mL
Cocoa, sifted if lumpy	1/4 cup	60 mL
Baking soda	1/4 tsp.	1 mL
Salt	1/8 tsp.	0.5 mL

MIDDLE LAYER

Hard margarine (or butter), softened	2/3 cup	150 mL
Icing (confectioner's) sugar	2 cups	500 mL
Milk	1 1/2 tbsp.	25 mL
Peppermint flavouring	1 tsp.	5 mL
Drops of green food colouring	5 – 6	5 – 6

TOP LAYER

Semi-sweet chocolate chips	1 cup	250 mL
Hard margarine (or butter)	3 tbsp.	50 mL

Bottom Layer: Cream margarine and brown sugar together in medium bowl. Beat in eggs, 1 at a time, beating well after each addition. Add vanilla. Mix.

Add next 4 ingredients. Beat until moistened. Turn into greased 9 × 9 inch (22 × 22 cm) pan. Bake in 350°F (175°C) oven for 15 minutes. Do not overcook. Cool thoroughly.

Middle Layer: Beat all 5 ingredients together in separate medium bowl. Spread over bottom layer.

Top Layer: Heat and stir chocolate chips and margarine in small heavy saucepan on low until melted and smooth. Spread over mint layer. Chill overnight until set. Cuts into 36 squares.

1 square: 153 Calories; 9.1 g Total Fat; 109 mg Sodium; 1 g Protein; 18 g Carbohydrate; 1 g Dietary Fibre

Pictured on page 3 and on page 87.

Top: Peanut Butter Bites, page 88
Centre: Grasshopper Squares, above
Centre Right: Rum And Butter Balls, page 84
Bottom Left: Ambrosia Orange Cookies, page 85

Peanut Butter Bites

Always a favourite combo—soft peanut butter log encased in a chocolate shell. More like candy than a cookie.

Smooth peanut butter	1 1/2 cups	375 mL
Hard margarine (or butter), softened	1/2 cup	125 mL
Graham cracker crumbs	1 cup	250 mL
Icing (confectioner's) sugar	2 1/2 cups	625 mL
White chocolate melting wafers	2/3 cup	150 mL
Green chocolate melting wafers	2/3 cup	150 mL
Red chocolate melting wafers	2/3 cup	150 mL

Mix peanut butter and margarine in large bowl.

Add graham crumbs and icing sugar. Mix well. Let stand for 10 minutes. Press or roll out between sheets of waxed paper into 7 × 10 inch (18 × 25 cm) rectangle 1/2 inch (12 mm) thick. Chill until firm. Peel off top layer of waxed paper. Cut into 1/2 × 1 3/4 inch (1.2 × 4.5 cm) bars. Arrange close together on baking sheet. Freeze.

Heat melting wafers separately in glass bowls over simmering water in small saucepan, stirring occasionally, until just melted. Remove from heat. Dip 1/3 of frozen bars into white chocolate, allowing excess to drip back into bowl. Place on foil or waxed paper to set. Repeat with remaining frozen bars and green and red chocolate. Makes about 6 dozen bites.

1 bite: 92 Calories; 5.8 g Total Fat; 54 mg Sodium; 2 g Protein; 9 g Carbohydrate; 1 g Dietary Fibre

Pictured on page 3 and on page 87.

Butterscotch Cookies, below

Butterscotch Cookies

These no-bake cookies are golden and crunchy. Sweet with a mild peanut butter flavour!

Smooth peanut butter	3 tbsp.	50 mL
Butterscotch chips	1 cup	250 mL
Corn flakes cereal	3 cups	750 mL
Chopped pecans (or walnuts)	1/2 cup	125 mL

Heat and stir peanut butter in large saucepan on medium until hot. Add butterscotch chips. Stir until melted. Remove from heat.

Add cereal and pecans. Stir until well coated. Drop by rounded tablespoonfuls into mounds onto waxed paper. Let stand until firm. Makes about 2 1/2 dozen cookies.

1 cookie: 53 Calories; 2.4 g Total Fat; 36 mg Sodium; 1 g Protein; 8 g Carbohydrate; trace Dietary Fibre

Pictured above.

Choc-A-Nut Fudge

Smooth and creamy fudge with a nut crunch.
The best indulgence ever.

Granulated sugar	2 cups	500 mL
Cocoa, sifted if lumpy	1/3 cup	75 mL
Salt	1/8 tsp.	0.5 mL
Corn syrup	2 tbsp.	30 mL
Hard margarine (or butter)	2 tbsp.	30 mL
Milk	3/4 cup	175 mL
Smooth peanut butter	1/2 cup	125 mL
Chopped unsalted peanuts (or walnuts)	1/2 cup	125 mL

Combine first 6 ingredients in 3 quart (3 L) heavy saucepan. Heat and stir on medium until boiling. Reduce heat to medium-low. Boil gently, without stirring, for 20 to 30 minutes until mixture reaches soft ball stage (234° to 240°F, 112° to 116°C) on candy thermometer or until small amount dropped into very cold water forms a soft ball that flattens on its own accord when removed. Remove from heat. Cool, without stirring, for 10 minutes.

Stir in peanut butter and peanuts. Beat with electric mixer for about 2 minutes until thick and colour lightens. Turn into greased 8 × 8 inch (20 × 20 cm) pan. Pat smooth. Chill until firm. Makes 1 1/2 lbs. (680 g) fudge. Cuts into 36 squares.

1 square: 94 Calories; 3.8 g Total Fat; 38 mg Sodium; 2 g Protein; 15 g Carbohydrate; 1 g Dietary Fibre

Pictured below.

Ragged Chocolate Drops

Sweet, crunchy and chewy all in one.
Kids will love these no-bake confections.

Shoestring potato chips (original flavour)	2 cups	500 mL
Unsalted peanuts	1 cup	250 mL
Sultana raisins (or dried cranberries)	1/2 cup	125 mL
Miniature multi-coloured (or white) marshmallows	2 cups	500 mL
Smooth peanut butter	1/4 cup	60 mL
Milk chocolate chips	2 cups	500 mL
White chocolate chips	2 cups	500 mL

Toss first 4 ingredients together in large bowl.

Heat and stir peanut butter and both chocolate chips in small heavy saucepan on low until chocolate is almost melted. Remove from heat. Stir until smooth. Immediately pour over marshmallow mixture. Toss until well coated. Drop by rounded tablespoonfuls into mounds onto waxed paper. Let stand at room temperature until firm. Makes about 50 chocolate drops.

1 chocolate drop: 120 Calories; 7.1 g Total Fat; 24 mg Sodium; 2 g Protein; 13 g Carbohydrate; 1 g Dietary Fibre

CHUNKY FUDGE: Press warm chocolate mixture into 9 × 9 inch (22 × 22 cm) foil-lined pan, using a sheet of waxed paper to protect your hands. Chill until set, if desired. Turn out of pan and remove foil before cutting. Cuts into 54 squares.

Pictured below.

Left: Caramel Nut Squares, page 91   Bottom Centre: Choc-A-Nut Fudge, above   Right: Chunky Fudge, above

New Year's Fritters, below

New Year's Fritters

The little bits of fruit are so pretty peeking out. Many different cultures have a similar recipe—Olie Bollen in Holland and Portzelky within the Mennonite community are versions of this yummy snack.

Diced dried apricots	1/2 cup	125 mL
Dried cranberries (or other dried fruit)	1/2 cup	125 mL
Golden raisins	1/2 cup	125 mL
Boiling water	2 cups	500 mL
Chopped glazed red and/or green cherries	1/2 cup	125 mL
Large eggs, room temperature	3	3
Granulated sugar	3 tbsp.	50 mL
Salt	1/2 tsp.	2 mL
Hot milk	1 1/2 cups	375 mL
Hard margarine (or butter)	1 tbsp.	15 mL
All-purpose flour	2 cups	500 mL
Instant yeast	1 tbsp.	15 mL
All-purpose flour, approximately	2 – 2 1/2 cups	500 – 625 mL

Cooking oil, for deep-frying

Icing (confectioner's) sugar (optional)

Mix apricots, cranberries and raisins in small bowl. Add boiling water. Let stand for 5 minutes. Drain. Spread fruit on dry tea towel or paper towels. Let stand until no moisture remains. Return to bowl.

Add cherries. Stir.

Beat eggs, granulated sugar and salt together in large bowl using fork. Slowly stir in hot milk and margarine until margarine is melted. Mixture should feel very warm but not hot.

Combine first amount of flour and yeast in separate small bowl. Stir into egg mixture. Vigorously stir for 2 to 3 minutes until batter is smooth, very sticky, and yeast is dissolved. Stir in fruit mixture.

Add second amount of flour, 1/2 cup (125 mL) at a time, until soft sticky dough forms that is too soft to knead but leaves the side of bowl while mixing. Place dough in large greased bowl, turning once to grease top. Cover with greased waxed paper and tea towel. Let stand in oven with light on and door closed for about 1 hour until doubled in bulk. Stir dough down.

Drop 4 to 5 rounded tablespoonfuls into hot (375°F, 190°C) cooking oil. Deep-fry for 4 to 4 1/2 minutes, turning to cook evenly, until deep golden colour. Remove fritters to paper towels to drain. Repeat with remaining dough.

Dust with icing sugar before serving. Makes about 5 dozen fritters.

1 fritter: 77 Calories; 2.9 g Total Fat; 29 mg Sodium; 2 g Protein; 11 g Carbohydrate; 1 g Dietary Fibre

Pictured on this page.

Fritters are best eaten the same day but can be frozen in airtight containers after cooking and cooling. To cook from frozen, do not thaw. Heat in 350°F (175°C) oven for about 10 minutes until warmed through. Or dough can also be measured out in fritter-sized portions onto lightly floured baking sheet and frozen. Once frozen solid, they can be stored in resealable freezer bags. Deep-fry, 3 at a time, in hot 360°F (182°C) cooking oil for about 5 minutes, turning to cook evenly, until deep golden colour.

Caramel Nut Squares

Sweet caramel with butter-crunch chocolate bar pieces.

All-purpose flour	1 2/3 cups	400 mL
Pecans	1/2 cup	125 mL
Brown sugar, packed	1/3 cup	75 mL
Hard margarine (or butter), chilled, cut into 8 pieces	1 cup	250 mL
Can of sweetened condensed milk	11 oz.	300 mL
Large eggs	2	2
Corn syrup	1/4 cup	60 mL
Vanilla	1 tsp.	5 mL
Chopped pecans	1 cup	250 mL
Chocolate-covered crispy toffee bars (such as Skor or Heath), 1 1/2 oz. (39 g) each, coarsely chopped	3	3

Measure flour, first amount of pecans and brown sugar into food processor. Process for a few seconds until just combined. Add margarine to flour mixture. Pulse with on/off motion several times until margarine is size of small peas. Firmly press into bottom of greased foil-lined 9 × 13 inch (22 × 33 cm) pan. Bake in 350°F (175°C) oven for 12 to 14 minutes until edges are golden. Cool for 10 minutes.

Beat condensed milk, eggs, corn syrup and vanilla together in medium bowl until blended.

Stir in second amount of pecans and chocolate bar pieces. Pour over crust. Spread evenly. Bake for 25 to 30 minutes until wooden pick inserted in centre comes out clean. Cool. Remove from pan. Remove foil. Cut into 1 1/2 inch (3.8 cm) squares. Cuts into 54 squares.

1 square: 131 Calories; 8.4 g Total Fat; 69 mg Sodium; 2 g Protein; 13 g Carbohydrate; trace Dietary Fibre

Pictured on page 89.

Toasted Popcorn Snack, below

Toasted Popcorn Snack

You get just a little nip from the Parmesan cheese and cayenne. A savoury, chunky snack that people will congregate around at your next party.

Hard margarine (or butter), melted	1/2 cup	125 mL
Grated Parmesan cheese	1/4 cup	60 mL
Worcestershire sauce	4 tsp.	20 mL
Salt	1/4 tsp.	1 mL
Garlic powder	3/4 tsp.	4 mL
Onion powder	1/2 tsp.	2 mL
Cayenne pepper	1/2 tsp.	2 mL
Popped corn (about 1/4 cup, 60 mL, unpopped)	8 cups	2 L
Rice squares cereal	3 cups	750 mL
Mini pretzels	5 cups	1.25 L

Combine first 7 ingredients in large bowl.

Add remaining 3 ingredients. Stir until coated well. Spread in large roasting pan. Bake in 300°F (150°C) oven for about 20 minutes, stirring occasionally, until lightly toasted. Makes 16 cups (4 L).

1/2 cup (125 mL): 84 Calories; 3.7 g Total Fat; 260 mg Sodium; 2 g Protein; 11 g Carbohydrate; 1 g Dietary Fibre

Pictured above.

Condiments

Honey Mustard Sauce

This sauce has a sweet flavour and a rich mustard colour.
Great with Maple And Rye Gravlax, page 48.

Grainy mustard	1/4 cup	60 mL
Brown sugar, packed	1 tbsp.	15 mL
Liquid honey	1 tbsp.	15 mL
Ground ginger	1/8 tsp.	0.5 mL

Combine all 4 ingredients in small bowl. Makes 1/3 cup (75 mL).

2 tbsp. (30 mL): 64 Calories; 1.5 g Total Fat; 311 mg Sodium; 1 g Protein; 13 g Carbohydrate; trace Dietary Fibre

Pictured on page 46.

Savoury Orange Dipping Sauce

Strong orange and mild mustard tastes in this sauce which may also be served cold. Good with Spring Rolls, page 167, meatballs, grilled chicken, chicken nuggets or pork.

Orange marmalade	1/2 cup	125 mL
Prepared horseradish	2 tsp.	10 mL
Grainy mustard	2 tsp.	10 mL

Combine all 3 ingredients in small saucepan. Heat and stir on medium until marmalade is melted. Makes 1/2 cup (125 mL).

2 tbsp. (30 mL): 103 Calories; 0.2 g Total Fat; 63 mg Sodium; trace Protein; 27 g Carbohydrate; trace Dietary Fibre

Pictured on page 164.

Fresh Herb Sauce

The perfect sauce for fish with its tarragon and thyme flavours. Good with Crab And Cheddar Waffles, page 81.

Mayonnaise (not salad dressing)	1 cup	250 mL
Milk	3 tbsp.	50 mL
Chopped fresh parsley	1 tbsp.	15 mL
Chopped fresh tarragon leaves	1 1/2 tsp.	7 mL
Fresh thyme leaves	1/2 tsp.	2 mL

Combine all 5 ingredients in small bowl. Chill until ready to serve. Makes 1 1/3 cups (325 mL).

2 tbsp. (30 mL): 155 Calories; 16.9 g Total Fat; 111 mg Sodium; trace Protein; trace Carbohydrate; trace Dietary Fibre

Pictured on page 78.

Horseradish Beet Relish

This is a delicious condiment served with turkey, beef and even egg dishes. Easy to double or even triple the recipe for hostess gifts.

Coarsely grated cooked beets	1 cup	250 mL
White vinegar	1/4 cup	60 mL
Creamed horseradish	1 tbsp.	15 mL
Granulated sugar	1 tbsp.	15 mL
Salt	1/4 tsp.	1 mL
Pepper	1/8 tsp.	0.5 mL

Combine all 6 ingredients in small bowl. Chill until ready to serve. Makes 1 1/4 cups (300 mL).

2 tbsp. (30 mL): 12 Calories; trace Total Fat; 69 mg Sodium; trace Protein; 3 g Carbohydrate; trace Dietary Fibre

Pictured on this page.

Fresh Tomato Relish

Red tomatoes and green peppers give this condiment the colours of Christmas. Delicious served with fish, chicken and roast beef or pork.

Chopped, seeded roma (plum) tomato	1 cup	250 mL
Finely chopped red onion	1/4 cup	60 mL
Finely chopped green pepper	1/4 cup	60 mL
Garlic clove, minced (or 1/4 tsp., 1 mL, powder)	1	1
Chopped fresh parsley (or cilantro), or 1 1/8 tsp. (6 mL) flakes	1 1/2 tbsp.	25 mL
Chopped fresh sweet basil (or 3/4 tsp., 4 mL, dried)	1 tbsp.	15 mL
Snipped fresh chives (or 1/4 tsp., 1 mL, dried)	1 1/2 tsp.	7 mL
Red wine vinegar	1 1/2 tsp.	7 mL
Hot pepper sauce	1/4 tsp.	1 mL
Salt	1/4 tsp.	1 mL
Freshly ground pepper, sprinkle		

Combine all 11 ingredients in medium bowl. Let stand for 2 hours at room temperature to blend flavours. Makes 1 1/3 cups (325 mL).

2 tbsp. (30 mL): 6 Calories; 0.1 g Total Fat; 58 mg Sodium; trace Protein; 1 g Carbohydrate; trace Dietary Fibre

Pictured on page 36.

Rhubarb Relish

Traditional chutney with a bit of tangy rhubarb. Serve with Handlheld Tourtières, page 166.

Chopped frozen (or fresh) rhubarb	2 cups	500 mL
Chopped onion	2 cups	500 mL
Brown sugar, packed	1 cup	250 mL
White vinegar	3/4 cup	175 mL
Ground allspice	1/2 tsp.	2 mL
Ground cinnamon	1/2 tsp.	2 mL
Ground cloves	1/2 tsp.	2 mL
Salt	1/2 tsp.	2 mL
Pepper	1/16 tsp.	0.5 mL

Combine all 9 ingredients in large saucepan. Simmer, uncovered, for about 60 minutes until rhubarb is tender and liquid is thickened. Makes 1 2/3 cups (400 mL).

2 tbsp. (30 mL): 99 Calories; 0.1 g Total Fat; 117 mg Sodium; 1 g Protein; 25 g Carbohydrate; 1 g Dietary Fibre

Pictured below.

Top Left & Right: Rhubarb Relish, above
Bottom Left: Horseradish Beet Relish, this page

Desserts

Strawberry Pizza Pie

Beautiful fruit topping on a cake crust.

CRUST		
Hard margarine (or butter), softened	1/4 cup	60 mL
Granulated sugar	1/4 cup	60 mL
Brown sugar, packed	1/4 cup	60 mL
Large egg	1	1
Milk	1/4 cup	60 mL
Vanilla	1/2 tsp.	2 mL
All-purpose flour	1 3/4 cups	425 mL
Cream of tartar	1 tsp.	5 mL
Baking soda	1/2 tsp.	2 mL
Salt	1/4 tsp.	1 mL
FILLING		
Block of cream cheese, softened	8 oz.	250 g
Icing (confectioner's) sugar	1 1/4 cups	300 mL
Lemon juice	1 tsp.	5 mL
Frozen whipped topping, thawed	2 cups	500 mL
Sliced fresh strawberries	2 1/2 cups	625 mL
Sliced ripe kiwifruit	1 cup	250 mL
Apple jelly	1/3 cup	75 mL

Crust: Cream margarine and both sugars together in medium bowl. Add egg. Beat. Add milk and vanilla. Beat until smooth.

Mix flour, cream of tartar, baking soda and salt in small bowl. Add to margarine mixture. Mix well. Turn out and spread evenly onto greased 12 inch (30 cm) pizza pan. Bake in 375°F (190°C) oven for about 20 minutes until golden. Cool thoroughly.

Filling: Beat cream cheese, icing sugar and lemon juice together in separate medium bowl until light and fluffy. Fold in whipped topping. Spread evenly over crust.

Arrange strawberries and kiwifruit over cream cheese mixture to make attractive pattern.

Heat jelly in small saucepan on medium-low, stirring occasionally, until liquefied. Dab surface of fruit with glaze to give shine and to prevent fruit from drying out. Chill until ready to serve. Serves 10 to 12.

1 serving: 440 Calories; 18.7 g Total Fat; 277 mg Sodium; 6 g Protein; 64 g Carbohydrate; 3 g Dietary Fibre

Pictured on page 95.

Left: Strawberry Pizza Pie, page 94   Top Right: Mango Rum Fluff, page 96   Bottom Right: Peaches And Cream Cake, this page

Peaches And Cream Cake

A saucy cream forms around the peach slices.
Garnish with peach slices and whipped cream.

All-purpose flour	1 cup	250 mL
Vanilla pudding powder (not instant), 6 serving size	1	1
Baking powder	1 tsp.	5 mL
Salt	1/2 tsp.	2 mL
Hard margarine (or butter), softened	3 tbsp.	50 mL
Large egg	1	1
Milk	2/3 cup	150 mL
Can of sliced peaches, drained, juice reserved	14 oz.	398 mL
Block of cream cheese, softened	8 oz.	250 g
Granulated sugar	1/2 cup	125 mL
Reserved peach juice	3 tbsp.	50 mL
TOPPING		
Granulated sugar	2 tbsp.	30 mL
Ground cinnamon	1 tbsp.	15 mL

Measure first 7 ingredients into large bowl. Beat well until smooth. Turn into greased 8 × 8 inch (20 × 20 cm) pan.

Arrange peach slices over batter.

Beat cream cheese, sugar and peach juice together in medium bowl. Drop dabs here and there over peach slices. Spread as best you can.

Topping: Stir sugar and cinnamon together in small cup. Sprinkle over cream cheese mixture. Bake in 350°F (175°C) oven for 60 to 70 minutes until wooden pick inserted in centre comes out clean. Cuts into 16 pieces.

1 piece: 193 Calories; 8.2 g Total Fat; 252 mg Sodium; 3 g Protein; 28 g Carbohydrate; 1 g Dietary Fibre

Pictured above.

PEACHES AND COCONUT CREAM CAKE: Omit vanilla pudding powder. Use coconut cream pudding powder (not instant), 6 serving size.

Mango Rum Fluff

And a light bit of fluff it is!
A fresh taste after a heavy meal.

Envelope of unflavoured gelatin (1/4 oz., 7 g)	1	1
Cold water	1/4 cup	60 mL
Granulated sugar	1/2 cup	125 mL
Lemon juice	1 tbsp.	15 mL
Salt	1/16 tsp.	0.5 mL
Can of sliced mango in syrup, drained, puréed	14 oz.	398 mL
Amber (or dark) rum (or 1/2 tsp., 2 mL, rum flavouring)	1 tbsp.	15 mL
Almond flavouring	1/4 tsp.	1 mL
Whipping cream	1 cup	250 mL
Amber (or dark) rum (or 1/4 tsp., 1 mL, rum flavouring)	1 1/2 tsp.	7 mL
Slivered (or flaked) almonds, toasted (see Tip, page 100)	1 tbsp.	15 mL
Edible red glitter, for garnish		

Sprinkle gelatin over cold water in small saucepan. Let stand for 5 minutes until softened. Heat and stir on medium until gelatin is dissolved.

Add sugar, lemon juice and salt. Stir until sugar is dissolved. Remove from heat.

Add mango, first amount of rum and almond flavouring. Mix well. Transfer to large bowl. Chill for 50 to 60 minutes, stirring occasionally, until mixture mounds softly.

Beat whipping cream in separate large bowl until stiff peaks form. Reserve 1/2 cup (125 mL) in refrigerator. Fold remaining whipped cream into mango mixture. Chill. Makes 4 cups (1 L).

Stir second amount of rum into reserved whipped cream. Spread in centre or around rim of dessert in serving bowl. Sprinkle with almonds and edible red glitter. Serves 6.

1 serving: 259 Calories; 14.3 g Total Fat; 45 mg Sodium; 2 g Protein; 31 g Carbohydrate; trace Dietary Fibre

Pictured on page 95.

To beat whipping cream faster, chill the bowl and beaters first. To keep whipped cream from separating, add 2 tsp. (10 mL) vanilla pudding powder (not instant) per 1 cup (250 mL) whipping cream.

Chilled Chocolate Cheesecake

A good no-bake, make-ahead dessert.

VANILLA WAFER CRUST		
Hard margarine (or butter)	6 tbsp.	100 mL
Vanilla wafer crumbs	1 1/2 cups	375 mL
Cocoa, sifted if lumpy	1 tbsp.	15 mL
FILLING		
Envelopes of unflavoured gelatin (1/4 oz., 7 g, each)	2	2
Cold water	2 cups	500 mL
Semi-sweet chocolate chips	1 cup	250 mL
Block of light cream cheese, softened	12 oz.	375 g
Granulated sugar	1/2 cup	125 mL
Vanilla	1 tsp.	5 mL
Envelope of dessert topping (not prepared)	1	1
Milk	1/2 cup	125 mL
Chocolate ice cream topping	1/2 cup	125 mL

Vanilla Wafer Crust: Melt margarine in medium saucepan. Add wafer crumbs and cocoa. Stir until well mixed. Firmly press into bottom of ungreased 10 inch (25 cm) springform pan. Chill.

Filling: Sprinkle gelatin over cold water in separate medium saucepan. Let stand for 1 minute until softened. Heat and stir until gelatin is dissolved. Remove from heat.

Add chocolate chips. Stir until melted. Cool.

Beat cream cheese, sugar and vanilla together in large bowl until smooth. Beat in chocolate mixture. Chill for about 1 hour until beginning to thicken.

Beat dessert topping and milk together in medium bowl until stiff peaks form. Fold into chocolate mixture. Turn into crust. Chill for at least 6 hours or overnight.

Drizzle 2 tsp. (10 mL) ice cream topping over individual wedges. Cuts into 12 wedges.

1 wedge: 350 Calories; 20.9 g Total Fat; 332 mg Sodium; 6 g Protein; 38 g Carbohydrate; 1 g Dietary Fibre

Pictured on page 97.

Butterscotch Peanut Treat

The perfect finale to any meal.

CRUST

Hard margarine (or butter), melted	1/2 cup	125 mL
Chocolate wafer crumbs	2 cups	500 mL
Ice cream (your choice), softened	8 cups	2 L
Dry-roasted peanuts, coarsely chopped	1 cup	250 mL
Butterscotch ice cream topping	1 cup	250 mL
Chocolate ice cream topping	1 cup	250 mL
Frozen whipped topping, thawed (or whipped cream)	2 cups	500 mL

Crust: Melt margarine in medium saucepan. Add wafer crumbs. Stir until well mixed. Reserve 1/2 cup (125 mL). Firmly press remaining crumb mixture into ungreased 9 × 13 inch (22 × 33 cm) pan.

Spoon ice cream in dabs here and there over crust. Spread evenly. Sprinkle with peanuts. Drizzle both ice cream toppings over peanuts. Cover. Freeze for about 1 1/2 hours until set.

Spread whipped topping over top. Sprinkle with reserved crumb mixture. Freeze until firm. Remove from freezer about 10 minutes before cutting. Store in freezer. Serves 15 to 18.

1 serving: 510 Calories; 27.9 g Total Fat; 341 mg Sodium; 8 g Protein; 63 g Carbohydrate; 1 g Dietary Fibre

Pictured below.

Creamsicle Dessert

A cool, light dessert that's easy to make.
Good chilled or frozen.

CRUST

Hard margarine (or butter)	1/4 cup	60 mL
Graham cracker crumbs	1 cup	250 mL
Granulated sugar	1 tbsp.	15 mL
Package of orange-flavoured gelatin (jelly powder)	3 oz.	85 g
Boiling water	1 cup	250 mL
Lemon juice	1 tbsp.	15 mL
Vanilla ice cream	2 cups	500 mL

Crust: Melt margarine in medium saucepan. Add graham crumbs and sugar. Stir until well mixed. Reserve 3 tbsp. (50 mL). Firmly press remaining crumb mixture into bottom of ungreased 9 × 9 inch (22 × 22 cm) pan. Set aside.

Combine jelly powder and boiling water in medium bowl. Stir until jelly powder is dissolved.

Add lemon juice and ice cream. Stir until smooth. Pour over crust. Sprinkle with reserved crumb mixture. Chill overnight or freeze until firm. Cuts into 9 pieces.

1 piece: 194 Calories; 9.8 g Total Fat; 172 mg Sodium; 3 g Protein; 25 g Carbohydrate; trace Dietary Fibre

Pictured below.

Top Left: Chilled Chocolate Cheesecake, page 96
Top Right: Butterscotch Peanut Treat, this page
Bottom Centre: Creamsicle Dessert, above

Butterscotch Sauce

An easy make-your-own sauce. Serve hot over ice cream or warm over Spice Coffee Cake, page 77.

Hard margarine (or butter)	1/2 cup	125 mL
Brown sugar, packed	1 1/3 cups	325 mL
Corn syrup	3/4 cup	175 mL
Salt	1/8 tsp.	0.5 mL
Half-and-half cream	1 cup	250 mL
Vanilla	1 tsp.	5 mL

Measure first 4 ingredients into medium saucepan. Heat and stir on medium until starting to boil and brown sugar is dissolved. Boil gently on medium-low for 5 minutes, stirring frequently. Remove from heat.

Slowly stir in cream and vanilla. Mixture may sputter a bit. Stir until well blended. Makes 2 3/4 cups (675 mL).

2 tbsp. (30 mL): 134 Calories; 5.3 g Total Fat; 86 mg Sodium; trace Protein; 22 g Carbohydrate; 0 g Dietary Fibre

Pictured on page 78.

Vanilla Sauce

A slightly sweet sauce, nice over puddings, pound cakes or fresh fruit. Drizzle over Fruit Pudding, page 100.

Granulated sugar	1 cup	250 mL
All-purpose flour	3 tbsp.	50 mL
Salt	1/2 tsp.	2 mL
Hot water	1 1/2 cups	375 mL
Hard margarine (or butter)	2 tbsp.	30 mL
Vanilla	1 tsp.	5 mL

Mix sugar, flour and salt in small saucepan.

Stir in hot water, margarine and vanilla. Heat and stir on medium until boiling and thickened. Sauce will thicken as it cools. Makes 2 cups (500 mL).

2 tbsp. (30 mL): 67 Calories; 1.4 g Total Fat; 88 mg Sodium; trace Protein; 14 g Carbohydrate; trace Dietary Fibre

Pictured on page 98 and on page 99.

Top Right: Fruit Pudding, page 100, with Vanilla Sauce, above
Centre Left: Honey Jewel Cake, page 101
Centre Right: Vanilla Sauce, above
Bottom Left & Right: Fruit Pudding, page 100

Fruit Pudding

Chewy, fruity and mildly spiced.
This pudding is a great gift-giving idea.
Drizzle Vanilla Sauce, page 98, over this tasty dessert.

Raisins	1 cup	250 mL
Currants	1 cup	250 mL
Chopped mixed glazed fruit	1 cup	250 mL
Chopped dates	1 cup	250 mL
Rolled oats (not instant)	2 cups	500 mL
Hard margarine (or butter), softened	1 cup	250 mL
Corn syrup	1 cup	250 mL
Large egg	1	1
All-purpose flour	1 1/2 cups	375 mL
Salt	1 1/2 tsp.	7 mL
Ground cinnamon	1 tsp.	5 mL
Baking soda	1 tsp.	5 mL
Ground cloves	1/4 tsp.	1 mL
Milk	1 cup	250 mL

Combine first 5 ingredients in large bowl. Toss well to coat fruit.

Beat margarine, corn syrup and egg together in separate large bowl until thick and smooth.

Stir next 5 ingredients together in small bowl.

Add flour mixture to margarine mixture in 3 additions, alternating with milk in 2 additions, beginning and ending with flour mixture. Stir in fruit mixture. Turn into greased 10 cup (2.5 L) pudding pan or large heatproof bowl. Cover with double layer of greased foil, domed slightly to allow for expansion. Secure foil by tying string around pan. Place pan in steamer or Dutch oven with rack (or metal jar rings). Pour boiling water into steamer until water comes 2/3 of the way up sides of pan. Cover. Simmer on low for 3 hours. Add more boiling water to keep level up as needed. Carefully remove pan from steamer. Let stand for 20 minutes before turning out onto wire rack to cool completely. Cover with plastic wrap and foil. Store in freezer for up to 2 months or in refrigerator for 2 to 3 weeks. Reheat before serving. Serves 14.

1 serving: 463 Calories; 15.7 g Total Fat; 564 mg Sodium; 6 g Protein; 80 g Carbohydrate; 5 g Dietary Fibre

Pictured on page 98 and on page 99.

Variation: Grease bottom of four 28 oz. (796 mL) cans. Line greased bottoms with circles of waxed paper. Fill each can 2/3 full with pudding batter. Top each with 1 red glazed cherry (optional). Cover each can with double layer of greased foil. Secure foil by tying string around cans. Place all 4 cans in Dutch oven with rack (or metal jar rings). Pour boiling water into Dutch oven until water comes 2/3 of the way up sides of cans. Cover. Simmer on low for 2 1/2 hours. Add more boiling water to keep level up as needed. Carefully remove cans from Dutch oven. Run knife around sides of cans to loosen pudding. Turn each out onto wire rack. Cool. Puddings may be individually covered with plastic wrap and attractively tied with ribbon to be given away as gifts. Makes 4 individual puddings.

To toast almonds, flaxseeds, pine nuts, sesame seeds and walnuts, place in single layer in ungreased shallow pan. Bake in 350°F (175°C) oven for 5 to 10 minutes, stirring or shaking often, until desired doneness

Honey Jewel Cake

A pretty, golden cake with lots of "jewels" visible once cut.
Great for dipping in Eggnog Fondue, page 102.

Sultana raisins	1 cup	250 mL
Red and/or green glazed cherries, coarsely chopped	1 cup	250 mL
Glazed pineapple, chopped	1 cup	250 mL
Golden raisins	2/3 cup	150 mL
Diced mixed peel	1/2 cup	125 mL
Sherry (or alcohol-free sherry)	1/4 cup	60 mL
Ground almonds	1/2 cup	125 mL
Butter (not margarine), softened	1 cup	250 mL
Liquid honey	1/2 cup	125 mL
Granulated sugar	1/3 cup	75 mL
Large eggs	4	4
Finely grated lemon rind	2 tsp.	10 mL
Finely grated orange rind	2 tsp.	10 mL
All-purpose flour	1 3/4 cups	425 mL
Baking powder	1/2 tsp.	2 mL
Salt	1/4 tsp.	1 mL
Slivered almonds	1 1/2 cups	375 mL
Whole blanched almonds, for garnish	1/3 cup	75 mL
Red and green glazed cherries, for garnish	1/3 cup	75 mL
Sherry (or alcohol-free sherry)	3 tbsp.	50 mL
Cheesecloth, enough to wrap cakes in double thickness		

Combine first 5 ingredients in large bowl. Sprinkle with first amount of sherry. Mix well to moisten. Cover. Let stand overnight at room temperature.

Add ground almonds. Toss well to coat. Set aside.

Cream butter, honey and sugar together in separate large bowl. Add eggs, 1 at a time, beating well after each addition. Beat in lemon and orange rind.

Combine flour, baking powder and salt in separate large bowl. Gradually beat into butter mixture.

Stir in slivered almonds. Add to fruit mixture. Stir well. Spoon batter into 2 greased parchment paper-lined 8 x 4 x 3 inch (20 x 10 x 7.5 cm) loaf pans. Bake in 300°F (150°C) oven for 40 minutes. Remove from oven.

Gently lay whole almonds and second amount of cherries in attractive pattern over surface of cakes. Bake for 1 1/2 to 2 hours until cake is firm to touch, cracks appear on surface and wooden pick inserted in centre comes out clean. Remove from oven. Cool in pans on wire racks. Turn out of pans. Peel off parchment paper.

Poke several holes into cakes using skewer. Slowly drizzle 1 tbsp. (15 mL) second amount of sherry over each cake. Soak cheesecloth in remaining sherry. Wrap cakes in cheesecloth. Wrap in waxed paper. Tightly wrap in foil. Store in cool place for at least 2 weeks. To store uncut cakes, store in cool place for up to 10 weeks. Check cakes weekly and remoisten cheesecloth with more sherry if necessary. Cut into 1/2 inch (12 mm) thick slices. Cut each slice into thirds. Makes 2 cakes, each cutting into 48 pieces, for a total of 96 pieces.

1 piece: 85 Calories; 3.9 g Total Fat; 32 mg Sodium; 1 g Protein; 12 g Carbohydrate; trace Dietary Fibre

Pictured on page 98/99 and on page 102.

Use the front cover of last year's Christmas cards as this year's gift tags. Be sure to check that there isn't any writing on the back of the cards before cutting out design.

Top Left: Chocolate Almond Cookies, page 84
Top Centre: Honey Jewel Cake, page 101
Centre Right: Eggnog Fondue, below

Eggnog Fondue

Very good festive fondue. Great use for eggnog and Christmas fruitcake.

All-purpose flour	2 tbsp.	30 mL
Cornstarch	2 tbsp.	30 mL
Brown sugar, packed	1 tbsp.	15 mL
Salt, just a pinch		
Milk (not skim)	1 cup	250 mL
Eggnog	2 cups	500 mL
Large egg	1	1
Vanilla	1 tsp.	5 mL
Ground nutmeg, sprinkle		
Ground cinnamon, sprinkle		
Dark rum	2 tbsp.	30 mL

Combine first 4 ingredients in large saucepan.

Slowly stir in milk and eggnog until smooth. Cook on medium, stirring frequently, until boiling and slightly thickened. Remove from heat.

Beat egg, vanilla, nutmeg and cinnamon together in small bowl using fork. Add 2 large spoonfuls eggnog mixture to egg mixture. Mix well. Stir into hot eggnog mixture. Heat and stir on medium-low for 2 minutes. Remove from heat.

Stir in rum. Carefully pour into fondue pot to no more than 2/3 full. Place over low heat. Add more eggnog or rum as necessary to keep proper dipping consistency. Makes 3 cups (750 mL).

2 tbsp. (30 mL): 46 Calories; 1.9 g Total Fat; 20 mg Sodium; 1 g Protein; 5 g Carbohydrate; trace Dietary Fibre

Pictured on this page.

Suggested dippers: Chocolate Almond Cookies, page 84; Honey Jewel Cake pieces, page 101; angel food cake; banana; doughnut pieces; firm chocolate cake cubes; fruitcake; kiwifruit; marshmallows; mini muffin halves; soft ginger cookies; strawberries.

Peach Mousse

A great dessert for a light finish.
Very nice served in individual glasses.

Package of peach (or lemon) flavoured gelatin (jelly powder)	3 oz.	85 g
Boiling water	1 cup	250 mL
Cold water	1/2 cup	125 mL
Jars of strained peaches (baby food), 4 1/2 oz. (128 mL) each	3	3
Brandy flavouring (optional)	1/4 tsp.	1 mL
Frozen whipped topping, thawed	2 cups	500 mL
Sliced fresh (or frozen or canned) peaches, for garnish		

Dissolve jelly powder in boiling water in large serving bowl.

Add cold water, peaches and flavouring. Stir. Chill for about 2 hours, stirring and scraping down sides of bowl occasionally, until slightly thickened.

Fold whipped topping into peach mixture until smooth. Chill for about 2 hours until softly set.

Garnish with peach slices. Serves 6.

1 serving: 182 Calories; 7.1 g Total Fat; 63 mg Sodium; 2 g Protein; 29 g Carbohydrate; 0 g Dietary Fibre

Pictured on page 103.

APRICOT MOUSSE: Omit strained peaches (baby food). Use strained apricots (baby food).

Eggnog Chantilly

This light eggnog dessert is perfect after all the turkey and heavy food! Best if chilled overnight.

Brown sugar, packed	1/4 cup	60 mL
All-purpose flour	6 tbsp.	100 mL
Ground nutmeg, sprinkle		
Ground cinnamon, sprinkle		
Eggnog	1 1/2 cups	375 mL
Milk	1 cup	250 mL
Large eggs	3	3
Unflavoured gelatin (1/2 of 1/4 oz., 7 g, envelope)	1 1/2 tsp.	7 mL
Dark rum	2 tbsp.	30 mL
Whipping cream	1 1/2 cups	375 mL

Edible gold glitter (or gold-coloured fine sugar or cinnamon sugar), for garnish

Combine first 4 ingredients in large saucepan.

Slowly add eggnog and milk, while whisking, until smooth. Heat and whisk on medium until boiling and thickened. Remove from heat.

Beat eggs in small bowl using fork. Add 2 large spoonfuls of hot eggnog mixture to eggs. Mix well. Stir into eggnog mixture. Heat and stir for about 2 minutes until beginning to boil and thicken.

Sprinkle gelatin over rum in small dish. Let stand for 1 minute until softened. Stir into hot eggnog mixture until gelatin is dissolved. Cover with plastic wrap directly on surface to prevent skin forming. Cool to room temperature. Turn into large bowl.

Beat whipping cream in small bowl until soft peaks form. Fold 2 large spoonfuls into cooled eggnog mixture. Fold in remaining whipped cream. Cover. Chill for several hours or overnight.

Sprinkle individual servings with edible gold glitter before serving. Makes 7 cups (1.75 L).

1/2 cup (125 mL): 178 Calories; 12.1 g Total Fat; 50 mg Sodium; 4 g Protein; 12 g Carbohydrate; trace Dietary Fibre

Pictured on this page.

Top Right: Eggnog Chantilly, above
Centre Left: Peach Mousse, page 102
Bottom Right: White Chocolate Liqueur Freeze, page 105

Pineapple Fluff Cake

A taste of the tropics. Make the day before to allow the pineapple flavour to intensify.

White cake mix (2 layer size)	1	1
Instant vanilla pudding powder (4 serving size)	1	1
Large eggs	4	4
Cooking oil	1/2 cup	125 mL
Vanilla	1 tsp.	5 mL
Pineapple juice	1 1/3 cups	325 mL
FILLING		
Block of cream cheese, softened	8 oz.	250 g
Envelope of dessert topping (prepared)	1	1
Can of crushed pineapple, drained and juice reserved	14 oz.	398 mL
ICING		
Hard margarine (or butter), softened	3/4 cup	175 mL
Icing (confectioner's) sugar	4 cups	1 L
Reserved pineapple juice	5 – 6 tbsp.	75 – 100 mL
Coconut (or vanilla) flavouring	1 tsp.	5 mL
Flake (or long thread) coconut, for garnish	2/3 cup	150 mL
Drops of yellow food colouring, for garnish	1 – 2	1 – 2

Empty cake mix into large bowl. Add pudding powder, eggs, cooking oil, vanilla and pineapple juice. Beat on low until just moistened. Beat on medium for about 2 minutes until smooth. Divide between 2 greased 9 inch (22 cm) round pans. Bake in 350°F (175°C) oven for about 35 minutes until wooden pick inserted in centre comes out clean. Let stand in pans for 15 minutes before turning out onto wire racks to cool completely. Cut each layer in half horizontally to make 4 cake layers.

Filling: Beat cream cheese in medium bowl until smooth. Add dessert topping. Beat well.

Place bottom cake layer on serving plate. Spread with 1/3 of filling. Sprinkle with 1/3 of pineapple. Repeat with 2 more cake layers. Top with remaining cake layer.

Icing: Beat first 4 ingredients together in separate medium bowl until smooth and spreadable. Ice top and sides of cake.

Combine coconut and food colouring in large plastic bowl with lid. Cover. Shake for about 2 minutes until coconut is coloured. Spread on paper towel to remove excess colour. Let stand for 10 minutes to air dry. Sprinkle over icing. Chill for 24 hours. Store, covered with plastic wrap, in refrigerator. Cuts into 16 wedges.

1 wedge: 548 Calories; 27.7 g Total Fat; 482 mg Sodium; 5 g Protein; 72 g Carbohydrate; trace Dietary Fibre

Pictured on page 105.

Cherry Mix-Up Cake

A moist and colourful cake with a cream cheese icing that adds even more sweetness.

Large eggs	2	2
Water	1/2 cup	125 mL
Cooking oil	1/4 cup	60 mL
White cake mix (2 layer size)	1	1
Can of cherry pie filling	19 oz.	540 mL
CREAM CHEESE ICING		
Block of cream cheese, softened	4 oz.	125 g
Hard margarine (or butter), softened	2 tbsp.	30 mL
Icing (confectioner's) sugar	2 1/2 cups	625 mL
Vanilla	1 tsp.	5 mL
Milk	1 tbsp.	15 mL

Beat eggs, water and cooking oil together in medium bowl until frothy.

Add cake mix. Beat on low until moistened. Spread in greased 9 x 13 inch (22 x 33 cm) pan.

Spoon pie filling in dabs here and there over batter. Swirl with knife or spoon to create marble effect. Bake in 350°F (175°C) oven for about 45 minutes until wooden pick inserted in centre comes out clean. Cool.

Cream Cheese Icing: Beat all 5 ingredients together well in small bowl, adding more milk or icing sugar if necessary, until proper spreading consistency. Drizzle icing over top or ice cake. Cuts into 24 pieces.

1 piece: 228 Calories; 8.1 g Total Fat; 180 mg Sodium; 2 g Protein; 38 g Carbohydrate; trace Dietary Fibre

Pictured on page 105.

Bottom Left: Cherry Nut Crumble, below   Top Centre: Cherry Mix-Up Cake, page 104   Bottom Right: Pineapple Fluff Cake, page 104

Cherry Nut Crumble

Slight almond and nutmeg flavours with warm cherry filling.
The topping is crispy and sweet. Great with ice cream!

Can of cherry pie filling	19 oz.	540 mL
Almond flavouring	1/4 tsp.	1 mL
Ground nutmeg	1/8 – 1/4 tsp.	0.5 – 1 mL
TOPPING		
Hard margarine (or butter), softened	6 tbsp.	100 mL
Brown sugar, packed	2/3 cup	150 mL
All-purpose flour	1/2 cup	125 mL
Quick-cooking rolled oats (not instant)	1/2 cup	125 mL
Sliced (or slivered) almonds	1/2 cup	125 mL

Combine pie filling, flavouring and nutmeg in ungreased 2 quart (2 L) casserole.

Topping: Mix first 4 ingredients in medium bowl until crumbly.

Add almonds. Mix. Sprinkle over pie filling mixture. Bake, uncovered, in 350°F (175°C) oven for about 30 minutes until lightly browned. Let stand for 10 minutes before serving. Serves 6.

1 serving: 455 Calories; 18.5 g Total Fat; 156 mg Sodium; 5 g Protein; 71 g Carbohydrate; 3 g Dietary Fibre

Pictured above.

White Chocolate Liqueur Freeze

A smooth, special dessert perfect when topped with a maraschino cherry.

Granulated sugar	3/4 cup	175 mL
Milk	2 1/2 cups	625 mL
Whipping cream	1 cup	250 mL
White chocolate baking squares (1 oz., 28 g, each), cut up	8	8
Milk	1/2 cup	125 mL
Egg whites (large), room temperature	3	3
Cherry-flavoured liqueur (such as Kirsch) or almond-flavoured liqueur (such as Amaretto)	3 tbsp.	50 mL

Combine first 3 ingredients in large bowl.

Heat and stir chocolate and second amount of milk in medium saucepan on low until smooth. Remove from heat. Add about 1 cup (250 mL) whipping cream mixture. Mix well. Add to whipping cream mixture. Stir well.

Beat egg whites in small bowl until stiff peaks form. Gently stir into whipping cream mixture. Stir in liqueur. Freeze until firm or freeze in ice-cream maker according to manufacturer's directions. Makes 6 cups (1.5 L).

1/2 cup (125 mL): 261 Calories; 13.1 g Total Fat; 70 mg Sodium; 5 g Protein; 30 g Carbohydrate; 0 g Dietary Fibre

Pictured on page 103.

Brownie Cake Dessert

*Serve this dense, chewy, rich chocolate cake
with ice cream for a finishing touch.*

Hard margarine (or butter)	1/2 cup	125 mL
Unsweetened chocolate baking squares (1 oz., 28 g, each), cut up	2	2
Large eggs	2	2
Granulated sugar	1 cup	250 mL
Vanilla	1 tsp.	5 mL
All-purpose flour	3/4 cup	175 mL
Baking powder	3/4 tsp.	4 mL
Salt	1/4 tsp.	1 mL
Chopped walnuts (optional)	1/2 cup	125 mL
CHOCOLATE GLAZE		
Semi-sweet chocolate baking squares (1 oz., 28 g, each), cut up	1 1/2	1 1/2
Milk	2 tbsp.	30 mL

Coarsely chopped walnuts, for garnish

Melt margarine and chocolate in medium saucepan on low, stirring often, until smooth. Cool.

Beat eggs in medium bowl until frothy. Beat in sugar and vanilla. Add chocolate mixture. Mix.

Add flour, baking powder and salt. Stir until just moistened.

Add walnuts. Stir. Turn into greased 8 x 8 inch (20 x 20 cm) pan. Bake in 350°F (175°C) oven for about 30 minutes until wooden pick inserted in centre comes clean. Do not overbake.

Chocolate Glaze: Combine chocolate and milk in small saucepan. Heat and stir on low until chocolate is melted. Smooth over warm cake.

Garnish with walnuts. Cuts into 12 pieces.

1 piece: 226 Calories; 12.6 g Total Fat; 180 mg Sodium; 3 g Protein; 28 g Carbohydrate; 1 g Dietary Fibre

Pictured on page 108.

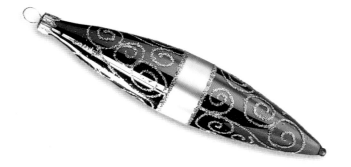

Chocolate Raspberry Biscotti

A wonderful biscotti with a hint of hazelnut.

Hard margarine (or butter), softened	1/3 cup	75 mL
Granulated sugar	1/2 cup	125 mL
Sweetened powdered raspberry-flavoured drink crystals	3 tbsp.	50 mL
Large egg	1	1
Egg yolk (large)	1	1
Cocoa, sifted if lumpy	1/4 cup	60 mL
Baking powder	1 1/2 tsp.	7 mL
Salt	1/4 tsp.	1 mL
All-purpose flour, approximately	1 1/2 cups	375 mL
Egg white (large)	1	1
Water	1 tsp.	5 mL
Flaked hazelnuts (filberts)	2 1/2 tbsp.	37 mL
White (or pink) chocolate melting wafers (optional)	1 cup	250 mL

Beat first 3 ingredients together in large bowl until thoroughly combined. Beat in egg and egg yolk until smooth.

Add cocoa, baking powder and salt. Mix well.

Gradually work in enough flour until stiff dough forms. Turn out onto lightly floured surface. Knead until smooth. Shape into log about 8 1/2 inches (21 cm) long. Flatten slightly to 1 1/2 inches (3.8 cm) high. Place on lightly greased baking sheet.

Beat egg white and water together in small dish using fork. Brush over log.

Sprinkle with hazelnuts. Bake in 375°F (190°C) oven for about 20 minutes until firm and wooden pick inserted in centre comes out clean. Remove to wire rack to cool for 1 hour. Reduce oven heat to 325°F (160°C). Cut, on slight diagonal, into 1/2 inch (12 mm) slices. Arrange, cut side down, on lightly greased baking sheet. Bake for 20 to 25 minutes, turning at halftime, until surface appears quite dry. Remove to wire rack to cool.

Heat chocolate in small glass bowl over saucepan with simmering water, stirring occasionally, until just melted. Dip biscotti halfway into chocolate, allowing excess chocolate to drip back into bowl. Place on waxed paper-lined baking sheets to dry. Makes 16 biscotti.

1 biscotti: 133 Calories; 5.7 g Total Fat; 129 mg Sodium; 3 g Protein; 19 g Carbohydrate; 1 g Dietary Fibre

Pictured on page 109.

Orange Cheesecake

A beautiful cheesecake with a decidedly orange flair.

CRUST

All-purpose flour	1 cup	250 mL
Granulated sugar	1/4 cup	60 mL
Hard margarine (or butter)	1/2 cup	125 mL

FILLING

Blocks of light cream cheese (8 oz., 250 g, each), softened	4	4
Granulated sugar	1 1/4 cups	300 mL
All-purpose flour	2 tbsp.	30 mL
Frozen concentrated orange juice, thawed	3 tbsp.	50 mL
Finely grated orange rind	2 tbsp.	30 mL
Large eggs	4	4

GLAZE

Can of mandarin orange segments, drained and juice reserved	10 oz.	284 mL
Frozen concentrated orange juice	2 tbsp.	30 mL
Water	1/4 cup	60 mL
Cornstarch	1 1/2 tbsp.	25 mL
Granulated sugar	2 tbsp.	30 mL
Whipped topping, for garnish	1/2 cup	125 mL
Chocolate curls, for garnish	24	24

Crust: Combine flour and sugar in medium bowl. Cut in margarine until crumbly. Press into ungreased 9 inch (22 cm) springform pan. Bake in 350°F (175°C) oven for 15 minutes. Cool.

Filling: Beat cream cheese, sugar, flour, concentrated orange juice and orange rind together in large bowl until smooth. Beat in eggs, 1 at a time, on low until just blended. Turn into crust. Bake on bottom rack in 350°F (175°C) oven for about 60 minutes until set. Run knife around side to allow cheesecake to settle evenly. Cool. Remove side of pan.

Glaze: Arrange orange segments in attractive pattern on top of cheesecake.

Pour reserved mandarin orange juice into medium saucepan. Add frozen orange juice and water. Stir well. Stir in cornstarch and sugar. Heat and stir on medium until clear and slightly thickened. Pour over cheesecake. Chill.

Garnish with whipped topping and chocolate curls. Cuts into 16 wedges.

1 wedge: 349 Calories; 19.5 g Total Fat; 524 mg Sodium; 9 g Protein; 36 g Carbohydrate; 1 g Dietary Fibre

Pictured on page 109.

Chocolate Oatmeal Cake

Moist, dark chocolate cake.
Top with Tropical Fruit Sauce, page 110.

Quick-cooking rolled oats (not instant)	1 cup	250 mL
Cocoa, sifted if lumpy	1/3 cup	75 mL
Boiling water	1 1/2 cups	375 mL
Hard margarine (or butter), softened	1/2 cup	125 mL
Brown sugar, packed	1 cup	250 mL
Large eggs	2	2
Vanilla	1 tsp.	5 mL
All-purpose flour	1 1/4 cups	300 mL
Baking soda	1 tsp.	5 mL
Salt	1 tsp.	5 mL
Mini semi-sweet chocolate chips	1/3 cup	75 mL

Combine rolled oats and cocoa in small bowl. Pour boiling water over top. Let stand for 15 minutes.

Cream margarine and brown sugar together in large bowl. Beat in eggs, 1 at a time, beating well after each addition. Add vanilla and rolled oat mixture. Beat until blended.

Add flour, baking soda and salt. Beat on medium for about 1 minute until well mixed.

Stir in chocolate chips. Turn into greased 9 inch (22 cm) round pan. Bake in 350°F (175°C) oven for about 55 minutes until wooden pick inserted in centre comes out clean. Cuts into 8 to 10 pieces.

1 piece: 409 Calories; 17.2 g Total Fat; 633 mg Sodium; 7 g Protein; 60 g Carbohydrate; 3 g Dietary Fibre

Pictured on page 108.

Photo Legend next page:

1. White Chocolate Cherry Cheesecake, page 110
2. Chocolate Raspberry Biscotti, page 106
3. Orange Cheesecake, this page
4. Chocolate Oatmeal Cake, above
5. Tropical Fruit Sauce, page 110
6. Brownie Cake Dessert, page 106

White Chocolate Cherry Cheesecake

So pretty when cut and the bits of cherry peek out.
A decadent dessert!

CRUST

Hard margarine (or butter)	1/2 cup	125 mL
Digestive biscuit crumbs (about 12 biscuits)	1 1/2 cups	375 mL
Cocoa, sifted if lumpy	3 tbsp.	50 mL
Ground almonds	1/2 cup	125 mL

FILLING

Blocks of cream cheese (8 oz., 250 g, each), room temperature	3	3
Sour cream	1 cup	250 mL
Granulated sugar	1/2 cup	125 mL
Cherry-flavoured liqueur (such as Kirsch) or maraschino cherry syrup	3 tbsp.	50 mL
Large eggs	4	4
White chocolate baking squares (1 oz., 28 g, each), cut up	6	6
All-purpose flour	2 tbsp.	30 mL
Quartered maraschino cherries, blotted dry	2/3 cup	150 mL
Whipping cream (or 1 envelope dessert topping, prepared)	1 cup	250 mL
Icing (confectioner's) sugar	1 tbsp.	15 mL
Maraschino cherries, for garnish		
Shaved white chocolate, for garnish		

Crust: Melt margarine in medium saucepan on low. Add biscuit crumbs, cocoa and almonds. Stir until well mixed. Firmly press into bottom and 1 inch (2.5 cm) up side of ungreased 10 inch (25 cm) springform pan.

Filling: Beat cream cheese, sour cream and granulated sugar together in large bowl until light and fluffy.

Beat in liqueur. Add eggs, 1 at a time, beating on low until just mixed.

Heat chocolate in heavy medium saucepan on lowest heat, stirring often, until just melted. Beat into cream cheese mixture on low speed.

Toss flour and cherries together in separate small bowl until cherries are coated. Stir into cream cheese mixture. Turn into crust. Bake on bottom rack in 325°F (160°C) oven for 1 1/4 to 1 1/2 hours until centre is almost set and top is golden. Run knife around side to allow cheesecake to settle evenly. Cool. Remove side of pan.

Beat whipping cream and icing sugar together until stiff peaks form. Pipe rosettes over surface of cheesecake. Garnish with cherries and chocolate. Cuts into 12 wedges.

1 wedge: 607 Calories; 48.1 g Total Fat; 396 mg Sodium; 11 g Protein; 34 g Carbohydrate; 1 g Dietary Fibre

Pictured on page 108.

Tropical Fruit Sauce

A sweet sauce with visible cherries and mangoes.
Serve over Chocolate Oatmeal Cake, page 107.

Can of cherry pie filling	19 oz.	540 mL
Can of crushed pineapple, with juice	14 oz.	398 mL
Can of sliced mango, with syrup, diced	14 oz.	398 mL
Granulated sugar	1/3 cup	75 mL
Halved maraschino cherries	1/2 cup	125 mL
Coconut (or almond) flavouring	1 tsp.	5 mL

Heat first 5 ingredients in medium saucepan, stirring occasionally, until boiling.

Stir in flavouring. Store in airtight container in refrigerator for up to 4 weeks or freeze for up to 4 months. To serve, thaw at room temperature. Makes 6 1/2 cups (1.6 L).

2 tbsp. (30 mL): 28 Calories; trace Total Fat; 1 mg Sodium; trace Protein; 7 g Carbohydrate; trace Dietary Fibre

Pictured on page 108.

BANANA FRUIT SAUCE: Stir 1/2 cup (125 mL) broken up banana chips into sauce with flavouring. Banana chips will soften in sauce.

COCONUT FRUIT SAUCE: Stir 1/2 cup (125 mL) flake (or fancy) coconut into sauce with flavouring.

Main Dishes

Cajun Chicken

*This slow cooker recipe is tops in flavour!
The tender chicken falls off the bones. Serve with
a hearty rye or pumpernickel bread.*

Large onion, chopped	1	1
Garlic cloves, minced (or 1 tsp., 5 mL, powder)	4	4
Large red pepper, chopped	1	1
Large celery rib, chopped	1	1
Cooking oil	2 tbsp.	30 mL
All-purpose flour	2 tbsp.	30 mL
Green onions, sliced	4	4
Lean kielbasa (or ham) sausage ring, cut into 6 pieces, each piece halved lengthwise	10 oz.	300 g
Chicken thighs (about 10 pieces), skin removed	2 lbs.	900 g
Bay leaf	1	1
Can of condensed chicken broth	10 oz.	284 mL
Chili powder	1 1/2 tsp.	7 mL
Dried sweet basil	1/2 tsp.	2 mL
Dried whole oregano	1/2 tsp.	2 mL
Ground thyme	1/4 tsp.	1 mL
Pepper	1/4 tsp.	1 mL
Chili sauce	1/2 cup	125 mL

Sauté onion, garlic, red pepper and celery in cooking oil in large frying pan for 3 to 4 minutes until onion is soft.

Sprinkle flour over vegetable mixture. Stir well. Turn into 4 quart (4 L) slow cooker.

Layer green onion, sausage and chicken over vegetable mixture. Drop in bay leaf.

Combine remaining 7 ingredients in same frying pan. Heat and stir for 5 minutes, scraping up any brown bits from frying pan, until heated through. Pour over chicken. Cover. Cook on Low for 7 to 8 hours or on High for 3 1/2 to 4 hours. Serves 6 to 8.

1 serving: 341 Calories; 16.5 g Total Fat; 1103 mg Sodium; 32 g Protein; 16 g Carbohydrate; 3 g Dietary Fibre

Pictured on page 112.

Top Left: Cajun Chicken, page 111   Bottom Centre: Beef Bourguignon, below   Top Right: Slow-Cooker Lamb Curry, page 113

Beef Bourguignon

A wonderful, rich and hearty stew that can be made ahead for a crowd. Serve over egg noodles or mashed potatoes.

Boneless sirloin tip roast, cut into 1 1/4 inch (3 cm) cubes	5 lbs.	2.3 kg
Hard margarine (or butter)	1 tbsp.	15 mL
Dried rosemary, crushed	1 tsp.	5 mL
Dried thyme, crushed	1 tsp.	5 mL
Dried whole oregano	1 tsp.	5 mL
Medium onions, cut lengthwise in 8 wedges	5	5
Brown (cremini) mushrooms, halved if large	6 cups	1.5 L
Garlic cloves, minced (or 1 tsp., 5 mL, powder)	4	4
Sliced carrot, cut 1/4 inch (6 mm) thick	3 1/2 cups	875 mL
Can of condensed beef broth	10 oz.	284 mL
Dry red (or alcohol-free) wine	2 cups	500 mL
Water	1 cup	250 mL
Can of tomato paste	5 1/2 oz.	156 mL
Parsley flakes	1 tbsp.	15 mL
Salt	1 tsp.	5 mL
Granulated sugar	1/2 tsp.	2 mL
Coarsely ground pepper	1/2 tsp.	2 mL
Water	1 1/2 cups	375 mL
All-purpose flour	3/4 cup	175 mL

Brown beef, in 3 batches, in margarine in large frying pan on medium-high, adding more margarine as needed. Transfer to large roasting pan.

Add rosemary, thyme and oregano. Stir.

Sauté onion, mushrooms and garlic in same frying pan for about 5 minutes, scraping up any browned bits from frying pan, until onion is clear and soft. Add to beef mixture.

Add carrot.

Combine next 8 ingredients in same frying pan. Reduce heat to medium. Heat and stir for about 5 minutes until boiling. Add to beef mixture. Stir. Cover. Cook in 325°F (160°C) oven for 1 1/2 hours until beef is tender.

Stir water into flour in small bowl until smooth. Stir into beef mixture. Cover. Cook in oven for 30 minutes until boiling and thickened. Makes twenty 3 oz. (84 g) servings.

1 serving: 240 Calories; 6.9 g Total Fat; 312 mg Sodium; 28 g Protein; 12 g Carbohydrate; 2 g Dietary Fibre

Pictured above.

Slow-Cooker Lamb Curry

Lots of mild curry sauce, with a subtle coconut flavour, to serve over rice or potatoes.

All-purpose flour	2 tbsp.	30 mL
Seasoned salt	1 tsp.	5 mL
Cayenne pepper	1/4 tsp.	1 mL
Lean lamb stew meat, trimmed of fat and cut into 1 inch (2.5 cm) pieces	1 lb.	454 g
Cooking oil	2 tbsp.	30 mL
Sliced carrot	1 1/2 cups	375 mL
Cauliflower florets	1 cup	250 mL
Coarsely chopped green pepper	1 cup	250 mL
Medium onion, coarsely chopped	1	1
Garlic cloves, minced (or 1/2 tsp., 2 mL, powder)	2	2
Curry powder	1 tbsp.	15 mL
Can of condensed chicken broth	10 oz.	284 mL
Reserved pineapple juice	1/4 cup	60 mL
Can of pineapple chunks, drained and juice reserved	14 oz.	398 mL
Grated solid coconut cream (1/2 of 7 1/2 oz., 200 g, package)	2/3 cup	150 mL
All-purpose flour	2 tbsp.	30 mL
Plain yogurt	1/2 cup	125 mL
Chopped fresh cilantro (or mint), optional	2 tbsp.	30 mL

Combine first amount of flour, seasoned salt and cayenne pepper in large resealable plastic bag. Add lamb. Shake until completely coated.

Brown lamb in cooking oil in large frying pan. Turn into 3 quart (3 L) slow cooker.

Add carrot, cauliflower and green pepper. Stir.

Sauté onion, garlic and curry powder in same frying pan for 2 minutes.

Slowly add chicken broth and reserved pineapple juice. Heat and stir for about 5 minutes, scraping up any browned bits from pan, until boiling. Add to lamb mixture. Stir. Cover. Cook on Low for 6 hours or on High for 3 hours.

Stir pineapple and coconut cream into lamb mixture.

Stir second amount of flour into yogurt in small bowl until smooth. Stir into lamb mixture with heat on High. Cover. Cook for about 1 hour until sauce is thickened.

Sprinkle with cilantro. Makes 7 cups (1.75 L).

1 cup (250 mL): 297 Calories; 14.7 g Total Fat; 521 mg Sodium; 18 g Protein; 24 g Carbohydrate; 4 g Dietary Fibre

Pictured on page 112.

Tangy Beef Rolls

Mild horseradish and rich tomato flavours in these rolls. Serve with rice or noodles.

Cream cheese, softened	2 oz.	62.5 g
Prepared horseradish	2 tsp.	10 mL
Minute steaks (about 1 lb., 454 g, in total)	4	4
Cooking oil	1 tsp.	5 mL
Chopped fresh mushrooms	1 cup	250 mL
Hard margarine (or butter)	1/2 tsp.	2 mL
Can of tomato sauce	7 1/2 oz.	213 mL
Dried marjoram, crushed	1/2 tsp.	2 mL
Salt	1/2 tsp.	2 mL
Pepper	1/4 tsp.	1 mL

Combine cream cheese and horseradish in small bowl. Spread over 1 side of each steak. Roll up. Secure with wooden picks. Brown rolls in cooking oil in non-stick frying pan. Remove rolls to plate. Keep warm.

Sauté mushrooms in margarine in same frying pan for 2 minutes.

Stir in tomato sauce, marjoram, salt and pepper. Add rolls. Bring to a boil. Reduce heat. Cover. Simmer for 10 minutes. Serves 4.

1 serving: 258 Calories; 13.6 g Total Fat; 752 mg Sodium; 28 g Protein; 6 g Carbohydrate; 1 g Dietary Fibre

Pictured on page 115.

Don't remove the lid on your slow cooker unless instructed to do so in the recipe. Each time the cover is removed, quite a lot of heat is lost, lengthening the cooking time.

Roast Duck

Succulent duck with a different, yet scrumptious, dressing.
Serve with applesauce, chutney or relish.

SAGE STUFFING		
Medium onions, chopped	2	2
Hard margarine (or butter)	1 tbsp.	15 mL
Coarse dry bread crumbs	4 cups	1 L
Parsley flakes	2 tsp.	10 mL
Dried sage	2 tsp.	10 mL
Salt	1 tsp.	5 mL
Pepper	1/4 tsp.	1 mL
Prepared orange juice, approximately	1 cup	250 mL
Domestic duck	6 lbs.	2.7 kg
GRAVY		
Fat drippings	1/4 cup	60 mL
All-purpose flour	1/4 cup	60 mL
Salt	1/2 tsp.	2 mL
Pepper	1/8 tsp.	0.5 mL
Drippings without fat (if any), plus water to make	2 cups	500 mL

Sage Stuffing: Sauté onion in margarine in frying pan until soft.

Combine next 5 ingredients in medium bowl. Add onion. Stir.

Add enough orange juice until stuffing is moist and holds together when squeezed.

Stuff duck with stuffing. Fasten with skewer. Tie wings to body with string. Tie legs to tail. Pierce skin all over with tip of paring knife to allow fat to run out. Put into roasting pan. Cover. Roast in 350°F (175°C) oven for about 2 1/2 hours until duck is tender, skin is crisp and meat thermometer registers 180°F (82°C). Remove cover. Roast for about 15 minutes until browned. Remove duck to serving platter. Tent with foil. Let stand for 10 minutes before carving.

Gravy: Pour off all but 1/4 cup (60 mL) drippings in roaster. Mix in flour, salt and pepper until smooth.

Stir in drippings and water. Heat and stir until boiling and thickened. Taste for salt and pepper, adding more as needed. Makes 2 cups (500 mL). Serves 8.

1 serving: 779 Calories; 48.3 g Total Fat; 1032 mg Sodium; 33 g Protein; 51 g Carbohydrate; 3 g Dietary Fibre

Pictured on page 115.

Stuffed Chicken Rolls

The seasoned sauce and Swiss cheese are just the right things for this delicious chicken cooked in the slow cooker.

Boneless, skinless chicken breast halves (about 1 1/2 lbs., 680 g)	6	6
Thin deli ham slices, cut to fit chicken	6	6
Hot water	1/2 cup	125 mL
Chicken bouillon powder	2 tsp.	10 mL
White (or alcohol-free) wine (or apple juice)	1/2 cup	125 mL
Liquid gravy browner (optional)	1 tsp.	5 mL
Dried marjoram	1/2 tsp.	2 mL
Salt	1/2 tsp.	2 mL
Pepper	1/4 tsp.	1 mL
Grated Swiss cheese	1 cup	250 mL
Water	2 1/2 tbsp.	37 mL
Cornstarch	1 tbsp.	15 mL

Place chicken breasts between sheets of plastic wrap. Pound with meat mallet or rolling pin until very thin. Lay 1 ham slice on each chicken breast. Roll up. Secure with wooden picks. Arrange in 3 1/2 quart (3.5 L) slow cooker.

Measure next 7 ingredients into small bowl. Stir. Pour over chicken rolls. Cover. Cook on Low for 8 to 9 hours or on High for 4 to 4 1/2 hours.

Remove chicken rolls to serving dish using slotted spoon. Scatter cheese over chicken rolls to melt. Keep warm.

Stir water into cornstarch in separate small bowl until smooth. Stir into liquid in slow cooker with heat on High. Cover. Cook for 15 minutes, stirring occasionally, until slightly thickened. Makes about 1 1/3 cups (325 mL) sauce. Serves 6.

1 serving: 284 Calories; 11.1 g Total Fat; 932 mg Sodium; 37 g Protein; 3 g Carbohydrate; trace Dietary Fibre

Pictured on page 115.

Top Left: Greek Pea Salad, page 138
Top Right: Roast Duck, this page
Centre Left: Tangy Beef Rolls, page 113
Bottom Right: Stuffed Chicken Rolls, above

Portobello Penne

Rich mushroom, walnut and cheese flavours make this pasta dish very satisfying. Serve with a green salad.

Penne pasta (about 10 oz., 285 g)	3 1/3 cups	825 mL
Boiling water	12 cups	3 L
Salt	1 tbsp.	15 mL
Garlic clove, minced (or 1/4 tsp., 1 mL, powder)	1	1
Medium portobello mushrooms, black "gills" cut off and discarded, coarsely chopped	3	3
Olive (or cooking) oil	2 tsp.	10 mL
Dry white (or alcohol-free) wine	1/4 cup	60 mL
Can of evaporated milk	13 1/2 oz.	385 mL
Milk	1/3 cup	75 mL
Dijon mustard	2 tsp.	10 mL
Salt	1/2 tsp.	2 mL
Diced Havarti cheese (about 1/3 lb., 150 g)	1 cup	250 mL
Coarsely chopped walnuts, toasted (see Tip, page 100)	1/4 cup	60 mL

Cook pasta in boiling water and salt in large uncovered pot or Dutch oven for 12 to 15 minutes until tender but firm. Drain. Transfer to large bowl. Keep warm.

Sauté garlic and mushrooms in olive oil in large frying pan for about 5 minutes until mushrooms are barely tender.

Add wine. Boil, uncovered, until liquid reduces by half.

Add next 4 ingredients. Bring to a boil. Reduce heat. Simmer, uncovered, for about 10 minutes, stirring occasionally, until sauce reduces slightly. The sauce will still be quite thin but will thicken when combined with pasta. Add to pasta.

Add cheese and walnuts. Toss gently until cheese begins to melt and some sauce is absorbed into pasta. Makes 6 cups (1.5 L).

1 cup (250 mL): 429 Calories; 17.7 g Total Fat; 497 mg Sodium; 20 g Protein; 47 g Carbohydrate; 2 g Dietary Fibre

Pictured on this page.

Chicken Raspberry

Nicely browned, tender chicken enhanced by raspberry vinegar and rosemary.

Hard margarine (or butter)	1 tbsp.	15 mL
Cooking oil	1 tbsp.	15 mL
Boneless, skinless chicken breast halves (about 1 1/2 lbs., 680 g)	6	6
Salt, sprinkle		
Pepper, sprinkle		
Ground rosemary	1/4 tsp.	1 mL
Finely chopped onion	1/4 cup	60 mL
Raspberry vinegar	1/3 cup	75 mL
Water	1/2 cup	125 mL
Chicken bouillon powder	1 tsp.	5 mL
Dried chives	1 tsp.	5 mL

Heat margarine and cooking oil in frying pan. Add chicken. Brown both sides, sprinkling with salt, pepper and rosemary. Transfer to plate. Keep warm.

Sauté onion in same frying pan, scraping up any browned bits from pan, until golden.

Add vinegar, water and bouillon powder. Boil for 5 minutes until slightly reduced. Makes 1/3 cup (75 mL) sauce.

Add chives. Stir. Add chicken. Bring to a boil. Reduce heat. Cover. Simmer for about 5 minutes to blend flavours. Serves 6.

1 serving: 173 Calories; 6.3 g Total Fat; 132 mg Sodium; 26 g Protein; 2 g Carbohydrate; trace Dietary Fibre

Pictured on this page.

Centre Left: Portobello Penne, above
Bottom Right: Chicken Raspberry, this page

Left: Creamy Onion Sauce, page 118   Top Centre: Shrimp Marinara Sauce, page 118   Bottom Right: Creamy Seafood Sauce, this page

Creamy Seafood Sauce

A rich sauce you won't believe is low in fat! A lot of great colour in this delicious sauce. Serve over pasta.

Raw medium shrimp (about 15), peeled and deveined (or frozen, thawed)	1/2 lb.	225 g
Fresh (or frozen, thawed) small scallops	1/2 lb.	225 g
Water	1/2 cup	125 mL
White (or alcohol-free) wine (or sherry)	1/4 cup	60 mL
Seafood (or chicken) bouillon powder	1 tsp.	5 mL
Garlic clove, minced (or 1/4 tsp., 1 mL, powder)	1	1
Small zucchini, diced	1	1
Small broccoli florets	2 cups	500 mL
Sliced fresh mushrooms	1 cup	250 mL
Diced red pepper	1/2 cup	125 mL
Green onions, sliced	2	2
Ripe medium roma (plum) tomato, diced	1	1
Basil pesto	2 tbsp.	30 mL
Can of skim evaporated milk	13 1/2 oz.	385 mL
All-purpose flour	3 tbsp.	50 mL

Combine first 5 ingredients in medium saucepan on medium-high. Bring to a boil. Reduce heat to medium. Simmer, uncovered, for 3 minutes until shrimp is pink. Do not drain. Remove seafood to small bowl using slotted spoon. Cover. Keep warm.

Add garlic, zucchini, broccoli and mushrooms to liquid in saucepan. Bring to a boil. Reduce heat to medium. Cover. Simmer for 3 minutes.

Add red pepper, green onion, tomato and pesto. Bring to a boil. Reduce heat. Cover. Simmer for 3 minutes.

Stir evaporated milk into flour in small bowl until smooth. Stir into vegetable mixture until boiling and thickened. Gently stir in shrimp and scallops until heated through. Makes 7 cups (1.75 L).

3/4 cup (175 mL): 125 Calories; 2.4 g Total Fat; 204 mg Sodium; 14 g Protein; 11 g Carbohydrate; 1 g Dietary Fibre

Pictured above.

Creamy Onion Sauce

A thin, sweet, versatile sauce with a hint of nutmeg. Serve over pasta or as an accompaniment to beef, chicken or fish.

Medium Spanish (or white) onions, coarsely chopped	2	2
Hard margarine (or butter)	2 tbsp.	30 mL
Brown sugar, packed	1 tsp.	5 mL
Water	1 cup	250 mL
Vegetable (or chicken) bouillon powder	2 tsp.	10 mL
Can of evaporated milk	13 1/2 oz.	385 mL
Cornstarch	2 tsp.	10 mL

Salt, sprinkle
Pepper, sprinkle
Ground nutmeg, sprinkle

Fresh sprigs of parsley, for garnish

Sauté onion in margarine in large frying pan until soft. Reduce heat to low.

Stir in brown sugar. Cover. Cook for about 15 minutes, stirring occasionally, until onion is very soft and beginning to turn golden.

Add water and bouillon powder. Stir well. Bring to a boil. Reduce heat. Cover. Simmer for 30 minutes. Cool slightly.

Combine onion mixture and 1/2 of evaporated milk in blender. Process until very smooth. Return to frying pan.

Stir remaining evaporated milk into cornstarch in small bowl until smooth. Stir into onion mixture.

Add salt, pepper and nutmeg. Heat and stir until boiling and slightly thickened.

Garnish with parsley. Makes 3 cups (750 mL).

1/4 cup (60 mL): 76 Calories; 4.7 g Total Fat; 168 mg Sodium; 3 g Protein; 6 g Carbohydrate; trace Dietary Fibre

Pictured on page 117.

To warm your plates just before using, place them in the oven on lowest heat for 2 minutes. Turn heat off.

Shrimp Marinara Sauce

The sweet tang of vinegar and herbs is nicely balanced with shrimp. Thin, tomato-coloured broth with chunky pieces. Serve over your favourite pasta. Garnish with finely grated Parmesan cheese.

Garlic cloves, minced (or 1/2 tsp., 2 mL, powder)	2	2
Chopped onion	1/2 cup	125 mL
Olive (or cooking) oil	2 tbsp.	30 mL
Can of diced tomatoes, with juice	28 oz.	796 mL
Dried whole oregano	1 1/2 tsp.	7 mL
Dried sweet basil	1 1/2 tsp.	7 mL
Red wine vinegar	1 tbsp.	15 mL
Granulated sugar	1 1/2 tbsp.	25 mL
Salt	1/2 tsp.	2 mL
Pepper	1/2 tsp.	2 mL
Cooked salad shrimp	8 oz.	225 g

Sauté garlic and onion in olive oil in large frying pan until onion is soft.

Add next 7 ingredients. Stir. Bring to a boil. Reduce heat. Simmer, uncovered, for 30 minutes.

Stir in shrimp. Cook for 3 to 4 minutes until heated through. Makes 3 2/3 cups (900 mL).

3/4 cup (175 mL): 148 Calories; 6.3 g Total Fat; 586 mg Sodium; 11 g Protein; 13 g Carbohydrate; 2 g Dietary Fibre

Pictured on page 117.

Paprika Stew With Zucchini Biscuits

A hearty, chunky stew with puffy golden biscuit topping and very tender beef.

Beef stew meat, cut into 1 1/2 inch (3.8 cm) pieces	2 lbs.	900 g
Cooking oil	2 tbsp.	30 mL
Medium onions, cut into 6 wedges each	4	4
Garlic clove, minced (or 1/4 tsp., 1 mL, powder)	1	1
Paprika	4 tsp.	20 mL
Hot water	1 cup	250 mL
Cans of diced tomatoes (14 oz., 398 mL, each), with liquid	2	2
Can of tomato paste	5 1/2 oz.	156 mL
Seasoned salt	1 tsp.	5 mL
Pepper	1/4 tsp.	1 mL
Medium carrots, sliced into 1/2 inch (12 mm) pieces	5	5
Celery ribs, cut into 1 1/2 inch (3.8 cm) pieces	4	4
Red (or alcohol-free) wine	1/3 cup	75 mL
ZUCCHINI BISCUITS		
Biscuit mix	2 1/2 cups	625 mL
Grated zucchini, with peel	2/3 cup	150 mL
Sour cream	1/2 cup	125 mL

Brown beef, in 2 batches, in cooking oil in large frying pan. Remove to ungreased 4 quart (4 L) casserole using slotted spoon.

Add onion, garlic and paprika to same frying pan. Sauté for 3 to 4 minutes, scraping up any browned bits from pan, until onion is soft.

Stir in hot water. Bring to a boil. Pour over beef.

Add next 7 ingredients to beef mixture. Stir. Cover. Bake in 325°F (160°C) oven for 2 1/2 hours. Increase heat to 425°F (220°C).

Zucchini Biscuits: Combine biscuit mix, zucchini and sour cream in medium bowl until just moistened. Turn out onto lightly floured surface. Knead 5 or 6 times until dough holds together. Pat out to same diameter as casserole surface. Cut into wedges or pieces. Assemble on top of beef mixture. Bake, uncovered, for about 15 minutes until biscuits are golden. Serves 8.

1 serving: 500 Calories; 20.5 g Total Fat; 945 mg Sodium; 32 g Protein; 46 g Carbohydrate; 5 g Dietary Fibre

Pictured on page 120.

Saucy Chicken

Good homemade flavour with a little bite and lots of excellent sauce to serve over fettuccine noodles or rice.

Chicken parts, skin and visible fat removed	4 lbs.	1.8 kg
Envelope of dry onion soup mix	1 1/2 oz.	42 g
Can of whole cranberry sauce	14 oz.	398 mL
French dressing	1 cup	250 mL

Arrange chicken in roasting pan.

Combine soup mix, cranberry sauce and dressing in medium bowl. Spoon over chicken, being sure to get some on every piece. Cover tightly with lid or foil. Bake in 350°F (175°C) oven for 1 hour. Remove cover. Baste chicken with sauce. Cover. Bake for 30 minutes until chicken is tender. Serves 6 to 8.

1 serving: 488 Calories; 22.5 g Total Fat; 1464 mg Sodium; 32 g Protein; 40 g Carbohydrate; 1 g Dietary Fibre

Pictured on page 120.

Gypsy Stew

Comfort food with very Old World flavour.
Serve over buttered noodles or mashed potatoes.

Bacon slices, chopped	6	6
Lean pork stew meat	2 1/4 lbs.	1 kg
Large onions, halved lengthwise and thinly sliced	2	2
Garlic cloves, minced (or 3/4 tsp., 4 mL, powder)	3	3
Paprika	4 tsp.	20 mL
Caraway seed	1 tsp.	5 mL
Water	2 cups	500 mL
Jar of sauerkraut, rinsed and drained	17 1/2 oz.	500 mL
Chicken bouillon powder	1 tsp.	5 mL
All-purpose flour	2 tbsp.	30 mL
Sour cream	1 cup	250 mL
Salt, sprinkle		
Pepper, sprinkle		
Bacon slice, cooked crisp and crumbled, for garnish	1	1

Fry first amount of bacon in large uncovered pot or Dutch oven until browned. Drain all but 1 tbsp. (15 mL) drippings.

Add pork, onion, garlic, paprika and caraway seed to bacon. Sauté for about 10 minutes, stirring frequently, until onion is soft.

Stir in water. Bring to a boil. Reduce heat. Cover. Simmer for 1 hour.

Stir in sauerkraut and bouillon powder. Bring to a boil. Reduce heat. Cover. Simmer for 45 to 60 minutes until pork is tender.

Stir flour into sour cream in small bowl until smooth. Stir into pork mixture for about 10 minutes on low until boiling and slightly thickened.

Add salt and pepper. Stir.

Sprinkle second amount of bacon over individual servings. Makes 8 cups (2 L).

1 cup (250 mL): 307 Calories; 16.5 g Total Fat; 565 mg Sodium; 29 g Protein; 10 g Carbohydrate; 2 g Dietary Fibre

Pictured below.

Top Left: Paprika Stew With Zucchini Biscuits, page 119
Top Right: Saucy Chicken, page 119
Bottom Centre: Gypsy Stew, this page

Stuffed Turkey Breast

The cranberry stuffing imparts a tart but subtle sweetness. A very impressive presentation. This may look complicated and fussy, but is really very easy. The drippings can be used for making gravy. Leftover turkey can be used to make Meaty Turkey Rice Soup, page 157.

SPICED CRANBERRY STUFFING

Chopped onion	1/2 cup	125 mL
Chopped celery	1/2 cup	125 mL
Garlic cloves, minced (or 1/2 tsp., 2 mL, powder), optional	2	2
Hard margarine (or butter)	1/4 cup	60 mL
Chopped cranberries	2/3 cup	150 mL
Grated peeled tart cooking apple (such as Granny Smith)	1/2 cup	125 mL
Fine dry bread crumbs	1/2 cup	125 mL
Brown sugar, packed	1 tbsp.	15 mL
Ground cinnamon	1/4 tsp.	1 mL
Ground nutmeg	1/8 tsp.	0.5 mL
Ground allspice	1/8 tsp.	0.5 mL
Cayenne pepper	1/8 tsp.	0.5 mL
Salt	1/2 tsp.	2 mL
Pepper	1/8 tsp.	0.5 mL
Apple juice (or water), approximately	1 tbsp.	15 mL
Whole bone-in turkey breast (see Note)	6 lbs.	2.7 kg
Margarine (or butter), melted	2 tbsp.	30 mL
Seasoned salt	1/2 tsp.	2 mL
Pepper, sprinkle		

Spiced Cranberry Stuffing: Sauté onion, celery and garlic in margarine in large frying pan for about 4 minutes until onion is soft. Remove from heat.

Add next 10 ingredients. Mix well.

Add enough apple juice until stuffing is moist and holds together when squeezed.

Cut turkey crosswise into 1 inch (2.5 cm) thick slices right to the bone on both sides. You should be able to cut about 6 slices on each side. Use very sharp knife to keep skin intact. Divide stuffing among "pockets" cut into turkey. Tie butcher's string horizontally around turkey once or twice to hold slices with stuffing together. Place turkey, cut side up, in medium roasting pan.

Drizzle second amount of margarine over turkey. Sprinkle seasoned salt and second amount of pepper over top. Cover. Roast in 325°F (160°C) oven for 1 3/4 to 2 hours, basting turkey several times with juices from bottom of roasting pan, until meat thermometer registers 180°F (82°C). Increase heat to 400°F (205°C). Remove cover. Roast for about 15 minutes until skin is browned. Serves 10 to 12.

1 serving: 404 Calories; 13.9 g Total Fat; 433 mg Sodium; 58 g Protein; 9 g Carbohydrate; 1 g Dietary Fibre

Pictured on page 122.

Note: A 14 to 15 lb. (6.4 to 6.8 kg) turkey will yield a 6 lb. (2.7 kg) turkey breast.

Plan your Christmas meals ahead of time, being realistic and time conscious. Planning ahead will save you the headache of last minute rushes or forgotten items. Check our Menu Suggestions section starting on page 38.

Photo Legend next page:

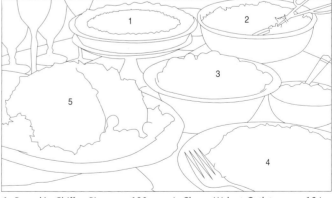

1. Pumpkin Chiffon Pie, page 130
2. Slaw Special, page 137
3. Sautéed Sprouts, page 146
4. Cherry Walnut Cutlets, page 124
5. Stuffed Turkey Breast, this page

Cherry Walnut Cutlets

Feed a bunch with this hearty main dish.

All-purpose flour	1/2 cup	125 mL
Walnuts	1/2 cup	125 mL
Lemon pepper	2 tsp.	10 mL
Seasoned salt	2 tsp.	10 mL
Chicken breast cutlets (about 5 oz., 140 g, each)	12	12
Hard margarine (or butter)	4 tsp.	20 mL
CHERRY SAUCE		
Chopped onion	1 cup	250 mL
Garlic clove, minced (or 1/4 tsp., 1 mL, powder)	1	1
Chopped celery	1/2 cup	125 mL
Grated carrot	1 cup	250 mL
Hard margarine (or butter)	3 tbsp.	50 mL
All-purpose flour	1/4 cup	60 mL
Chicken (or vegetable) bouillon powder	2 tsp.	10 mL
Salt	1/2 tsp.	2 mL
Pepper	1/4 tsp.	1 mL
Ground cloves, just a pinch		
Water	1 cup	250 mL
Red (or alcohol-free) wine	1/2 cup	125 mL
Can of pitted Bing cherries, with juice, halved	14 oz.	398 mL
Chopped walnuts	1/4 cup	60 mL

Measure first 4 ingredients into blender. Process until walnuts are finely chopped. Transfer to shallow dish or onto waxed paper.

Press cutlets in flour mixture on both sides to coat completely. Heat 2 tsp. (10 mL) margarine in large frying pan on medium-high until hot. Brown cutlets, in batches, for about 1 minute per side. Add remaining margarine as needed. Put cutlets into small roasting pan.

Cherry Sauce: Sauté onion, garlic, celery and carrot in margarine in same frying pan until onion is soft.

Add flour, bouillon powder, salt, pepper and cloves. Stir. Stir in water and wine until boiling and thickened.

Add cherries and juice. Bring to a boil. Pour over cutlets. Cover. Bake in 350°F (175°C) oven for about 40 minutes until cutlets are no longer pink in centre.

Arrange cutlets on serving platter. Sprinkle walnuts over cutlets. Serves 12.

1 serving: 318 Calories; 12.8 g Total Fat; 572 mg Sodium; 33 g Protein; 15 g Carbohydrate; 1 g Dietary Fibre

Pictured on page 123.

Beef Melt

A different kind of hot beef sandwich with an interesting mix of flavours. A great way to use leftover roast beef.

Whole wheat bread slices (buttered, optional), see Note	4	4
Cooked (or deli) roast beef slices (about 4 oz., 113 g)	4	4
Chili sauce	3 tbsp.	50 mL
Prepared horseradish	1 tsp.	5 mL
Grated Swiss (or medium Cheddar or Monterey Jack) cheese	1/2 cup	125 mL
Pepper, sprinkle (optional)		

Arrange bread slices, buttered side up, on ungreased baking sheet. Top with beef slices.

Combine chili sauce and horseradish in small cup. Spread over beef.

Sprinkle with cheese and pepper. Broil about 8 inches (20 cm) from heat until cheese is melted and lightly browned. Makes 4 melts.

1 melt: 196 Calories; 7.6 g Total Fat; 378 mg Sodium; 16 g Protein; 17 g Carbohydrate; 3 g Dietary Fibre

Pictured on page 125.

Note: Toast 1 side of bread first, if desired. Layer ingredients on untoasted side and broil as directed.

Bottom Left: Beef Melt, page 124

Top Right: Beef Curry Hotpot, this page

Beef Curry Hotpot

The mild curry flavour is complemented by the raisins, apricots and very tender beef. Serve over rice.

Inside round (or blade) steak, trimmed of fat and cubed	2 lbs.	900 g
Cooking oil	1 tbsp.	15 mL
Medium onions, sliced	2	2
Medium cooking apples (such as McIntosh), peeled, cored and chopped	3	3
Chopped tomato	2 cups	500 mL
Curry powder	2 tsp.	10 mL
Water	1 cup	250 mL
Can of condensed beef broth	10 oz.	284 mL
Dark raisins	1/3 cup	75 mL
Chopped dried apricots	1/2 cup	125 mL
Brown sugar, packed	1 tbsp.	15 mL
All-purpose flour	1 tbsp.	15 mL
Pepper, sprinkle		

Brown beef in cooking oil in large frying pan. Transfer to ungreased 4 quart (4 L) casserole.

Sauté onion and apple in same frying pan. Add to beef.

Sauté tomato and curry powder in same frying pan, stirring up any browned bits from pan, until hot and fragrant. Add to beef mixture.

Add water, broth, raisins and apricots to beef mixture. Stir. Cover. Bake in 325°F (160°C) oven for about 2 hours until beef
is tender.

Combine brown sugar, flour and pepper in small dish. Stir into beef mixture. Cover. Bake for 10 to 15 minutes until boiling and thickened. Makes 8 cups (2 L).

1 cup (250 mL): 261 Calories; 5.9 g Total Fat; 305 mg Sodium; 28 g Protein; 25 g Carbohydrate; 3 g Dietary Fibre

Pictured above.

Slow Cooker Method: Put browned beef mixture into 4 1/2 quart (4.5 L) slow cooker. Cook on Low for 6 to 8 hours or on High for 3 to 4 hours until beef is tender. Stir brown sugar mixture into beef mixture with heat on High. Cover. Cook for 15 minutes until thickened.

Seafood And Shell Stew

A shrimp and fish stew with shell pasta.
Serve with plenty of crusty bread to soak up the broth.

Medium shell pasta	1 cup	250 mL
Boiling water	4 cups	1 L
Salt	1 tsp.	5 mL
AÏOLI SAUCE		
Mayonnaise (not salad dressing)	1/2 cup	125 mL
Garlic clove, minced (or 1/8 tsp., 0.5 mL, powder)	1/2	1/2
Chopped fresh parsley (or 1/4 tsp., 1 mL, flakes)	1 tsp.	5 mL
Medium leeks (white and tender parts only), thinly sliced	2	2
Garlic cloves, minced (or 1/2 tsp., 2 mL, powder)	2	2
Small red pepper, diced	1	1
Fennel seed, crushed	1/4 tsp.	1 mL
Olive (or cooking) oil	1 tbsp.	15 mL
Clam tomato beverage	1 cup	250 mL
Can of stewed tomatoes, with juice, chopped	14 oz.	398 mL
White (or alcohol-free) wine	1/2 cup	125 mL
Water	1 cup	250 mL
Finely grated lemon peel	1/2 tsp.	2 mL
Dried thyme, crushed	1/8 tsp.	0.5 mL
Saffron threads (or turmeric), just a pinch		
Raw medium shrimp (about 30), peeled and deveined (or frozen, thawed)	1 lb.	454 g
Halibut fillets, cut into 1 inch (2.5 cm) chunks	8 oz.	225 g
Cod fillets, cut into 1 inch (2.5 cm) chunks	8 oz.	225 g
Chopped fresh cilantro (optional)	1 tbsp.	15 mL
Chopped fresh parsley (or 3/4 tsp., 4 mL, flakes), optional	1 tbsp.	15 mL
Hot pepper sauce (optional)	1/4 – 1/2 tsp.	1 – 2 mL

Cook pasta in boiling water and salt in medium saucepan for 6 minutes until partially cooked. Drain. Rinse under cold water. Drain. Set aside.

Aïoli Sauce: Combine mayonnaise, garlic and parsley in small bowl. Chill for 30 minutes to blend flavours.

Sauté next 4 ingredients in olive oil in large uncovered pot or Dutch oven for about 5 minutes until leeks are soft.

Add next 7 ingredients. Stir. Cover. Bring to a simmer. Simmer for 15 minutes.

Add remaining 6 ingredients and pasta. Stir. Bring to a boil. Reduce heat. Cover. Simmer for about 10 minutes until fish flakes easily when tested with fork and pasta is tender but firm. Serve with Aïoli Sauce. Makes 8 cups (2 L).

1 cup (250 mL): 353 Calories; 15.7 g Total Fat; 462 mg Sodium; 26 g Protein; 24 g Carbohydrate; 2 g Dietary Fibre

Pictured on page 127.

Stuffed Ham Casserole

Lots of bite-sized ham cubes with a pineapple bread stuffing.

Boneless ham, cut into 1/2 inch (12 mm) pieces (about 5 cups, 1.25 L)	2 lbs.	900 g
PINEAPPLE STUFFING		
Chopped onion	1/2 cup	125 mL
Chopped celery	1/2 cup	125 mL
Hard margarine (or butter)	2 tsp.	10 mL
Can of crushed pineapple, drained, juice reserved	14 oz.	398 mL
Dry coarse bread crumbs	2 cups	500 mL
Poultry seasoning	1 tsp.	5 mL
Parsley flakes	1/2 tsp.	2 mL
Salt (optional)	1/8 tsp.	0.5 mL
Pepper	1/8 tsp.	0.5 mL
Reserved pineapple juice	2 tbsp.	30 mL
SAUCE		
White vinegar	1 tbsp.	15 mL
Cornstarch	1 1/2 tbsp.	25 mL
Brown sugar, packed	1/4 cup	60 mL
Reserved pineapple juice, plus water to make	3/4 cup	175 mL

Scatter 1/2 of ham in greased 3 quart (3 L) casserole.

Pineapple Stuffing: Sauté onion and celery in margarine in non-stick frying pan until soft.

Add next 6 ingredients to onion mixture. Stir.

Drizzle reserved pineapple juice over pineapple mixture. Stir well until stuffing is moist and holds together when squeezed. Lightly pack stuffing over ham. Scatter remaining ham over stuffing.

Sauce: Mix all 4 ingredients in small saucepan. Heat and stir on medium until boiling and thickened. Drizzle over ham. Cover. Bake in 350°F (175°C) oven for 30 minutes. Serves 8.

1 serving: 352 Calories; 10.9 g Total Fat; 1530 mg Sodium; 22 g Protein; 41 g Carbohydrate; 2 g Dietary Fibre

Pictured on page 127.

Bottom Left: Rich Chicken Stew, below   Top Centre: Stuffed Ham Casserole, page 126   Bottom Right: Seafood And Shell Stew, page 126

Rich Chicken Stew

Very tender and flavourful chicken in a creamy sauce made in a slow cooker. Serve over potatoes or pasta.

Bacon slices, diced	2	2
Medium onion, sliced	1	1
Chopped fresh mushrooms	1 cup	250 mL
All-purpose flour	2 tbsp.	30 mL
Diced carrot	1 1/2 cups	375 mL
Diced celery with leaves	1 1/2 cups	375 mL
Chicken parts, skin removed	3 lbs.	1.4 kg
Can of condensed chicken broth	10 oz.	284 mL
Parsley flakes	1 tbsp.	15 mL
Dried sage	1/2 tsp.	2 mL
Dried thyme	1/2 tsp.	2 mL
Salt	1/4 tsp.	1 mL
Pepper	1/4 tsp.	1 mL
Sour cream	2/3 cup	150 mL
All-purpose flour	2 tbsp.	30 mL

Fry bacon in large frying pan on medium-high until crispy. Do not drain.

Add onion and mushrooms. Sauté for 3 to 4 minutes until onion is beginning to brown and is soft.

Sprinkle first amount of flour over mushroom mixture. Stir well. Turn into 4 1/2 quart (4.5 L) slow cooker.

Layer carrot, celery and chicken over mushroom mixture.

Combine next 6 ingredients in same frying pan. Heat and stir for 5 minutes, scraping up any browned bits from pan, until heated through. Pour over chicken. Cover. Cook on Low for 7 to 8 hours or on High for 3 1/2 to 4 hours. Remove chicken to serving dish using slotted spoon. Keep warm.

Stir sour cream into second amount of flour in small bowl until smooth. Stir into carrot mixture with heat on High. Cover. Cook for about 5 minutes until slightly thickened. Pour sauce over chicken to serve. Serves 6.

1 serving: 274 Calories; 11.4 g Total Fat; 600 mg Sodium; 29 g Protein; 13 g Carbohydrate; 2 g Dietary Fibre

Pictured above.

Pies

Arctic Freeze

This pie changes every time you use a different ice cream.

VANILLA WAFER CRUST

Hard margarine (or butter)	1/3 cup	75 mL
Vanilla wafer crumbs	1 1/4 cups	300 mL
Brown (or granulated) sugar, packed	2 tbsp.	30 mL

FILLING

Hot fudge ice cream topping	1 cup	250 mL
Ice cream (your choice), softened	4 cups	1 L
Frozen whipped topping, thawed (or whipped cream)	2 cups	500 mL
Apricot-flavoured liqueur (such as Crème d'abricots) or peach schnapps (optional), see Note	1 tbsp.	15 mL

TOPPING

Hard margarine (or butter)	1 1/2 tsp.	7 mL
Sliced almonds	1/4 cup	60 mL
Granulated sugar	2 tsp.	10 mL
Ground cinnamon	1/4 tsp.	1 mL

Vanilla Wafer Crust: Melt margarine in medium saucepan. Add wafer crumbs and brown sugar. Stir until mixed well. Press firmly into bottom and up side of 9 inch (22 cm) pie plate. Bake in 350°F (175°C) oven for 10 minutes. Cool.

Filling: Spread ice cream topping over crust. Freeze until firm.

Spread ice cream over ice cream topping. Freeze until firm.

Fold whipped topping and liqueur together in medium bowl. Smooth over ice cream. Freeze until firm.

Topping: Melt margarine in medium saucepan on medium-low. Add almonds, granulated sugar and cinnamon. Heat and stir until almonds are toasted. Cool. Sprinkle over whipped topping. Freeze. Cuts into 8 wedges.

1 wedge: 533 Calories; 31.3 g Total Fat; 265 mg Sodium; 6 g Protein; 62 g Carbohydrate; trace Dietary Fibre

Pictured on page 131.

Note: Choose a liqueur that complements your choice of ice cream. For example, coffee-flavoured liqueur (such as Kahlúa) with mocha ice cream. Or mint-flavoured liqueur (such as Créme de Menthe) with mint chocolate chip ice cream.

Orange Chocolate Pie

Dark chocolate crust complements orange filling so nicely.
A splendid dessert.

CHOCOLATE CRUST

Hard margarine (or butter)	6 tbsp.	100 mL
Chocolate wafer crumbs	1 1/2 cups	375 mL
Icing (confectioner's) sugar	2 tbsp.	30 mL

FILLING

Cream cheese, softened	12 oz.	375 g
Granulated sugar	1/2 cup	125 mL
Hard margarine (or butter), softened	2 tbsp.	30 mL
Water	2 tbsp.	30 mL
Skim milk powder	1/2 cup	125 mL
Frozen concentrated orange juice, thawed	1/2 cup	125 mL
Finely grated orange peel	2 tsp.	10 mL
Frozen whipped topping, thawed	2 cups	500 mL

Candied orange slices, for garnish

Chocolate Crust: Melt margarine in medium saucepan. Add wafer crumbs and icing sugar. Stir until well mixed. Reserve 1 tbsp. (15 mL). Firmly press remaining crumb mixture into bottom and up side of 10 inch (25 cm) pie plate. Bake in 350°F (175°C) oven for 10 minutes. Cool.

Filling: Beat cream cheese and granulated sugar together in large bowl until smooth. Add margarine, water and milk powder. Beat well. Add concentrated orange juice and orange peel. Beat until mixed well.

Fold in whipped topping. Turn into crust. Sprinkle with reserved crumb mixture. Chill.

Garnish with orange slices. Cuts into 10 wedges.

1 wedge: 435 Calories; 29 g Total Fat; 361 mg Sodium; 7 g Protein; 39 g Carbohydrate; trace Dietary Fibre

Pictured on page 131.

Peach Blueberry Pie

Moist juicy blueberries contrasted by golden peach slices.
A delicious combination.

Pastry for a 2 crust (9 inch, 22 cm) pie, your own or a mix		
Minute tapioca	1 tbsp.	15 mL

Peach Blueberry Pie, this page

Frozen blueberries	1 1/2 cups	375 mL
Cans of sliced peaches (14 oz., 398 mL, each), drained	3	3
Granulated sugar	1/2 cup	125 mL
Minute tapioca	1 tbsp.	15 mL
Salt	1/4 tsp.	1 mL
Granulated sugar	1/2 tsp.	2 mL

Roll out large 1/2 of pastry. Line pie plate. Sprinkle first amount of tapioca over bottom. Roll out top crust slightly larger than top surface of pie plate using remaining pastry. If desired, cut out shapes with cookie cutter.

Toss next 5 ingredients together in large bowl. Turn into pie shell. Dampen pastry edge with water. Cover pie with top crust. Tuck edge under bottom crust. Press lightly to seal. Trim and crimp (see Pretty Pastry, page 134). Cut small vents in top crust if not doing cut-outs.

Sprinkle second amount of sugar over crust. Bake on bottom rack in 400°F (205°C) oven for about 45 minutes until crust is golden. Cuts into 8 wedges.

1 wedge: 275 Calories; 10.7 g Total Fat; 284 mg Sodium; 2 g Protein; 44 g Carbohydrate; 3 g Dietary Fibre

Pictured on front cover and above.

Pear And Ginger Pie

*An excellent pie with mild pear flavour
and the occasional burst of ginger.*

Brown sugar, packed	1/2 cup	125 mL
All-purpose flour	3 tbsp.	50 mL
Ground cardamom	1/4 tsp.	1 mL
Ground cinnamon	1/4 tsp.	1 mL
Salt	1/4 tsp.	1 mL
Minced candied ginger	1 tbsp.	15 mL
Large egg	1	1
Lemon juice	1 tbsp.	15 mL
Vanilla	1 1/2 tsp.	7 mL
Large firm pears, peeled, cored and thinly sliced (about 2 lbs., 900 g)	5	5
Pastry for a 2 crust (9 inch, 22 cm) pie, your own or a mix		
Hard margarine (or butter), cut into small pieces	1 tbsp.	15 mL
Milk	1 tbsp.	15 mL
Granulated sugar	1 tsp.	5 mL

Combine first 6 ingredients in large bowl.

Beat egg, lemon juice and vanilla together in small bowl using fork. Stir into brown sugar mixture.

Fold pears into brown sugar mixture until well coated.

Roll out large 1/2 of pastry. Line pie plate. Turn pear mixture into pie shell. Drop margarine pieces here and there over pear mixture. Dampen pastry edge with water. Roll out top crust slightly larger than top surface of pie plate using remaining pastry. Cover pie with lattice top (see Pretty Pastry, page 135). Trim and crimp edge.

Brush milk over lattice top. Sprinkle granulated sugar over top. Bake on bottom rack in 450°F (230°C) oven for 10 minutes. Reduce heat to 350°F (175°C). Bake for about 40 minutes until starting to bubble and crust is golden. Cuts into 8 wedges.

1 wedge: 291 Calories; 12.5 g Total Fat; 313 mg Sodium; 3 g Protein; 42 g Carbohydrate; 2 g Dietary Fibre

Pictured on page 131.

Pumpkin Chiffon Pie

Lighter in texture than the typical pumpkin pie.

Egg yolks (large)	3	3
Can of pure pumpkin (not filling)	14 oz.	398 mL
Granulated sugar	3/4 cup	175 mL
Ground cinnamon	3/4 tsp.	4 mL
Ground nutmeg	1/2 tsp.	2 mL
Ground ginger	1/2 tsp.	2 mL
Ground cloves	1/8 tsp.	0.5 mL
Salt	1/4 tsp.	1 mL
Sour cream	1 cup	250 mL
Egg whites (large), room temperature	3	3
Unbaked 9 inch (22 cm) pie shell	1	1
Whipped cream, for garnish	1/2 cup	125 mL

Beat egg yolks well in large bowl. Add next 7 ingredients. Beat.

Add sour cream. Beat.

Beat egg whites with clean beaters in medium bowl until stiff peaks form. Fold into pumpkin mixture.

Turn into pie shell. Bake on bottom rack in 450°F (230°C) oven for 10 minutes. Reduce heat to 350°F (175°C). Bake for about 40 minutes until set and knife inserted in centre comes out clean. Cool.

Decorate with whipped cream. Cuts into 8 wedges.

1 wedge: 252 Calories; 11.5 g Total Fat; 216 mg Sodium; 5 g Protein; 34 g Carbohydrate; 1 g Dietary Fibre

Pictured on page 122/123.

Top: Orange Chocolate Pie, page 129
Centre: Pear And Ginger Pie, this page
Bottom: Arctic Freeze, page 128

Pineapple Cheese Pie

A light and fluffy pie with bits of pineapple.
A very delicious dessert.

GRAHAM CRUST

Hard margarine (or butter)	1/3 cup	75 mL
Graham cracker crumbs	1 1/3 cups	325 mL
Granulated sugar	2 tbsp.	30 mL
Block of cream cheese, softened	8 oz.	250 g
Granulated sugar	1 cup	250 mL
Can of crushed pineapple, drained	8 oz.	227 mL
Lemon juice	1/2 tsp.	2 mL
Salt, just a pinch		
Frozen whipped topping, thawed	2 cups	500 mL

Graham Crust: Melt margarine in small saucepan. Add graham crumbs and first amount of sugar. Stir until well mixed. Reserve 2 tbsp. (30 mL). Firmly press remaining crumb mixture into bottom and up side of 9 inch (22 cm) pie plate. Bake in 350°F (175°C) oven for 10 minutes. Cool.

Beat cream cheese and second amount of sugar together in medium bowl until smooth.

Add pineapple, lemon juice and salt. Stir. Fold in whipped topping. Turn into crust. Sprinkle with reserved crumb mixture. Chill. Cuts into 8 wedges.

1 wedge: 430 Calories; 25.4 g Total Fat; 281 mg Sodium; 4 g Protein; 49 g Carbohydrate; 1 g Dietary Fibre

Pictured on page 133.

Pineapple Pie

A takeoff from the traditional Southern chess pie that tastes mildly of pineapple.

Large eggs	3	3
Granulated sugar	1 1/2 cups	375 mL
All-purpose flour	6 tbsp.	100 mL
Hard margarine (or butter), softened	6 tbsp.	100 mL
Can of crushed pineapple, drained	14 oz.	398 mL
Milk	6 tbsp.	100 mL
Vanilla	1 1/2 tsp.	7 mL
Salt	1/2 tsp.	2 mL
Unbaked 9 inch (22 cm) pie shell	1	1

Beat eggs in medium bowl until frothy. Add sugar, flour and margarine. Beat until smooth.

Add pineapple, milk, vanilla and salt. Stir.

Turn into pie shell. Bake on bottom rack in 350°F (175°C) oven for about 60 minutes until set and golden. Cool. Cuts into 8 wedges.

1 wedge: 385 Calories; 16 g Total Fat; 383 mg Sodium; 4 g Protein; 57 g Carbohydrate; 1 g Dietary Fibre

Pictured on page 136.

Forgotten Apple Pie

A golden brown crumb topping and a creamy white filling with bits of pale yellow apple. The tartness of the apple is a nice contrast to the sweet topping. Serve with ice cream.

Large egg	1	1
All-purpose flour	2 tbsp.	30 mL
Salt	1/4 tsp.	1 mL
Sour cream	1 cup	250 mL
Granulated sugar	2/3 cup	150 mL
Vanilla	1/2 tsp.	2 mL
Peeled and chopped cooking apple (such as McIntosh)	3 1/2 cups	875 mL
Unbaked 9 inch (22 cm) pie shell	1	1

TOPPING

Brown sugar, packed	1/3 cup	75 mL
All-purpose flour	1/3 cup	75 mL
Hard margarine (or butter), softened	1/4 cup	60 mL

Beat egg, flour and salt together in medium bowl until smooth. Beat in sour cream, granulated sugar and vanilla until sugar is dissolved.

Add apple. Stir. Turn into pie shell. Bake on bottom rack in 400°F (205°C) oven for 10 minutes. Reduce heat to 350°F (175°C). Bake for 20 minutes.

Topping: Mix brown sugar, flour and margarine until crumbly. Sprinkle over pie. Bake for about 40 minutes until apple is tender. Cuts into 8 wedges.

1 wedge: 352 Calories; 16.4 g Total Fat; 273 mg Sodium; 3 g Protein; 50 g Carbohydrate; 1 g Dietary Fibre

Pictured on page 136.

Top Left: Rocky Road Pie, below

Bottom Left & Right: Pineapple Cheese Pie, page 132

Rocky Road Pie

*A favourite among big and little kids with
the chocolate and marshmallows.*

CHOCOLATE CRUST

Hard margarine (or butter)	1/3 cup	75 mL
Chocolate wafer crumbs	1 cup	250 mL
Graham cracker crumbs	1/4 cup	60 mL
Finely chopped almonds	1/4 cup	60 mL
Granulated sugar	1 tbsp.	15 mL

FILLING

Miniature marshmallows	1 2/3 cups	400 mL
Semi-sweet chocolate baking squares (1 oz., 28 g, each), cut up	3	3
Milk	6 tbsp.	100 mL
Salt	1/8 tsp.	0.5 mL
Block of cream cheese, softened and cut up	8 oz.	250 g
Frozen whipped topping, thawed	2 cups	500 mL
Miniature marshmallows	1 cup	250 mL
Milk chocolate candy bar, coarsely chopped	3 1/2 oz.	100 g

Chocolate Crust: Melt margarine in medium saucepan. Add wafer and graham crumbs, almonds and sugar. Stir until well mixed. Reserve 2 tbsp. (30 mL). Firmly press remaining crumb mixture into bottom and up side of 9 inch (22 cm) pie plate. Bake in 350°F (175°C) oven for 10 minutes. Cool.

Filling: Put first 4 ingredients into large saucepan. Heat and stir on medium-low until melted and smooth.

Add cream cheese. Stir until melted. Whisk to blend well. Chill for about 20 minutes, stirring occasionally, until slightly thickened.

Fold in whipped topping. Fold in second amounts of marshmallows and chocolate. Turn into crust. Sprinkle with reserved crumb mixture. Chill. Cuts into 8 wedges.

1 wedge: 521 Calories; 35.7 g Total Fat; 358 mg Sodium; 7 g Protein; 48 g Carbohydrate; 1 g Dietary Fibre

Pictured above.

Pretty Pastry

When you learn how to make these pretty pastry edges, you will want to bring your pie and plates to the table for serving to hear the exclamations of delight from your guests. Whether a single or double-crust pie, your filling will be presented in a pretty frame of pastry.

Make your favourite single-crust pie pastry. Roll out pastry to line 9 inch (22 cm) pie plate. Trim pastry, leaving a 1 inch (2.5 cm) overhang. Fold edge under to width of pie plate. Gently press down to flatten. Choose one of the methods shown below, or on page 135, and follow the instructions.

FLUTED EDGE

Squeeze pastry edge between thumb and forefinger at an angle. Continue around pastry edge.

PINCHED EDGE

Have thumb and forefinger of one hand pointing outward towards edge of pastry, and have forefinger of other hand pointing inward towards edge of pastry, in between fingers. Push towards each other at the same time, crimping the edge. Continue around pastry edge.

FORKED EDGE

Press underside of fork tines along pastry edge at a straight angle. Next, press down at a 45° angle to first mark. Repeat pattern around pastry edge.

PINWHEEL EDGE

Make 45° cuts at alternating angles to form triangles around entire pastry edge. Remove cut triangles from edge, leaving attached triangles. Fold back every other triangle to stand up.

DECORATIVE EDGE

Gather up and roll out leftover pastry. Cut out desired shapes. Dampen bottom of shapes with water using fingertips. Arrange shapes on pastry edge and gently press down.

CUT-OUTS

Make enough pastry for a double-crust pie. Roll out large 1/2 of pastry to line pie plate. Fill as desired. Roll out remaining pastry slightly larger than top surface of pie. Cut out desired shapes from centre of pastry. Dampen bottom of shapes with water using fingertips. Place shapes on pastry and gently press down. Carefully lift and lay pastry over filling. Dampen around bottom pastry edge. Pinch flute edge (see page 134).

LATTICE TOP

Make enough pastry for a double-crust pie. Roll out large 1/2 of pastry to line pie plate. Fill as desired. Roll out remaining pastry. Using fluted pastry cutter, cut into eight 1 inch (2.5 cm) strips about 6 inches (15 cm) in length.

Dampen 1 end of 1 strip with water using fingertips. Twist strip. Place dampened end on pastry edge and lay other end in centre on filling. Repeat at equal intervals around pastry edge with remaining 7 strips. Gather and pinch ends together in centre, using a bit more water.

Berry Blend Pie

Such a festive colour and lots of fruity berries in this pie.

Granulated sugar	1 cup	250 mL
Cornstarch	3 tbsp.	50 mL
Reserved mixed berries juice (plus water to make)	1 cup	250 mL
Package of raspberry-flavoured gelatin (jelly powder)	3 oz.	85 g
Bag of frozen mixed berries, thawed, drained and juice reserved	21 oz.	600 g
Baked 9 inch (22 cm) pie shells, cooled	2	2
TOPPING		
Envelope of dessert topping (prepared), optional	1	1

Fresh blueberries (or raspberries or strawberries), for garnish

Stir sugar, cornstarch and reserved juice together in large saucepan until smooth. Heat and stir until boiling and thickened. Remove from heat.

Add jelly powder. Stir until dissolved. Chill, stirring and scraping down sides often, until beginning to gel.

Fold mixed berries into jelly mixture. Divide between pie shells.

Topping: Pipe or place dollops of dessert topping over pies.

Garnish with blueberries. Chill until ready to serve. Makes 2 pies, each cutting into 8 wedges, for a total of 16 wedges.

1 wedge: 182 Calories; 5.3 g Total Fat; 117 mg Sodium; 1 g Protein; 33 g Carbohydrate; 1 g Dietary Fibre

Pictured below.

Bottom Left: Berry Blend Pie, above   Top Centre: Pineapple Pie, page 132   Bottom Right: Forgotten Apple Pie, page 132

Salads

Slaw Special

*A brightly coloured and crunchy salad
with a hint of Thai flavours.*

DRESSING

White vinegar	1/4 cup	60 mL
Cooking oil	3 tbsp.	50 mL
Dark sesame (or cooking) oil	1 tbsp.	15 mL
Granulated sugar	1/4 cup	60 mL
Minced onion flakes	1 tbsp.	15 mL
Reserved seasoning packet from instant noodles		
Shredded savoy (or green) cabbage, packed	2 cups	500 mL
Bag of broccoli coleslaw (about 4 cups, 1 L) or broccoli stems and carrots, cut julienne	12 oz.	340 g
Green onions, chopped	5	5
Fresh sugar snap peas, sliced diagonally (about 5 oz., 140 g)	1 1/2 cups	375 mL
Dry (or honey) roasted peanuts, chopped	1/2 cup	125 mL
Package of instant noodles with beef- flavoured packet, broken up and seasoning packet reserved	3 oz.	85 g

Dressing: Stir first 6 ingredients together in small bowl until sugar is dissolved. Can be prepared 1 to 2 days ahead and chilled.

Toss next 5 ingredients together in large bowl. Can be prepared 1 to 2 days ahead and chilled.

To serve, add noodles and dressing to salad. Toss well. Makes about 11 cups (2.75 L).

3/4 cup (175 mL): 120 Calories; 6.6 g Total Fat; 56 mg Sodium; 3 g Protein; 13 g Carbohydrate; 2 g Dietary Fibre

Pictured on page 123.

HOT SLAW STIR-FRY: Heat non-stick wok or frying pan on medium-high. Add leftover Slaw Special. Stir-fry for 3 to 5 minutes until heated through.

Blackened Chicken Caesar Salad, this page

Greek Pea Salad

A creamy salad with a nice pea and feta cheese combination.
Great with Spinach And Olive Braid, page 76.

Frozen peas	2 cups	500 mL
Water		
Crumbled feta cheese	1 cup	250 mL
Hard-boiled egg, chopped	1	1
Deli ham slice (about 1 oz., 28 g), cut into short narrow strips	1	1
Sliced ripe olives	1/4 cup	60 mL
Green onions, sliced	3	3
Small red pepper, diced	1	1
DRESSING		
Salad dressing (or mayonnaise)	1/4 cup	60 mL
Red wine vinegar	1 tsp.	5 mL
Greek seasoning	2 tsp.	10 mL

Cook peas in water in medium saucepan for about 3 minutes until tender. Drain. Rinse with cold water. Drain well. Transfer to medium bowl.

Add next 6 ingredients. Stir.

Dressing: Mix all 3 ingredients in small bowl. Makes 1/4 cup (60 mL) dressing. Drizzle over salad. Stir to coat. Chill for at least 1 hour to blend flavours. Makes 3 cups (750 mL) salad.

1/2 cup (125 mL): 201 Calories; 13.1 g Total Fat; 626 mg Sodium; 9 g Protein; 12 g Carbohydrate; 3 g Dietary Fibre

Pictured on page 115.

Blackened Chicken Caesar Salad

A full-meal salad with a bit of bite from the chicken.

Large heads of romaine lettuce, cut up or torn	2	2
Croutons	1 cup	250 mL
Finely grated Parmesan cheese	1/4 cup	60 mL
DRESSING		
Cooking oil	3 tbsp.	50 mL
Sour cream	3 tbsp.	50 mL
White wine vinegar	1 tbsp.	15 mL
Lemon juice	1 tsp.	5 mL
Worcestershire sauce	1 tsp.	5 mL
Garlic salt	1/2 tsp.	2 mL
Pepper	1/4 tsp.	1 mL
Finely grated Parmesan cheese	1/2 cup	125 mL
BLACKENED CHICKEN		
Cooking oil	1 tbsp.	15 mL
Boneless, skinless chicken breast halves, cut into 3/4 inch (2 cm) pieces	2 lbs.	900 g
Ketchup	2 tbsp.	30 mL
Paprika	1 tbsp.	15 mL
Salt	2 tsp.	10 mL
Pepper	1/2 tsp.	2 mL
Onion powder	1/2 tsp.	2 mL
Ground thyme	1/2 tsp.	2 mL
Chili powder	1/2 tsp.	2 mL
Cayenne pepper	1/2 tsp.	2 mL

Finely grated Parmesan cheese, to taste

Toss lettuce, croutons and Parmesan cheese together in large bowl. Chill.

Dressing: Mix all 8 ingredients in small bowl. Let stand for 10 minutes to blend flavours.

Blackened Chicken: Heat wok or frying pan until hot. Add cooking oil. Add chicken. Stir-fry for 6 to 7 minutes until partially cooked.

Add next 8 ingredients. Stir-fry until chicken juices run clear. Add dressing to salad. Toss. Divide among 8 large plates. Divide chicken over individual salads.

Sprinkle Parmesan cheese over individual salads. Serves 8.

1 serving: 284 Calories; 13.2 g Total Fat; 947 mg Sodium; 32 g Protein; 9 g Carbohydrate; 3 g Dietary Fibre

Pictured on this page.

Elegant Eggnog Mold

So practical—this salad can stand out for up to 3 hours.

Reserved mandarin orange juice (plus water to make)	1/2 cup	125 mL
Envelopes of unflavoured gelatin (1/4 oz., 7 g, each)	2	2
Granulated sugar	1/4 cup	60 mL
Eggnog	2 cups	500 mL
Orange-flavoured liqueur (such as Grand Marnier), optional	1/4 cup	60 mL
Cranberry cocktail	1 cup	250 mL
Package of cranberry (or raspberry) flavoured gelatin (jelly powder)	3 oz.	85 g
Large ice cubes	3	3
Whipping cream	1 cup	250 mL
Can of mandarin orange segments, drained and juice reserved	10 oz.	284 mL

Fresh mint leaves, for garnish
Fresh raspberries, for garnish

Measure mandarin orange juice into small saucepan. Sprinkle unflavoured gelatin over top. Let stand for 5 minutes until softened. Stir. Add sugar. Heat and stir on medium until gelatin and sugar are dissolved. Remove from heat. Let stand at room temperature, stirring several times, until lukewarm but still liquid. If beginning to set, heat on low or microwave on medium (50%) for about 30 seconds until liquefied. Transfer to large bowl.

Add eggnog and liqueur. Chill for about 20 minutes, stirring several times, until slightly thickened and beginning to curdle slightly. Stir vigorously. Keep at room temperature to prevent further thickening, stirring several times to keep soft.

Heat cranberry cocktail in separate small saucepan on medium-high until boiling. Remove from heat. Stir in cranberry-flavoured gelatin until dissolved. Stir in ice cubes until melted. Chill, stirring several times, until syrupy.

Beat whipping cream in medium bowl until stiff peaks form. Add 2 large spoonfuls eggnog mixture to whipped cream. Stir. Add to eggnog mixture. Fold in orange segments. Pour into lightly greased 6 1/2 to 7 cup (1.6 to 1.75 L) mold or bundt pan. Mixture should stay softly mounded when 1 spoonful is placed on top of another. Chill for 10 minutes. Pour cranberry mixture over eggnog mixture. Poke soft spatula deeply into eggnog mixture 8 to 10 times, particularly around side of mold, allowing cranberry mixture to fill spaces. Chill for at least 4 hours or overnight until firmly set. Invert onto dampened serving plate. Dampness makes it easier to centre mold. To loosen salad in mold, place hot tea towel over top. Let stand until tea towel is cool. Repeat 6 to 8 times. Shake mold slightly. Chill until firm.

Garnish with mint and raspberries. Serves 14.

1 serving: 166 Calories; 8.7 g Total Fat; 47 mg Sodium; 3 g Protein; 20 g Carbohydrate; trace Dietary Fibre

Pictured on page 140.

Vegetable Salad

A brightly coloured salad.

Can of kernel corn, drained	12 oz.	341 mL
Can of peas, drained	14 oz.	398 mL
Can of cut green beans, drained	14 oz.	398 mL
Thinly sliced celery	1 cup	250 mL
Medium onion, finely chopped	1	1
Diced red pepper	1/2 cup	125 mL
Diced green pepper	1/2 cup	125 mL
DRESSING		
Granulated sugar	1 cup	250 mL
White vinegar	3/4 cup	175 mL
Water	1/3 cup	75 mL
Cooking oil	2 tbsp.	30 mL
Salt	1/2 tsp.	2 mL

Combine first 7 ingredients together in large bowl. Transfer to airtight container.

Dressing: Stir all 5 ingredients together in small bowl until sugar is dissolved. Pour over salad. Stir until coated. Cover. Chill for 24 hours to blend flavours. Store in refrigerator for up to 4 weeks. Makes 8 cups (2 L).

1/2 cup (125 mL): 101 Calories; 1.9 g Total Fat; 190 mg Sodium; 1 g Protein; 21 g Carbohydrate; 2 g Dietary Fibre

Pictured on page 140.

Top Left: Elegant Eggnog Mold, page 139   Bottom Centre: Potato And Bean Salad, below   Top Right: Vegetable Salad, page 139

Potato And Bean Salad

A creamy and tangy dressing over crunchy red radishes and bright green peas. The potato salad for Christmas.

Whole medium potatoes, with peel (about 2 lbs., 900 g)	5	5
Water	2 cups	500 mL
Salt	1 tsp.	5 mL
Can of garbanzo beans (chick peas), drained	19 oz.	540 mL
Frozen peas, thawed (or fresh, barely cooked)	1 cup	250 mL
Thinly sliced radish	1/2 cup	125 mL
Green onions, thinly sliced	3	3
GARLIC MUSTARD DRESSING		
Buttermilk (or reconstituted from powder)	1/2 cup	125 mL
Plain yogurt	1/2 cup	125 mL
Mayonnaise (not salad dressing)	1/4 cup	60 mL
Garlic cloves, minced (or 1/2 tsp., 2 mL, powder)	2	2
Dijon mustard	1 1/2 tbsp.	25 mL
White vinegar	2 tsp.	10 mL
Salt	1 1/2 tsp.	7 mL
Granulated sugar	1/2 tsp.	2 mL
Pepper	1/8 tsp.	0.5 mL

Thinly sliced radish, for garnish
Fresh sugar snap peas, for garnish

Simmer potatoes in water and salt in large covered saucepan for about 35 minutes until tender. Drain. Cool. Peel. Dice into 3/4 inch (2 cm) pieces. Put into large bowl.

Add beans, peas, radish and green onion. Stir gently.

Garlic Mustard Dressing: Stir first 9 ingredients together in small bowl until smooth. Add to potatoes. Stir until coated. Cover. Chill for at least 2 hours to blend flavours.

Garnish with radish and peas. Makes 9 1/2 cups (2.4 L).

1 cup (250 mL): 181 Calories; 6.3 g Total Fat; 547 mg Sodium; 6 g Protein; 26 g Carbohydrate; 3 g Dietary Fibre

Pictured above.

For an attractive way to catch dripping wax from lighted candles, and to protect delicate wood surfaces, place large plant leaves, such as magnolia or lemon, under the candle. To make candles last longer, freeze before burning.

Side Dishes

Barley And Rice Pilaf

*A chewy side dish that makes a nice substitution
for plain rice or mashed potatoes.*

Chopped onion	1 cup	250 mL
Chopped celery	1 cup	250 mL
Garlic cloves, minced (or 1/2 tsp., 2 mL, powder)	2	2
Olive (or cooking) oil	1 tbsp.	15 mL
Olive (or cooking) oil	1 tbsp.	15 mL
Long grain brown rice, uncooked	1 cup	250 mL
Pearl barley	1 1/4 cups	300 mL
Julienned carrots	1 cup	250 mL
Chicken (or vegetable) bouillon powder	3 tbsp.	50 mL
Parsley flakes	1 tbsp.	15 mL
Dried crushed chilies (optional)	1/4 – 1/2 tsp.	1 – 2 mL
Boiling water	6 cups	1.5 L

Sauté onion, celery and garlic in first amount of olive oil in large frying pan until onion is soft. Turn into ungreased 3 quart (3 L) casserole.

Add second amount of olive oil to same frying pan. Sauté rice and barley for about 5 minutes until starting to turn golden. Add to onion mixture.

Stir in remaining 5 ingredients. Cover. Bake in 350°F (175°C) oven for 1 1/2 to 1 3/4 hours until liquid is absorbed and barley is tender. Stir to distribute vegetables. Makes 9 1/2 cups (2.4 L).

1/2 cup (125 mL): 112 Calories; 2.2 g Total Fat; 319 mg Sodium; 3 g Protein; 21 g Carbohydrate; 2 g Dietary Fibre

Pictured on page 143.

For best results when cooking rice, choose a saucepan with a tight-fitting lid to prevent steam escaping. Avoid lifting the lid or stirring the rice while cooking. Better yet, put an automatic rice cooker on your Christmas wish list. It cooks rice perfectly every time.

Corn And Bean-Stuffed Peppers

Beautiful stuffed peppers that are made in the slow cooker.

Large red peppers	6	6
Long grain white (or brown) rice, uncooked	1/4 cup	60 mL
Lean ground chicken	11 oz.	310 g
Sliced green onion	1/4 cup	60 mL
Garlic clove, minced (or 1/4 tsp., 1 mL, powder), optional	1	1
Frozen kernel corn	1 cup	250 mL
Can of black beans (19 oz., 540 mL, size), drained (see Note)	1/2	1/2
Seasoned salt	1/2 tsp.	2 mL
Dried sweet basil	1/4 tsp.	1 mL
Dried whole oregano	1/4 tsp.	1 mL
Pepper	1/4 tsp.	1 mL
Can of diced tomatoes, with juice	14 oz.	398 mL
Couscous, approximately	2/3 cup	150 mL
Chopped fresh parsley (or cilantro), for garnish		

Slice tops off red peppers. Discard core, seeds and ribs. If necessary, cut small slice from bottom of each pepper, without making a hole, to allow peppers to stand upright. Sprinkle 2 tsp. (10 mL) rice into each pepper shell. Stand in 6 quart (6 L) slow cooker.

Combine next 9 ingredients in medium bowl. Evenly divide and spoon into each pepper shell.

Pour tomatoes with juice over and around stuffed peppers. Cook on Low for 5 hours or on High for 2 1/2 hours. Remove stuffed peppers to serving dish. Keep warm.

Pour liquid from slow cooker into 2 cup (500 mL) liquid measure. Add same amount of couscous to liquid. Let stand for about 5 minutes until liquid is absorbed. Spoon couscous onto stuffed peppers.

Sprinkle with parsley. Serves 6.

1 serving: 289 Calories; 8 g Total Fat; 299 mg Sodium; 16 g Protein; 41 g Carbohydrate; 5 g Dietary Fibre

Pictured on page 143.

Note: Freeze remaining beans to use another time.

Broccoli With Lemon Cheese Sauce

A very delicious change from Cheddar cheese sauce and broccoli. Serve in Hot Carrot Ring, page 146.

Fresh broccoli	1 1/2 lbs.	680 g
Boiling water		
Salt	1/2 tsp.	2 mL
LEMON CHEESE SAUCE		
Milk	1/2 cup	125 mL
Block of cream cheese, cut into chunks	4 oz.	125 g
Finely grated lemon peel	1/2 tsp.	2 mL
Lemon juice	1 tsp.	5 mL
Ground ginger	1/4 tsp.	1 mL
Salt, sprinkle		

Cut broccoli into bite-size florets. Peel stalks. Cut into thin slices or julienne. Cook in boiling water and salt in large covered pot or Dutch oven for about 5 minutes until bright green and tender-crisp. Drain well. Keep warm.

Lemon Cheese Sauce: Heat milk in small saucepan until hot.

Add cream cheese. Stir on low until cream cheese is melted and smooth.

Stir in lemon peel, lemon juice, ginger and salt. Makes 3/4 cup (175 mL) sauce. Pour over broccoli. Makes 6 cups (1.5 L).

1/2 cup (125 mL): 57 Calories; 4 g Total Fat; 51 mg Sodium; 3 g Protein; 4 g Carbohydrate; 1 g Dietary Fibre

Pictured on page 143.

Centre Left: Corn And Bean-Stuffed Peppers, this page
Top Right: Barley And Rice Pilaf, page 141
Bottom Right: Hot Carrot Ring, page 146, with Broccoli With Lemon Cheese Sauce, above

Potato Ruffles
In Mushroom Sauce

*Potato rolled in pasta and covered
in a mushroom and pepper sauce.*

Lasagna noodles	7	7
Spinach lasagna noodles	7	7
Boiling water	16 cups	4 L
Salt	4 tsp.	20 mL

MUSHROOM SAUCE

Sliced brown (cremini) mushrooms	3 cups	750 mL
Hard margarine (or butter)	2 tbsp.	30 mL
All-purpose flour	1/2 cup	125 mL
Water	2 1/2 cups	625 mL
Can of skim evaporated milk (or half-and-half cream)	13 1/2 oz.	385 mL
Beef bouillon powder	1 tbsp.	15 mL
Granulated sugar	1 tsp.	5 mL
Dill weed	3/4 tsp.	4 mL
Salt	1/2 tsp.	2 mL
Pepper	1/4 tsp.	1 mL

FILLING

Medium potatoes (about 1 1/2 lbs., 680 g), cut into chunks	4	4
Coarsely chopped onion	1 cup	250 mL
Water	2 cups	500 mL
Salt	1 tsp.	5 mL
Dry curd cottage cheese	1 cup	250 mL
Salt	1 tsp.	5 mL
Pepper	1/4 tsp.	1 mL
Grated white Cheddar (or mozzarella) cheese	3/4 cup	175 mL

Fresh dill sprigs, for garnish

Cook both noodles in boiling water and salt in large uncovered pot or Dutch oven for 10 to 12 minutes until tender but firm. Drain. Rinse in cold water. Drain well. Cover noodles with plastic wrap. Set aside.

Mushroom Sauce: Sauté mushrooms in margarine in large frying pan until liquid from mushrooms has evaporated.

Sprinkle flour over mushroom mixture. Stir well on medium-low for 2 to 3 minutes until flour mixture begins to brown.

Gradually stir in water and evaporated milk. Add next 5 ingredients. Heat and stir until mixture is boiling and slightly thickened. Makes 4 cups (1 L) sauce. Keep warm.

Filling: Cook potato and onion in water and first amount of salt in medium saucepan for about 15 minutes until potato is soft. Drain. Return to saucepan. Mash until no lumps remain.

Add cottage cheese, second amount of salt and pepper. Mash well. Makes about 3 3/4 cups (925 mL) filling. Spoon 4 to 5 tbsp. (60 to 75 mL) filling at 1 end of each noodle. Roll up, jelly roll-style, pressing down slightly halfway through rolling to force potato mixture to fill noodle more evenly. Spoon 1/3 of sauce into greased deep casserole. Place potato ruffles, in single layer, ruffled edges up, on sauce. Spoon remaining sauce over and around potato ruffles. Cover casserole with greased foil. Bake in 350°F (175°C) oven for 40 minutes. Remove foil. Spoon sauce in casserole over potato ruffles.

Sprinkle with Cheddar cheese. Bake, uncovered, for 12 to 15 minutes until cheese is melted and sauce is bubbly.

Garnish with dill. Makes 14 potato ruffles.

1 potato ruffle: 212 Calories; 4.6 g Total Fat; 484 mg Sodium; 10 g Protein; 32 g Carbohydrate; 2 g Dietary Fibre

Pictured on page 147.

Cabbage Rolls

A regular at the holiday table of many families with Ukrainian roots.

Large head of cabbage (thin-leafed cabbage works best), about 5 lbs. (2.3 kg), see Note	1	1
Boiling water		
FILLING		
Short grain white (or pearl) rice, rinsed	1 1/2 cups	375 mL
Water	2 1/4 cups	550 mL
Salt	1 1/2 tsp.	7 mL
Pepper	1/2 tsp.	2 mL
Bacon slices, diced	6	6
Finely chopped onion	2 cups	500 mL
Tomato juice	1 cup	250 mL
Water	1/3 cup	75 mL
Hard margarine (or butter)	1 tbsp.	15 mL
Water	1/4 – 1/2 cup	60 – 125 mL

Remove core from cabbage and about 1/2 inch (12 mm) of surrounding leaf stems. Put cabbage, core-side down, into Dutch oven. Cover with boiling water. Cover. Simmer for about 30 minutes until leaves begin to soften and loosen. Peel leaves, layer by layer, using tongs. Place on tea towel to drain. If leaves are too soft, run under cold water to stop cooking process. Place leaves on cutting board. Remove hard centre ribs by cutting long, narrow "V" from larger leaves. Cut larger leaves into 3 equal pieces and smaller leaves into 2 equal pieces, keeping size of pieces uniform. You should end up with 4 to 4 1/2 inch (10 to 11 cm) pieces. Stack leaves on plate. Line bottom of greased medium roasting pan with some of very small and torn leaves.

Filling: Combine rice, water and 1 tsp. (5 mL) salt in medium saucepan. Bring to a boil. Reduce heat to medium-low. Cover. Simmer for 10 minutes until water is absorbed and rice is very firm. Remove cover. Cool. Fluff with fork several times while cooling to break up any clumps. Turn into large bowl. Sprinkle remaining salt and pepper over rice. Mix.

Fry bacon in large frying pan on medium for about 10 minutes until beginning to brown. Do not drain.

Cabbage Rolls, this page

Add onion. Sauté for about 10 minutes until very soft. Add to rice. Mix well. Place 1 to 1 1/2 tbsp. (15 to 25 mL) filling in centre of each leaf. Fold 1 end over filling. Fold sides in. Roll up to enclose filling. Arrange cabbage rolls close together, in layers if necessary, in roasting pan.

Heat tomato juice, first amount of water and margarine in small saucepan until almost boiling. Pour over cabbage rolls. Place any extra cabbage leaves over cabbage rolls. Cover. Cook in 350°F (175°C) oven for 1 hour. Tip pan to check amount of liquid. If dry, add second amount of water. Cover. Bake for 30 to 45 minutes until all liquid is absorbed and cabbage rolls are golden. Makes 7 to 8 dozen cabbage rolls.

1 cabbage roll: 29 Calories; 1 g Total Fat; 69 mg Sodium; 1 g Protein; 5 g Carbohydrate; trace Dietary Fibre

Pictured above.

Note: If cabbage leaves are especially white and seem tough, arrange in layers on baking sheet after steaming. Cover. Freeze overnight. Thaw completely before using.

To remove cabbage rolls easily from pan, let stand for 15 minutes after baking. Gently shake pan from side to side to loosen cabbage rolls. They should separate without breaking. Tip pan and use soft spatula to help direct cabbage rolls into serving bowl.

Hot Carrot Ring

Dress up your table with a soft, moist ring of carrots. Fill the centre with Broccoli With Lemon Cheese Sauce, page 142, or Sautéed Sprouts, this page, if desired.

Medium carrots, cut up (about 3 cups, 750 mL, cooked and mashed)	2 lbs.	900 g
Water		
Salt	1/2 tsp.	2 mL
Milk	1/2 cup	125 mL
Fine dry bread crumbs	1 cup	250 mL
Grated medium Cheddar cheese	1 1/2 cups	375 mL
Parsley flakes	2 tsp.	10 mL
Seasoned salt	1 tsp.	5 mL
Large eggs, fork-beaten	3	3
Pepper	1/4 tsp.	1 mL

Cook carrot in water and salt until tender. Drain. Mash until no lumps remain. Transfer to large bowl.

Add remaining 7 ingredients. Mix well. Turn into well-greased ring-shaped pan. Bake in 350°F (175°C) oven for 45 to 50 minutes until knife inserted in centre comes out clean. Let stand in pan for 10 minutes before turning out onto serving plate. Serves 10 to 12.

1 serving: 184 Calories; 8.4 g Total Fat; 385 mg Sodium; 9 g Protein; 19 g Carbohydrate; 3 g Dietary Fibre

Pictured on page 143.

Ginger Honey-Glazed Beans

Tangy, yet sweet, beans with a nice ginger taste.

Hard margarine (or butter)	3 tbsp.	50 mL
Soy sauce	2 tsp.	10 mL
Finely grated gingerroot (or 1/2 tsp., 2 mL, ground ginger)	2 tsp.	10 mL
Frozen (whole or cut) green beans (about 6 cups, 1.5 L)	1 lb.	454 g
Water	1 tbsp.	15 mL
Cornstarch	2 tsp.	10 mL
Liquid honey	3 tbsp.	50 mL
Roasted peanuts, coarsely chopped	2 tbsp.	30 mL

Melt margarine in large frying pan on medium. Stir in soy sauce and ginger until bubbling. Add green beans. Stir to coat. Cover. Cook for 10 to 11 minutes until beans are tender-crisp.

Stir water into cornstarch in small cup until smooth. Stir into beans.

Add honey. Heat and stir until sauce is boiling and thickened. Turn into serving dish.

Sprinkle peanuts over top. Makes about 3 1/2 cups (875 mL).

1/2 cup (125 mL): 113 Calories; 6.4 g Total Fat; 160 mg Sodium; 2 g Protein; 14 g Carbohydrate; trace Dietary Fibre

Pictured on page 147.

Sautéed Sprouts

Grapes and almonds give a uniqueness to ordinary sprouts. Serve in Hot Carrot Ring, this page, if desired.

Fresh (or frozen) Brussels sprouts, trimmed	1 lb.	454 g
Boiling water		
Salt	1 tsp.	5 mL
Hard margarine (or butter)	2 tbsp.	30 mL
Seedless red (or green) grapes	1 cup	250 mL
Slivered almonds	2 tbsp.	30 mL
Salt, sprinkle		
Pepper, sprinkle		

Cook Brussels sprouts in boiling water and salt in medium saucepan for about 10 minutes until tender. Drain. Quickly cool in cold water. Drain.

Melt margarine in large frying pan until sizzling. Add Brussels sprouts, grapes and almonds. Gently stir for 3 to 4 minutes until heated through.

Sprinkle with salt and pepper. Makes 4 cups (1 L).

1/2 cup (125 mL): 77 Calories; 4.3 g Total Fat; 49 mg Sodium; 3 g Protein; 9 g Carbohydrate; 3 g Dietary Fibre

Pictured on front cover and on page 123.

Top Left: Potato Ruffles In Mushroom Sauce, page 144   Bottom Left: Ginger Honey-Glazed Beans, page 146   Bottom Right: Chutney-Glazed Squash, this page

Chutney-Glazed Squash

Sweet, buttery squash rings that are soft and tender and have a slight tang.

Hard margarine (or butter)	1/2 tsp.	2 mL
Acorn squash, with peel, cut into 3/4 inch (2 cm) slices, seeds removed	3	3
Seasoned salt	1/2 tsp.	2 mL
Hard margarine (or butter)	3 tbsp.	50 mL
Mango chutney, large pieces finely chopped	1/2 cup	125 mL
Orange (or apple) juice (or water)	2 tbsp.	30 mL
Ground cinnamon	1/4 tsp.	1 mL
Ground nutmeg	1/8 tsp.	0.5 mL
Chopped pecans	1/4 cup	60 mL

Line large baking sheet with foil. Grease with first amount of margarine.

Arrange squash in single layer on foil. Sprinkle with seasoned salt. Cover with foil, sealing sides. Bake in 350°F (175°C) oven for about 30 minutes until slightly firm.

Melt second amount of margarine in small saucepan on medium. Heat and stir in next 4 ingredients until hot. Brush over both sides of squash. Bake, uncovered, for about 20 minutes until squash is tender.

Sprinkle pecans over squash. Makes about 13 squash slices.

1 squash slice: 87 Calories; 4.5 g Total Fat; 81 mg Sodium; 1 g Protein; 12 g Carbohydrate; 1 g Dietary Fibre

Pictured above.

Scalloped Tomatoes And Corn

*This very good side dish is a
nice addition to any dinner buffet!*

Cans of stewed tomatoes, with juice (14 oz., 398 mL, each)	3	3
Garlic clove, minced (or 1/4 tsp., 1 mL, powder)	1	1
Finely diced celery	1/3 cup	75 mL
Finely diced onion	1/3 cup	75 mL
Finely diced green pepper	1/3 cup	75 mL
All-purpose flour	3 tbsp.	50 mL
Granulated sugar	2 tsp.	10 mL
Dried marjoram	1/2 tsp.	2 mL
Dried thyme	1/4 tsp.	1 mL
Salt	1 tsp.	5 mL
Pepper	1/4 tsp.	1 mL
Whipping cream	1/2 cup	125 mL
Frozen kernel corn	1 cup	250 mL
White bread slices, toasted and buttered, cut into small cubes	4	4
French-fried onions (from can)	3/4 cup	175 mL
Grated Swiss cheese	1 cup	250 mL

Heat first 5 ingredients in large saucepan on medium-high until boiling. Reduce heat to medium-low. Cover. Simmer for about 15 minutes until onion is soft.

Combine next 6 ingredients in small bowl. Slowly stir in whipping cream until smooth. Stir into tomato mixture.

Add corn. Heat and stir until boiling and thickened.

Stir toast cubes into tomato mixture. Turn into greased 2 1/2 quart (2.5 L) casserole.

Crumble french-fried onions into small bowl. Add cheese. Toss. Sprinkle over tomato mixture. Cover. Bake in 350°F (175°C) oven for 30 minutes. Remove cover. Cook for about 10 minutes until browned. Let stand for 5 minutes before serving. Serves 8 to 10.

1 serving: 268 Calories; 12.8 g Total Fat; 902 mg Sodium; 9 g Protein; 33 g Carbohydrate; 3 g Dietary Fibre

Pictured on page 149.

Sweet Apple And Turnip

Pretty to serve and even better to eat.

Medium yellow turnip (about 1 3/4 lbs., 790 g), cut into 1/4 inch (6 mm) slices	1	1
Water		
Medium cooking apples (such as McIntosh), with peel	2 – 3	2 – 3
Liquid honey	1/4 cup	60 mL
Lemon juice	2 tbsp.	30 mL
Ground cinnamon	1/16 tsp.	0.5 mL
Salt	1/4 tsp.	1 mL
Pepper, sprinkle		
Hard margarine (or butter)	1 tbsp.	15 mL
Coarsely chopped pecans	1/4 cup	60 mL

Place turnip slices on rack over simmering water in large saucepan. Cover. Steam for about 20 minutes until barely tender. Cool.

Core apples, leaving whole. Cut apples into 1/2 inch (12 mm) thick rings. You should have same amount of apple slices as turnip slices.

Combine next 5 ingredients in small cup. Pour into small pie plate. Coat turnip and apple on both sides. Arrange overlapping, alternating turnip and apple in rows, in greased shallow 2 1/2 quart (2.5 L) casserole.

Melt margarine in small frying pan. Stir in pecans. Heat and stir on medium until bubbly and pecans are lightly browned. Sprinkle over turnip and apple. Drizzle any remaining margarine over top. Cover. Bake in 350°F (175°C) oven for about 30 minutes until turnip is soft. Serves 8 to 10.

1 serving: 131 Calories; 4.4 g Total Fat; 109 mg Sodium; 1 g Protein; 24 g Carbohydrate; 3 g Dietary Fibre

Pictured on page 149.

To Make Ahead: Turnip can be prepared 2 to 3 days ahead of time, stored covered in refrigerator and assembled with apple rings when needed.

Spicy Sausage And Bread Stuffing

A large recipe that can be served from the slow cooker. Has a nice kick from the jalapeño peppers.

Package of frozen sausage meat, thawed	13 oz.	375 g
Finely chopped pickled jalapeño pepper	2 tbsp.	30 mL
Herb (or garlic) seasoned croutons	10 cups	2.5 L
Chopped onion	2 cups	500 mL
Chopped celery, with leaves	2 cups	500 mL
Hard margarine (or butter)	1/2 cup	125 mL
Chopped fresh parsley (or 2 tbsp., 30 mL, flakes)	1/2 cup	125 mL
Dried sage	2 tsp.	10 mL
Dried thyme	1 tsp.	5 mL
Dried whole oregano	1 tsp.	5 mL
Pepper, sprinkle		
Can of condensed chicken broth	10 oz.	284 mL
Hot water, approximately	1/2 cup	125 mL
Hard margarine (or butter)	1 tbsp.	15 mL

Scramble-fry sausage in large frying pan until browned. Drain. Turn into large bowl.

Add jalapeño pepper and croutons. Stir.

Sauté onion and celery in first amount of margarine in same frying pan for about 10 minutes until soft.

Add next 5 ingredients. Stir. Add to sausage mixture. Stir.

Drizzle with chicken broth and enough hot water until stuffing is moist and holds together when squeezed. Mixture should not be mushy.

Grease inside liner of 3 1/2 to 4 quart (3.5 to 4 L) slow cooker with second amount of margarine. Lightly pack stuffing into liner. Cover. Cook on Low for about 2 hours until heated through and flavours are blended. Makes 7 3/4 cups (1.9 L).

1/2 cup (125 mL): 253 Calories; 16.4 g Total Fat; 648 mg Sodium; 6 g Protein; 21 g Carbohydrate; 2 g Dietary Fibre

Pictured below.

Top Left: Sweet Apple And Turnip, page 148
Top Right: Spicy Sausage And Bread Stuffing, this page
Bottom Right: Scalloped Tomatoes And Corn, page 148

Spiced Cauliflower

Nutty and aromatic with identifiable East Indian influence.
A great make ahead.

Large head of cauliflower (about 2 lbs., 900 g), large green leaves removed	1	1
Water	1 cup	250 mL
Hard margarine (or butter)	3 tbsp.	50 mL
Garlic cloves, minced (or 1/2 tsp., 2 mL, powder)	2	2
Grated gingerroot (or 1/4 tsp., 1 mL, ground ginger)	1 tsp.	5 mL
Salt	1/2 tsp.	2 mL
Ground coriander	1/2 tsp.	2 mL
Ground cumin	1/4 tsp.	1 mL
Dried crushed chilies	1/4 tsp.	1 mL
Plain yogurt	1/4 cup	60 mL
Hot water	1/4 cup	60 mL
Granulated sugar	1/2 tsp.	2 mL
Garam masala (optional)	1/2 tsp.	2 mL
Shelled and chopped pistachios (or almonds)	2 tbsp.	30 mL

Place cauliflower, root-end down, on rack in large pot or Dutch oven. Add water. Bring to a boil. Cover. Reduce heat to medium-low. Cook for about 15 minutes until cauliflower is tender-crisp. Cool under cold running water until able to handle. Drain well. Cut away and discard very thick core. Cut cauliflower into serving-size pieces.

Heat margarine in large saucepan on medium. Stir in next 6 ingredients.

Add yogurt and hot water. Stir in cauliflower until coated. Cover. Cook on medium-low for about 15 minutes, stirring occasionally, until soft. Remove cover.

Sprinkle with sugar and garam masala. Heat and stir until most of liquid is absorbed and sauce is thickened. Turn into serving bowl.

Sprinkle pistachios over cauliflower mixture. Makes about 5 1/2 cups (1.4 L).

1/2 cup (125 mL): 51 Calories; 4.1 g Total Fat; 171 mg Sodium; 1 g Protein; 3 g Carbohydrate; 1 g Dietary Fibre

Pictured on page 151.

Orange Couscous With Sultanas

The perfect side dish to serve with poultry, pork or fish.

Diced onion	1/2 cup	125 mL
Diced celery	1/2 cup	125 mL
Garlic clove, minced (or 1/4 tsp., 1 mL, powder)	1	1
Hard margarine (or butter)	2 tbsp.	30 mL
Can of condensed vegetable broth	10 oz.	284 mL
Prepared orange juice	1 cup	250 mL
Water	2/3 cup	150 mL
Dried crushed chilies	1/4 tsp.	1 mL
Sultana raisins	1/2 cup	125 mL
Chopped fresh parsley (or 1 1/2 tsp., 7 mL, flakes)	2 tbsp.	30 mL
Finely grated orange zest	1 tsp.	5 mL
Couscous	2 cups	500 mL
Mandarin orange segments, for garnish	2	2
Strips of orange peel, for garnish	2	2

Sauté onion, celery and garlic in margarine in large saucepan until soft.

Stir in next 6 ingredients. Bring to a boil.

Stir in orange zest and couscous. Cover. Let stand for 10 minutes.

Garnish with orange segments and orange peel. Makes 6 cups (1.5 L).

1/2 cup (125 mL): 189 Calories; 2.6 g Total Fat; 195 mg Sodium; 5 g Protein; 36 g Carbohydrate; 2 g Dietary Fibre

Pictured on page 151.

To reheat food in the microwave, always use some form of cover. To prevent moisture loss when cooking, cover food loosely with plastic wrap and make air vents. If moisture loss is not a concern, cover food with a paper towel.

Top & Bottom: Spiced Cauliflower, page 150   Centre: Orange Couscous With Sultanas, page 150   Left & Right: Green Beans With Bacon, this page

Green Beans With Bacon

*Try this yummy way to get fussy eaters to eat their
vegetables. Recipe is easily doubled or tripled to serve more.*

Frozen cut green beans	2 cups	500 mL
Water		
Bacon slices, diced	2	2
Chopped onion	1/4 cup	60 mL
Soy sauce	2 tsp.	10 mL
Granulated sugar	1/2 tsp.	2 mL
Salt	1/4 tsp.	1 mL
Pepper	1/16 tsp.	0.5 mL

Cook beans in small amount of water in medium saucepan
for about 5 minutes until tender. Drain.

Sauté bacon and onion in medium frying pan until
browned. Drain.

Add remaining 4 ingredients. Stir. Add beans. Toss to coat
with sauce. Cook until heated through. Makes 2 1/4 cups
(550 mL). Serves 4.

*1 serving: 46 Calories; 1.7 g Total Fat; 380 mg Sodium; 2 g Protein;
6 g Carbohydrate; 2 g Dietary Fibre*

Pictured above.

Maple Yams

*Creamy smooth yam sprinkled with dark specks of cinnamon.
Has a light maple syrup flavour.*

Fresh yams, peeled and cubed	3 lbs.	1.4 kg
Water		
Maple syrup	1/4 cup	60 mL
Hard margarine (or butter)	2 tbsp.	30 mL
Salt	1/4 tsp.	1 mL
Ground cinnamon	1/2 tsp.	2 mL
Fresh parsley, for garnish		

Cook yams in water in large saucepan until tender. Drain.
Mash until no lumps remain.

Add next 4 ingredients to yams. Stir.

Garnish with parsley. Makes 5 1/4 cups (1.3 L).

*1/4 cup (60 mL): 69 Calories; 1.3 g Total Fat; 48 mg Sodium; 1 g Protein;
14 g Carbohydrate; 1 g Dietary Fibre*

Pictured on page 172/173.

Soups

Cheese-Topped Soup

Chunks of carrots and mushrooms are nicely complemented by the melting cheese in this hearty soup.

Chopped onion	2 cups	500 mL
Diced potato	3 1/2 cups	875 mL
Sliced carrots	1 cup	250 mL
Chopped celery	1 cup	250 mL
Diced fresh mushrooms	1 cup	250 mL
Water	6 cups	1.5 L
Beef bouillon powder	1 tbsp.	15 mL
Chicken bouillon powder	1 tsp.	5 mL
Hard margarine (or butter)	1/3 cup	75 mL
All-purpose flour	1/3 cup	75 mL
Salt	1 tsp.	5 mL
Pepper	1/4 tsp.	1 mL
Grated medium Cheddar (or your favourite) cheese	1 1/2 cups	375 mL

Combine first 8 ingredients in large pot or Dutch oven. Bring to a boil. Reduce heat. Cover. Simmer for about 35 minutes until vegetables are tender.

Melt margarine in small saucepan. Mix in flour, salt and pepper until smooth. Heat and stir until golden. Stir into vegetable mixture until boiling and thickened.

Sprinkle individual servings with cheese. Makes 10 cups (2.5 L).

1 cup (250 mL): 215 Calories; 12.7 g Total Fat; 687 mg Sodium; 7 g Protein; 19 g Carbohydrate; 2 g Dietary Fibre

Pictured on page 153.

If you saved your poinsettias from last Christmas, October is the time to start getting them ready for this Christmas. Keep the plants in complete darkness during the night and leave them in a spot with lots of natural sunshine during the day.

Top Left: Barley Vegetable Soup, below

Bottom Right: Cheese-Topped Soup, page 152

Barley Vegetable Soup

*Lots of colourful vegetable chunks with
plump barley in this pot of comfort food.*

Can of condensed tomato soup	10 oz.	284 mL
Water	6 cups	1.5 L
Pearl barley	1/2 cup	125 mL
Frozen mixed vegetables, chop before measuring	2 cups	500 mL
Shredded cabbage	2 cups	500 mL
Sliced carrot	2 cups	500 mL
Beef bouillon powder	2 tbsp.	30 mL
Granulated sugar	2 tbsp.	30 mL
Salt	1/2 tsp.	2 mL
Pepper	1/2 tsp.	2 mL
Dried sweet basil	1/2 tsp.	2 mL
Dried whole oregano	1/4 tsp.	1 mL

Combine all 12 ingredients in large pot or Dutch oven. Bring to a boil. Reduce heat. Cover. Simmer for about 1 1/4 hours until vegetables are tender. Makes 9 cups (2.25 L).

1 cup (250 mL): 126 Calories; 1.2 g Total Fat; 796 mg Sodium; 4 g Protein; 27 g Carbohydrate; 3 g Dietary Fibre

Pictured above.

Smoky Lentil Chowder

A very good chowder for those cold days.

Medium onion, chopped	1	1
Small green pepper, chopped	1	1
Hard margarine (or butter)	1 1/2 tbsp.	25 mL
Water	6 cups	1.5 L
Cans of tomatoes, with juice (14 oz., 398 mL, each), broken up	2	2
Hickory smoke barbecue sauce	1/2 cup	125 mL
Green lentils	2 cups	500 mL
Salt	1 tsp.	5 mL
Pepper	1/4 tsp.	1 mL
Smoked pork hock (or meaty ham bone), about 1 1/3 lbs. (600 g), optional	1	1

Sauté onion and green pepper in margarine in large uncovered pot or Dutch oven until onion is soft.

Add remaining 7 ingredients. Stir. Bring to a boil. Reduce heat. Cover. Simmer for about 40 minutes until lentils and vegetables are tender. Remove pork hock. Cut off meat. Discard skin, fat and bone. Dice meat. Return meat to soup. Makes 12 cups (3 L).

1 cup (250 mL): 156 Calories; 2.2 g Total Fat; 418 mg Sodium; 11 g Protein; 25 g Carbohydrate; 5 g Dietary Fibre

Pictured on page 154.

Scotch Broth

Tender lamb in a broth with a hint of thyme.

Lamb (or beef) stew meat, diced	1 lb.	454 g
Yellow split peas	1/4 cup	60 mL
Dried green peas	1/4 cup	60 mL
Pearl barley	1/4 cup	60 mL
Water	10 cups	2.5 L
Medium carrots, diced	2	2
Diced yellow turnip	1/2 cup	125 mL
Medium onions, chopped	2	2
Medium leeks (white and tender parts only), chopped	2	2
Chopped cabbage	1/2 cup	125 mL
Salt	2 tsp.	10 mL
Pepper	1/2 tsp.	2 mL
Ground thyme	1/4 tsp.	1 mL

Place first 5 ingredients in large pot or Dutch oven. Bring to a boil. Reduce heat. Cover. Simmer for 1 hour, stirring occasionally.

Add remaining 8 ingredients. Bring to a boil. Reduce heat. Cover. Simmer for 30 to 45 minutes until vegetables are tender. Makes 13 cups (3.25 L).

1 cup (250 mL): 115 Calories; 2.1 g Total Fat; 402 mg Sodium; 10 g Protein; 14 g Carbohydrate; 2 g Dietary Fibre

Pictured on page 154/155.

Top Left: Smoky Lentil Chowder, page 153
Top Right: Cream Of Mushroom Soup, page 156
Bottom Left: Scotch Broth, above
Bottom Right: Wonton Soup, page 156

Cream Of Mushroom Soup

A creamy, smooth soup with lots of mushroom flavour
and a good tang from the sour cream and vinegar.

Mayonnaise (not salad dressing)	1/2 cup	125 mL
Water	2 1/2 cups	625 mL
Beef bouillon powder	1 tbsp.	15 mL
Fresh mushrooms, large ones cut smaller	1 lb.	454 g
Sour cream	1 1/2 cups	375 mL
White vinegar	4 tsp.	20 mL
Salt	1/2 tsp.	2 mL
Pepper	1/4 tsp.	1 mL

Freshly ground pepper, for garnish
Sliced fresh mushrooms, for garnish

Process first 4 ingredients, in 2 batches, in blender until smooth. Pour into large saucepan. Bring to a boil. Reduce heat to medium-low. Cook, uncovered, for 2 minutes.

Add sour cream, vinegar, salt and pepper. Stir. Heat for about 5 minutes, stirring often, until hot.

Garnish with pepper and mushroom slices. Makes 6 cups (1.5 L).

1 cup (250 mL): 258 Calories; 24.6 g Total Fat; 625 mg Sodium; 4 g Protein;
7 g Carbohydrate; 1 g Dietary Fibre

Pictured on page 155.

Wonton Soup

A distinctive soup with a hint of orange.
You'll want to make extra to freeze. Delicious!

Lean ground pork	1/4 lb.	113 g
Water chestnuts, chopped	4	4
Chopped fresh mushrooms	3/4 cup	175 mL
Grated orange peel	1/4 tsp.	1 mL
Large egg, fork-beaten	1	1
Cornstarch	1 tbsp.	15 mL
Soy sauce	1 tbsp.	15 mL
Pepper, sprinkle		
Wonton wrappers	18	18
Large egg	1	1
Water	1 tbsp.	15 mL
Chicken broth	6 cups	1.5 L
Chopped bok choy	1/2 cup	125 mL
Sliced celery	1/4 cup	60 mL
Chopped broccoli	1/4 cup	60 mL
Raw medium shrimp, peeled and deveined (about 5)	3 oz.	85 g

Scramble-fry ground pork in medium frying pan until no pink remains. Remove from heat. Drain.

Add next 7 ingredients. Mix well.

Place scant 1 tbsp. (15 mL) filling on each wrapper.

Beat second egg with water in small bowl using fork. Dampen 3 sides of each wonton wrapper with egg mixture. Roll up, tucking in sides. Pinch to seal.

Combine chicken broth, bok choy, celery and broccoli in large saucepan. Bring to a boil. Boil for 1 minute. Add wontons. Bring to a boil.

Stir in shrimp. Cook for 3 to 4 minutes until shrimp is pink. Makes 7 1/2 cups (1.9 L).

1 cup (250 mL): 174 Calories; 6.3 g Total Fat; 956 mg Sodium; 13 g Protein;
15 g Carbohydrate; trace Dietary Fibre

Pictured on page 155.

To make the most of the holiday season, make a difference in your community. Call a local charity and ask what they need, then plan a party to provide it—whether it's serving meals, carolling or decorating a tree. Or find out what items are needed (blankets, toys, canned food), and have a party to assemble these donations as well as to celebrate the holidays.

Meaty Turkey Rice Soup, below

Meaty Turkey Rice Soup

Uses remaining turkey from Stuffed Turkey Breast, page 121.
Count on two days to do this soup: one day to boil, strain and chill
the broth, and the next day to make the soup. A lot of flavour.

DAY 1		
Water	12 cups	3 L
Turkey parts, with skin	6 lbs.	2.7 kg
Whole celery heart (see Note)	1	1
Medium onions, halved	2	2
Large carrot, halved	1	1
Bay leaves	2	2
Peppercorns	10	10
Fresh parsley sprigs	2	2
Salt	1 tbsp.	15 mL
DAY 2		
Water		
Chopped onion	1 cup	250 mL
Chopped celery	1 cup	250 mL
Diced carrot	1 cup	250 mL
Reserved diced cooked turkey	4 cups	1 L
Cooked long grain white rice	1 1/2 cups	375 mL
Frozen peas	1 cup	250 mL
Chopped fresh parsley (or 1 tbsp., 15 mL, flakes)	1/4 cup	60 mL
Salt, to taste		
Pepper, to taste		

Day 1: Combine water and turkey parts in at least 6 quart (6 L) Dutch oven or stockpot. Bring to a boil. Boil, uncovered, for 5 minutes. Remove from heat. Carefully spoon off and discard foam from surface. Bring to a boil.

Add next 7 ingredients. Reduce heat. Simmer, partially covered, for about 3 hours until meat is almost falling off bones. Pour through sieve over large liquid measure. Remove meat from turkey bones as soon as cool enough to handle. Dice meat. Reserve 4 cups (1 L). Cover. Chill. Discard skin, turkey bones and strained solids. Chill broth overnight until fat comes to surface and solidifies.

Day 2: Carefully spoon off and discard fat from surface of broth. Add water, if necessary, to make 10 cups (2.5 L). Pour into Dutch oven or stockpot. Bring to a boil. Add onion, celery and carrot. Reduce heat. Simmer, partially covered, for 1 hour.

Add remaining 6 ingredients. Cook gently for about 10 minutes until heated through. Makes about 10 1/2 cups (2.6 L).

1 cup (250 mL): 289 Calories; 6.9 g Total Fat; 431 mg Sodium; 40 g Protein; 14 g Carbohydrate; 2 g Dietary Fibre

Pictured above.

Note: The celery heart is the very centre of a celery bunch, including the small white-coloured stalks with leaves. Celery hearts are available in ready-to-use packages from the produce section in grocery stores.

Boxing Day— Help Yourself!

Now it's time to relax and settle down for a true day of rest during the holidays. Here are some simple-to-make recipes and menu suggestions that will keep everyone, including the cook, satisfied without a lot of work.

Making It Easy

Ribbons and wrappings, boxes and bows—another hectic but memorable Christmas Day has come and gone! But not so your guests! Grandma and Grandpa will be with you for a few more days and the kids won't be going back to school until the new year.

There's been baking goodies since November, wrapping gifts since mid-December and your house has been given a complete Christmas makeover. Everyone's worked hard to be ready and it was all worth it! But now it's Boxing Day—a day to take it easy. Children want to play with their new toys and games or head outdoors to try the new toboggan. Teens want to sleep in and have a lazy day. Some people want to curl up and start reading the book that was in their stocking. No one wants to make any hard and fast plans. Friends or relatives may drop in, or may even come for dinner. Regardless of what your household might do on Boxing Day, it will no doubt be casual, casual, casual.

Plan for a day of "grazing," that is, serve the food so that it can be eaten at will. Everyone simply roams around, nibbling and eating when they feel like it. In the morning, pull Gingerbread Muffins, page 63, and Cranberry Scones, page 64, from the freezer and place them in a basket lined with a Christmas napkin. Lay another napkin over top to keep them from drying out. Place some butter and jams beside them, along with a stack of plates. Set a platter of fresh fruit and cheeses, covered loosely with plastic wrap, on the counter or table beside the basket. Arrange knives, rolled individually in paper napkins, in a pretty Christmas container to complete this oh-so-simple early to late morning fare.

Around midday, bring out the leftover turkey and all the fixings for Turkey Salad Wraps, page 37, or Turkey Cristo Sandwich, page 161, and let people make their own when they're ready. Replace the muffins and cheese with a tray of Christmas cookies and squares.

At the same time, or even earlier in the morning when the household is still quiet, assemble Cajun Chicken, page 111, in your slow cooker. Set it on Low to cook all day. When it's ready, serve with a simple lettuce and tomato salad, some buns and refill the Christmas goodies tray. Supper is on the table!

There are numerous ways to mix and match the recipes found in this book to accommodate the kind of Boxing Day that your family would enjoy. Following are a few menu suggestions to get you started.

Come-And-Go Boxing Day

Ricotta And Jalapeño Tarts, page 44

Hot Mushroom Dip, page 51 (with crackers)

Holiday Whirls, page 50

Peanut Butter Dip, page 54 (with fresh fruit)

Turkey Mixed Bean Soup, page 161 (with buns)

Tray of Christmas goodies, pages 82 to 91

Leftovers Party

Turkey Salad Wraps, page 37

Christmas Bread, page 72

Feta Spinach Mushroom Caps, page 43

Chocolate Almond Cookies, page 84

Travellers' Take-Away Lunch

Turkey Cristo Sandwich, page 161

(with carrot and cucumber sticks, and pickles)

Ragged Chocolate Drops, page 89

Boxing Day Buffet

Cranberry Cheese, page 55 (with crackers)

Honey Mustard Turkey Salad, page 34

Sweet Potato Biscuits, page 65

Beef Bourguignon, page 112

Peaches And Cream Cake, page 95

Boxing Day Trivia

When is Boxing Day?

In some countries, Boxing Day is celebrated on December 26, the day after Christmas Day. But in other countries, it falls on the first weekday following Christmas Day.

Who celebrates Boxing Day?

For many people, the day after Christmas Day is a holiday from work and generally schools are closed, but they have no idea there is a name, let alone a reason, for the day. Commonwealth countries such as Australia, Canada and New Zealand, along with Britain, are widely known to celebrate Boxing Day.

What is the origin of Boxing Day?

There are differing stories and folklore attached to this après Christmas holiday, but there are a few basic facts that almost everyone agrees upon when discussing the origin of Boxing Day: This annual holiday began in Britain in the 19th century under Queen Victoria and it has to do with giving presents such as money or household goods to the less fortunate. Beyond that, the details grow hazy.

The following are the more popular of the Boxing Day stories:

* Churches used to open their alms boxes that contained money from people making special holiday donations. The clergy would distribute the contents to the poor the following day.

* English servants were required to work on Christmas Day to help their masters' celebrations run smoothly. They were, therefore, given leave the next day to visit their own families. Typically, their employers would give each servant a box containing gifts and bonuses to take home.

* Masters gave their servants an allotment of practical goods at Christmas, the amount and value being determined by the status of the workers and the size of their family. Spun cloth, durable food supplies, tools and leather goods were packed into one box per family for easy travelling. These gifts were not voluntary but more of an obligation by masters because often servants were completely dependent on their masters for food and clothing.

* British servants used to take boxes to their masters in which the masters would place coins as a special year-end gift. Or the servants would smash open small earthenware boxes filled with money given specifically to them by their masters.

* The poor would carry empty boxes door-to-door the day after Christmas and people would fill these boxes with clothing, goods, sweets and money.

* Centuries ago, the merchant class gave boxes of food and fruit to the tradespeople and servants the day after Christmas as a form of a tip for service done. In the same way, nowadays, we might give the piano teacher or paper boy a little something extra at Christmas to show our gratitude—only now it's in an envelope rather than a box!

The common theme in all of these stories is that the rich (landowners, employers, royalty) gave gifts to the poor (servants, tradespeople, the general poor), sometimes out of obligation and sometimes out of simple generosity. It should be noted that the poor never gave a gift back to the rich as this would have been seen as a presumptuous act of claiming equality with the rich.

What does Boxing Day mean today?

It would seem that Boxing Day has nothing to do with the empty boxes piled in the corner by the Christmas tree. The origin of the name seems to have something to do with boxes, but the true meaning has been lost over time. Boxing Day in the 21st century is a day to be together with family, celebrating the holidays with food, fun and love. Many people use this day to go shopping to exchange gifts or to purchase sale-priced items. Many churches and organizations follow the original tradition of donating special money and goods collected to assist families who are in need.

Turkey Cristo Sandwich, below

Turkey Cristo Sandwich

An excellent and easy-to-make sandwich.
A very filling meal for one person or perfect for
two people, along with a leafy green side salad.

Cooked turkey slices (1 oz., 28 g), to cover	2	2
Salt, sprinkle		
Pepper, sprinkle		
Process Swiss cheese slice	1	1
Whole wheat (or white) bread slice (buttered, optional)	1	1
Cooked ham slice (about 3/4 oz., 21 g)	1	1
Process Swiss cheese slice	1	1
White bread slices (buttered, optional)	2	2
Large egg	1	1
Water	1 tbsp.	15 mL
Hard margarine (or butter)	2 tsp.	10 mL

Layer first 7 ingredients, in order given, on white bread slice. Top with remaining white bread slice.

Beat egg and water together in shallow bowl using fork. Dip sandwich on both sides to soak up all of egg mixture.

Heat margarine in frying pan on medium until sizzling. Place sandwich in frying pan. Cook for 3 to 4 minutes per side until golden and cheese is melted. Serves 1 or 2.

1 serving: 580 Calories; 30.1 g Total Fat; 974 mg Sodium; 36 g Protein; 41 g Carbohydrate; 3 g Dietary Fibre

Pictured above and on page 36.

Turkey Mixed Bean Soup

A great way to use up leftover holiday turkey.
Serve with Two-Toned Buns, page 65.

Turkey carcass	1	1
Water	12 cups	3 L
Bay leaves	2	2
Large onion, chopped	1	1
Celery ribs, with leaves, chopped	2	2
Medium carrots, chopped	3	3
Can of mixed beans, with liquid	19 oz.	540 mL
Can of diced tomatoes, with juice	14 oz.	398 mL
Chicken bouillon powder	1 tbsp.	15 mL
Dried whole oregano	1 tsp.	5 mL
Salt	1 tsp.	5 mL
Pepper	1/4 tsp.	1 mL

Bring turkey carcass, water and bay leaves to a boil in large pot or Dutch oven. Skim off and discard foam that forms on top. Reduce heat. Cover. Simmer for 1 1/2 hours. Remove turkey carcass. Remove meat from bones. Dice meat. Discard bones. Pour stock through sieve over large saucepan. Discard solids. Add meat to soup.

Add remaining 9 ingredients. Bring to a boil on medium. Reduce heat to medium-low. Simmer, uncovered, for 30 to 45 minutes, stirring occasionally, until vegetables are tender. Makes about 19 cups (4.75 L).

1 cup (250 mL): 188 Calories; 4.5 g Total Fat; 399 mg Sodium; 27 g Protein; 9 g Carbohydrate; 1 g Dietary Fibre

Pictured on page 35.

Turkey Mixed Bean Soup, above

International Buffet

Import a new tradition into your array of holiday menus
with this collection of recipes with influences from
around the world. There's a mosaic of flavours to match
our country's diverse cultural background.

Slow-Cooker Dolmades

Pronounced dohl-MAH-dehs. The name of this Greek dish comes from the Arabic word for "something stuffed." Makes a big batch. Serve garnished with fresh lemon slices. Delicious with Greek tzatziki dip or plain yogurt.

Medium-large grapevine leaves (see Note)	4 cups	1 L
Cold water, several changes		
Long grain white rice, uncooked	1 3/4 cups	425 mL
Water	2 1/2 cups	625 mL
Salt	1 tsp.	5 mL
Diced onion	1 1/2 cups	375 mL
Olive (or cooking) oil	1 tbsp.	15 mL
Garlic cloves, minced (or 3/4 tsp., 4 mL, powder)	3	3
Lean ground lamb	1 lb.	454 g
Raisins, chopped (optional)	1/2 cup	125 mL
Dried mint leaves	1 tsp.	5 mL
Parsley flakes	1 tsp.	5 mL
Dried whole oregano	1 tsp.	5 mL
Salt	1 tsp.	5 mL
Pepper	1/4 tsp.	1 mL
Boiling water	4 1/3 cups	1.1 L
Olive (or cooking) oil	3 tbsp.	50 mL
Lemon juice	1/2 cup	125 mL
Garlic cloves, cut in half (or 1/4 tsp., 1 mL, powder)	4	4
Granulated sugar	1/2 tsp.	2 mL

Carefully unroll grapevine leaves. Put into large bowl. Cover with cold water. Let stand for 10 minutes. Drain and repeat twice more with cold water until brine is rinsed from grapevine leaves. Set aside.

Combine rice, water and first amount of salt in medium saucepan. Bring to a boil. Stir. Reduce heat. Cover. Simmer for about 12 minutes until liquid is absorbed and rice is firm. Remove cover. Cool. Fluff with fork several times while cooling to break up any clumps.

Sauté onion in first amount of olive oil in large frying pan for about 5 minutes until soft.

Add first amount of garlic and ground lamb. Scramble-fry for about 5 minutes, breaking up large pieces, until lamb is no longer pink. Drain. Turn into large bowl.

Add rice and next 6 ingredients. Stir well. Carefully separate grapevine leaves, reserving any torn or small leaves to separate layers. Trim off and discard any hard stems. Line bottom of 5 quart (5 L) slow cooker with few torn or small grapevine leaves. Place 1 to 2 tbsp. (15 to 30 mL) filling (depending on size of leaves) in centre of each grapevine leaf on rough side. Roll up, from stem end, tucking in sides to enclose filling. Do not roll too tightly as rice will expand. Arrange rolls close together, seam-side down, in layers in slow cooker. Separate layers with torn or small grapevine leaves. Place any remaining grapevine leaves over top layer of dolmades.

Stir remaining 5 ingredients together in medium bowl. Slowly pour enough water mixture over dolmades, allowing all air spaces to fill, until almost covered and water mixture is just visible on sides. Reserve any remaining water mixture. Cook on Low for 3 1/2 to 4 hours, checking after 2 1/2 hours to see if more water mixture is needed. Turn off slow cooker. Do not uncover. Let stand in slow cooker for at least 30 minutes to set rolls. Drain off and discard liquid. Carefully remove dolmades to serving plate or airtight containers for freezing. Serve at room temperature. Large rolls can be cut in half diagonally. Makes about 6 dozen dolmades.

1 dolmade: 46 Calories; 2.3 g Total Fat; 111 mg Sodium; 2 g Protein; 5 g Carbohydrate; trace Dietary Fibre

Pictured on page 165.

Note: Grapevine leaves can be purchased fresh or in various sized jars. Some jars have a lot of very small leaves that are unusable for rolling in this type of recipe, so you may need 1 to 2 jars, or possibly more, if all the leaves in one jar are small.

Photo Legend next page:

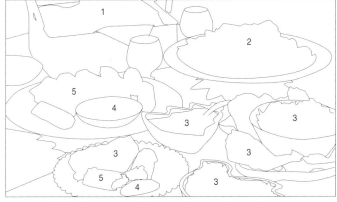

1. Handheld Tourtières, page 166
2. Slow-Cooker Dolmades, this page
3. Shrimp Salad Rolls, page 166
4. Savoury Orange Dipping Sauce, page 92
5. Spring Rolls, page 167

Shrimp Salad Rolls

The interesting contrast of ingredients provides
excellent colour to this Asian appetizer.

CHILI MAYONNAISE
Mayonnaise (not salad dressing)	1/3 cup	75 mL
Plain yogurt	1/4 cup	60 mL
Seafood cocktail sauce	2 tbsp.	30 mL
Sambal oelek (chili paste)	2 tsp.	10 mL
Finely chopped green onion	1 tbsp.	15 mL

SAUCE
Water	2 tbsp.	30 mL
Chili sauce	1 tbsp.	15 mL
Sherry (or alcohol-free sherry)	1 tbsp.	15 mL
Hoisin sauce	1 tbsp.	15 mL
Dark sesame (or cooking) oil	1 tsp.	5 mL
Granulated sugar	1 tsp.	5 mL
Cornstarch	2 tsp.	10 mL

FILLING
Garlic clove, minced (or 1/4 tsp., 1 mL, powder)	1	1
Finely grated gingerroot (or 1/4 tsp., 1 mL, ground ginger)	1 tsp.	5 mL
Finely chopped broccoli, with stems	1 cup	250 mL
Grated carrot	1/4 cup	60 mL
Cooking oil	2 tbsp.	30 mL
Raw medium shrimp (about 15), peeled, deveined and chopped (about 2 cups, 500 mL)	1/2 lb.	225 g
Green onions, sliced	2	2
Salt	1/2 tsp.	2 mL
Cellophane (mung bean) noodles	2 oz.	57 g
Cold water, to cover		
Large butter (or iceberg) lettuce leaves	24	24
Chopped roasted peanuts, for garnish		

Chili Mayonnaise: Combine all 5 ingredients in small bowl. Cover. Chill. Makes 2/3 cup (150 mL) chili mayonnaise.

Sauce: Stir all 7 ingredients together in separate small bowl. Set aside.

Filling: Sauté garlic, ginger, broccoli and carrot in cooking oil in wok or large frying pan on medium-high for 1 minute.

Add shrimp and green onion. Stir-fry for 2 to 3 minutes until shrimp is pink. Add salt. Stir. Stir sauce. Add to shrimp mixture. Stir-fry for 1 to 2 minutes until sauce is thickened. Transfer to large bowl.

Soak noodles in cold water for 5 minutes. Drain well. Snip noodles with scissors to make more manageable for serving. Add to shrimp mixture. Toss. Makes about 3 cups (750 mL) filling.

Place lettuce leaves in stacks around filling. Individuals serve themselves by placing about 2 tbsp. (30 mL) filling on each lettuce leaf. Serve with peanuts and Chili Mayonnaise. Serves 6 to 8.

1 serving: 259 Calories; 16.9 g Total Fat; 508 mg Sodium; 10 g Protein; 17 g Carbohydrate; 1 g Dietary Fibre

Pictured on page 164 and on page 165.

Handheld Tourtières

Meat-filled French-Canadian pastries.
Serve with Rhubarb Relish, page 93.

Lean ground beef	1 lb.	454 g
Lean ground pork	1/2 lb.	225 g
Diced onion	1 cup	250 mL
Seasoned salt	1 1/2 tsp.	7 mL
Beef bouillon powder	1 tsp.	5 mL
Pepper	1 tsp.	5 mL
Poultry seasoning	1 tsp.	5 mL
Water	1 1/2 cups	375 mL
Instant potato flakes, approximately	1 cup	250 mL
Pastry for three 2 crust pies, your own or a mix		

Put first 8 ingredients into large saucepan. Bring to a boil on medium. Boil slowly, uncovered, for 30 minutes. Remove from heat.

Add enough instant potato flakes, 1/4 cup (60 mL) at a time, until liquid is absorbed. Mixture should be thick enough to hold its shape. Cool. Makes 5 cups (1.25 L) filling.

Roll out 1/3 of pastry into 16 x 16 inch (40 x 40 cm) square on lightly floured surface. Cut into 16 squares. Place about 1 1/2 to 2 tbsp. (25 to 30 mL) filling in centre of each square. Dampen edges with water. Fold diagonally. Seal edges using fork. Cut small slits in top using tip of sharp knife. Arrange on ungreased baking sheet. Repeat with remaining pastry and filling. Bake in 375°F (190°C) oven for about 25 minutes until golden. Makes 4 dozen tourtières.

1 tourtière: 119 Calories; 7.6 g Total Fat; 162 mg Sodium; 3 g Protein; 9 g Carbohydrate; trace Dietary Fibre

Pictured on page 164.

Spring Rolls

*Traditionally these Asian appetizers are deep-fried
but are also very good baked. Serve with
Savoury Orange Dipping Sauce, page 92.*

Cooking oil	1 tbsp.	15 mL
Boneless, skinless chicken breast halves (about 2), finely chopped	1/2 lb.	225 g
Medium carrot, grated	1	1
Finely grated gingerroot (or 1/4 tsp., 1 mL, ground ginger)	1 1/2 tsp.	7 mL
Garlic clove, minced (or 1/4 tsp., 1 mL, powder)	1	1
Grated cabbage, lightly packed	2 cups	500 mL
Fresh bean sprouts	2 cups	500 mL
Chopped green onion	1/3 cup	75 mL
Soy sauce	1 1/2 tbsp.	25 mL
Salt	1 tsp.	5 mL
Pepper	1/8 tsp.	0.5 mL
Spring roll wrappers (6 inch, 15 cm, size)	24	24
Cooking oil, for deep-frying	5 cups	1.25 L

Heat cooking oil in wok or large frying pan on medium. Add chicken, carrot, ginger and garlic. Stir-fry for 5 minutes.

Add cabbage and bean sprouts. Stir-fry for 2 minutes. Add green onion. Stir-fry for 2 minutes. Remove from heat.

Stir in soy sauce, salt and pepper. Makes 3 cups (750 mL) filling.

Place 1 spring roll wrapper on work surface with 1 point towards you. Spread about 2 tbsp. (30 mL) filling in between point and centre (see Figure 1). Fold point over filling (see Figure 2). Moisten open edges with water. Fold each side point toward centre (see Figure 3). Roll up. Seal. Repeat with remaining spring roll wrappers and filling, stirring filling occasionally to keep moisture evenly distributed.

Deep-fry, in batches, in hot (375°F, 190°C) cooking oil for about 5 minutes, turning at halftime, until golden. Remove to paper towels to drain. Makes 24 spring rolls.

1 spring roll: 136 Calories; 3.6 g Total Fat; 350 mg Sodium; 6 g Protein; 20 g Carbohydrate; trace Dietary Fibre

Pictured on page 164.

BAKED SPRING ROLLS: Arrange, seam-side down, on greased baking sheet. Bake in 375°F (190°C) oven for about 18 minutes until golden.

Sauerkraut Salad

*This German salad is very good and
very colourful with red and green bits showing.
Must be made the day before serving.*

Can of sauerkraut, rinsed, drained and squeezed dry	28 oz.	796 mL
Chopped onion	1 cup	250 mL
Chopped celery	1 cup	250 mL
Green pepper, chopped	1	1
Jars of pimiento (2 oz., 57 mL, each), chopped	2	2
Large tart cooking apple (such as Granny Smith), peeled and grated	1	1
Granulated sugar	3/4 cup	175 mL

Combine all 7 ingredients in large bowl. Chill for 24 hours to blend flavours. Stir. Store in airtight container in refrigerator for about 1 month. Makes about 4 cups (1 L).

1/2 cup (125 mL): 124 Calories; 0.3 g Total Fat; 673 mg Sodium; 2 g Protein; 31 g Carbohydrate; 4 g Dietary Fibre

Pictured on page 168.

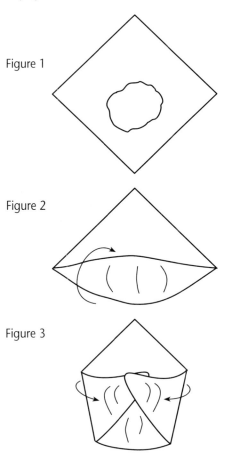

Figure 1

Figure 2

Figure 3

Bottom Left: Mexican Christmas Salad, below

Top Right: Sauerkraut Salad, page 167

Mexican Christmas Salad

A beautiful, colourful, crunchy salad using
crunchy jicama, fresh and canned fruit and beets.

BALSAMIC DRESSING

Cooking oil	1 tbsp.	15 mL
All-purpose flour	1 tbsp.	15 mL
Reserved pineapple juice	1/3 cup	75 mL
Balsamic vinegar	2 tbsp.	30 mL
Brown sugar, packed	2 tbsp.	30 mL
Medium navel oranges (or other seedless oranges), peel and outside membrane removed, cut in half and cut crosswise into 1/4 inch (6 mm) slices	4	4
Medium red grapefruit, peeled, sectioned, membrane and seeds discarded, cut bite size	1	1
Can of pineapple tidbits, juice drained and reserved	14 oz.	398 mL
Ripe kiwifruit, peeled and diced	2	2
Peeled and julienned jicama	1 cup	250 mL
Can of sliced beets, rinsed, drained and cut julienne	14 oz.	398 mL
Crisp romaine lettuce and/or Belgian endive leaves	8	8
Roasted unsalted peanuts, chopped	2 tbsp.	30 mL
Shelled, roasted sunflower seeds	1 tbsp.	15 mL

Balsamic Dressing: Stir cooking oil into flour in small saucepan until smooth. Stir in pineapple juice, vinegar and brown sugar. Heat and stir on medium until boiling and thickened. Cool. Makes about 1/2 cup (125 mL) dressing.

Put next 5 ingredients into large bowl. Drizzle with dressing. Toss to coat. Chill until ready to serve.

Just before serving, add beets. Mix well.

Pile salad onto lettuce leaf-lined serving dish. Sprinkle with peanuts and sunflower seeds. Makes 8 1/2 cups (2.1 L).

3/4 cup (175 mL): 115 Calories; 2.7 g Total Fat; 55 mg Sodium; 2 g Protein; 23 g Carbohydrate; 2 g Dietary Fibre

Pictured above.

Variation: Add 2 medium bananas, sliced, to salad at same time as beets.

Variation: Add 1 pomegranate, peeled and membranes discarded, at same time as oranges, reserving 1/4 cup (60 mL). Sprinkle reserved pomegranate over top of finished salad.

Pineapple Coconut Curry

Lots of sauce with a mild curry flavour in this Asian dish. Serve with a variety of condiments, such as chopped cashew nuts, diced cucumber and chutney. Best to make the whole recipe the day before and reheat.

Beef inside round steak, cut into 3/4 inch (2 cm) cubes	2 lbs.	900 g
Lean boneless pork loin, cut into 3/4 inch (2 cm) cubes	2 lbs.	900 g
Cooking oil	2 tbsp.	30 mL
Sliced onion	1 1/2 cups	375 mL
Mild (or medium) curry paste	1 1/2 tbsp.	25 mL
Slivered crystallized ginger	1/4 cup	60 mL
Chopped fresh mint leaves (or 1 1/2 tsp., 7 mL, dried)	2 tbsp.	30 mL
Salt	1 tsp.	5 mL
Pepper	1/8 tsp.	0.5 mL
Ground cloves, just a pinch		
All-purpose flour	3 tbsp.	50 mL
Can of crushed pineapple, with juice	14 oz.	398 mL
Can of condensed beef consommé	10 oz.	284 mL
Coconut milk	1 cup	250 mL
Flake coconut	1 cup	250 mL
Lime juice	2 tbsp.	30 mL

Brown beef and pork, in batches, in cooking oil in large frying pan. Remove beef and pork, using slotted spoon, to ungreased 3 quart (3 L) casserole.

Add next 7 ingredients to drippings in same frying pan. Heat and stir for about 5 minutes until onion is soft. Remove from heat.

Sprinkle flour over onion mixture. Stir well. Slowly stir in pineapple with juice and beef consommé. Pour over beef and pork. Cover. Bake in 300°F (150°C) oven for about 1 3/4 hours until meat is very tender. Chill overnight to blend flavours. Skim fat from top if desired. Cook in 350°F (175°C) oven for 60 to 80 minutes, stirring once, until heated through.

Stir in coconut milk, coconut and lime juice. Makes 10 cups (2.5 L).

1 cup (250 mL): 499 Calories; 30.3 g Total Fat; 494 mg Sodium; 41 g Protein; 16 g Carbohydrate; 2 g Dietary Fibre

Pictured on page 170.

Shrimp Creole

This richly flavoured dish will remind you of Southern U.S.A. Serve over rice.

Chopped celery	1 cup	250 mL
Chopped onion	1 cup	250 mL
Green pepper, diced	1	1
Garlic clove, minced (or 1/4 tsp., 1 mL, powder)	1	1
Cooking oil	1 tbsp.	15 mL
Can of diced tomatoes, with juice	14 oz.	398 mL
Tomato paste	2 tbsp.	30 mL
Granulated sugar	2 tsp.	10 mL
Lemon juice	1 tbsp.	15 mL
Louisiana hot sauce (optional)	1 – 3 tsp.	5 – 15 mL
Bay leaf	1	1
Dried thyme	1/2 tsp.	2 mL
Salt	1/2 tsp.	2 mL
Pepper	1/4 tsp.	1 mL
Raw medium shrimp (about 60), peeled and deveined (or frozen, thawed)	2 lbs.	900 g

Sauté celery, onion, green pepper and garlic in cooking oil in large wok or Dutch oven until lightly browned.

Add next 9 ingredients. Stir. Bring to a boil. Reduce heat. Simmer, uncovered, for 10 minutes to blend flavours.

Add shrimp. Bring to a boil. Reduce heat. Simmer for 10 minutes, stirring occasionally, until shrimp is pink. Makes 6 3/4 cups (1.7 L). Serves 6.

1 serving: 226 Calories; 5.3 g Total Fat; 553 mg Sodium; 32 g Protein; 12 g Carbohydrate; 2 g Dietary Fibre

Pictured below.

Shrimp Creole, above

Varenyky With Onion Butter

This popular Ukrainian and Polish dish is also known as pyrohy, perogies or potato dumplings. Cheesy potato filling surrounded by a tender, almost non-existent, dough that melts in your mouth.

DOUGH

All-purpose flour	2 cups	500 mL
Baking powder	1/4 tsp.	1 mL
Salt	1 tsp.	5 mL
Cooking oil	2 tsp.	10 mL
Warm water, approximately	2/3 cup	150 mL

ONION BUTTER

Finely diced onion	1/2 cup	125 mL
Butter (not margarine)	1/4 cup	60 mL

TWO-CHEESE POTATO FILLING

Hot mashed potatoes (3 to 4 medium)	1 3/4 cups	425 mL
Grated sharp Cheddar cheese	3/4 cup	175 mL
Creamed cottage cheese, mashed with fork	1/3 cup	75 mL
Pepper	1/8 tsp.	0.5 mL
Boiling water	16 cups	4 L
Salt	1 tbsp.	15 mL

Dough: Combine flour, baking powder and salt in food processor. Process for 3 seconds.

With motor running, slowly add cooking oil and enough warm water through feed chute until a ball begins to form. Turn dough out onto lightly floured surface. Knead 3 to 4 times until smooth. Cover with plastic wrap. Let stand for 20 minutes.

Onion Butter: Sauté onion in butter in small saucepan on medium-low for about 10 minutes until onion is soft but not brown. Keep hot.

Two-Cheese Potato Filling: Mix first 4 ingredients in medium bowl until Cheddar cheese melts and mixture is evenly moist. Makes about 2 1/4 cups (550 mL) filling. Divide dough into 4 equal portions. Roll out 1 portion into a rope about 12 inches (30 cm) long. Keep other portions covered. Cut at 1 inch (2.5 cm) intervals. Press balls slightly to flatten. Cover with plastic wrap. Stretch and press 1 ball to about 2 1/2 inches (6.4 cm) in diameter. Place in palm of hand. Place about 2 tsp. (10 mL) filling in centre.

Left & Bottom: Pineapple Coconut Curry, page 169
Top Right: Baccalà, page 172

Fold dough in half. With floured fingers, pinch edges firmly together to seal. Edges of dough may be moistened if desired. Arrange in single layer on lightly floured tea towel-lined baking sheet. Cover with tea towel to prevent drying. Repeat with remaining dough and filling.

Cook varenyky, in batches, in boiling water and salt in large pot or Dutch oven for 3 to 4 minutes, stirring occasionally, until varenyky float to top. Allow to bob for 1 minute. Remove using slotted spoon. Drain. Turn into large bowl. Drizzle some Onion Butter over each varenyky batch. Gently shake to mix and prevent sticking. Makes 4 dozen varenyky.

1 varenyky: 47 Calories; 2 g Total Fat; 104 mg Sodium; 1 g Protein; 6 g Carbohydrate; trace Dietary Fibre

Pictured on page 172/173.

Variation: Add 6 bacon slices, cooked crisp and crumbled, to Two-Cheese Potato Filling.

Variation: After varenyky are cooked, sauté, in batches, in 2 tsp. (10 mL) butter in frying pan until lightly browned.

To Make Ahead: Place filled varenyky (cooked or uncooked) on baking sheet, in layers between waxed paper or parchment paper. Cover. Freeze until solid. To remove varenyky, hit baking sheet on counter to pop them off. Store in resealable freezer bags in freezer. To cook from frozen, do not thaw. Boil, as above, increasing cooking time after they float to top.

Many Jewels Stir-Fry

The jewels are evident in the vibrant colours,
crisp texture and great shapes. Serve over rice vermicelli.

SAUCE

Water	1/3 cup	75 mL
Oyster sauce	1/3 cup	75 mL
Soy sauce	1/4 cup	60 mL
Sherry (or alcohol-free sherry)	1 tbsp.	15 mL
Cornstarch	2 tbsp.	30 mL
Brown sugar, packed	2 tsp.	10 mL
Cooking oil	2 tbsp.	30 mL
Garlic cloves, minced (or 3/4 tsp., 4 mL, powder)	3	3
Grated gingerroot (or 1/4 – 3/4 tsp., 1 – 4 mL, ground ginger)	1 – 3 tsp.	5 – 15 mL
Fresh small chili pepper, seeded and finely diced (see Note)	1	1
Medium carrot, decoratively cut	1	1
Small green pepper, cut into 3/4 inch (2 cm) diamond shapes	1	1
Small yellow pepper, cut into 3/4 inch (2 cm) diamond shapes	1	1
Small red pepper, cut into 3/4 inch (2 cm) diamond shapes	1	1
Medium zucchini, with peel, quartered lengthwise and sliced into 1/2 inch (12 mm) pieces	1	1
Quartered fresh mushrooms	1 1/2 cups	375 mL
Can of sliced water chestnuts, drained	8 oz.	227 mL
Sesame seeds, toasted (see Tip, page 100)	1 tbsp.	15 mL

Sauce: Stir first 6 ingredients together in small bowl. Set aside.

Heat cooking oil in wok or large frying pan on medium-high. Add garlic, ginger, chili pepper and carrot. Stir-fry for about 1 minute until fragrant. Add all 3 peppers. Stir-fry for 2 minutes.

Add zucchini, mushrooms and water chestnuts. Stir-fry for 2 to 3 minutes until zucchini is tender-crisp. Stir sauce. Add to vegetable mixture. Heat and stir until sauce is thickened and coats vegetables.

Sprinkle sesame seeds over vegetable mixture. Makes 6 1/2 cups (1.6 L).

1 cup (250 mL): 135 Calories; 5.4 g Total Fat; 1768 mg Sodium; 3 g Protein; 20 g Carbohydrate; 3 g Dietary Fibre

Pictured on page 172/173.

Note: Wear gloves when chopping chili peppers and avoid touching your eyes.

Greek Lemon Potatoes

A light lemon flavour with a hint of oregano
in these light golden potatoes.

Medium potatoes (about 2 lbs., 900 g), peeled and quartered	8	8
Olive (or cooking) oil	2 tbsp.	30 mL
Hard margarine (or butter), melted	2 tbsp.	30 mL
Freshly squeezed lemon juice	3 tbsp.	50 mL
Dried whole oregano	1 1/2 tsp.	7 mL
Salt	1 1/2 tsp.	7 mL
Pepper, generous sprinkle		
Hot water	2/3 cup	150 mL

Rinse potatoes. Turn into shallow roasting pan. Drizzle olive oil, margarine and lemon juice over potatoes. Sprinkle with oregano, salt and pepper. Stir to coat.

Carefully pour hot water down 1 side of pan, being sure not to rinse coating from potatoes. Roast, uncovered, in 400°F (205°C) oven for 45 to 60 minutes, shaking pan and adding more hot water as necessary to keep potatoes from sticking to bottom of pan, until golden brown. Serves 8.

1 serving: 147 Calories; 6.5 g Total Fat; 486 mg Sodium; 2 g Protein; 21 g Carbohydrate; 2 g Dietary Fibre

Pictured on page 173.

Baccalà

Pronounced bah-kah-LAH. An Italian dish made from salted cod, traditionally served as one of the many meatless dishes on Christmas Eve. We've adapted the very salty traditional recipe to suit most tastes by substituting regular cod for some of the salted cod that would normally be used.

Dried bone-in salted cod	10 1/2 oz.	300 g
Cold water, several changes		
Garlic clove, minced (or 1/4 tsp., 1 mL, powder)	1	1
Medium red peppers, cut into 3/4 inch (2 cm) pieces	3	3
Olive (or cooking) oil	1 tbsp.	15 mL
Can of roma (plum) tomatoes, with juice, chopped	19 oz.	540 mL
Dried sweet basil	2 tsp.	10 mL
Dried whole oregano	1 tsp.	5 mL
Pepper	1/4 tsp.	1 mL
Fresh (or frozen, thawed) cod fillets, cut bite size	16 oz.	500 g

Cut salted cod into large pieces. Put into large bowl. Cover with cold water. Soak for 24 hours, draining and changing water 3 to 4 times. Drain. Put into large saucepan. Cover with fresh water. Bring to a boil. Reduce heat. Simmer, uncovered, for 10 minutes. Drain. Let stand until cool enough to handle. Remove skin and bones from cod. Cut into bite-size pieces. Set aside.

Sauté garlic and red pepper in olive oil in large frying pan for about 4 minutes until red pepper is tender-crisp.

Add tomatoes with juice, basil, oregano and pepper. Bring to a boil. Reduce heat. Simmer, uncovered, for 30 minutes.

Stir in salted cod and fresh cod. Heat for 5 to 10 minutes until fresh cod flakes easily when tested with fork. Makes 8 1/2 cups (2.1 L). Serves 6 to 8.

1 serving: 292 Calories; 4.6 g Total Fat; 1954 mg Sodium; 48 g Protein; 14 g Carbohydrate; 3 g Dietary Fibre

Pictured on page 170.

Top Left: Maple Yams, page 151
Top Right: Greek Lemon Potatoes, page 171
Centre Left: Varenyky With Onion Butter, page 170
Bottom Right: Many Jewels Stir-Fry, page 171

Norwegian Almond Pastry

A very rich European pastry with crisp pastry and soft creamy filling. A bit fussy and time-consuming, so make in two or three stages and then have the rolls in the freezer to bake up fresh any time.

BUTTER PASTRY

All-purpose flour	4 cups	1 L
Baking powder	1 1/2 tsp.	7 mL
Salt	1/2 tsp.	2 mL
Cold butter (not margarine), cut into 16 pieces	1 lb.	454 g
Ice water	1 cup	250 mL

ALMOND FILLING

Blocks of almond paste (8 oz., 225 g, each), about 2 cups (500 mL), room temperature	2	2
Granulated sugar	2/3 cup	150 mL
All-purpose flour	1 tbsp.	15 mL
Water	1 tbsp.	15 mL
Large egg, fork-beaten	1	1
Ground almonds	1 cup	250 mL
Egg white (large), lightly fork-beaten	1	1
Granulated sugar, sprinkle		

Butter Pastry: Stir flour, baking powder and salt together in large bowl. Cut in butter until crumbly and consistency of small peas. Make a well in centre.

Pour ice water into well. Mix, bringing in flour from side of bowl, until no flour remains and dough is wet and sticky. Press into ungreased waxed paper-lined 8 × 8 inch (20 × 20 cm) or 9 × 9 inch (22 × 22 cm) pan. Cover. Chill overnight. Store in refrigerator for up to 2 days.

Almond Filling: Crumble almond paste into medium bowl using hands. Microwave on high (100%) for 10 seconds if too hard to crumble. Add first amount of sugar, flour, water and egg. Beat until smooth. Add almonds. Stir. Cover. Chill overnight. Store in refrigerator for up to 2 days. Makes about 2 cups (500 mL) filling. Cut pastry in pan into 8 equal pieces. Roll out 1 pastry piece on floured surface to 8 × 10 inch (20 × 25 cm) rectangle. Turn filling out onto lightly floured surface. Form 1/4 cup (60 mL) filling into 9 inch (22 cm) long rope. Place rope down long side of pastry, about 1 inch (2.5 cm) in from long edge. Brush edges of pastry piece with water. Roll up, jelly roll-style, to enclose filling. Pinch to seal. Cover securely with plastic wrap. Repeat with remaining pastry and filling. Freeze until firm.

Arrange frozen rolls, seam-side down, on large ungreased baking sheet. Pierce each roll in several spots, through to filling, using wooden pick dipped in flour. Brush with egg white. Sprinkle second amount of sugar over top. Bake in 400°F (205°C) oven for 20 to 25 minutes until golden. Let stand until rolls are lukewarm. Cut, on diagonal, into 3/4 inch (2 cm) pieces. Makes 8 rolls, each roll cutting into about 12 pieces, for a total of about 96 pieces.

1 piece: 87 Calories; 5.7 g Total Fat; 59 mg Sodium; 1 g Protein; 8 g Carbohydrate; 1 g Dietary Fibre

Pictured on page 175.

Rice Pudding

This just might be the best rice pudding you'll ever eat. A Danish tradition at Christmastime gives an extra present to the lucky person finding the almond in their dish. Recipe reprinted from Dinners of the World, page 133.

Long grain white rice, uncooked	1 cup	250 mL
Water	2 cups	500 mL
Cinnamon stick (4 inch, 10 cm, length)	1	1
Milk	4 cups	1 L
Granulated sugar	1 cup	250 mL
Raisins	1/2 cup	125 mL
Salt	1/4 tsp.	1 mL
Egg yolks (large)	3	3
Vanilla	1 tsp.	5 mL
Whole blanched almond	1	1

Combine rice, water and cinnamon stick in medium saucepan. Cover. Bring to a boil. Reduce heat. Simmer for about 15 minutes until water is absorbed and rice is tender. Remove and discard cinnamon stick.

Heat milk in large heavy saucepan. Stir in sugar, raisins and salt. Add rice. Bring to a boil. Reduce heat. Gently simmer, uncovered, for about 15 minutes, stirring often, until thick but still soft.

Beat egg yolks in small bowl using fork. Stir in vanilla. Add about 1/2 cup (125 mL) hot rice mixture to egg yolk mixture. Mix well. Stir into hot rice mixture.

Add almond. Heat and stir for about 1 minute. Makes 6 cups (1.5 L).

3/4 cup (175 mL): 298 Calories; 3.5 g Total Fat; 144 mg Sodium; 7 g Protein; 60 g Carbohydrate; 1 g Dietary Fibre

Pictured on page 175.

Top Left: Rice Pudding, page 174   Bottom Left: Norwegian Almond Pastry, page 174   Right: Old Country Yogurt Slice, this page

Old Country Yogurt Slice

This dessert square, hailing from old Eastern Europe, is not very sweet, just very satisfying. Serve with fresh fruit.

DOUGH

Hard margarine (or butter), softened	1/2 cup	125 mL
Granulated sugar	1/2 cup	125 mL
Egg yolks (large)	4	4
Light sour cream	1 tbsp.	15 mL
All-purpose flour	2 1/2 cups	625 mL
Baking powder	1 tbsp.	15 mL

FILLING

Low-fat vanilla yogurt (not fat-free)	3 cups	750 mL
Light sour cream	1 2/3 cups	400 mL
Cream of wheat (unprepared)	1/2 cup	125 mL
All-purpose flour	1/2 cup	125 mL
Vanilla	2 tsp.	10 mL
Egg whites (large), room temperature	4	4
Icing (confectioner's) sugar	1/2 cup	125 mL

Dough: Cream margarine, sugar, egg yolks and sour cream together in medium bowl.

Mix in flour and baking powder until mixture is crumbly. Divide in half. Press 1 portion of dough into ungreased 9 x 13 inch (22 x 33 cm) pan. Set remaining dough aside.

Filling: Stir first 5 ingredients together in large bowl until well mixed.

Using clean beaters, beat egg whites in separate medium bowl until soft peaks form. Gradually beat in icing sugar until stiff peaks form. Gently fold into yogurt mixture. Spread evenly over dough in pan. Crumble remaining dough evenly over filling. Bake in 400°F (205°C) oven for 40 minutes. Cool. Cuts into 20 to 24 pieces.

1 piece: 225 Calories; 8.2 g Total Fat; 162 mg Sodium; 7 g Protein; 31 g Carbohydrate; 1 g Dietary Fibre

Pictured above.

Table Decorations

Bring some true holiday glitter to the feast—enhance your
culinary efforts amidst these enchanting table decorations.
Here's a marvelous opportunity to show off
your creative side with stunning results!

Setting the Table

When you ask your family and guests to "please come and sit down" at the Christmas dinner table, you want their first impression to set the stage for the meal you have prepared. The art of creating can be quite simple—but with elegant and wowing results! Our creations for your Christmas dinner table couldn't be simpler. A beautiful red and silver table runner that doubles as the placemats, red and silver poinsettia centrepieces and red and green felt poinsettia napkin rings combine to present a gorgeous vision of Christmas splendor. No sewing or gluing is required for any of these ideas.

Woven Ribbon Runners

Take a plain, solid-coloured tablecloth and 2 or 3 colours of ribbon and you will transform your dining table setting from a conversation piece to a conversation topic for years to come. Build a colour scheme around your china by choosing ribbon of complementary or contrasting colours. Choose soft, heavier ribbon that will lie flat and straight throughout the course of the evening's meal. The ribbons can be of varying widths as well as texture and you can space them equal distance apart or with a pattern—the possibilities are endless! Use all one kind of ribbon for a less dramatic, but still effective, look. Each woven runner will make two "placemats" on opposites sides (or ends) of the table.

For our design for 8 place settings, you will need:
Silver ribbon (3 inches, 7.5 cm, wide), enough to cover
  2 lengths and 6 widths of table, plus additional
  48 inches (120 cm)
Red ribbon (2 inches, 5 cm, wide), enough to cover
  1 length and 3 widths of table, plus additional
  24 inches (60 cm)
Tape measure
Scissors

White tablecloth

Cut 2 lengths of silver ribbon and 1 length of red ribbon to each measure length of table plus 6 inches (15 cm). Cut 6 lengths of silver ribbon and 3 lengths of red ribbon to each measure width of table plus 6 inches (15 cm).

Place tablecloth over table. Place long red ribbon lengthwise down centre of tablecloth. Lay long silver ribbons down either side, leaving about 1 inch (2.5 cm) in between. Take end of 1 short silver ribbon and feed it, across width of table, over, under and over the three longer ribbons about where the edge of the outside placemats would be. Pull ribbon through to hang about 3 inches (7.5 cm) over opposite side. Take end of 1 short red ribbon and feed it, about 1 inch (2.5 cm) beside first ribbon, under, over and under the same longer ribbons. Pull ribbon through to hang same as first ribbon.

Repeat with second silver ribbon to complete pattern. Repeat complete pattern two more times, moving down length of table.

Poinsettia Cups Centrepiece

This centrepiece can be used in a variety of ways. Make as many as you want for the centre of your dinner table, or place individual cups at each place setting. For a buffet meal, have a large arrangement of poinsettia cups in the back and a few placed randomly around the food. Although we have chosen a red poinsettia with red ribbon and a silver cup to complement our Woven Ribbon Runners, page 177, you can choose colours, ribbon and cups to match your china.

For 5 centrepieces, you will need:

White ribbon (1/4 inch, 6 mm, wide), cut into
   five 6 inch (15 cm) lengths
5 silver martini goblets
Small paring knife
5 small blocks of florist's (foam) oasis

Green florist's moss
Poinsettia bush with at least 5 flowers
   (or 5 individual poinsettia picks)
Wire cutters
20 to 30 Christmas picks (pine cones, evergreen,
   berries, holly, pine branches, etc.)

Place enough moss in goblet to cover oasis. Separate poinsettia bush using wire cutters. Push 1 flower through moss into centre of oasis. Push 3 or 4 Christmas picks in and around flower. Repeat with remaining supplies. (Note: Do not glue in place; goblets can then be used for their intended purpose at a later date.)

Tie 1 piece of ribbon around stem of 1 goblet. Cut and shape 1 oasis to fit down about 1 1/2 inches (3.8 cm) inside goblet.

Poinsettia Napkin Ring

Whether or not we use cloth napkins on a day-to-day basis, we can't seem to help but get them out for Christmas dinner. What table setting would be complete without them? And napkin rings add the final touch to the overall presentation. We have continued the poinsettia theme of the centrepiece with this napkin ring design.

For 1 napkin ring, you will need:
Piece of brown paper (or other heavier paper),
  6 × 12 inch (15 × 30 cm) size
Scissors

Piece of red felt (about 7 × 7 inch, 18 × 18 cm, size)
Piece of green felt (about 4 × 12 inch, 10 × 30 cm, size)

To enlarge pattern: Mark brown paper into 1 inch (2.5 cm) squares. Transfer pattern to grid, matching lines within each square. Cut out patterns.

POINSETTIA PATTERN

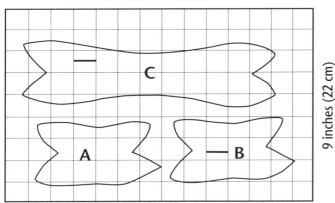

14 inches (35 cm)

9 inches (22 cm)

Bring folded ends of (A) together. Slip through slit in (B). Unfold to make flower.

Take long end of (C) and tuck back into itself. Leave loose to make ring for napkin.

Cut out both petals (A and B) from red felt and leaf (C) from green felt. Fold (A) in half lengthwise and insert halfway into slit in (C). Do not unfold (A).

Dessert Buffets

The dessert buffet is a pretty presentation for an afternoon tea, baby shower or engagement party.
It provides a relaxing alternative after a more formal main course. After a play, ballet
or concert, invite people back to your place for dessert and coffee with a flair.

Après Dinner Dessert Buffet

Mango Rum Fluff, page 96

Pineapple Cheese Pie, page 132

Dessert, served buffet-style after a formal sit-down dinner, is a pleasant way to get guests to move from the table to the sitting area to finish conversations and let the first course settle a bit longer. Dessert, in this case, would be a fork dessert such as a pie, layer cake or fancy dessert. It may already be cut and served on individual plates, ready to be picked up along with a cup of tea or coffee and perhaps a liqueur. Or it may be uncut with a serving utensil and stack of plates or bowls set beside it. In either case, guests can go over and serve themselves at their leisure. Sometimes a choice of two desserts is just as easy as making twice as much of just one dessert.

Dessert Buffet (After Main Course)

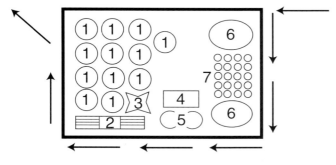

Dessert Buffet (Variety)

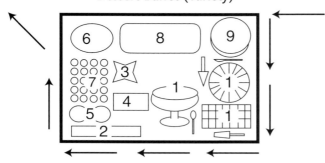

Chocolate Dessert Buffet

Chocolate-Coated Mint Patties, page 26

White Chocolate Fudge Truffles, page 83

Chocolate Orange Treats, page 84

Ragged Chocolate Drops, page 89

Chocolate Raspberry Biscotti, page 106

Brownie Cake Dessert, page 106

White Chocolate Cherry Cheesecake, page 110

Chilled Chocolate Cheesecake, page 96

Rocky Road Pie, page 133

As part of a cocktail party, a dessert buffet would be an assortment of pick-up-with-your-fingers treats such as squares, candies and confections or small cakes. But the truly sumptuous dessert offering is in the middle of the afternoon or later in the evening when an array of both fork and finger desserts are offered in an aesthetically picturesque way. The line should flow in one direction and towards the seating area so that if bottlenecks are going to occur, they won't interfere with people who have already gotten their food.

Buffet Table Legend
1. Dessert
2. Napkins, Cutlery
3. Mints
4. Coffee Spoons
5. Cream, Sugar
6. Coffee, Tea
7. Cups, Saucers
8. Centrepiece
9. Plates, Bowls

Measurement Tables

Throughout this book measurements are given in Conventional and Metric measure. To compensate for differences between the two measurements due to rounding, a full metric measure is not always used. The cup used is the standard 8 fluid ounce. Temperature is given in degrees Fahrenheit and Celsius. Baking pan measurements are in inches and centimetres as well as quarts and litres. An exact metric conversion is given on this page as well as the working equivalent (Metric Standard Measure).

Oven Temperatures

Fahrenheit (°F)	Celsius (°C)	Fahrenheit (°F)	Celsius (°C)
175°	80°	350°	175°
200°	95°	375°	190°
225°	110°	400°	205°
250°	120°	425°	220°
275°	140°	450°	230°
300°	150°	475°	240°
325°	160°	500°	260°

Spoons

Conventional Measure	Metric Exact Conversion Millilitre (mL)	Metric Standard Measure Millilitre (mL)
1/8 teaspoon (tsp.)	0.6 mL	0.5 mL
1/4 teaspoon (tsp.)	1.2 mL	1 mL
1/2 teaspoon (tsp.)	2.4 mL	2 mL
1 teaspoon (tsp.)	4.7 mL	5 mL
2 teaspoons (tsp.)	9.4 mL	10 mL
1 tablespoon (tbsp.)	14.2 mL	15 mL

Cups

1/4 cup (4 tbsp.)	56.8 mL	60 mL
1/3 cup (5 1/3 tbsp.)	75.6 mL	75 mL
1/2 cup (8 tbsp.)	113.7 mL	125 mL
2/3 cup (10 2/3 tbsp.)	151.2 mL	150 mL
3/4 cup (12 tbsp.)	170.5 mL	175 mL
1 cup (16 tbsp.)	227.3 mL	250 mL
4 1/2 cups	1022.9 mL	1000 mL (1 L)

Pans

Conventional - Inches	Metric - Centimetres
8x8 inch	20x20 cm
9x9 inch	22x22 cm
9x13 inch	22x33 cm
10x15 inch	25x38 cm
11x17 inch	28x43 cm
8x2 inch round	20x5 cm
9x2 inch round	22x5 cm
10x4 1/2 inch tube	25x11 cm
8x4x3 inch loaf	20x10x7.5 cm
9x5x3 inch loaf	22x12.5x7.5 cm

Dry Measurements

Conventional Measure Ounces (oz.)	Metric Exact Conversion Grams (g)	Metric Standard Measure Grams (g)
1 oz.	28.3 g	28 g
2 oz.	56.7 g	57 g
3 oz.	85.0 g	85 g
4 oz.	113.4 g	125 g
5 oz.	141.7 g	140 g
6 oz.	170.1 g	170 g
7 oz.	198.4 g	200 g
8 oz.	226.8 g	250 g
16 oz.	453.6 g	500 g
32 oz.	907.2 g	1000 g (1 kg)

Casseroles

Canada & Britain

United States

Standard Size Casserole	Exact Metric Measure	Standard Size Casserole	Exact Metric Measure
1 qt. (5 cups)	1.13 L	1 qt. (4 cups)	900 mL
1 1/2 qts. (7 1/2 cups)	1.69 L	1 1/2 qts. (6 cups)	1.35 L
2 qts. (10 cups)	2.25 L	2 qts. (8 cups)	1.8 L
2 1/2 qts. (12 1/2 cups)	2.81 L	2 1/2 qts. (10 cups)	2.25 L
3 qts. (15 cups)	3.38 L	3 qts. (12 cups)	2.7 L
4 qts. (20 cups)	4.5 L	4 qts. (16 cups)	3.6 L
5 qts. (25 cups)	5.63 L	5 qts. (20 cups)	4.5 L

Tip Index

How-To Index

Recipe Index

DANIELLE
JACLYN
MARLENE
MARGARET
MARY
PETE
PATRICIA
STEPHE
MARILYN
WENDY
ELIZABETH
LAURIE
LESLIE
BRENDA
SARAH
ALLISON
SANDRA
SHERRI
VICKI
TAMM
DON
LEAH
ROXANNE
JESSICA
PAT
BLAIR
RUTH
KAREN
DARLANE
AUDREY
DERRICK
RICHARD
DEANNA
ELEANOR
JOHN
GRANT
GEORGE
SHELLY
SHEILA
LAUREL
DAWNA
AMANDA
CONNIE
SUZANNE
GAIL
PENNY
CHARLENE
DANA
PAULA
CATHY
LOVONI
TEQUITA
DIANE
ROSE
NORA
CINDY
SHELLEY
JODIE
KATHY
STEPHANIE
LINDA
JAMES
BOB
NADINE
CARA
RENDI
LYNDA
LORRAINE